Ancestry: The Deep Field of Reality

Eugenio Ordóñez

Published by Quechelah Publishing, 2021.

---

1. http://www.quechelah.org

Table of Contents

Dedication

This book is dedicated to *my mother and my father,* to whom I owe the most important gift and blessing: Life. Knowing that I will never be able to give them back what I received from them, this book is an attempt to acknowledge their greatness. In most ways this is their work, because without them it would have not been possible. This book is the response to a calling: the calling of my ancestors. What seems to be my effort is nothing but their love, support, and guidance that never stopped flowing to me. It is an honor to present as mine something that belongs to a lineage of people.

At the same time this book was only possible because of the help, support, and care of innumerable persons, from family, friends, and colleagues, to unexpected visitors, brief acquaintances, and strangers, directly and indirectly. In such a sense, I openly acknowledge that for this book to occur it required all of them. Being unable to mention them one by one, and fearing that I could inadvertently omit someone, I bow in gratitude to all of you.

Introduction

What is the aim of this book? What is its purpose?

The chief intention of this book is to bring attention to the importance, influence, and impact of the ancestors in one's existence. In order to achieve this objective, this book undertakes a hermeneutic revision of ancestry; in simpler prose, it is a revision of important literature regarding ancestry from different domains of knowledge, largely based on the work of four major contributors to the field: Carl G. Jung and James Hillman, two depth psychologists; Bert Hellinger, the developer of the Family Constellations method; and Malidoma Somé, an African elder, diviner, and shaman whose purpose has been to share ancient indigenous spiritual technologies with the Western world. My approach is not purely hermeneutic and interpretative, but rather experiential, anecdotal, and inquisitive. Thus, I incorporate ideas and theoretical contributions from old Greek philosophy, phenomenology, Homeopathic medicine, Native American traditions, as well as insights from poetry, especially from Sufism. Hence, the goal of this extensive text is not merely to develop a psychological view of ancestry, but to awaken an awareness of those deep hidden influences that can shift the perspectives upon which many practices are based, from psychotherapy and social work, to medicine and the healing arts. Rather than establishing fixed and clear conclusions, this weaving of theoretical arguments, therapeutic observations, lived experiences, and practical ideas aims to open a field of studies that can contribute directly on the ways and methods of practicing the healing arts (therapies), the different ways of knowing (epistemologies), and, ultimately, the studies of being (ontologies) and the praxis of happiness and well-being (eudaimonia).

What is my part on it? And, more importantly, is the book relevant at all?

To try to identify the first moment when I became interested in the topic of ancestry is as ambiguous and fruitless a quest as it is to pinpoint the beginning of ancestry itself. I cannot specify when my interest in ancestry began for that would depend upon a kind of false chronological origin—a moment in time which I do not remember. It is equally hard to try to find the first few facts that directed my attention to the topic, as if events in life were separated and just some facts produced, afterwards, some interest in certain topic I can only say that I came across a few situations which deeply moved me and for which I could not find an explanation that satisfied my rational mind. The central experience that I can recall is attending a "Family Constellations" workshop, led by a very bright and incisive woman in Mexico City, Ingala Robl. She facilitated an all-day workshop on constellations using Hellinger's theories and approach.

That day I saw and experienced situations that were out of the ordinary, yet powerfully healing and strongly emotive. By out of the ordinary, I mean out of the ordinary realm of psychotherapy and the mainstream schools of psychology. Nowadays, as it can be the case in many countries, it might sound ordinary that a day of constellations is a deeply moving experience.

This is not the place to explain what a constellation is, how it works, what it produces, and so on, because that will be explained later in the work; but it is important to mention family constellations as a catalyst for what happened after that workshop, and which led to this book about ancestry.

My interest in the topic of ancestry goes back (in time) to moments and memories that I do not relate to ancestry per se, and which are not that important to tell. For as long as I can recall, I have been interested in the so-called human *body and its affections.* This interest led me to inquire in an uncommon and sometimes provocative way about issues and situations that pertain to and dramatically perturb the physicality of a person, including severe illnesses, fatal accidents, unexpected events, and bodily disturbances, whether congenital or acquired. I kept these inquiries into the lived notion of "the body" mostly to myself, either because they were outside the conventional mainstream, i.e., the allopathic medicine to which I was exposed, or they due to some irrational factor—not so much in denying rationality, but rather in escaping its grasp. As I followed this path of thought, sometimes I found myself drawn to unconventional ideas and at other times simply dissatisfied with most of the explanations given by physicians, professors, priests, and particularly psychologists and psychotherapists; so I kept a silent and persistent uncertainty about embodiment.

Some of the answers to problems of the body given by professionals—such as "It is your biological inheritance and nothing can be done about it," "It is God's will that you are like that, that you have this or that disease," or "Such is life"—were unsatisfactory to me. Often, in my early years, my attention was drawn to physicality and circumstantial happenings in life that were inexplicable or did not have convincing explanations, but which usually were labeled and accepted as fate, or in the more fashionable word from Eastern philosophies: karma.

A few anecdotes will serve here to illustrate the point about the tough manifestations of fate. When I was in elementary school, a lively classmate of my brother's, who was just a little bit older than I was, died of leukemia. Some time later, when I was in secondary school, a car hit a dedicated and bright classmate of mine as he was walking across the street, becoming severely injured and disabled for life and unable to walk normally. When I was in high school, a seemingly joyful classmate, not too close to me but from my group of friends, unexpectedly shot himself in the head and subsequently died. Some years later when I was in college, a friend of my father's, a hardworking, friendly man who I had known since I was a child, died after struggling for several years with spinal cancer. These four persons are examples of what led me to a deep inquiry about the unfolding of fate, which turns mysteriously and suddenly shifts the lives of those who seem to be *good people.*

Hence, for some uncanny and strange reason, by an inexplicable shift of destiny, after I had navigated in the uncertainty of psychological reflection, the notion of ancestry gave me a wider perspective on the mysteries of soul. After reading this book, you might find that the answer to those shifts of fate might not be answered, but perhaps a deeper questioning will arise, a more profound inquiry into matters of life and death, misery and joy, tragedy and peace. This book does not start with the assumption that the answers that one can find in the different professional fields are incorrect, but rather that some may be insufficient.

Therefore this topic of ancestry arose organically in me as a need to deepen into some of the concerns of psychological reflection and ultimately to step boldly into the wilder dimensions of the psyche, where some "fixed" certainties might not be accurate anymore. This psychologized re-vision of ancestry seems to come at the same time in which some concepts in the laws of physics—which were useful for the development of current societies—are being also challenged. Hence this work, without being scientific in its narrative, could very well parallel some of the recent discoveries in some fields of science, including biology and physics. However, pertaining to psychology, this research into the importance of the ancestors is needed because so far not much has been written on the topic, and, moreover, ancestry has not played an important role in depth psychological reflections, in the many schools of psychotherapy, or in the studies of soul.

This book attempts to make a contribution of particular import to depth psychological approaches, which to date have not focused much attention on the trans-generational stream of consciousness or the flow of psychic energy along the biological and, not often mentioned, psychological inheritance. In addition to being relevant for Jungian, Freudian, and Archetypal psychologies, the examination of ancestry may also prove fruitful for other disciplines of study that have been interested in matters pertaining to soul, embodiment, and integral life practices. In such a way, this book will address those questions which Jung, in his old age, called "the Unanswered, Unresolved, Unredeemed" (1961/1965, p. 191). This exploration into the importance of ancestry is also an attempt to find responses to those issues and figurations that many psychotherapeutic schools have left unattended and unresolved. The aim of this book is to return psychology's attention to the oftentimes forgotten notion of ancestry and ancestors, which have an impact and calling in ways that so far have not been recognized clearly, nor been attended properly.

What does it delve into?

This book's crucial question and main inquiry is related to the impact of the past (or "the time before") on the present; in other words, *how are we living in relation to our ancestry?* To answer this question, a brief re-vision of texts will be needed, along with some seemingly wild reflections. In addition, a few more questions need to be explored, including: Are we free from the issues that concerned the psyches of our ancestors? Are we completely detached from the lives of our ancestors? Are we continuing in our life something that occurred in "their" time? Can we disentangle ourselves from the unresolved situations that pertained to our ancestors? This book is not necessarily intended to convince people of a certain truth by answering yes or no to such questions, but rather to open a little discussed domain that could be of immense value in its theoretical and practical contributions. The questions are rhetorical and not meant to be promptly answered, but rather to be considered, pondered, and reflected upon.

For some people, these questions might sound altogether unreasonable and invalid. It seems easier to attach oneself to the belief that life begins with one's birth and that one's life has nothing to do with ancestors or blood lineage. To some people, this idea has been a successful escape, and actually many so-called depth psychotherapeutic schools have dealt with concerns regarding soul without looking into the blood lineages. In other words, many psychotherapeutic approaches have overlooked ancestry and have built a practice around the concerns of soul as if everything—life experience, physical problems, psychological wounds—came into being with the birth of the person. From a biological standpoint, meaning the fact that one is embodied as a living organism, this idea that soul begins at birth is quite narrow and myopic; clearly there is such a thing as a biological inheritance, which is a crucial consideration in any serious inquiry about the body and its pathological manifestations as well as essential for any medical intervention. In the same way, from a depth psychological standpoint, it has been observed that many issues a person has to cope with during life—such as diseases—have not only the well-accepted genetic component, but also those psychic remnants that come from that person's blood lineage and which tincture many domains of existence, not just embodiment, but also the social, professional, vocational, and spiritual aspects of life.

So far, there have not been enough depth psychological reflections regarding the impact, importance, and influence of ancestry on the concerns of soul. Despite the lack of literature on the topic, there are practices that consider ancestry's affect in our lives which have powerfully brought healing, health, and happiness to people. A couple of such practices will be reviewed here in order to expand more thoroughly on the topic. One such practice is the already controversial and provocative work on constellations, developed by Hellinger, in which he strongly challenges traditional psychotherapeutic approaches and theories, as it is the idea of exploring personal and childhood stories deeply—like psychoanalysis. A constellation in this sense —and in my words—is a phenomenological approach that consists of an embodied configuration of personified presences and issues that circumstantially affect a person in order to find a view, and at times a resolution, from the soul. Soul or psyche—the terms will be used interchangeably throughout the book[1]—refers to a mysterious factor, an uncanny agent, which unites one to the family of origin, to the ancestors, to other people, and even to other beings and places beyond spatial or temporal physical causality. In such a sense, soul is that irrational, indefinable force, whose affections are often sensed and felt, for good or bad; and whose effects can be experienced, in suffering or healing, sickness or health, failure or success, misery or happiness.[2] The other practice to be reviewed is a specific ritual (in relation to the ancestors) that comes from Africa; this practice will be considered to a lesser extent, however, as there is no literature about it.

What is this book based on? In other words, what sustains the arguments?

Fundamentally, the book uses four main theoretical lenses to follow four particular thinkers, each of them having a peculiar praxis and a personal way to find an *empirical* approach to the issues discussed. By empirical approach, I do not mean that the results are measurable, repeatable, and predictable, but instead that the approach is or was *observed in lived experience*. In this sense, what could seem to be a highly philosophic argument about one or two issues comes mainly from people who have dealt with it practically—including myself—, and not merely linguistically and theoretically. However, in order to expose and explain clearly the main observations and experiences about ancestry, it is highly valuable to take a look at the current literature, which is often the result of a lifetime of serious investigation and dedication.

Firstly, to deepen the discourse into the *domains of soul* from the perspective of depth psychology,[3] some of Jung's writings and insights will be addressed and revisited to articulate terms for this book's examination of ancestry and to help the arguments remain coherent. Some ideas, notions, and insights of Jung's will be useful to structure the topic. However, it is Jung's *Complex Theory*[4], conceived when he was a young man and then reviewed later in his life, what is the crucial text with which to unfold other issues that appear later in this work. To get a notion of this theory's importance, it is worth mentioning that Jung originally considered naming his particular psychotherapeutic theory and practice "Complex Psychology" rather than "Analytical

Psychology" as he eventually decided to call it[5]. According to Jung, *a complex* is "a certain psychic situation . . . strongly accentuated emotionally and . . . incompatible with the habitual attitude of consciousness"[6]. This idea of an unconscious psychic factor will be foundational for further reflections on the soul. Along with the complex there is another notion that requires attention, this being Jung's idea of "psychic energy," which "is always experienced specifically as *motion and force* (italics added) when actual, and as a state or condition when potential"[7]. In this way the importance of the relationships in every domain of life are acknowledged; from the psychological point of view, psychic energy is not a substance moving in space but *the interrelations*, which are experienced as energy.

Alongside the ideas of the complex and psychic energy, the notion of the *autonomous psyche*[8] is of critical value, because it helps one understand the autonomy of the complexes as well as the nature of psychic energy. The notion of the autonomous psyche also turns some popular psychological ideas inside out—as the unconscious moves from being simply intrapersonal to being interpersonal, transpersonal, and even trans-generational and trans-temporal. These ideas open up a different mode of seeing into the phenomenal world and allow for the possibility of an autonomous unconscious, a somatic manifestation of unconscious relations due to unknown psychodynamics; such concepts also remind us of *the forgotten due to the presences* that do not dwell in the physical realm, but whose affects and effects nonetheless are felt in our daily lives; "as if outside circumstances were simply projections of your own psychological structure"[9].

Jung's ways of describing psyche, along with some of his other contributions, provided sufficient ground for James Hillman to contribute to the field years later. Hillman, a trained analytical psychologist and self-defined Jungian[10], took bold steps which allowed him to move beyond some of the constraints found in Jungian orthodoxy (which arose following Jung's death) and provided him with a powerfully insightful *way of knowing*—an epistemology—which he described in his book *Re-visioning Psychology*[11]. There, he described four *basic moves* for a new way of looking into matters pertaining to the soul, which are in fact and according to many of the sources used in this book, actually *old* ways of looking and knowing, and ultimately old ways of being. Hillman's insightful psychological moves are: *personifying* as an epistemology of the heart; *pathologizing* as the soul's callings through that which is falling apart, also known as the symptomatic; *psychologizing* as the way of seeing phenomena through psyche, which is also from and for psyche; and *de-humanizing* as a main move to see how relative it is the anthropo-centeredness, and in order to gain a broader vista of a soul that embraces more than humans—in other words, bringing back the old notion of *Anima Mundi*[12].

However, Hillman made other equally important theoretical contributions to depth psychology, some from early in his career and some from later. Some of these contributions arose from what he, inspired by the mythic imagination, called the *Dionysian consciousness*, which allows one to perceive a fragmented psyche[13]. This is a highly important notion for further reflections on a world that is autonomously psychoactive. Hillman also wrote about the importance of the *Erotic*—not with a sexual connotation, but again inspired by mythic imagination—as the realization of soul's fate to be in psychic relations[14]. The notion of destiny, which is also an important issue along with Hillman's concerns about soul, has played an important role in the expositions of his perspectives. Therefore, destiny also becomes a medullar stream from which other reflections and figuring outs arise. In this sense, what Hillman colloquially described in one of his latest books as the *soul's code*[15]—a term inspired by a Heraclitus' fragment—turns out to be useful in understanding one's lived experiences concerning family, society, vocation, and death in a soul that might not be static but as I prefer to conceive it, *riverrunning*.

Even with Jung's and Hillman's contributions, coming as they do out of years of therapeutic practice, the topic could still seem too theoretical for some readers; however, when the work and insights of Hellinger are introduced, the book's argument that seemed fixed in theories becomes alive with practices that have occurred in recent years and continue to be in use today.

Hellinger's radical and controversial approach is not based solely on academic theories and sophisticated speculations, but rather on what he calls a *"phenomenological epistemology"* and a *"participative knowing"*[16]. His approach might be like an affective empiricism; and even when seemingly coming from branches of psychotherapy other than Jungian or Archetypal (the later founded by Hillman), Hellinger's insights allow one to get a profound and vivid experience of the Soul, and in his latest work, a vivid experience of the movements of the Spirit-Mind. *Family constellations*, the approach developed by Hellinger to deal with human relationships, becomes suddenly and unexpectedly a different, powerful and fully embodied way of knowing, which ultimately expands one's notions of being and well-being.

First and foremost, it is necessary to mention what Hellinger called the *orders of love*, which became the grounds for any further understanding and development of his work, compiled mostly in the first book about constellations, *Felicidad Dual*[17], and further explained and extended with its consequences in the book *Órdenes del amor—Orders of Love*[18]. These "orders of love" which help individuals find their right place in their existence, are groundbreaking contributions if bridged to the literature by Jung and Hillman mentioned before and to some of the notions explained there—the complex, psychic energy, autonomous psyche—and give a very different reading to them. If someone were to ask, "What would be the point of this?" the answer would lie in the *praxis*. Hellinger, or so it seems, has been primarily interested in that which is empirical—that which he evidences by the senses and proves—and not merely on theories, no matter how convincing or how sophisticated. One can read that it was in the *praxis* that many of his insights came to him, and that from there he developed a refined phenomenological approach.

Hence, the material from Hellinger's books and videos is altogether mixed; there are some writings by Hellinger where he explains respect towards others' destiny[19]; some works on *religion, psychotherapy, and cure of souls*[20] where he writes about the consequences of the images of God; some books offer insights on the entanglements with *the dead* and how to cope with *fate*[21]; some focus more on *reconciliation* among family members, families, and peoples[22]; some writings consider the *movements of the spirit-mind*[23] where he writes extensively on *the ways of love*; and several transcribed seminars that contain examples of his work are given, along with his commentary. In addition, I review some video recordings from live seminars in which lived experiences, insights and reflections on death, the dead, fate, the past, lineage, ancestors, and many other topics are mentioned. The work of Hellinger, some of his followers, and people inspired by him, such as van Kampenhout speaking about the notion of a *tribal soul* and the similarities and common ground with shamanism[24], and Hausner's work regarding diseases and chronic symptoms[25] provide a solid support for some of the issues regarding ancestry, ancestors, and their impact on life, health, and healing.

However, there is a fourth man whose work and perspective offers a strong and powerful deepening into the main topic. This man is Malidoma Somé, an African elder, diviner, and shaman of the Dagara people in Burkina Faso, who has written, lectured, given workshops, and literally dedicated his life to reawaken the old forgotten notion of the ancestors and their importance. In *Ritual: Power, Healing and Community*[26], he addressed the vital importance of the ancestors to those who still are walking on earth, asserting that the past generations provide guidance and help to the living and ultimately the community itself; for, according to the Dagara worldview, "human beings are collectively oriented"[27]. In *Healing Wisdom from*

Africa[28] Somé goes on to explain in further detail some African ways for healing the psyche that arise out of the "relationships with the visible worlds of nature. . . [and] with invisible forces of the ancestors"[29]. According to Somé and the traditions of the Dagara people, it is those ancestors who must be addressed for deep healing. In later audio recordings from Somé's lectures, he firmly expresses the deep need to reclaim the gifts and "wisdom of the past"[30], because, in his words, the purpose of his work regarding ancestors "is really [the] continuity of community and family"[31]; which is very similar indeed to Hellinger's aim to be in *service of life*.

These four main theoretical and practical lenses of Jung, Hillman, Hellinger, and Somé with which the book unfolds further will not be so clearly categorized and separated from one another. Instead, each thread will be considered alongside the others and even woven together with other thinkers not yet mentioned in order to create an intricate tapestry of connected ideas. The four main lenses will help maintain a particular way of wording ideas, notions, and images in order to keep the discourse under a certain coloring and patterning—those of the tapestry. The aim of the investigation is to weave the philosophical and psychological strings tightly enough—referencing and making use of the books, recordings and videos as well as honoring the oral traditions— and in such a way bring together some written works with some speeches, some profoundly thoughtful books with some deeply moving experiences from recorded workshops, some ancient ways with some new ways—so that it will become a carpet with which to fly the one thousand nights of the soul, and even more, no matter how dark.

What are the book's commitments?

Before this book unfolds, a brief description of the *points of departure* is needed. The first and most important are the philosophical commitments that inform my work and which offer a frame of understanding.

To begin with, I have a deep concern with the nature of being human—an ontological concern—that aims to look into the aspects of ancestry and embodiment from a perspective that pertains to the studies of soul—*psychology*. Such an examination has far-reaching implications for the practical and actual living situations in which individuals are immersed, moved, and strangely maintained for the time-being. In this sense, the re-vision of the notion of ancestry is not interested simply in the relation of one's life to those of the ancestors, as if it were merely a sociological, anthropological, or historical account of facts up to where memory and imagination begin, following one another to our actual days in a cause and effect conception of linear time.

This book has a different and deeper approach to this re-vision, allowing a psychological commitment to the impact of ancestry to unfold an unexpected manifestation of life circumstances and events. A bold view into one's ancestry can strangely change where one stands and where one is—one's *circumstances*—and also what one encounters as random happenings in life—one's life *events*. But, as a *philosophical commitment*, it is necessary to keep in mind and in sensed feeling, a concern that relates to soul—psyche—and not merely to a psychological discursive vanity. The commitment is a compromise that involves *the heart*—"the organ which produces true knowledge"[32]—and depending on the conditions of its participation, the whole organism responds in one way or another[33]. Therefore, the basic concerns of the psychological reflections about ancestry are bound to a serious *courage to face life and a nod to fate*. To make this first philosophical commitment, that of considering the full implications of the nature of being human, a little bit clearer, maybe a brief story titled *Blood bondage* will help.

Two men, with not so white skin, were talking about their genealogy, and they decided to find out more about where they came from and from whom they came. Since both were from the same country of origin, they helped one another with some of the facts about their families and their biological origins.

After some research into the historical facts that occurred in the country of their ancestors, they found out that the village where their forebears had lived had been colonized by an imperialistic nation; that their ancestors had been enslaved and brought to another country where they had to work under inhumane conditions; and that after a few generations of struggle, they had freed themselves. So the two men found that they both were coming from ancestors who had been slaves.

One of them, feisty and critical, kept researching into sociological and political facts and ultimately felt that he wanted the descendants of those who enslaved his ancestors to pay for what they had done, or at least wanted some kind of compensation. He kept thinking that those who had done the enslaving ought to be punished, but since they were dead already, he kept this emotion inside himself and decided to keep researching. The other, humble and graceful, imagined that all the ancestors were behind him; he looked at them, and he saw that in their faces there was pain, suffering, and the effects of injustice. However, he turned his head a little, and to his surprise saw all those who had enslaved them. He remained awhile looking at them, without doing anything, and suddenly felt that if he were to feel revengeful he would be tied to them. Seeing both in front of him—his ancestors and their colonizers and enslavers—he put his head down, nodded, and then looked up at them again. He said, "Thank you. Because of what you lived through, and because of the fate you endured, I am here now, and as a way to honor your suffering, I will live a good life," and he turned around and walked away.

Some time later, the one who had felt offended still wanted revenge and continued to feel angry, indignant, and resentful. The other, grateful for life as it was, moved away from a fate that wanted him to be outraged and incensed, a fate that linked him to the enslavers, and so he made out of his life something that freed him from a fight that pertained to the ancestors.

As a consequence of this concern about ancestry in relation to the nature of being human, there is an embedded way of knowing what is known—an epistemology—which is second commitment. Rather than being exclusively linguistic, legitimated by logical premises, or sustained by conceptual speculative rhetoric, this epistemology is deliberately originated from a sentient intelligence. In other words, it is *a way of knowing from and for the heart*. Of course, for the purposes of a written work such as this book, there needs to be a relation to previous psychological and philosophical works, in which some interpretation could occur. However, the most important aspect of this work cannot be forgotten or put aside at any time, that being the effects on the heart. As implied by this first ontological concern, the heart affects the totality of the organism and its circumstances. This approach is, in a way, similar to the importance that the Buddhists put on the *heart*, as the core for fully understanding the philosophical and religious implications of their tradition, or, as the Dali Lama expresses it, "it is only through the cultivation of the qualities of the human heart that we can begin to address and overcome our mental suffering"[34]. Zavala, who compared Jung's views and practice with old Mexican cultures and traditions, also emphasized the importance of the heart for the Aztecs and their sacred activities, from which, he said, one could attain a godly light[35].

A way of knowing from the heart requires a sentient intelligence, which means a necessarily embodied perspective, based on the afflictions of the body and the affections of the soul. In simpler words, it requires sensing and feeling in tune with what one thinks one knows, in tune with what one does, and in tune with one's life entanglements and happenings. In this way, a sentient intelligence cannot be detached, in any way, from one's activities, even if these are philosophical activities. It is not as in some other philosophical perspectives where one thoughtfully and verbally agrees and defends thoughtfully and verbally an idea, but one, not consciously, feels different about it, and even produces somatic disturbances because this idea is not the best kind of *knowledge for life*. But to clarify this point we need another brief story. It is titled *Seminal Love*.

Two men in their twenties were talking about their father. Both had grown up and lived only with their respective mothers, and in both cases they were told that their fathers had just left and had been mere brutes—lazy, irresponsible, stupid, and altogether useless. The two young men, wanting to do something about it, went into psychotherapy. However one of them, after a few sessions, decided to stop going.

The one who had remained in therapy for a while thought that he was ultimately better than his father, that he didn't need him, and that he was better off without him. In front of others, he constantly reaffirmed his mother's view that his father had been an idiot. He was a dedicated intellectual and found out that society was oppressed by various structures of domination. He had constant struggles with authority figures and was always criticizing the economy, politics, social occurrences, and even patriarchal religions of his country. He was a smart young man who would constantly point out what was wrong with society and its practices.

The other, not an intellectual, found out that deep inside he missed his father. One day he sat on the edge of his bed and despite what his mother had told him about his father, he closed his eyes and imagined the presence of a man; he felt that it was his father, although he had never met him. He said to the man that he had missed him in life. He kept looking at him and suddenly saw two other figures behind him, which also had powerful presences. One was a woman and the other a man. Then he looked back at his father and said, "I have forgotten what Mama said about you," and suddenly he felt connected to his father and through him to the other two presences and to even to a bigger force behind them. He said, "Whatever you did to Mama is between you and her. For me, you are my father and I thank you for my life," and he remained with his eyes closed and felt a sense of peace in his heart. Sitting at the edge of the bed, he felt strangely loved, and an unexpected love for the world and mankind kindled in his heart.

The one who convinced himself that his father was an idiot eventually wrote an acclaimed philosophical book about the anti-father, and the academic world applauded his theories, but afterwards he was diagnosed with lung cancer and then threw himself out of the window, killing himself. The other, definitely not an intellectual, decided to live according to the convictions of his heart and not according to the convictions of his mother. Yet every time he visited his mother he silently told himself, "Thank you, Mama, for having picked the right and only father for me."[36]

This knowing from the heart is hard to master; if it were not so, one could live easily from the time of being a small child. Therefore, some people have started using phenomenological practices, rather than only obtaining knowledge from written material; they have obtained knowledge from experience in an empirical form. This does not mean necessarily in a numerical, statistical, or quantitative modality, but rather from the experiences that when displayed produce an effect that can be observed qualitatively—and proved. This is exactly where it becomes challenging. Using philosophical rhetoric, many can convince themselves about one thing or its opposite, but often the afflictions of embodiment—bodily illnesses, chronic disturbances, and even suicidal impulses—point to a deeper affection that pertains to soul and fate. Hence, sentient intelligence is needed, because for matters of the soul it is not the best or most logically convincing arguments that heal or restore one to peace, and as is often the case, it is not medical treatments but heartfelt solutions that satisfy the soul.

At this point, a crucial third philosophical commitment is required for a better understanding of this book. This third commitment implies a way of looking into the written material and into the examples and stories from the *perspective of psyche*—or, as it can also be called, the soul. This commitment posits that the understanding of the text exists in one's own experience of soul, but without making it just personal. Therefore, this third philosophical commitment is called *psychologizing*, which means looking from the standpoint of the soul, and realizing that all *seeing through* into phenomena is a perspective of psyche[37]. In this way, it is possible to "*remove discussion of ideas from the realm of thought to the realm of psyche*"[38], for ideas themselves are "ways of seeing and knowing." Hence, the most appropriate methodology to re-engage actively with the idea of "ancestry and ancestors" is one that not only fits an elaborated philosophy—through sophisticated discourse—as mere hermeneutics could do, but one that keeps the perspectives rooted in soul, whether in one's own flesh, family situation, and fantasies, or one's own capacity to envision the situation and see through it.

Borrowing the hermeneutic methodology—the interpretation of texts—to re-view the ideas will be a key aspect of this book, but this work ultimately is not simply an exercise in rhetoric, but also an examination of *the thought of the heart*[39] in order to deepen into the embodiment and the vicissitudes of love. However, it is acknowledged that everything said is what Nietzsche calls "*perspectival knowing*"[40], and it is assumed that every reading—and critique—of material will be as well. Therefore, by stating that this work starts as an hermeneutic re-vision but always follows a *psychologized* stance, I recognize the inherent "capacity to have all arguments for and against *at one's disposal*," depending on the perspectives of the *psychic pre-disposition*. The methodological aim is not to achieve academic grandiosity that refers to theories, names, and books, but instead to attempt to enrich the poverty of ideas about the soul through a discourse that wishes to be imagined, sensed, felt, smelt, touched, tasted, and even—following Nietzsche again—"*ruminated*"[41].

The unfolding of the book, which will review and re-vision imaginatively texts in order to describe, explain, clarify, inquire, and even wonder about the topic and idea of ancestry, at times relates to the perspectives of depth psychology. This means that that which is done in order to make this work readable and understandable—the methodology—is an approach into the phenomenon of ancestry from the eyes and hearts of people who studied and were committed to psyche, so that despite the fact that there might be a bridge between texts and that some theories might run parallel, overlap, or expand upon others' ideas, the whole vision of ancestry is not based on a hermeneutic re-vision, but on a *psychologized reading*—for which the texts are necessary. To illustrate this, another brief story will be told. It is titled: *Moving images*.

A young woman is watching a movie with another female friend. Near the conclusion of the movie—which has a tragic end—the young woman feels deeply moved and cries unexpectedly. She realizes that it is just a movie, but despite that there's something about it that makes her sad. The movie was about some Jewish families during the Holocaust. She tries to convince herself that their suffering doesn't pertain to her; that she should not cry for something that happened decades ago in a distant land to people from another religion. However, there's something deeply moving in their story. On the other hand, while her friend felt emotionally moved by the film, she did not cry.

From merely an interpretation of texts, there can be some logical and coherent argumentation, which if enriched by other texts might point to some kind of convincing explanation of a situation—a so-called theory. This explanation might hit on a truth, or not, regardless of its clarity and elusiveness, and the theory might be correct or not. However, if the explanation is left at that, it might result in an intellectual exercise that tries to explain a deeply moving experience, eventually cheapening the experience or taking the juice out of it. This often happens when life is intellectualized and interpreted, even if done by a person who has read extensively and is familiar with many theories. Another path is not to explain, but instead to keep the experience and *psychologize* it, that is, to ask: *what* happened and *what* does it have to do with my psyche, my soul? Such an approach is by no means about being sentimental or trying to decipher the occult meaning of the experience; instead, by focusing on the "what," it is possible to "stay right with the matter"[42] and to be truthful to the soul affections and thereby gain a deeper and broader view of the situation[43]. To psychologize an experience does not imply that one needs to build reflections that will fit a psychological theory; it simply means that one inquires about the significance and relevance of the experience to one's soul.

This book re-visions some texts, not merely for the sake of elaborating on sophisticated interpretations, but to expand the horizons of how soul is experienced, reaching out into the domain of ancestry, where some actual life concerns can be attended to, in the present, if a proper tending for the (ancestral) presences is sought.

The young woman from the last story had the right intention and attitude towards her experience, and weeks later she unexpectedly found out that her great grandfather had been an SS officer. Rather than finding an understanding of her experience from a compilation of arguments from here and there, from this or that book, she followed her affection—a deep sadness, which connected her with the victims, as if tears could bring them back from death. She realized that those tears pulled her to look back into her lineage, to her forgotten and excluded great grandfather, and to ultimately see him beyond his acts.

For this book, the notion of looking at ancestry through interpretation came first from a *psychologized approach*. In addition, any reading of this work must be related—vividly or imaginatively—to one's own notion of psyche. With these three philosophical commitments serving as the first point of departure, there is a need to move to the second point: the theoretical lenses with which the phenomena of ancestry will be examined. No doubt, there are many other lenses that I could use, but for this book, based on the commitments and approaches mentioned above and my own experience, I focus on the four theoretical lenses mentioned before—those of Jung, Hillman, Hellinger, and Somé. Clearly there may be a much wider hermeneutic compilation of different sources that I could use, but what truly matters is that all the writing to come will be "*written with blood*"[44], with the blood in which ancestral forces run free.

The topic of ancestry constellates itself and is autonomous. The relation to "the topic" *is not* just an abstraction, for one cannot reduce a multifold relation into one concept. There is no such a thing as *a* relationship to the ancestors, but rather multiple numbers of relations regarding them. The "choice" to write about this topic, the elusiveness of its unfolding, the insights discovered, the opportunity to delve into its phenomenology, the possibility to experience profound healing, and all that inspired the work arise from a relationship of *gratitude towards the ancestors for having given life*. In no way can this topic be viewed as limited or confined, for it is by nature an expansive examination of the multi-dimensionality of soul. On the contrary, it would be a hindrance *not* to look at the ancestors, even worse to blame them, or, as too often happens, fatally to curse them.

There is, however, a common disagreement regarding what the notion of ancestry is. Some sociologists and anthropologists contend that ancestry is the whole continuum of events that happened in the past that caused our present situation. Others believe that ancestry ought to be viewed as pertaining only to personal issues. Still others do not even bother to reflect on ancestry and instead simply stumble forward with what is given. Reading this work may provide a wider notion of ancestry. To form an image of this issue a brief story, called *Ancestrælity,* will be of help.

There was a man named Albert, who had a friend named Niels, and both agreed that they disagreed about the meaning of ancestry. Niels often insisted that ancestry was a whole continuum of energy that had passed from generation to generation, and that due to this interrelated set of events, there was an implied order—and disorder—in the world. He was sure that ancestry had to be an unbroken series of events from which nothing could be excluded, and that the present was the consequence of this movement across time. Albert, however, fervently insisted that that ancestry required particularized presences, and that this could be proven if one would observe the particularities of individuals.

Neils believed that ancestry had to be seen in its massive scale, a full continuum of interrelated and sequenced events that had occurred in the past. For example, according to his view, a war would have arisen from a bad economy, that had to do with a poor harvest, that in turn was the consequence of bad weather, that had been caused by pollution, which came from factories and industries that had been built to manufacture products to satisfy consumers who were buying too much, and so on.

Albert disagreed, saying that if what Neils said was true, then there was not much that could be done and we would be, in principle, at the mercy of uncertainty. Albert insisted that ancestry needed to be looked at in particular ways, by looking into the presences that would ultimately reflect effects. He was adamant about this fact, which he called the ancestor effect, and he said that those effects could be observed. Both men held firmly to their views, and agreed to disagree.

It was not until a friend of theirs named Little Paul proposed a different view that the notion of ancestry was experienced differently. Little Paul was never able to make Albert and Niels agree; however, he realized that both Niels and Albert were right: the way to look at ancestry differently was actually to look at it! Little Paul then understood that rather than thinking and speculating about ancestry, that he could feel it and sense it. Consequently, he moved from an understanding that he was such and such because certain events had occurred, to the perception that he was as he was because he felt such and such, and at the moment he realized this, he questioned whether he could feel differently in relation to his ancestry.

Unfortunately, the followers of Niels kept speculating on all the possible sets of events and remained amazed by the movements of the un-fragmented continuum, the wave of life. Albert's followers, fewer it's true, didn't know what to do about it. Little Paul eventually died, but in his personal writings one finds some clues to what he meant.

A suggestion before beginning

This book can be read in at least three ways. One way is a slow and deliberate reading that requires one to pause at every footnote, thus interrupting the flow and rhythm of the main text. This kind of reading might be bothersome for some, but it enriches the arguments and even points out ideas that could be commented upon or written about in some other work. A second method is to read only the main text, with a few footnotes if necessary, an approach that would keep the reader moving forward at an enjoyable and virtually uninterrupted pace. A third possibility, and probably the most advisable, is to read only the main text first, and, if it is found to be interesting, to read it again with the footnotes.

Chapter 1
The Complex: A View of One's Psychic Situation

"... physics and the description of nature were no longer described as a way of 'revealing the true nature of phenomena', but as a way of 'tracing connections in the diversity of our experience.'"

The innermost kernel[45]

At the beginning of the twentieth century, when scientists were drastically revolutionizing the theories of physics and matter, Jung discovered an insightful way of investigating and looking into the situations of the people he was working with—patients who were at the time considered to be insane—a method that helped him develop a unique diagnostic view of psychic matters[46]. Through the popularized "word association" test, he realized that patients reacted in certain ways to specific spoken words and not to the other words with which he was testing them. However, he knew that the claim of association was too misleading, and that it would have been better to call it a *"linguistic reaction"* that "represent[ed] the psychological connection in only a remote and imperfect way"[47]. He was well aware in these experiments that he was not classifying the associations, "but merely their objective symptoms"[48], and, beyond that, only those symptoms which he could perceive. He came to the conclusion that the people being studied were involved in what he called a "collection of imaginings" which had an *autonomy* that was "relatively independent of the central control of consciousness"[49]. This set of imaginings kept them captive, and would make them *react* with a certain "feeling-toned"[50] response when a certain word was mentioned[51]. In other words, he discovered that individuals live within a circumstantial psychic pattern that powerfully affects their volition, sentiments, and intellection.[52] He named this psychic circumstance *the complex*[53], and later elaborated the concept to form what he called *the complex theory,*[54] and which he reviewed decades later, in 1934[55],[56].

When Jung reviewed the complex he was much older and more experienced, he realized that the complex is "a psychic factor which, in terms of energy, possesses a value that sometimes exceeds that of our conscious intentions"[57]. This observation is crucial for further understanding related to this book, where the overrated notion of being conscious of something does not exclude other factors that play a role in the unfolding of psychic manifestations and their physical consequences. These other factors might be called un-conscious, or unknown factors that are psycho-active, and with which one is in ineffable relation.[58] This way of looking into one's own life and body expands and populates the psychic territories in which one dwells, for one comes to realize that there are many more aspects that influence (the personal notion of the) psyche than those of which one is aware and "conscious."[59]

Sticking to Jung, who said that "[c]onsciousness is primarily *an organ of orientation* (italics added)," one might assume that consciousness is not a product of the mind, good thoughts, good behavior, or being a good person, but rather a faculty that allows and prohibits movement, sets direction, and limits action, decision, and choice through perception. "First and foremost, it establishes the fact that something is there [,]" said Jung, who also "called this faculty *sensation*"[60],[61]. From this perspective, it can be said that consciousness is not a substance, a thing, or something one acquires in increments throughout life, nor is it something that "good people" possess in greater quantity than others. Instead, consciousness, as an organ of orientation, is closer to the function of a compass and a map working together.[62] *Consciousness structures, and in a way tinctures, the perception of what is sensed; but at the same time, the sensed is limited by the structures and tinctures of consciousness.*[63] By means of consciousness, one perceives the world, but always according to one's own degree of clarity; by means of one's consciousness one also delimits it, distorts it, disfigures it, and moves in it.[64] From this perspective, consciousness is not the map of the world or its contents, but rather what allows one to perceive or not perceive, to move or not to move, and to do or not to do. Understanding consciousness only as something personal seems all too narrow, deceptive, delusional, distorted, and dismembered from the infinite continuum of life; quite possibly, as such, "all our consciousness relates to errors," as Nietzsche observed[65]. Aside from what "our consciousness" lets us perceive, there are still worlds, unknown and undiscovered dimensions of being human, or so to speak, not-conscious territories.[66] The unconscious, therefore, is the name for all those no doubt unlimited possibilities of "world" contents that are still unperceived and that, as a consequence, do not figure out on the maps of one's so-called "reality." From Jung's standpoint, one might say that the unconscious is not simply vast, but also the great psychic—perhaps infinite—unknown, and consciousness is one's own way of navigating this immense sea of uncertainty.[67]

Naturally, this way of looking into one's own being departs from the premise that psychic reality is not derived from the physical world, as if the soul were an outcome of the body, or as if its psychic contents were only related to something of physical or material nature. It comes close to Hillman's warning about and avoidance of what he calls "the naturalistic fallacy in psychology" that "insists that material reality is first and psychic reality must conform with it"[68].

Hence, when speaking of the complex, it is not meant only as a configuration of physically visible situations in which an individual is held captive or entangled, but also includes the psychic situations that affect the person regardless of his or her physical freedom. Therefore, it can be easily observed that individuals suffer and live with psychological afflictions even when their life might appear to be easy, smooth, and enjoyable to an outsider. When observing such cases, it becomes clear that the idea of the supremacy of the will and the overvalued notion that the human will can conquer anything seem false,[69] and if one is honest about the afflictions of the body, one realizes that there are aspects of illnesses that man has not understood yet, and which still seem far from human comprehension when they are explored merely from the standpoint of physiology, anatomy, genetics, and neurology. This is not to deny the scientific contributions made to health, healing, and well being, but by acknowledging and looking through the complex theory, understanding what it means to be an embodied human acquires a wider, perhaps unfathomable, spectrum.

An idea that is "not so well known" that Jung emphatically argued "is that complexes *have us*"[70]. In other words, we do not have these complexes; they are not inside us, and they are not in our so-called "psychological interiority." Complexes, from this vantage point, are not understood as personality traits that burden our life; they are not the mere outcome of some failure in our so-called psychological development. The term complexes is a way of naming the observation of psychic circumstances which tincture life issues in many settings. But complexes cannot be reduced to something which only belongs to the individual, or—even worse—to something that was exclusively produced by the individual. The individual belongs to the complex in the same way that the individual belongs to a family, a city, a country, the world, etc. It would sound rather clumsy to say that the family or the city belong to the individual.

If one seriously considers Jung's description of a complex as "the image of a certain psychic situation which is strongly accentuated emotionally and . . . incompatible with the habitual attitude of consciousness,"[71], then one can only ask humbly how to cope with something one does not know; otherwise one is at the mercy of factors one is neither aware of nor perceives, which leave one defenseless at times and often blind.[72] I believe this is a common issue in the existence of most people, when life suddenly takes a shift and things go from bad to worse, or when unexpectedly the body fails and some organ seems to be deteriorating, as if it were following a physical path of its own, regardless of whether the individual ate healthy food, exercised, meditated, and kept a balanced life. Jung went on to assert that the complex has "a relatively high degree of autonomy"[73];[74] considering this idea allows one to deepen into reflections about it, and one might question how much we are influenced by other factors, other presences, and even other people that we do not have the ability to recognize under the normal circumstances of ordinary life.[75]

The complex, one can then say, is the pattern of psychic energy that holds the individual under a certain way of feeling, thinking, and behaving; it is the pattern of ways in which the individual lives and loves. It influences all spheres of life at different times and to different degrees of intensity, even moving beyond the individual's volition, intellection, and understanding, as harsh as that may sound. From this standpoint, "the idea of [psychic] energy is not that of a substance moved in space; it is a concept abstracted from relations of movement"[76]. It is a concept that allows a way of perceiving and calibrating the dynamic intensities in the psyche and "therefore is founded not on the substances themselves but on their relations"[77].

Embodiment then, despite the fact that it might be seen as something tangible and substantial, is also a psychic dynamism in a web of interrelations, and as a consequence is energized by the quality and intensity of those relations. Unfortunately, being humanly embodied also means being vulnerable to reacting unconsciously to these relations, mostly without the possibility of avoiding such reactions, which at times can manifest in doing something obsessive, perverse, shameful, or even cruel, criminal, or murderous. Unconscious action does not mean merely behaving automatically or without awareness, as the term might be used in cognitive sciences; rather, it refers to a kind of acting that is *in relation to psychic contents that one is not conscious of*—that one does not perceive.[78] This does not mean that as individuals we have absolutely no will to decide how we behave, but instead that the decisions we make obey our consciousness and our usual ways of orienting in a world in which there is much more than we imagine or perceive—contents that exceed our everyday, ordinary, conscious capacities. From this viewpoint, many rationally incomprehensible actions, such as rape or murder, are understood differently. Jung clearly wrote how "an active complex puts us momentarily under a state of duress, of compulsive thinking and acting"[79].

By active complex Jung meant an active set of relations in regards to psychic contents, which can be imagined in motion and with direction towards others and oneself, producing a tension of forces and a felt intensity of energy as a direct result from which one cannot escape. Jung, no doubt in an attempt to be precise, chose an uncommon word to describe the felt influence of being under an activated complex: *duress*, a word that means: "threats, violence, constraints, or other action brought to bear on someone to do something against their will or better judgment"[80]. Looking at the etymological origin of the word duress, we see it is used in the sense of "hardness, harshness, forcible restraint, imprisonment, or constraint," and stems from the Latin word *duritia*, which means *hard*[81].

In essence, Jung observed that when one acts under the influence of a complex, one has no choice to do otherwise. When acting under the energy of the complex it is as if one were under threat from unseen people. Hence, in the view of depth psychology, any action committed by an individual under such conditions, no matter how terrible, seems to have been the only possible enactment for that individual at that time and setting. This interpretation is not meant to release the individual from any of the social, legal, or judicial consequences of committing a particular action, but rather, as Jung acknowledges, the complex is, at times, such a powerful and unavoidable force or set of forces that "under certain conditions the only appropriate term would be the judicial concept of *diminished responsibility*"[82]. A brief story, might illustrate the explanation.

Whom Does this Rage Belong to?

A young man, still in his teenage years, behaves aggressively at school and with his family, which consists of his brother, sister, mother, and maternal grandparents. He gets into trouble at school, because of constantly and violently fighting with his classmates. He admits to feeling anger and at times even an inexplicable and uncontrollable rage, but he also admits that he doesn't know why he feels this way, because conditions at school and home are not bad at all, and definitely not aggressive or threatening. His family situation, to which he does not give any importance, is quite complex. He stopped seeing his father when he was still a young boy. His mother told him that his father drowned at the sea while he was saving two children, but the young man suspects that this story is absurd, because how could his father have saved the children without saving himself? However, once the son grew up, he learned from his paternal uncles that his father had always been involved in politics in a very active way. His mother insists he stay away from his paternal uncles; in her eyes they are nothing but trouble. It seems to the young man as if she knows something, a secret perhaps. On the other hand, his uncles have openly offered him help whenever he needs it. He has come to suspect that his father was murdered.

Such a young man acts under a strong psychic complex, being completely involved by it, and blaming the mother for his actions would be utterly silly. The young man and the mother, as well as the "absent" father and the grandparents, are involved in a shared dynamic that is also populated by other important family members and/or psychic figures who *cannot be seen through thought*. The young man fulfills a psychic need within the family system, which might be in relation to family members other than his mother, or those related by blood. Under ordinary circumstances, however, where psychic relations are not explored or seen but instead enacted almost as if under obligation, the young man has no chance to act otherwise. His aggression, violence, and generalized anger are in relation to something that affects him, but which also includes other psychic members from his psychological life—any family member being a psychic member in one's psychological milieu. The psychic situation (the complex) is what compels him to behave in such a way, and if such a situation is not attended to properly, it can even push him into committing terrible and regretful deeds with severe legal consequences as had happened with the inexplicable fights he got in with his classmates.

When an individual acts in incomprehensible ways, outside of social logic or reason, Jung's notion of the complex as an "autonomous being capable of interfering with the intentions of the ego"[83] becomes quite clear. It is very important, however, to clarify that the complex is not simply a way of naming an issue with one person, one image, or one presence, as if it had to do only with his mother, or just with his mother and father, the way psychoanalysis might explore and overexploit such a condition for years. From his earliest reflections, Jung glimpsed that his investigation of the complex would go "beyond the scope of Freud's views"[84],[85]. In addition, the complex is not a way of naming a personality disorder, a personality trait, or even worse a so-called personality "defect," as if one could say in the case of the story that the young man has a "warrior complex." It is also a serious—and common—mistake to refer to a complex in relation to a "personality identification" with a concept or with an archetypal image, as if one could say arbitrarily that the man is under a "Mars complex." All these ways of applying the notion of a complex seem to be cheap and all-too-easy deviations due to semi-rational elaborations of thought, professional laziness, and a lack of phenomenological work, because psychologists prefer to talk things out rather than literally seeing the phenomena.[86]

The complex is, by definition, a dynamic situation in which the individual is involved, and in which the mother and father and even grandparents, great-grandparents, siblings, and many other important people are involved. All of them together configure an energetic set of patterns, that, of course, at the core, are archetypal in nature, and consequently not new at all to the history of human experience. It has been observed, then, that to be in a complex—as we all are—is a situation where there are no individuals to blame, but where everyone is a result of the dynamic situation that moves through the generations. This understanding carries with it a total implication of the consequences—whether those may be called good, bad, sane, insane, stupid, destructive, perverse, or whatever the name with which one labels human actions.

However, most complexes are an energetic situation in relation to presences and psychic contents that are out of the range of consciousness, and that one is not aware of, but which are important in some way to the individual. For example, there may be other psychic contents with which individuals are in relation, but which do not necessarily have a physical presence such as a dead family member—whether that be a parent, sibling, partner, grandparent, or someone further back in the lineage.

In the case of criminal acts, for instance, taking the complex theory as a point of departure, one can see that the individuals are not able to disentangle themselves from the complexities of their own energetic patterns; consequently, those patterns keep them involved in scenarios with many *unconscious relationships*—bonds to psychic contents for which they might have no other way of orienting. The complex, therefore, can be seen as a configuration of a fragment of the psychic reality of the individual, where there are contents, presences, and entities that do not follow the conscious desires and decisions the person would make under ordinary circumstances. Hence, as Jung described it, "an autonomous complex [is] divorced from consciousness, leading a life of its own in the psychic non-ego and instantly projecting itself whenever it is constellated in any way"[87],[88]. In other words, whenever a complex is activated by a word, memory, encounter, situation, place, or event, such psychic contents participate, for good or bad, directly or indirectly, in either a weak or strong way.

Most of the time, what an individual might call a volitional act, whether it is a thought, a choice, a deed, and the subsequent feeling about it, is *the only possible act, oriented by that person's consciousness under the immersion of that particular complex.* The so-called ego, the notion of "I," is one actor, who is never alone in the theater of existence, but always surrounded by the entire company of characters that belong to the script of life—even when those characters are seemingly invisible to ordinary ways of seeing. This does not mean in any way a mere representation of one's own personality characteristics into fictional imaginations of personae that populate one's psychic surrounding. Rather, the psyche has an autonomous quality. The contents that dwell in the psychic surrounding of an individual, and which eventually configure the complex, are independent of the individual's will and consciousness. Those contents exist independently of the individual having the capacity to see or imagine them. One is inescapably in relation to them, and one cannot make them disappear by not seeing them. It would be utterly preposterous to deny someone's existence, say, a miserable homeless man, just because one has avoided or refused to see him. Certainly it is not just a matter of "being conscious," as has been widely popularized, and attempting to make the individual *have* more and more of the usual consciousness. If it were so, then very mindful and meditative people would not become suddenly ill with terminal diseases.

Jung warned against "the arrogant claim of the conscious mind to be the whole of the psyche"[89]; the false belief he refers to has been severely overvalued in many modern cultures, where there is almost a cult to consciousness, and an almost absolute lack of psychological awareness about the unconscious factors that play a role in life, factors which often display their effect in the actualities of chance and fate, tragedy and luck, and blessings and misfortunes.[90] As Jung humbly wrote, "experience, not books, is what leads to understanding"[91]. One has to remember that the complex, as previously mentioned, has an energy value that exceeds the conscious intentions and the possibilities of the individual's orientation. Hence, when dealing with complexes it is not as if suddenly one can get rid of them simply by trying to become a better, nicer, kinder, "more conscious" person. The fatal consequences of some complexes can be the result of good intentions that arise from a so-called *"good conscience"* (that is, one that is conscious only of that which it is allowed to perceive[92]).

The way to deal with complexes requires challenging the consciousness of the individual, for the energetic situation in which the individual is immersed is frequently sustained and maintained by that individual's attitude and intentions, even when those are seemingly good, nice, just, and kind. The deception of a complex lies in the fact that it is activated in situations that seem to have nothing to do with the problems the individual experiences. For instance, take the case of someone having trouble finding and relating with a romantic partner. That individual might overlook the fact that in any resulting conflicts or hindrances with possible partners—whether caused by dissatisfaction, insufficient charm, lack of commitment, repetitive patterns, jealousy, infidelity, or any other trouble—it is the complex itself that is active and directing the interaction. Most of the times the complex is activated not in the situations where the one anticipates failure, but rather in crucial relationships where one feels one is on good terms, as it is often the case within the family of origin and the blood lineage.[93] This is just an example, and, of course, it does not attempt to reduce the complex theory into the triad relationship of mother-father-son.[94] There are many more relations, maybe innumerable psychic relations, in an individual's life. To confine one's explorations only to the mother and/or father is to fall short, fool oneself, and remain deliberately blind towards other active psychic influences of existence that in fact do affect the mother and the father, too, in different ways, but that involve them in own their specific complexes, which are especially shared among family members.[95]

This way of seeing into one's own ways of being opens up *ways of knowing* which were otherwise hidden from the habitual attitudes of consciousness and the habitual ways of explaining one's sufferings. What to other branches of psychology might seem to be personality disorders—such as a lack of ego strength, the absence of a functional psychological structure, fixations and ruptures in development, failures in the adaptation process, or some other sophisticated theory—are often an inability to recognize the forces that are the result of intense relationships, which generate a psychoactive complexity that moves along with the individual wherever he or she goes. In an uncanny way, the complex, which is just the way of naming the psychic complexities in which one is involved, moves through life, changing, sometimes becoming more active than others, but always affecting and being affected by the unfolding of one's existence. This complex in turn flows through the generations, passing from parents, to children, to grandchildren, to great-grandchildren and so on.

This does not mean that the complex is necessarily repeated in the same way in succeeding generations. That would be too simplistic, and if it does happen, it cannot be generalized. If it is taken as a rule, it just burdens perception, obscures understanding, defiles intuition, and limits reflection. The familial repetition of complexes rather implies that psychic patterning is a dynamic flow in which every individual is immersed, and in which every person lives and suffers, according to his or her own individuality. In addition, it is also obvious that since two, three, or more individuals are siblings does not necessarily mean that it is a given that they will suffer the same affections[96] and consequences of the complex. Every individual, despite the fact that he or she shares some psychic relations with others, lives, loves, suffers, acts, and dies following the peculiarities of his or her own *way of relating*.[97]

By being born into a family, which possesses a given family history and family consciousness, and which resides within a given social group and in a given place that itself possesses a culture with its own ideologies, religion, and traditions, an individual is already in several spheres of psychic influence, manifestation, movement, possibilities, limitations, and psychic unfolding. There is, however, a problem when only dealing with complexes theoretically, analytically, dialectically, or linguistically. Although reaching into the cultural and social domains in order to understand the psychic contents of a complex can appear to provide lucidity, this apparent clarity can be misleading. There is an inevitable danger that psychologists and psychotherapists have overlooked, and which has become a strong and difficult to break deception. Complexes cannot be dealt with by means of thought and elaborations of rhetoric. Complexes are not to be explored and explained by means of the intellect, with effective writing or persuasive speaking alone. Such approaches fail to render the necessary accuracy and promote a generalized flaw in perception. To write about the complexes in generalized ways, trying to cover whole cultures and peoples, with one's arguments and philosophies can quickly fall short. It is too easy to fall prey to the tricks of one's own consciousness, where the content of the argument is more than often distorted by the *orienting limitations* of the person doing the writing, whether motivated by a desire for academic recognition, publication, or grandiosity.[98]

A similar situation happens when people start to explore a complex independently or with the help of a therapist, without benefit of a phenomenological approach. When a complex is dealt with through analytic or interpretative means, the individual often makes observations and reaches conclusions that involve duping true perception and making up all kind of hyper-interesting explanations, at times amplified with mythological images. Unfortunately, the end result often reinforces the position of the individual without ever addressing or dealing with the actual psychic autonomous contents.

Dealing with the complex of a person does not mean improving that person. It does not mean enhancing a human's development, nor does it provide personality polishing or charisma improvement. To deal with a complex implies dealing with psychic contents that are independent and autonomous from the notion of I-ness, yet with which the "I" is in relation. Jung mentioned that it was "of some importance . . . to understand that there are contents which do not belong to the ego-personality, but must be ascribed to a psychic non-ego" (1960/1969, p.481). This understanding does not refer only to human-to-human relations, but it might encompass other-than-human beings and entities that can possibly influence the life of the individual, even going so far as to possess it. Jung was very well aware of how his psychological view of the complex was quite close to the notion of "possession" from the Middle Ages[99]. From his earliest writings he considered "the superstition held by all races that hysterical and insane persons are 'possessed' by demons [to be] right in conception"[100]. Jung argued that the complex, "by not fitting into the hierarchy of the conscious mind . . . [was the reason] why psychoneuroses and psychoses have from time immemorial been regarded as states of *possession*"[101]. It is worth clarifying that Jung did not refer only to the Church's idea of possession (which he acknowledged "is limited to extremely rare cases"), but he used the term "in a wider sense as designating a frequently occurring psychic phenomenon [,]" which he realized meant that, "any autonomous complex not subject to the conscious will exerts a possessive effect on consciousness proportional to its strength and limits the latter's freedom"[102],[103].

The complex, in this sense, prompts us to reflect on the multidimensionality and mysteries of the soul, where the notion of the psyche as solely personal and only on the human level is too narrow. According to Jung, it is advisable for psychology "to admit that there are other forms of psychic life besides the acquisition of personal consciousness"[104]. If considered carefully, this insight diminishes much of the importance of consciousness and consciousness studies, and shifts them to psyche, soul, a realm that Heraclitus long ago claimed remains "undiscovered, though explored forever to a depth beyond report"[105],[106].

Understanding the complex is crucial for further investigations in the domain of depth psychology and any field of study interested in deepening into the body and the human nature, for as Jung pointed out, "[t]he *via regia* to the unconscious is not the dream . . . but the complex, which is the architect of dreams and symptoms"[107],[108]. Explorations and investigations of the phenomenology of the complex allow us to observe the effects of psychic energy and its impact on the body, health, and healing. Departing from a standpoint that defines psyche as the primal phenomenon one can talk about and the physical world itself as psyche in a material form, although not limited solely to that, it then becomes clear that researching the impact of psychic energy deserves primary attention, for, as Jung observed, "some kind of energy underlies the changes in phenomena"[109], whether this occurs from circumstances that happen in an individual's life or from relationships or physical and corporeal conditions.

In the professions of service, health, and help, when exploring any issue related to an individual, it is important to start with psychic energy, for the complexes have a clear impact, first and foremost, on the body and its related issues. Many counseling and psychotherapeutic techniques focus on improving the conscious aspects of the individual by exploring and solving only the affairs of the individual's life and childhood. However, using the complex as a point of departure addresses not only the individual, but also the wider psychic sphere to which the individual inevitably belongs. This means that the complexes hold the aspects that require attention and need to be resolved or redeemed in some way, because they are, *in an individual notion*, the *"characteristic expressions of the psyche"*[110].

If the person or therapist is inexperienced, however, there is a common problem in the explorations of the psyche. It often occurs that the individual does not know where to start or what to explore. As a result, in the case of psychotherapy, the process might become excessively long, ambiguous, impractical, messy, and without a confined scope, as the person becomes lost in all sort of images and ideas that create a delusional miasma of self-discovery. In such cases, therapists frequently miss the important issues.

In order to approach the complex and see into and through it, two things are required. Firstly, it is necessary to have a setting in which psychic contents can be explored under a certain framework. Secondly, one should bring to the work an experimental and phenomenological attitude that does not rigidly depend on theories or approaches derived from books, but instead boldly follows *clear* perceptions and responds to what is shown. Jung, I believe, aware of the difficulties regarding an empirical and reliable approach to the complexes, wrote near the end of his Review on the Complex Theory, "[t]hree important problems have to be dealt with: The therapeutic, the philosophical, and the moral"[111]. It makes one think that he had glimpsed the problem of dealing with the complex in a phenomenological way, but had not arrived at clear method by which that could happen—and which he could demonstrate and teach.

Hillman, however, without addressing the problem of how to approach and display the complex, wrote extensively on how to deal with psyche and psychic contents. In the mid nineteen-seventies he proposed four basic moves that would re-vision—and deconstruct—many psychological assumptions, presuppositions, fallacies, and so-called certainties than in many cases had kept psychology without soul. These works, although they deal primarily with soul and ways to re-imagine a psychology with soul, can also be read for insights regarding the complex. Ultimately Hillman was not solely a Jungian analyst and a therapist, but also a meticulous scholar. The four psychological moves, which are not simply methods, but rather ways of knowing and being, are: personifying, pathologizing, psychologizing, and de-humanizing[112]. By personifying, Hillman meant: "envisioning and speaking of the configurations of existence as psychic presences"[113]. He recognized that the energetic patterns could be seen through images. In other words, he posited that the complex, rather than being considered as an abstraction or ideation of a psychic configuration and spoken of as a noun, could well be imagined with figures that would take the place, the body, and even the posture and gesture of the psychic contents, in other words, a sort of a psychic scenario with a plot.[114] This move would engage the complex, *through imagination*, in a participatory and phenomenological way.[115]

The second move, pathologizing, is a "mode of speech," but also a way of seeing into that which is metaphorically, and at times literally, "falling apart"[116]: the body with its afflictions, diseases, illnesses, symptoms, pains, and sicknesses. Hillman claimed that this move is actually "a royal road of soul-making" because it "returns us to soul"[117], to the important issues in life, issues that might have nothing to do with our egoistical intentions and desires. In this way, pathologizing clearly seems a "way of soul"[118], where the actual pathology one suffers points to psychic contents and to something or someone with which one is in (psychic) relation. It is not just a royal road to soul, but it is the imperative calling of the complex.

The third move, psychologizing, which he meant as "seeing through"[119], is a way of deliteralization, because, he claims, "[l]iteralism prevents mystery by narrowing the multiple ambiguity of meaning into one definition"[120], so, in a way, psychologizing is a meta-methodology, which is aware of its knowledge as always bound to perspective, and, therefore, avoiding fixed conclusions. It is not a way of seeing, but the action of *seeing through* while realizing that "soul's first habitual activity is reflection"[121]. In this sense, by psychologizing one can see through life, either in routines, events, circumstances, tragedies, misfortunes, dreams, dramas, or even in ideas, a reflection of one's (personal notion of) psyche. This move allows one to "move from the literal to the metaphorical"[122] in every situation, and consequently events "gain the element of significance for soul"[123]. Psychologizing as the activity of reflection could be said to be the act of awareness by which one engages psychic reality with life, bringing psyche into existence, and allowing psychic contents to be remembered and viewed through memory and the eyes of the heart.

The fourth move, de-humanizing, is a very important one. Hillman strongly argued for the need to detach psychology from being merely a branch of humanism, or, even worse, a science under the fantasy of the scientific method. As he presented it, de-humanizing means not becoming inhumane, but realizing that "[i]f our souls are not ours . . . our psychological afflictions and emotions too are not truly ours"[124]. He even dared to question the so-called "human faculties" and not take them for granted as human[125]. Hence, based on the idea that "a human life is a personification of the soul"[126], Hillman argued on the one hand how urgent it is to *dehumanize emotion,* and on the other hand, how crucial it is to *demoralize psychology*[127]. He also called this move *soul-making,* meaning that life is not important because of human interests, desires, wishes, goals, needs, and intentions, but for the sake of soul, which in many domains is "beyond our human reach"[128]. In this fourth move, without directly addressing or referring to the complex, he presented a psychological way of seeing and knowing, even a way of being, which is entirely aware of the psychic contents and dynamics that configure and constellate the frailty of human existence.[129]

Using imagination, mythological studies, and the notion of the imaginal,[130] Hillman took Jung's reflection a step further, and opened the possibility of exploring the complexes with a phenomenological approach that was image-based, not concept-based.[131] Rather than relying on a loyal faith and blind belief in grammar and semiotics to explain psychological issues, he examined them with bold acuteness and aesthetic sensitivity. Rather than having individuals (patients) formulate their issues with abstract considerations, and then explain them back with obscure but fancy concepts, he did it with the aid of imagination, as in dreams. Therefore, rather than sticking to theories and attaching his understanding to academic and clinical conventions, he followed the motto: *Stick to the image.*[132] With these four moves he detached from the analytical methods and from interpretations altogether, remaining with that which appeared through an individual's imagination, whether in dreams, daydreams, life stories, fictions, fantasies, pathologies, or *any kind of image.*[133] However, even though the approach revolutionized psychological approximations and explorations of psychic contents, there seemed to be something missing. Hillman's approach was, and still is, chaotic and oceanic, where one can easily fall into speculations about every image, and one can suddenly get lost in delusions, drowning in a *Neptunian* world where "psyche is all and everywhere." Hillman's four moves proposed for re-visioning psychology harbor a danger. Despite being strongly phenomenological, soul-centered (without meaning that the soul is the center), and psychically oriented, his approach carries the danger in the infinity of possibilities to imagine and get interested in.

In Hillman's work one can notice a *Saturnian*, always grounding, aim that does not get lost in transcendental realms or other-worldly interests. His *Martial* and penetrating insights opened deep ways to explore the complexes and the psychic realms, where he addressed *the therapeutic, the philosophical, and the moral.* But to remain only in the realms of images and the imaginal, regardless of the elusiveness of its highly mytho-poetic style, does not always address the practical, the mundane, the relational, the immediate, and immanent dimension of earthly life. In some ways, Hillman's style can be a great risk to others, with the threat of making psychological explorations mere literature, or making of psychology a creative process that entertains, that is interesting, and that might be controversial and radical, but that is also useless, vague, and mostly a rhetorical game of great sophistication.[134]

Jung first and then Hillman discovered and wrote extensively on the patterns of psychic energy that could be imagined and amplified archetypally through the myths of any culture. In my opinion, the practical result of such activities, however, seems to have remained in darkness for many years. It was there, but hard to see. The therapeutic aspect was affected in some circles; the philosophical aspect gained the perspective of depth psychology, and particularly archetypal psychology and the imaginal; and the moral aspect got severely challenged. Those three domains were enriched, but all this happened primarily in a theoretical way, with rich sophistry, but little impact. Jung's last line in the Review of the Complex Theory, addressing those aspects said that, "[a]ll three await discussion"[135], and that discussion indeed took place. It occurred for several years in very interesting ways and with radical perspectives, but the three aspects have remained in discussions, mere discussions.

Jung, knowing that "in the realm of complicated psychic processes … the experimental procedure cannot be restricted to certain definite possibilities," was well aware of the need to explore and experiment with the effects of the complex "without the safeguards afforded by specific aims," and most probably without definite intentions, giving rise to what he called a "constellation."[136] He realized the need to explore the psychic circumstances of the individuals far beyond their conscious attitudes, and far beyond his own interpretative ideations. Jung used the word constellation when referring to a circumstantial display of the psychic atmosphere, where "the outward situation releases a psychic process in which certain contents gather together and prepare for action"[137]. He knew from his early word-association tests that certain stimuli (an outward situation) could trigger reactions (psychological and physiological), and could keep the individual under an action pattern that was directly in relation to the psychic contents that the stimuli activated. However, Jung also knew that such psychic contents could be activated without a deliberate presentation of the stimuli; in other words, they could be activated by the outward (worldly) situations in which the individual typically and ordinarily moves.[138]

For instance, an individual has a discussion with someone important in his or her life, that is, a partner, mother, or boss, and then later while on a road far away from that person, the individual has an accident and crashes the car. Beyond the legal matters that determine whose fault it was, who is guilty, and who will pay, it is as if the life situation constellated the psychic atmosphere that the individual did not want to face honestly. What "outwardly" seems like an unexpected rupture, an abrupt stop, an unseen crossing element, a sudden failure, or the like, and that would popularly be called chance, might be due to *a flaw in one's conscious attention*. It is as if a deeper (not-conscious) quality of attention, with its own intentions, had directed such an event. In such situations, it is said that *psyche constellates fate*, as if fate puts the pieces together and moves them in such a way that the individual inevitably gets into it.[139] Jung knew that psychic contents were autonomous for the individual, just as the outward world is. In this sense, considering that everyone lives within energetic patterns (complexes) of love and action, everyone also experiences life in regard to what gets autonomously constellated, according to one's psychic atmosphere, whether one recognizes it or not.[140]

Somehow Jung also knew that the complex could be elicited, explored, displayed, seen, and then worked out or worked off, in order to shift certain psychic processes that otherwise would remain occult or invisible to the ordinary way of seeing.[141] Therefore, he used the noun "constellation" and the verb "to constellate" when referring to the way of manifestation that showed the psychic contents with their peculiar dynamics in a phenomenological and somehow *visible* manner (at least to the eye of imagination). However, he did not seem to know how to facilitate empirically the constellation within a public consensus, it all remained imaginative speculation (from the Latin *speculari*) derived from his insights, experiences, investigations, and *ways of seeing into and through psyche*. In other words, Jung seemed to have been aware of the reality and tremendous impact of psychic processes that were not visible by means of ordinary sight, that were not perceived equally by everyone, but that somehow could be changed, although they were impossible to explore under the scientific paradigms of his time. In spite of all that, I would say that he opened this field and way of knowing in a professional, serious, committed, and grounded fashion.

Many decades later, Hellinger offered a method that seems to be a contemporary answer to Jung's concern about *the therapeutic, the philosophical, and the moral* aspects of the complex theory. Today, more than seventy years after Jung's essay on The Review of Complex Theory was first published, a method has fully emerged that engages those three aspects in a practical, empirical, and sensuous way: the Family Constellations method. Hellinger developed this method after many years of dedicated study and praxis. Despite the fact that Hellinger was not trained as a Jungian analyst nor particularly Jung-oriented, at least as far as anyone knows, his work and discoveries powerfully and successfully address what Jung defined as the complex.

It is worth noticing what Jung wrote in 1922 in what would later become his *Red Book* about a conversation he had with his soul regarding the "new religion." His soul told him that the new religion "expresses itself only in the transformation of human relations[,]" because "[r]elations do not let themselves be replaced by the deepest knowledge"[142]. Indeed, after decades of having worked with Family Constellations, Hellinger ventured to call his method the *Hellinger Sciencia*, also known as, the science of all human relations.[143]

A brief story, titled *The Spheres of Reality*, might illustrate these insights.

A young man woke up in a beautiful valley where an eagle had eaten a snake (although some say it was a falcon that ate a serpent), that region of Earth watched over by Iztlaccíhuatl and Popocatépetl, and permanently grieved by Malintzin. The young man was an ordinary fellow, but he was eager to know the wonders of life. One day, while walking on the periphery of the old city, he met an old man; so old and rare was this man that the young man felt that he was in front of an ancient man, a man from another time, almost a mythical time. The young man greeted him and the old man replied kindly. The young man asked him where he was from, and the old man told him that he was from the same city, but that in his time life had been different. When the younger man asked in what ways, the old man answered that in his time it had been more wonder-full. The young man naïvely asked what wonders he was referring to, and the old man answered, "The wonders of life." The younger man begged him to tell him how to recognize them.

"I'll tell you," the old man said, "although it's difficult to understand. You'll think it absurd, but it is the only possible way to see these wonders, the so-called miracles. First of all you need to know that we live in almost absolute darkness. Most people live this way most of their life, if not all of it. However, everyone believes, with childish faith, that after dawn and until dusk there is light."

"And it is so, indeed," replied the youngster.

"I told you it was difficult to understand," the old man said, "but leave your indulgent comments to someone else, and allow yourself to see the landscape that I will describe for you." He took a deep breath and, looking into the young man's eyes, said, "There is a physical domain, which most people foolishly call 'reality', but that is only a limited version of reality. Most people believe with great confidence that reality is the same to everybody, but it is only the physical version of it that which is publicly shared, in a consensus, so to speak. Therefore, the most important thing you have to know is that we all live in different settings, almost as if we were living at different times, even though it might seem to you that the people you meet are in the same place at the same time."

"If that's not so, how is it possible to meet them?" asked the youngster.

"Let me continue, and if you leave your stubbornness aside at least you'll be able to wonder. All the people that you know and that you have met also live in other domains of reality, not just in the limited version of it. Those other versions, however, are not seen consensually; that is, those other

versions do not look the same to one and all. For some they look one way, for others in a different way. The majority of people, unfortunately, have no clue that these different realities exist, so people share the domain of 'physical reality,' and because of that they get along, get married, and do businesses, and so on. But there are other domains of reality in which they also participate, in which they are deeply interrelated, and through which they become powerfully connected, but which they, most often, do not experience in consensus, but privately."

"Oh, I see," said the youngster.

"The most important issue of all this deep obscurity that we call 'physical reality' is that if you do not at least recognize that there are other domains of reality, then you'll end up believing that physical reality, in a materialistic sense, is all there is. But worst of all, you'll end up trying to fix things and problems seeing only physicality and materiality, when in fact all issues that you call problematic, from tooth decay and bankruptcy to cancer and unhappiness, have their cause in these other domains. That's why physical reality is often referred to as the great darkness. Living in physicality without acknowledging the other domains of reality is like always walking and doing things without any light. Even though you can live half of your days with common sunlight, from dawn till dusk, you might as well be living in plain obscurity, without ever venturing to wonder that there are other worlds, which are quite powerful actually," said the old man. Then, after another deep breath, he continued: "The paradox of the other domains of reality is that they are nowhere. They aren't somewhere else, but right here. The world, as you see it, is a sphere superimposed and interpenetrated by other spheres, all of them forming this Earth, right now. This paradox might give you one blessing or many curses. The curses are the limitations to physicality, not only in terms of perception, movement, and knowledge, but also in terms of decay, sickness, and mortality, as well as many others that I need not name. The one blessing is bliss," said the old man before becoming quiet again.

"But, what does this have to do with the wonders of life?" inquired the young man.

"All the wonders in life come from the realization of bliss. The more you realize your actuality and activity in the other spheres of reality, the more you'll be blessed. If you remain unaware of it, it is not that you'll be cursed, but you'll feel as if casualties, failures, and accidents are a lack of something," said the old man. "The feeling of lack moves people to uncontrolled desire, from lust, gluttony, laziness, and greed, to envy, pride, and rage. But the fact is that all those afflictions are physical manifestations produced by a lack of acknowledgement of the other domains, and a misdirected desire. In the end, no one wants any of those mundane desires. The only 'real' desire is the taste of the bliss, and, little by little, taste by taste, to strive towards fulfillment and ecstasy. In principle this is all you need to know."

When the old man had finished speaking, his whole body smiled. He walked away, and as he went into the old city, he vanished out of sight.

Chapter 2

The Constellation: A Display of the Complex

"After accepting the pragmatic existence of the other reality, the brujo would only have to learn the mechanical aspect of such a movement."

Las enseñanzas de Don Juan[144]

In Hellinger's work and words, a constellation is a phenomenological procedure[145] that occurs in a group setting, where:

> a person with a serious problem or that is severely ill, chooses representatives [from the rest of participants in the group] as members of his family and *places them in a special relation to one another* (italics added). . . As soon as these representatives stand in the places that were assigned, they experiment feelings that seem to reflect something from the persons they represent[146].

This method has nothing to do with theater, acting, performing, or role-playing in its popular sense.[147] It is merely an experience that opens up through a sentient intelligence, where one does not think or analyze what should be done; one, as a representative within a deliberate and intentional field of manifestation, only lets the body be exposed to feelings and sensations and slowly moves accordingly.[148] As simple as this sounds, however, this method has revolutionized psychotherapy and even left it behind. What is crucial about this method is its phenomenological approach, where one gets fully exposed to that which shows itself, without using it as a basis any kind of analytical methodology or an interpretative procedure. If one would have to explain phenomenology in a single sentence, the best rendering would probably be found in the following fragment from Heraclitus: "Those things which are learned by sight and hearing (i.e. by the sense organs) I honour [*sic*] more"[149],[150] as if the awareness to *sensation* were that which propitiates veritable knowledge—or consciousness, as Jung mentioned.[151] It is important to mention, however, that, "awareness not only is receptive, but it creates a field of energy and has an external effect"[152].[153]

This method for helping people opened up and offered a radical way of knowing. Starting in the nineteen seventies and eighties, it began working from a systemic standpoint,[154] where people's problems were considered from a perspective that embraced much more than just the individual, and their solutions were often sought while facilitating a *systemic psychotherapy*[155]. In the realm of this therapy, *the family of origin* was considered to be the main and most important system. Therefore, the aim of the procedure was to look at the whole system and to attend to it in the best and most balanced way, and not solely for the sake of the person seeking for help. At the time, the constellations were basically a therapeutic approach with representatives for the literal people of the individual's family, people of that lineage from the past, people related to the lineage but not necessarily blood relations, and some ancestors. These "representatives," to use Hellinger's words, would feel and sense in ways that were foreign to them, having nothing to do with the representatives' actual life situations, in most cases. It was observed, then, that these feelings, sensations, and even thoughts pertained to the people they were representing. This reporting of feelings and sensations was what allowed the phenomenological method to work; it allowed the consultant to observe a family dynamic in which the person was involved yet to which he or she was blind, a dynamic which he or she would never be able to describe accurately with words or through simple talk therapies.[156] The therapeutic aim was to disentangle the individual from ways of relating that would keep him or her under a difficult—and at times sickening—family dynamic, and where it would be nearly impossible to do so otherwise. It is important to mention that the notion of "family dynamic" is not reduced to situations in which one lives with, or close to, the family of origin, as if once out of the parents' sight and house one were free of it.[157]

While dealing in essence with family members, either from two, three, or four generations back, or one or two generations in the future, using this method revealed that many issues that disturb or perturb an individual are *related to issues* that happened in previous generations, dynamics that transcend the notions of physical space and time. Hence, it was not just family therapy working with the members that were alive, but also a therapeutic approach that worked with those family members who had been dead for decades who were important and relevant to the family system. Therefore, it has always been a trans-generational method for doing therapy. In its beginnings, it started to revolutionize the taken for granted ways of knowing that would sustain themselves merely on an interpretative understanding. Psychotherapy, as a consequence, and in my opinion, was radically challenged, never to be the same.

In the beginnings of the constellations work it was observed that many life issues that individuals seeking help wanted to solve were in fact *related* to family events that the individual knew from one, two, three, or even four generations back. Such events from the past were not necessarily the same in content, and, moreover, could have been actually entirely different. For example, an individual seeking help for a problem in his marriage might discover that his marital conflicts were *in relation* to a murderous act committed by some ancestor in his blood lineage. These kinds of conclusions were not assumed, but seen and perceived through a phenomenological approach when the people involved in such issues from the past were brought into the present through the embodiment of the representatives.[158] But the further the explorations went "back" in time (allowing this metaphor of linear time for the sake of *this* explanation), trying to reach several generations "back," the more those facts and events were uncertain, and for most individuals completely unknown. It is very common that people do not know the history of their family for more than three generations back. However, just because the facts about the past remain unknown does not mean that they are unimportant. It might be advisable not to think that the therapeutic aspect of the constellations work is limited solely to the nuclear family and factual family events that the individual knows or can learn about. Rather, it is better to see that Hellinger's work is only the beginning of something radical, because the constellations are able to open a multidimensional field of consciousness that might transcend literality, allowing symbolic expressions of the psyche.

It is important to mention that Hellinger's way of doing constellations follows a very structured way of dealing with issues and problems. Before anything else, it is crucial to point out what he calls the "rigorous distinction" between perception and observation: "Observation leads to partial units of knowledge united to the loss of a global vision[;]" on the contrary, while being "exposed to perception," he said, "details get lost and I immediately capture the essential, the nucleus, and all these, also, in the service of the rest"[159]. It is from *this kind* of perception that one enters into a qualitative way of being, from where one participates in what shows up, allowing it to happen, getting exposed to what needs to appear, and refraining from judging or making quick interpretations. This I believe to be *a very clear grade of, or even transparent, perception*, not flawed by the tinctures or frames of one's own personal conscious contents; as such, it sets the stage for anything to occur, anything, no matter how horrendous and terrible.[160] Furthermore, I believe this is why Hellinger called his way of knowing a *participative knowing*, where one is active simply by perceiving fully and seemingly without fear, doing by non-doing.[161] It is an entirely different "therapeutic attitude"[162] from the normal attitude where, Hellinger once mentioned, "theory burdens the praxis"[163].[164] Hellinger's comment is similar to Jung's advice when he said: "Learn the best, know the best—and then forget everything when you face the patient"[165]. In other words, dare to perceive clearly and vastly.[166]

Perception, therefore, is the basis of this method, but one could say that it also follows some structures of attention. In this method, the first structure is the physical body of the individual, which is the gateway to any phenomenological method that aims for an empirical experience. In this way, it could be said that Hellinger's work starts with the "body" of the individual seeking help and the bodies of the "representatives," where the effects are observed qualitatively through gestures, postures, movements, gazes, looks, and mostly felt-presence, as well as their positions in relation to the others (distance, closeness, angle) while they are displayed on a physical terrain.

The second structure is quite important for it prevents getting lost in any so-called emotional issue; otherwise, the attention deviates from the essential into the consequential. This structure is the family system, with which, according to Hellinger, "we form a community with a common fate"[167]. This therapeutic frame on the family allows the phenomenological work to remain focused on the essential and important, which otherwise could encompass virtually anything, from causalities, dreams, excuses, justifications, failures, ideas, images of any kind, emotions, or any sort of "conscious" conflict. Hellinger claims to have obtained this frame of the family system structure from his therapeutic trainings in transactional analysis, family therapy, and family constellations according to McClendon and Kadis first, and according to Schönfelder later[168]. However, the "order of origin" has been recognized as his insightful discovery[169], from which he was able to explain the "conditions for the development of a family net"[170].

A third structure properly speaking relies already on the "conditions," also commonly known as the *orders of love.* The first order is the "right of belonging," in which Hellinger explained who belongs to the family net or family system (this will be detailed further in the chapter called "Family"). The second order is the "law of complete number," where he asserts that one feels genuinely complete when one has included all those who belong to the family system. The third order is the "law of priority of those who were first," in which he argues that those who came before have priority in the right of belonging. And the fourth order is "to recognize that everything is ephemeral"[171], which, of course, is one of life's greatest paradoxes.[172]

With this therapeutic setting and framework, Hellinger continued to develop his work, helping people from being sidetracked by unimportant issues in their lives, and keeping them focused on what he considered crucial: family bonds, family of origin, fate, and an earthly life. Even today, to some people this method of helping people might still seem very basic and fundamental.

However, by focusing only on the family system issues, that is, on *events* that changed the individuals' lives, Hellinger reduced the possibility of hitting unimportant aspects to almost none, and by exploring issues in a phenomenological way, the possibilities to fail are proportional to the lack of accurate perception. Hellinger's therapeutic method, which he named "Family Constellations," is in a way failure-proof and very efficient, although it can be done at varying levels of depth.

It is not certain how much Hellinger knew the about the psychic aspects of life, for he did not mention them in his first books. However, when Hellinger's work and discoveries are woven into Jung's reflections and writings, one can see that Hellinger developed a method that directly addresses what Jung called the complexes. It might not have been Hellinger's interest, but he discovered an empirical way for dealing therapeutically, and in front of a public consensus, with the psychic energetic patterns, which manifest themselves primarily and most vividly in the affectivity of the family system's members.[173]

Affectivity,[174] interestingly, is the core of the complexes—although affects are better imagined and viewed as akin to weather, something that involves the individual, but never something that he or she possesses. According to Jung, "A complex would not be a complex at all if it did not possess a certain, even considerable, affective intensity"[175]. Somehow, affect is the most important and energizing aspect, making the complex relevant in terms of relations. As a consequence affects generate either movement towards or against something (or someone), or an attitude about something (or towards someone). It is worth noticing in the early writings of Jung where he mentioned that, "affects have a dissociating (distracting) effect on consciousness, probably because they put a one-sided and *excessive emphasis on a particular idea* (italics added), so that little attention is left over for investment in other conscious psychic activities"[176]. However, it seems also crucial to mention that Jung, being influenced by his mentor, Bleuler, considered attention as "nothing more than a special form of affectivity" . . . "always directed by an affect". . . "[doing] nothing more than what we know affectivity does, i.e., it facilitates certain associations and inhibits others"[177].[178] The emphasis of attention, however, can fall unknowingly on a particular psychic person (whether dead or alive), which as a consequence takes over the intensity of attention from the individual, and, as a result, produces compulsive ideas or thoughts, strange or stubborn behaviors, weird dreams, inexplicable fears, pathological fantasies, or any sort of conduct—as if trapping the individual, without his or her consent or awareness, in such relation or issue, and not leaving enough energy for the rest of life's activities.[179]

A simple example regarding affects can be observed in the relation one has with one's first sexual partner, with whom one often is (or was) deeply in love, because affective intensity produces a very strong bond.[180] Many life events receive less importance at the time, and such a relation absorbs a good amount of psychic attention and physical "energy." Years or even decades after the couple has separated there is a psychological reaction regarding the sphere of sexuality, which is tinctured by the affectivity from such a relation. Psychologically speaking, the relation never disappears; *it is* (psychoactive) as having happened, and as having been the first. It might elicit certain feeling-tone responses, either of joy and cheerfulness, rage and anger, or shame and indifference, but it remains a part of the individual's psychic life regardless of his or her attention, and regardless of whether or not the two actual physical people ever see each other again. Between such people there is an affective condition, which usually becomes active solely at the mention of the other's name. The affectivity, therefore, remains, not as a sentimental situation, but as a psychological complexity that elicits memories, moods, ideas, fantasies, states of mind, and that moves one's energy, producing emotion. Important people in one's life (such as the one just mentioned) and in one's family history are the main psychic presences that configure one's psychological complexes.

It seems then that without the charged atmosphere, due to its affectivity, the complex would not be of any relevance. However, affectivity might just be the way to designate and name the sensed psychic state that one recognizes, in particular moments, as one flows and navigates through life. Affectivity, in this sense, is not something that is inside the skin, or in some sort of secret interiority, or something that pertains more to introverts than extroverts. Rather, it comes close to a weather condition that one cannot predict, control, or change at will, something that one inevitably experiences and goes through. In this sense affectivity seems like the atmospheric current that elicits particularized ways of moving through it. "Thoughts and actions," and even feelings, are seen then as "only symptoms of [it]"[181].

From this perspective, the affective intensity is not something one experiences alone, in one's "inside," or as a reaction to one's "mental life." It is rather a tension between psychic contents that are physically present at some times and not at others. However, it is always a *tension produced in the relation between* these contents (persons or images) and the "I," which is also one more psychic content, a mere image.[182]

For instance, it could be observed that some people who chronically are emotionally perturbed or depressed, present an affective condition that is not in relation to their actual life situation. This happens often when one is being affected by contents that do not pertain to the physical reality, but which are psychically active, nevertheless. For example, the death of an important family member might disturb a person for years, and the bond between the person and the dead relative can be so intense that the living person might go through an atmosphere of interminable sadness, with an evident lack of vitality and indifference toward existence, until the relationship is healthily released. In cases such as this, it becomes clear that affectivity is not necessarily produced by actual physical circumstances, but instead by the relationships that inevitably move, change, shift, and end throughout one's life. Affectivity is like invisible weather, always happening, always felt, always moving and changing, always present and affecting one's own life unfolding, in one way or another. This metaphor, however, is not applicable in a spatial manner to the actual physical conditions, or to place. *Affectivity, somehow, is lived differently by every individual, according to one's own way of being and affected by one's own ways of relating (with the autonomous psychic contents).*

Hence Hellinger's discoveries and contributions to matters pertaining to family systems are quite important, for indeed he addressed matters pertaining to relationships that went far beyond only living family members. His systemic psychotherapy and the trans-generational approach, whether or not he knew about the complex theory, directly addressed and sought solutions for the affective dynamics that in many cases were not dynamics related to physical but to psychical contents (persons or images).

Hellinger observed with great clarity that many people were affected by contents that were beyond their capacity to perceive, contents even that those people were strongly denying, repressing, or simply not seeing; or contents that were disorienting because they were out of the range of people's consciousness—therefore un-conscious. Such a view of Hellinger's work fits the "[t]wo main grounds . . . in explaining the unconsciousness of the complex," one being the "repression of a content capable of becoming conscious," and also the "*strangeness* (italics added) of a content not yet capable of reaching consciousness"[183]. For example, the presence of a dead person often might not be recognized, or due to one's belief system, the very notion of that presence might be dismissed as a weird or absurd idea, a mere superstition, and therefore not considered or included into one's consciousness or one's heart; for it is often thought that dead people are simply not existent and gone.

Jung observed that "[t]he nuclear element [of the complex] is characterized by its feeling-tone, the emphasis resulting from the intensity of affect"[184], which is almost as if it would *infect* ordinary everyday circumstances. The reason behind this lies in the observation that "[t]he nuclear element has a constellating power corresponding to its energic [*sic*] value"[185]. In simpler words, the feeling-tone reactions, which are experienced personally and bodily, occur due to the affective atmosphere; that affective atmosphere, in turn, is the result of psychic contents being *in relation*, but those reactions affect the publicly shared circumstances in which the individual lives. Hence it is often said that these reactions autonomously constellate situations in everyday public life that reaffirm the energetic setting of contents, even if those are repeatedly problematic, sickening, isolating, or even deadening. Jung clearly saw that "complexes behave like independent beings"[186], where oneself (in the notion of I-ness) is merely one more participant in a psychic milieu. Therefore, he warned: "whatever you repress . . . is constellated outside of you; it works in your surroundings and influences other people"[187].

Hellinger's work started facilitating solutions regarding crucial relations for the individuals (mostly family and couple relationships), without being specifically directed towards other psychic contents. However, he opened up a method to deal with contents that can be outside of ordinary ways of seeing, or that were never in sight for individuals, such as matters related to people from several generations in the past. So, by looking into the trans-generational background of individuals, and by discovering that most issues that individuals suffered from had some relation to events from the past, Hellinger intuitively or purposively addressed psychic contents that were already out of sight for the individuals—as it is when a representative takes the place and position of someone who is not alive anymore, a dead person. The constellations method, focusing on all relations and ways of relating, revealed how to cope with contents that pertain to a psychic domain—the complex—and which can be invisible; but whose effects and consequences are physically felt and suffered.

Hellinger's practical, brief, and Zen-like work, which he once referred to as "the simplest and most ordinary"[188], might seem for some to have nothing to do with Jung's richly imaginative, mythic, and speculative work. But in fact, and in a practical sense, it is the most effective method yet devised to address *the therapeutic* aspect of the complex theory.[189] Hellinger, who considered his work to be purely phenomenological, has been called a great empiricist. But in this Hellinger does not differ from Jung, who claimed: "I am an empiricist and adhere to the phenomenological standpoint"[190]. Despite his great analytical and synthetical skills, Jung was also an acute perceiver of that which happens in the psychic fields. To better understand Jung's complex theory in relation to Hellinger's constellations, and vice versa, and in order to gain a deeper understanding of *the philosophical* and *the moral* aspects of such work, Hillman's contributions are required.

In *Re-visioning Psychology*[191], the touchstone of archetypal psychology, Hillman seemed to have already seen and revealed part of the method.[192] When he wrote about personifying,[193] although he was referring to an imagining process with which to deepen into imaginal realms, he was already doing something similar to Hellinger's constellation.[194] In this way, Hillman, leaving concepts aside and by means of images, knew how to address the contents of the complex. Initially he dealt with them by *figuring out* images, and then treating them as if they were persons, autonomous psychic persons, independent of one's will.[195] His psychological move called personifying was in fact close to the constellation's principle of representing anything (presences, the death, fate or even other people) with people who were present in the group setting.[196] It might be a coincidence, but constellations are also known as *configurations.*[197]

Rather than doing therapy by the aid of existential categories, psychoanalytic concepts, philosophical ideas, relating patterns, or even Jungian terms, Hillman proposed a therapeutic way of "imagining things"[198], problems, and relations, where all could be personified and ensouled—because all belongs to Soul.

Instead of speaking of the burst of anger, the incontrollable fear, the panic attack, or the saddening loneliness, and simply trying to deal with it or somehow solve it, by making sense of it, Hillman proposed looking into life issues as if they were entities—people. The fear or the anger can then be related to an actual psychic person, after which it is possible to depersonalize the feelings (which may simply be the result of the affective intensity in the relations with such people). Not in vain did Hillman call this psychological move "a way of soul-making"[199], where the important contents (psychic persons) of the psyche are attended to.

Hillman also proposed pathologizing as a way of seeing into that which is "falling apart." With this insight, he realized that symptoms, illnesses, and so-called incurable, chronic, or terminal diseases are soul's "autonomous ability"[200] to live through something that the soul wants one to see and attend to.[201] He cynically observed that "[t]he soul can exist without its therapists but not without its afflictions"[202]; which, if personified, might point to images that otherwise would have been forgotten and lost: ancestors, friends, dead people, relatives, family members, strangers, and who knows what else.

Hillman, by observing that "pathologizing forces the soul [in its individual notion] to a consciousness of itself as different from the ego and its life"[203], uncovered the insight that consciousness needs to perceive much more than what it usually does—either through images, or through pathologies.[204] For him "consciousness means psychic reflection of the *psychic* world about us and is part of adaptation to that reality"[205]. In its *function*, his definition aligns with Jung's, who said consciousness is what allows one to *perceive the psychic contents,* and adapt, orient, and relate one's personal life with, and to, them.[206]

By means of personifying and pathologizing, Hillman discovered a successful method to acknowledge, respect, honor, and deal with not-conscious contents; and in a certain way, his 'psychological moves' are close to and similar to the constellations method. Perhaps he opened the field with such insights, perhaps not. In either case, he furthered Jung's therapeutic ideas, and his contributions can be considered, *in some ways,* as precursors to the new[207] constellations method by Hellinger. However, Hillman's work and reflections, if not fully grounded on the immanent, can lift the individual into an imaginative, almost drug-like mist. On the other hand, Hellinger's to-the-point approach, based on family and systemic psychotherapy[208], provides a solid ground that keeps things in the earthly realm and even within the mundane.

The constellations method principally uses the family system as a basis to work with, but Hellinger also observed that conscience plays a very important role in the process, if not the crucial one. He defines conscience as the "organ of equilibrium" that watches over the relationships[209], and he distinguishes several types of it. First he acknowledges an "individual conscience," which operates on the principle of innocence or guilt, pleasure or displeasure. This conscience is recognized by the sensed effect it produces, which is always experienced in relationships. So, for example, when one does something that could damage the relation, one experiences guilt or displeasure, because one fears not being part of such relational system any longer[210],[211].

Hellinger also acknowledges what he calls a "family conscience" that is "not perceived through sensation or through feelings." Rather, this is a "participative conscience" that "looks for the *order and equilibrium* (italics added) for all the members of the family net [or system]." This conscience, Hellinger maintains, "remains unconscious" to the individual, and that one "has more possibility to know it is through the suffering that it causes to ignore its order, either in oneself or in others, especially the children"[212]. According to Hellinger, from this perspective the individual conscience can be sensed and felt, and according to the pleasure-displeasure principle, one acts and reacts to keep the equilibrium. But in the equilibrium of the family conscience "one can just find what helps through knowledge that comes from understanding"[213]. In other words, one has *to know* and respect the family orders—what Hellinger called *the orders of love*[214] (*in the family*). This means that one could feel a kind of pleasure while disrupting the orders of love, but in the long run one will pay the consequences—oftentimes difficult ones. However, there are other sorts of consciences, which include more people than simply the blood-related or family-related, and which Hellinger called *group conscience*[215]. While these might seem to be arbitrarily designated groups, they are what bring, and keep, people together within certain ideologies, traditions, religions, cultures, or practices of any sort—and they impose rules, codes, and limits. And there can be groups within bigger groups.[216]

For example, an individual belongs to a family, and its family conscience; and the family, by living in a certain region, belongs to that region in a given country; but ultimately the family (as a group) also feels that it belongs to that country—and behaves, feels, and thinks accordingly. These groups are limited by a "participative conscience" that is *exclusive* only to those who belong, and so it keeps people's actions (in thought, speech, discourse, and behavior) limited and delimited. For instance, in Westernized countries people do not stone women to death, because it would seem wrong and cruel. But in some of the same countries a person can be legally killed by the death penalty, and it might be considered fine, and people might consent to it and approve of it.[217] The danger is that individuals or groups, following their group conscience, can perform terrible deeds in the name of what they perceive to be good and just, like going to war, for instance.[218] Hellinger also called these groups' consciences the collective conscience[219]. But he mentioned yet another conscience that is wider and *all-inclusive*, perhaps unfathomable. This he called the *spiritual conscience*, where one "overcomes the limits of the personal conscience and the collective [or group's] conscience"[220]. It becomes clear then, that for Hellinger, conscience seems to be that which limits and delimits perception—and action as a consequence—and it functions in a way that tinctures and frames the perception with what is permitted in the family, group, and the collective, and perhaps not letting the individual perceive clearly, as Hellinger often plainly said: "*as it is*"[221]. In this sense, a spiritual conscience might be thought of as the organ which allows one to perceive in full clearness and with an expansive vision, not having the perceptual tinctures and frames of one's family or one's groups, so that one sees the world as it is.

When Jung's notion of consciousness as an organ of orientation is woven into Hillman's notion of consciousness as the reflection of the psychic world around an individual, and then that combination is woven into Hellinger's notion of conscience (whether the personal, familial or group) as an organ of equilibrium and limitation, then the philosophical and the moral aspects of the complex theory acquire a deeper and wider vision (which will be reviewed later in this book). For Jung, consciousness is a sense-based function that establishes the perceived; for Hillman, it is the reflective function that perceives, or not, the psychic contents about oneself; and for Hellinger, it seems to be the awareness of the balancing function that is sense-based on an individual level, but "sanctioning and compensating"[222] on a familial and collective level.[223]

Consciousness, in any case, is affected and influenced by contents that go beyond the boundaries of the known. In Jung's notion it is affected by the vast un-conscious; in Hillman's notion it is affected by the unfathomable psychic world in which one dwells; and in Hellinger's notion it is affected mostly by the consciousness and fate of the family of origin, whether it is known or not—where "further members suffer the injustices committed to [or by] previous members"[224].

Consciousness, as a consequence, cannot be studied then from the individual perspective alone, where there is no room for other contents that come from beyond the individual sphere, beyond one's lifetime, and beyond one's ordinary comprehension. Consciousness studies might be completely different if they were to include the unconscious as defined by Jung—as that which escapes the domain of one's consciousness and perception, and which is autonomous.[225] In some sense, this might come close to the idea and word for consciousness in Tibetan, which "has a broader range of application than the English term in that it covers not only the whole range of conscious experiences but also those *forces* (italics added) that might be recognized as part of the so-called unconscious"[226].

The usual constellations method, which can be seen as *a phenomenological display of the complexes*, deals effectively with what Jung called the "autonomous unconscious," with what Hillman called "the invisibles" or "the imaginal or psychic figures", and with what Hellinger discovered to be "the family conscience" the "group's conscience" and "the trans-generational contents." In some ways, this method could be akin to some old ways of divination, where the aim is "not to learn what the future is going to be, but *to find out how the component parts of the present stand in relationship to each other* (italics added)," as it is with the Cherokee[227]. One of Hellinger's aim, I believe, and which contains a very profound insight, is the insistence on the importance of knowing, observing, respecting, and following the orders of love. It is not a coincidence that Jung conceived of and foresaw that the new religion "does not consist only in knowledge, but at its visible level in a new *ordering* (italics added) of human affairs"[228].

The constellations method, however, has not been static. It has been a common mistake and misinterpretation to consider Hellinger's work as *just* a systemic psychotherapy (in the common mainstream psychological way). His method is partly based on contributions from it, but it is not only that, and definitely it is not one more among the many family therapies. It certainly started there, but it moved further, kept developing, and reached a point where the chronological and factual dimension of historical time became fuzzy and unapproachable, and where the psychic contents (and presences) were ambiguous, uncertain, and indeterminate. The display of the complex with representatives for the literal persons that might have been involved in some issue or event from the past is useful, as long as there is a chronological ordering by generations when constellating, and a defined positioning and identification when dealing with the contents (the psychic persons and specific events).

In recent years, Hellinger has taken bold steps, which have opened up another dimension for working with psychic issues—with other-than-human presences. The constellations work, in the development of its new method, has become a qualitative and not extensive approach, quite suitable for the work regarding ancestry, where *time is not understood, and not displayed, as a line in space.* In this sense, the physical space (where the constellations takes place) is not used to extend time, placing the past and those who lived before behind and the future and the coming generations in front. This kind of constellation can open an intense experience that breaks the usual conception and notion of chronological time, where the past and the future are not far away (as if they were extended far behind or far ahead), but vividly and *intensely* present.[229] Therefore, the representatives for people of the past are not isolated units or people, but processes and movements of the multiplicity of soul that occur in the life-time of an individual. These movements are experienced as multiple influences, and are multiple in themselves. Therefore, time is often felt, and better understood, as a multiplicity without number, as *an intensity of experience* without numerical value or identifiable content, and something which in its core is *pure quality.* This is, in my words, what Hellinger has called the *multidimensional constellations*[230]—which, if not experienced, can hardly be debated.[231] Similarly, Deloria Jr. explained that, for Native Americans, "time, space, and substance do not have ultimate values in [what they call] a ceremony"[232], which I would rather refer to as a ritual—and the same would apply for the constellations.[233]

In any event, the new and recent method of constellations work seems to deal with contents that escape the pettiness of one's personal "conscious" understanding, but which are actual and powerful nevertheless. As such, they have widely extended the horizon of our human experience.

One might say that these new ways to constellate still deal with the complexes, but not just with what one remembers, knows, or can someday learn, and not even with what one's own family might know; but instead they deal with unknown and uncertain psychic contents that affect and move one's life, with unconscious contents that are dynamic and present, and with any 'representation' of the unfathomable and *multidimensional psyche.*[234] Even while this new method could sound unscientific, one might simply need to turn a little to consider other philosophical doctrines that claim that "[t]here is more to human existence and to reality itself than current science can ever give us access to"[235]. Through the family constellations method "we obtain access to a dimension of human existence that had been occult and that until now philosophy had not been able to comprehend or describe"[236].

There is one last important aspect about the constellations, in regard to this book. Constellations should not be discussed. They should not be debated, interpreted, or questioned. The work of constellations—and especially the "new constellations"—is not a topic to be dialogued among people and then scrutinized and analyzed by sophisticated argumentation, rhetoric, or thoughts of any kind. It comes close to a healing rite;[237] either it works or it doesn't, but there is nothing in between, and therefore nothing to talk about.[238] Jung also mentioned regarding his psychology that, "in certain respects there can be no 'principles' or valid judgments at all, but only *phenomenology*—in other words, *sheer experience*"[239].[240] A brief story, titled *Waphíyapi*, might illustrate this point.

Two chronically ill men were told by a mutual friend to go and see a great healer. They were given the address and the days when the healer would see people, and off they went. Once there, an assistant of the healer received them and told them to wait until it was dark, and so they did. A little later the assistant asked them to follow him and he gave them an introductory talk about the healer's work. He told them that the healer was a very powerful one, having helped a lot of people, and that they would go alone into a room to see him and ask him for help, just that. The assistant added, however, that it was not a dialogue or exchange of ideas with the healer, but just a petition. He also told them that just by virtue of seeing them the healer would start to help them and would know what medicine to prescribe. When it got dark, and there were more people gathered to see the healer, the two men were told that the healer would start seeing the people, one by one. When it was their turn, the two men went into the room, alone, and did as they were told. The process had been extremely brief, and once being back outside, they were told to go the next day to another address to pick up the medicine.

That night, while traveling back home, both were stunned and in awe. The next day they went to the address they had been given where the same assistant received them and, after waiting a little bit, they were given a bag each. The bags contained several packages with instructions for how to prepare and take the medicine for several months. They were told that they could keep their usual lives and activities, and that the medicine would do the healing. They paid for the medicine and left. By this time one was grateful and still in awe, hoping to be healed; the other was skeptical and thinking that the medicines had been expensive. On their way back home they walked together for a while. The skeptical wanted to talk about what he had perceived the night before and about the medicines, but the other man just wanted to remain silent. At some point, on the way back, each man went his own way.

Days passed and they stopped seeing each other because one wanted to discuss the process, and the other one did not have anything to say about it. Weeks later the one who was skeptical, and who would talk about the process with anyone and everyone, was persuaded by a friend to go and see a herbalist in order to know what stuff was he taking. The herbalist told him that those were not very powerful herbs, and he recommended he take some other herbs. This man told his friends and family that the herbalist had given him better herbs than the healer, and he felt that he had outwitted the healer. Weeks later, however, he was still in pain, and went to see an physician who told him that all those herbs were altogether useless, and gave him what he said were "real chemicals." The cynical man felt silly for having gone with the healer, but happy to have found "real medicine." Weeks passed by, and nothing seemed to change, so he went to see a psychotherapist who told him that maybe his condition was inevitable and fated, and that he needed to find meaning in it, through a process of dialogue.

The other man, the one who had remained silent about the whole process, became healed of his ailments after some months and felt infinite gratitude for a mystery that surpassed his understanding, but which nevertheless permitted him to live better, and in health. From then on he danced every day for the joy of being alive.

Chapter 3
Body: Instinct to Live; and the Inevitable Heaviness of Being

"Don't make the body do

what the spirit does best, and don't put a big load

on the spirit that the body could carry easily."

A basket of fresh bread[241]

The body is inescapable, "there can be no meaning without the body"[242] and maybe, like Nietzsche pointed out, most philosophy has been only a *misunderstanding of the body*[243]. Moreover, as Abram claims, "we *live* our own bodies and so know, from within, the possibilities of our own form"[244]. Therefore, a look into ancestry requires an exploration of the vicissitudes of how the complex constellates the physical body as one more element of a great psychic movement. Hence it is *a* primal structure of attention[245] for any comprehension that wishes to be not only intellectually pondered, but also empirically experienced.[246] This does not mean that it limits its scope and reach to that which is just experienced bodily, but it acknowledges the importance, and the pleasure and joy, of a healthy body—in one's own individual way to live, and be, in health. This is, in a way, very close to Jung's *criterion* for evaluating a concept: "I call an idea *right* or *true* only when it is helpful . . . . [and] see what the influence is on my digestion"[247],[248]; here he meant that he was attentive to the effect of ideas and beliefs upon the nervous and mental systems[249]. It seems that for him, too, the primal structure for attention, even when elaborating theories, was the physical body.[250] It is also worth noting that the resolution during a Constellation is lead by the best sensed-felt positions and movements, asking the representatives *where do they find themselves better (Befindlichkeit)*, never through a process of intellectual interpretation, elaborated reflection, refined logic, or analysis. Just as Jung said: "Logical arguments simply bounce off the facts felt and experienced"[251]. "Behind your thoughts and feelings" as Nietzsche was well aware, "stands a mighty commander, an unknown wise man . . . he is your body"[252]; and therefore, rather than joining *the despisers of the body,*[253] one ought to learn how to listen to the body. Damasio's acknowledgment might seem simple but it is indeed profound in wisdom: "We still need digestion in order to enjoy Bach"[254]. We need our most spontaneous, primal, autonomous, and most animalistic functions to work harmoniously in order to think with clarity and lucidity—otherwise, thoughts and feelings, no matter how mindfully observed and consciously justified, like Nietzsche wrote, might be a regurgitation of undigested experiences—personal, familial, or even cultural[255].

There are many ways to see our personal physical reality, from the perspective of a quantum physicist, a chemist, a Buddhist, a homeopathic physician, a shaman, an internist, too many altogether. But "since man is a living body, his body is ultimate reality"[256], and for the purposes of this book I will not give a clear definition of what the "body" is; on the contrary, I will leave the word deliberately ambiguous, *as it is*, a mystery in itself, in which one is embedded, so seemingly, without warning.[257] When exploring and talking about the body, we need, as Ortega claimed, "the most strict posture of humility in front of the permanent mystery of life and death"[258].[259] The answers to the question of "what is the body?" seem multiple and unfathomable; yet, the inevitability of being embodied pertains even to saints, monks, nuns, or extremely bright and gifted minds that sometimes reside in physically crippled bodies. At times, as Jung mentioned, "[t]he body is a most doubtful friend because it produces things we do not like"[260]. Moreover, the impulse of sexuality pertains also to all humans; it is, so to speak, inevitable, whether repressed, punished, acted out, "sublimated," or rejected.[261] In its all-too-instinctual impulse the flesh seems to show its force—a force that cannot be avoided, only taken or taken by it.[262]

The body has to be a starting point for any phenomenological inquiry about life, otherwise one can articulate the most eloquent thoughts and discuss very lucid arguments and have no effect on one's physical domain. The "body," however, seems to be an invention, a concept with which one struggles throughout life, and in some philosophical, religious, political, and cultural traditions the mere concept of "the body" separates what is corporeal from what is psychical or spiritual. This distinction and dissection seems to have been terrible in all cases, where the body is one thing, and the soul a different thing—and if not a mere obscenity—the spirit even something else.[263] "We philosophers are not free to divide body from soul, as the people do; we are even less free to divide soul from spirit"[264].

This deconstructing insight about embodiment is in no way a reductionist move in which the soul and the spirit "are only the body," "within the body," a "byproduct of the body," a "segregation of the body," a "product of the brain chemicals," a "mental ideation from the body," or, even worse, a "linguistic construct from one's phenomenology of perception." This insight rather strives towards other perspectives, where "the body" is as mysterious and ambiguous, unknown and uncertain, unfathomable and powerful as soul, the spirit, and life itself. Moreover, "the body," if not taken only as that which is material and tangible, observable and measurable, solid and fixed, becomes then *a field of qualitative possibilities*, as well as *quantum possibilities*; it is, in its original meaning, *a sensational field*, a realm of experience in a physical form, but not separated from the realm of psychic and spiritual experience, psyche and the spirit.[265] When thought of as a porous field of sensibility, "the body" acquires a different image; and the idea of "the body" as different and distinct from everything else—whether family, other people, animals, plants, places or even rocks, the ocean, and the world—becomes severely challenged.

The usual way of describing the physical domain, and everything related to the physical experience, as "the body" requires either a new word, or a wider and deeper approach to it. A very old word could serve to replace the fixed notions of the body as being merely material—because in fact one does not know what matter is.[266] The old Greek word *soma* (σῶμα)[267] refers to physical experience, and it does not create boundaries between the physical, the psychical, and the spiritual; nor does it clearly distinguish itself from those notions. In this sense, all somatic issues are also psychological and spiritual. The physical domain, which one might be used to calling "the body," can be in fact the shrine of the spirit and an image of a facet of the soul in movement. When the physical domain and its experience are lived and viewed in this sense, then physiological explanations for some physical ailments become at times too narrow and limited, if not absurd. This does not mean that one can stop cleansing the teeth and they will not get rotten. Rather it expands the vision of the physical domain, where many ailments, diseases, pains, and issues are in relation to something other than physical causality.[268] It is a view that comprehends that the physical domain—*soma*—is permanently affected by the psychical and spiritual movements. In fact, one could say that there is no difference while one still lives, as if the embodiment were just a qualitative and operational distinction that helps one to observe, move, and make sense of experiences for the time-being. Hence, as a way to ground the psychological investigations regarding ancestry, one needs to start with what is sensed, felt, experienced as movement—at times in joy and at other times in pain; in other words, it requires placing attention on that which one normally calls corporeal, but which actually could be better referred to as *somatic*.[269]

However, there is often a titanic mistake made regarding the term "somatic," where people confuse it with that which is only about the body (in its usual narrow sense), erroneously conceiving it as a psychology of the body. And there is also the common mistake about somatic studies and practices where it seems that somatic affairs have to be about some kind of aerobic exercise, ways to handshake, exploiting and cathartic screams, body tapping, eye movements, hypersensitivity training, massages, ways to hug and smile, and so on. Those kind of somatic approaches, without saying that they are harmful, useless, or wrong, are reaffirming the usual and narrow concept of "the body"; and, as such, they risk becoming thoughtless psychological approaches in which one is trapped with techniques that look at the organic "body" without soul, motility exercises without depth, breath techniques without spiritual insight, muscular elasticity without psychic engagement, neuronal connections without heartfelt interactions, the movement of limbs without psychic motion, eyeball patternings without imaginal perspectives, and body postures without psychological positioning.[270]

If by somatic one refers to matters pertaining to or disturbing "the body" and addresses them *just* with bodily (almost mechanical) techniques, as if the issue had nothing to do with psychological and psychical aspects, and as if the spirit were out of the question (and out of the solution), then such a perspective is doomed to fail.[271] It will favor the flesh over the soul and will forsake the world for an eventual corpse. D.H. Lawrence expressed this notion beautifully in his poem *Healing*:

I am not a mechanism, an assembly of various sections.

And it is not because the mechanism is working wrongly,

that I am ill.

I am ill because of wounds of the soul...[272]

It also seems the greatest mistake to use the word *psychosomatic*, as if psyche were not soma (bodily) already, as if only a few psychological issues would affect one's embodiment, as if the psychic were somewhere else beyond and apart from the physical domain, and as if the psychological aspects were mere phantasmagorical products of one's imagination and mental derangement.[273] It is better to keep present the knowledge that "all psychic processes have, at least, their physical correlates"[274].[275]

So, in spite of *soma* being a good way to describe the physical domain of experiences, the word *somatic* is not, because of its popularized and commercial misuse—in literature, therapy, and colloquial jargon[276]. Therefore, for this written work, the word "body" will *mostly* to be used to refer to this domain—but *in its psychically extensive, spiritually mysterious, and materially unfathomable sense.*

Life as a human inevitably involves living bodily. In a way, one can say, from a very grounded and earthly perspective, that there is a "superiority of flesh over spirit [that] is showed in the consummation of love"[277], meaning the sexual act.[278] Everybody is born out of it; it is the movement of the flesh through millions of human lives.[279] It is, in a way, the *instinct to live* that takes individuals for its purposes, the instinct to move through uncountable generations of human bodies, passing over one another, moving along the physicality of being (human).[280] Hence, existence could be perceived as the temporal embodiment of *indestructible life*, as Kerényi suggested[281],[282]. The "body" lives! The "body" has a will of its own; it is moved by a force that is instinctive, pre-rational, pre-linguistic, and pre-moral; it is pure will, it is the *instinct to live!* Suzuki called it the "will to live" which is "stranger than ratiocination"[283]. Humanity in all its rationality does not know what life is, and "[t]o give an explanation of life, or instinct in this case, is nothing more than to block the sun with a finger"[284].[285]

It can be observed often how "the instinctive shows its wisdom and strength where the reasonable and moral find their limits and fail"[286]. The *ways and wisdom of soma*, in its instinct to live, overwhelm the desires, wishes, rationalizations, and ideations of some people, as those who are old and sick who would like to die, but in whom the instinct to live persists for years, even decades. Certainly "[t]he body is meant to live"[287] even at times far beyond one's personal volition and comprehension. However, this instinct also follows paths which can sicken one's embodiment, because the instinct to live is not just free to do as the narrow personal will desires; instead it seems to be directed, moved, and affected by an occult and powerful movement—a *dynamic* reality.[288]

"The body is guided by a creative force that maintains all bind," all its organs and biological systems bound. "That force we know it as soul . . . and the body obeys determinate orders" given by such force[289]. The body, then, from this perspective, is ensouled, in soul—in a particular manifestation of soul. If we depart from the standpoint that the biological "body" does not function chaotically and randomly, but in an orderly fashion, then we get an idea of what this force is. One way to see this, and a very common way actually, is to think of us as having this force, possessing this "soul," which is a very strange idea. Does one *have* this force, really? Another way to think of it is as if this force were taking a body, getting embodied, taking us—with all its consequences. This book will look at the "body" in this second way, and will keep such a view for further reflections.

One always has to give due attention and care to the body, because "[w]e cannot get rid of ourselves, we carry our body, and our shadow and everything else as it always has been"[290]. One's body is one's physical reality—which does not necessarily mean that it is the only reality, or the primal reality, but it is one's unavoidable domain of physical experience, affection, and interaction in a human sense. "[I]t is a catastrophic illusion to think that one can jump out of one's skin and be an angel from henceforth"[291]. One is meant to live the actuality of embodiment, one way or another, for a short or long time, as a blessing or curse, in health or in pain, in agreement or in complaint, with an existential sense of purpose or without it. The physical domain, with all its consequences, has to be experienced while being human. Even when one could direct and invest attention in other domains of reality, as dreamscapes, refined ideation, or spiritual insights, "the body" requires its due.[292]

Being embodied, however, can be considered, imagined, sensed, and perceived differently than in the ways that one might have been accustomed or taught to use. If not arbitrarily and stubbornly detached from the domain of psyche and psychic experiences, the body is a deep field of sensations and affections, where causality is hard to establish, if not impossible, and where *all things and events* are intertwined in relations and interactions, with limitations and consequences.[293]

Hence, the complex is the key to open a gateway for addressing issues pertaining to or disturbing embodiment, where "it must be admitted that things exist in the psyche about which we know little or nothing at all, but which nevertheless affect our bodies in the most obstinate way"[294]. The display of the complex allows one to see, and literally look at, either imaginatively or with representations, the process of an affective situation where the psychic contents "possess at least as much reality as the things of the physical world which ultimately we do not understand either"[295].

The scientific explanation for such a view of the body—where the psychic contents affect, and at times infect, the physical domain—seems difficult if not impossible to provide.[296] One can agree with Jung's idea that there is a facet of soul that affects the body, because it *"dwells in the blood* (italics added) . . . as the psychic phenomenon that mediates between consciousness and the physiological functions of the body"[297]. In this sense, the insistence that one has to cope with one's own blood in body and soul becomes clear. One cannot run away from one's stream of life, even if it moves one to terrible urges of instinctual behavior. Inevitably, in everyone's blood there is a psychic history and prehistory that seems to surpass scientific and philosophical understandings. We all carry in our own blood the ancestral lineages and their psychic influence. "[I]t would be astonishing if the psyche were the only biological phenomenon not to show clear traces of its evolutionary history, and it is altogether probable that these marks are closely connected with the instinctual base"[298].[299] One way or another, in grace or disgrace, in plain delight or total misery, alone or with company, the human has to be embodied in order to live in this domain and intensity of being.

One only has to look aside a little bit, beyond the narcissistic mirror, and see that there are many people in deep and terrible physical suffering, from street children, to young girls and boys being used, sold, and traded for prostitution, to thousands of children dying out of hunger everyday, to people being tortured, raped, kidnapped, or mistreated in many ways. The domain of being human requires human "bodies" in order to experience the qualitative affections of such destinies—even when at time those affections involve tremendous suffering, unspeakable pain, and unending misery. Beyond one's capacity to detach as much as possible from the physical realm of experience, the crude manifestations of world happenings make one remember that one's embodiment can materialize tough affections and immeasurable pain[300].

When dealing with psychological issues or matters related to psyche, one ought not to leave aside the sensations of the body. One can think of the physical body *as if* it were immersed in the complex—which holds the psychic contents that constellate not just the life of a particular individual, but also the physiological unfolding and the individual's metabolism. In other words, the complex affects that which is known colloquially as "corporeal complexion." The unknown contents in one's complex can have severe affections on one's embodiment without one even thinking of those aspects as being related. This occurs because, somehow, "[t]he psychological side of the body *is* the unconscious, and we reach the body—psychologically, not physically—only through the unconscious"[301]. One only needs to think of those diseases that suddenly make a seemingly athletic, balanced, and harmonious individual quite sick, or those cases in which a so-called strong individual becomes severely ill and dies in a few months.[302] Aside from the explanations that claim that diseases are all due to the genes, the environment, or both, as if they were merely a physical malfunctioning of the organs or physical bad luck, the standpoint which considers and departs from a view of the unconscious and the complex reveals that there are more factors than what scientific measurements can perceive up to date (like family history, fateful events, etc.). These factors, which might be called psychic contents, require a method that allows them to be perceived and even empirically proven, because otherwise one feels that one is simply speaking of flimsy things—when in fact it is not the case.[303] This method, however, has to engage contents that are probably out of one's ordinary consciousness, and that one might not be able to perceive without a psychological eye. The phenomenological display of the complex, if experienced in one's body and proved, as in a constellation, allows one to acknowledge that, indeed, "[w]hat we call the unconscious is an avenue, an access to the body"[304].

There are many transcribed cases of situations in which individuals, after having been constellated by a professional, got physically better or even strangely healed—beyond medical comprehension[305]. One reason to understand this, without claiming it to be the only perspective, is that this method—the constellation—can engage and interact with contents whose nature is psychical (even when at times it is or was physical too), and whose relations are or were out of the range of conscious perception—in an autonomous unconscious. However, as Hausner humbly claims, whenever there is healing through his work, it is always a self-healing[306], meaning that it is not him (the constellations facilitator) who heals, but the process and movements that the individual is willing to face, look at, embody, and let happen.[307] Through the healing experiences of the work of constellations (as one example of many other healing processes), one can fully understand Jung's reflection that "the soul has the greatest power over the body"[308]; this notion is, indeed, close to Hellinger's reflection of the soul being a force that moves and directs the body.[309]

Jung, even when having been despised, rejected, and criticized for not engaging "the body," was well aware of the importance of an earthly life, bodily issues, and the grounding of one's psychological life in order not to lose oneself in mere theories, rhetoric, and speculations. In his alchemical writings he clearly indicates to "locate the mystery of psychic transformation in matter . . . as *theoria* for chemicals changes"[310], where "[t]he alchemical athanor or melting pot, signifies the body"[311]. Jung knew that the body can go from a rusty condition to a shiny one; but, as Rumi wrote: "Copper doesn't know it's copper, until it's changing to gold"[312],[313]. Just so, many times we do not know how ill we were because we had accustomed ourselves to live and cope with a few physical ailments (digestive, circulatory, skeletal, or so), and we convince ourselves that such is life and such are the ailments of age. But once we look into the depths, once we perceive a glimpse of the complex, the body moves and finds better places to reside in, a better positioning, and it starts to transform and heal. Therefore, Jung implied that any real psychological reflection and process that claims to address psychic issues, necessarily has to affect the material qualities of the individuals involved—if it does not want to remain in an obscurantist lucubration.[314]

The body, then, does not have to be detached from one's psychological life. It is one's sensitivity and sensuous engagement with the psychic realms; and by looking into those complexities one does not need to detach or anaesthetize one's physicality.[315] Jung realized that "the thing people are most afraid of is not so much the soul, which to them is practically non-existent, but the body"[316]; for the body can truly experience pain that one cannot forget, avoid or run away from, and which at times cannot be alleviated with exogenous chemicals. The body, said Jung, "is the Darkness, and very dangerous things could be called up. It is better to play the piano in order not to hear what the body says"[317],[318]. It is a real mystery, and despite the great efforts of science in trying to map the whole organism, from a perspective that considers the body as the sensuous and sensitive field of one's personal notion of soul, the body will remain an unfathomable field of happenings and miracles.[319] One just has to read the inexplicable healings by Pachita, the Mexican *curandera*—which, in fact, are being continued by her son—to realize how mysterious our embodiment still is, and will continue to be[320].

The recognition of the importance of the body for any psychological work and serious in-depth reflection opens up an entirely different way to deal with diseases, pains, symptoms and physical issues in general, a place where an imminent "rediscovery of the body [will occur,] after its long depreciation in the name of the spirit"[321]. Such an approach does not imply that the body is the most important focus of attention, or the only one, as if physicality were the only reality—even when matter is still unknown from a quantum physics perspective. It rather acknowledges that the actuality of embodiment, in all its conditions, is highly affected by other domains.

Moreover, the body, when not defined limitedly under narrow scopes, might appear as a psychic field in which relations take place—a sort of terrain. One has to be observant of the body's unfolding, because the important psychic issues in the life of an individual have a direct impact and influence on it in seemingly incomprehensible, but physiological, ways. No one claiming to do serious depth psychological work can avoid the body; and no one claiming to do therapeutic bodywork can ignore the psychic aspects of life. Anything bodily is already psychological, even when not acknowledged as such.

The body, if seen from a material perspective, is *just* matter in decay, whatever "matter" is;[322] seen from a psychic perspective, it is psyche in a sensuous experience.[323] This idea comes close to Jung's, when he mentioned "[t]he body is merely the visibility of the soul, the psyche; and soul is the psychological experience of the body"[324]. *Everything that one experiences and suffers belongs to one's psychological life*—there are no random casualties. As Nietzsche profoundly observed: "in the end one experiences only oneself"[325], and everything that one goes through, from diseases and pains, to traumas, accidents, or any happenings that involve one's body, belong to one's existence and fate. Being truly honest, one can ask oneself: "What *could* still fall to me now that would not already be my own"[326].[327]

In this way, if one *psychologizes* or sees through the body, then one gets a deep and ambiguous notion of it, where the medical perspectives, in all their usefulness and without being wrong, can be acknowledged as metaphors for what is happening in one's personal notion of psyche. Very often people believe that a heart attack, for instance, has nothing to do with their (personal notion of) psyche or psychic contents. It is usually treated and explored without any psychological insight, and most probably not cured, but only stabilized. Such limited perspectives about "the body" do not see with an embracing view and with depth, and definitely do not see what affects individuals "from outside" their bodies—in other words, from the psychic complex where the body resides and in which the body loves and lives.[328] Diseases, pains, and bodily disturbances in general, if looked from Jung's complex theory in combination with Hellinger's constellations method, open up a much wider vista that allows one to take immediate action, without undervaluing the contributions and necessities of the medical interventions and treatments. This view into what happens to the body is indeed what Hillman referred as *pathologizing,* which "is primarily a psychological reality that needs psychological insight"[329].

However, Hillman warned about finding a reduction or a cause for physical conditions. Otherwise, he claims, one remains with an idea of soul which is "lost in its literal perspective, or its identity with material life . . . stuck in coagulations of physical realities"[330]. Rather than following the fantasy of linear cause and effect thinking, and trying to find what produced what, Hillman suggests one stay with the issue and explore it psychologically—leaving the medical model to medical practitioners. This insight allows one to see differently and to see through, and via such an act, to find out what is it that the soul needs. In what may be Hillman's most central and significant insight about pathologizing, he said, "my symptoms point to my soul as my soul points to me through them"[331]. It becomes clear then, that no physical condition, whether inherited, congenital, acquired, or even accidental, is detached from the psychic life of the individual. Besides the varieties of medical metaphors to observe, diagnose, comprehend, treat, and cure people, either through acupuncture, homeopathic, allopathic, ayurvedic, quantum medicine, or even herbs and folk-healing, all physical conditions "have psychological significance, [and] are metaphors too"[332]. Most theories (or body-metaphors), however, are based *only* on sensation, which, according to Jung, is the perception through conscious sensory processes[333].[334]

It is important to make clear that the soul does not live inside the body, and it is not merely and only the body.[335] Unfortunately, the soul (or psyche) to some people is nothing but a philosophical metaphor with which one articulates sophisticated explanations and descriptions about existence, a kind of conceptual crutch to fill up linguistic meanings. For others, it is a religious metaphor with which one feels connected to a greater domain, a sort of wire to the source. Still others have lost the capacity to think metaphorically, and the idea of "soul" seems unscientific, primitive, esoteric, retrograde, or out of fashion to them. Those who deny soul because of its lack of concrete factuality are stuck in concreteness and literality; they limit their referent of existence to the current paradigms of what science can say about physical reality. Such people's capacities to experience and expand their life-view, as well as their capacities to love and act in their life, are dictated by the discoveries published in the science journals—that is, if their intellectual willingness allows them to understand.[336] Concrete factuality reduces the mystery of life to concrete and rigid thinking, concrete and ugly cities, concrete and dry hearts, and confines the views of life within a few concrete, supposedly philosophical or scientific, ideas about what it is to be human.[337] Western man has long insisted on cementing ideas and building upon them, constructing theories, and even deconstructing them later, but always aiming to concretize thought and life, rather than living wisdom and psyche as a continuous flow, as a moving truth.[338]

From another perspective, the body is the metaphor for the soul.[339] Instead of psyche being an idea and image about one's life, rather it seems that a human life is *simply* "a personification of the psyche"[340]. With this idea in mind, one can comprehend Hillman better when he says that "[t]he body has its home in the soul and every organic pathology is a cooperation between pathogenic agents and the human person as a host"[341]. *Pathologies, seen through psyche, are not inside the body*—regardless of the medical conclusions that see and insist that the organs have the pathogenic elements.[342] Considering the individual as an isolated, separate, and independent entity is the greatest fallacy, and in the same sense, human pathologies cannot be thought of as independent from the rest of life.[343] There are such phenomena as disease, but not as individual phenomenon; they always belong to the full continuum of life, to the whole display of soul, and, more importantly, to the psychic dynamism of the individual (which *by nature* includes contents and relations beyond one's consciousness). Ortega claims that disease is "a state of being"[344]. His definition seems correct, although it might be too abstract. Disease might be understood better if it were thought of as one's ways of relating. If the introspection of the body is *psychologized,* by looking into the complex, one finds out that the organs react to affective conditions produced by *psychic interrelations,* which might end up sickening the body. From this perspective of 'seeing through,' pathology can be considered and treated in a fuller context in which the individual lives, rather than just with the modernized bacteriological view of disease. But if the pathogenic aspects were to be looked in the physical atmosphere where the individual lives—out there, in the surroundings—it would only be a change in the locations where one looked, leaving one stuck with the same methodology.[345] Those who look for bacteria or viruses will find them, whether in an individual's organs or in the environment. *The change has to be in the way of seeing—allowing the eye to perceive differently, and allowing consciousness to see beyond its limitations and delimitations.* Intuition, defined by Jung as the "perception *by way of* (italics added) unconscious contents and connections"[346], is what allows this process to occur, implying that one ought to perceive a context which is beyond the range of sensory consciousness.[347]

The context which depth psychology explores and works with is not the literal environment under the paradigms of a scientific materialism. Instead, what interests depth psychology is the psychic energetic patterns—the complexes that are neither literally spaced out nor clearly displayed around the individual under ordinary circumstances. Moreover, the psychic contents might affect people who are nearby, but it does not mean that those are their issues. A complex, which is nothing but psychic energy, is not a substantial view of the world, people, and things, but instead a *relational* view. Psychic energy cannot be seen or be measured quantitatively with the usual yardstick in order to produce statistics, but can only be perceived and observed through its effects in the physical domain.[348]

The body is complexed, as if it were inside the complex, as if it were inside a sphere of psychic energy. The complex, however, is not the surrounding physical world; it is not visible by ordinary sight; and it is not shared in consensus with the people or situations around.[349] So, a man sitting at a table in a restaurant might be in a complex with particular contents that pertain to his psychic life. Another man sharing the same table and physical setting with him does not share the same psychic situations and is not inside nor seriously affected by the complex, unless he is a family member, or someone with whom the man shared an important life event. And even if this were the case, this would in no way mean that the two men would experience the complex in the same manner. Every individual experiences the complex according to his or her way of relating, living, and loving. In this sense, the people at the tables close to where the man is sitting do not share that complex either. The other diners are each in their own complex.[350] Physical reality, to a certain psychological way of seeing it, can be seen not as the only cause of the effects experienced in life, but also as the field of happenings, where one can only observe the psychic forces[351] manifest. In this sense, thought, feeling, and behavior, and any action in general is influenced, if not completely determined, by those contents. Complexes are not evil nor are they only about wrong or morbid aspects of one's life. They "are very much a part of the psychic constitution, which is the most absolutely prejudiced thing in every individual"[352]. One can say that complexes direct the life of the individual, up to the point of saying that one's elaborated thoughts, philosophical reflections, noble ideologies, firm convictions, willful decisions, premeditated actions, and unexpected reactions are in relation to the psychic (invisible) life; indeed "complexes are also a means of understanding other people"[353]. What on the surface seems as if it were attained from the educational, social, political, economical, or even the popular and traditional environment, is nothing but a reflection of psyche at its depths. The complexes tincture the whole life of the individuals, from the bodily unfolding to philosophical inclinations and spiritual beliefs—something that is frequently overlooked.[354]

However, it is the attention to the body that one ought to begin with, because life is bodily, and "the body" is not really affected by elusive speeches of rhetoricians, academicians, philo-sophists, doxophilists, and the like. If the psychic contents are not dealt with, not seen, honored, or attended to, then all intellectual life is nothing but a discursive vanity that is not in service of the body or in service of life.[355] As Jung said: "Well-being is a better judge than the law"[356], and a better parameter than many academic and (pseudo-) philosophical claims; sometimes peasants indeed live and die better than academicians and scholars.[357] It is advisable to ask oneself what Jung asked: "Of what use is philosophical knowledge in the head, if one is not also a philosopher at heart?"[358]. A brief story, titled *Apish Philosophy*, might illustrate this point

Not long ago in the zoo of the prettiest city in the world there used to be a couple of apes that were quite loud. They lived in the apes' area, which was fenced in with bars, but otherwise quite open and designed for their recreation and sojourn. However, two apes out of the group were strangely loud, and they would shout all day long, complaining about everything they possibly could. They would constantly encourage the rest of the apes to rise up against the zoo that kept them behind bars, as if they were prisoners of their politics of domination. The two would climb to the top of the poles and would start speeches on how the zoo had been enslaving them and had made them just a mere tourist attraction. The rest of the apes, who were many, would listen to their shouts, but would not care much about them. They knew from stories that their species had been originally from a place with no confinement, with plenty of fruit to eat and fresh water to drink, with innumerable trees, and even with other species to live with. But they also knew that such a place was a paradise lost, and that even if they would escape from the zoo, they would never survive in a city that was mostly made of cement, bricks and stones—an all-too-concrete world. The two apes who were bent on revolution, however, kept encouraging the rest to unite, so that all together they could open the bars of confinement, and finally break free and end their shameful captivity. But the rest of the apes would never follow them. They were happy with their lives under such conditions—some fruit, free peanuts, and an apish security granted.

One of the discontented apes shouted so often and for so long that one day it ended up with a collapsed lung, and became severely ill. The people of the zoo realized that the ape would never fully recover, but would remain injured for life. The other unhappy ape also shouted brutally, and become so ill from disliking his life in the zoo that it came down with a strange disease and started to feel weak. A little later, the one with the collapsed lung climbed to the top of a pole and threw itself to the ground, having shouted that it could not live caged up in a zoo. It died, of course. The other one kept shouting, but the more it shouted how it disliked its life, the more its disease spread out in its body. One day, fully miserable, it died, too. Both were remembered as loud speakers, but also as unhappy apes.

The rest of the apes observed their deaths with pity, but kept their life with free food and zoo security, knowing that once in such a city, the jungle and the wild were gone forever. They kept eating and drinking, mating, playing and sleeping, and once in while when a young ape with an eye to revolution would start shouting in the same way as the dead apes, one could hear the old apes say: "Oh, don't worry. Leave him alone. He has been listening to the so-called philosophers. Sooner rather than later he will come back to live in his animality."

The body, being on the one hand the most prosaic and matter-of-fact thing, and on the other a mystery, as Suzuki said[359], seems the path to the needs of soul. Pathologies point to the necessities of soul. The body is required to keep up with life activities in an earthly and material way, through sleep, nutrition, work, movement, rest, relationships, sexuality, and so on. It also must fulfill duties that seem to belong to another order of being—*matters pertaining to making-soul*. These matters are understood, only after psychological reflection, as diseases, pains, accidents, tragedies, misfortunes, failures, losses, separations, ruptures, death, and fatalities of all kinds. Strokes of luck, the sense of meaning, the direction in one's life, the notion of purpose, the fulfillment of one's deep desires, and the genuine joys of existence also make soul; for, in fact, the difficulties and the joys go along together, and often one precedes the other.

Even in his day, Jung observed that when people say: "[i]t's only psychological," they would often mean: "It's nothing!"[360]. Nowadays, unfortunately, people still seem to think this way, as if a psychological problem were some kind of secondary affair that did not require priority of attention and was not that serious. But how different it is when someone says, "Oh, it's only in your body," and then one feels the panic and the pain![361] However, there is a widespread erroneous idea that bodily issues do not pertain to the psyche, and that psychic issues do not matter to the body. There is a lot of confusion among people about what psychology is or ought to be. Some people understand it as only cognitive processes, behavioral improvements, emotional support, pampering consulting rooms, conduct conditioning, hypnotic trances, linguistic life-meanings, neuronal re-wiring, personal historicity analysis, family management, couples' solutions, confessional sessions, motivation techniques, artistic explorations, or some kind of personality enhancement; but all these approaches are "psychologies without psyche"[362]. Hence, the dealings with the "body" (in the common, mainstream ways) reveal that man has indeed lost soul, and *even the idea of soul*[363].

A way back to psyche is through the display of the complex, but always departing from and considering the affections and afflictions in the physical domain. One cannot avoid or negate oneself for "[t]he body is the truest thing: this is indubitable and undeniable even if it should fabricate poetry and philosophy or other illusions and delusions"[364].[365] One of *the philosophical* aspects of the complex theory is the imperative necessity of a phenomenological procedure, showing the *imminent in its immanence*—this means that it is close at hand in one's indwelling. If one does not want to remain in the realm of merely speculating with theories and sophisticated discourses, or as a discussion topic for academic journals and dusty psychological dissertations, then one has to rely on, and speak about, the phenomenology of embodiment, affliction, and its psychic interaction.[366]

When using this broad way of seeing one's physicality, one realizes that even one's most primal experience of reality has very deep notions—very often unexplored notions—as if they were unchartered territories, peopled with unknown presences that one might have just heard of.[367] In the physical body one can feel the force of the soul as something that keeps life bound to something else, and to someone else certainly, and to many human lives before; "there is nothing in our bodies that in principle did not come from our parents"[368], and from their parents before them, and so on. The physical body in this way is the flow of the soul incarnated, in flesh, with all its joys and pains, with all its pleasures and diseases, with all its implications, limitations, and consequences.[369] In addition to being seen as the forceful *instinct to live*, the body can also be considered as the *inevitable heaviness of being*. Despite all speculations, lucubration, refined thoughts, and sophisticated ideas, the body implies a heaviness that keeps us close to the soil and the Earth—as if the spirit of gravity pulled us.[370]

The body can also be seen as "a link of a long chain that bounds everybody before and after us, and everybody immediately around us, as if we were all part of a life and soul in common"[371]. What is the body, after all? A piece of the world—a luminous and knowing moment of the *world-soul moving* in any of its human tonalities of love[372] and strife.[373]

Chapter 4

The Miasma: An Excursus into a Medical View

"Ignorance lies at the root of all afflictions, and afflictions are inevitably at the root of suffering."

The essence of the heart sutra[374]

The psychic atmosphere conforms the dynamism of the individual's psychic structure through the general configuration of the individual in relation to psychic persons and contents—whether the individual knows them or not. In simpler words, psychically, the individual could be imagined and seen as always positioned *in a terrain* in which he or she stands, and in which is related to other presences or contents—and a terrain on which he or she must always find his or her place (*Befindlichkeit*). These contents mostly pertain to the family and the "community of fate",[375] because when *personifyied,*[376] as it has been often observed, they are in relation to living or dead family members, or members from previous generations—antecessors and ancestors (which are not the same and later in the work to be distinguished). Hence they are felt and carried in "the body," because in a way they constitute the body, and so they are hereditary; but it is important to mention that they are autonomous, and psychoactive. The psychic contents are not constructions of one's mind, will, or conceptual elaborations of one's lived experiences, but actual felt entities with which the individual is in a dynamic and fated relation; they constitute and configure that which is called in Homeopathic medicine as the miasma.

Miasma, according to its colloquial use, means: "an oppressive or unpleasant *atmosphere* (italics added) that surrounds or emanates from something"[377]. The word stems from the Greek *mianínem,* which means "to pollute"[378]. It is, in its old medical sense (in Western's views), an emanation that is present in the atmosphere, and which pollutes or defiles the individual. One can think of the effect it produces upon an unclean but constantly used toilette in a small apartment. If left unclean, but still in use, for days or weeks, the vapors from accumulated urine and feces would reach the whole place and would severely perturb the individuals living there—not just physically, maybe infecting them, but also affecting the mood, the thinking process, the states of mind, and all ways of relating and behaving in general. One does not have to experience an unclean atmosphere, as such, for years, in order to imagine the affections from such vaporous emanations and their fetid effect on the totality of the human being. However, if the idea of the miasma is not taken literally as a bad and polluted smell in the air, but as a psychic situation that gives "a bad atmosphere," an affectivity of suffering, darkness and pain, then it is pretty accurate to use such a word in its allegorical sense.[379] If one thinks of the *bad smell* that the unattended dead in one's own lineage produce, then one can start to comprehend the psychic atmosphere, and one also gets a different sense of the people with a so-called evil or with a *bad essence*. It is worth remembering Heraclitus fragment saying: "Thus in the abysmal dark the soul is known by scent"[380].[381]

The idea of the miasma seen from the bacteriological view is old-fashioned, obsolete, absurd, and out of consideration or something akin. Ortega, however, following Hahnemann, the founder of Homeopathic medicine, clearly stated that it is one of the touchstones of such theory and practice, and he differentiates between two different types of miasma, acute and chronic.[382]

The *acute miasma* according to the Hahnemannian view is "a morbific and morbigenic [*sic*] element capable of acting in the totality of the human genre or at least in the majority of its components because the man's nature is in general susceptible to its action"[383]. However, there might be a flaw in the definition (not necessarily in the understanding) of such concept, because the idea of an element, makes one think of a thing, either a bacteria, a virus, or something the like. In the same text, Ortega clarified that even when "it can be explained from the viewpoint of modern bacteriology and akin sciences, in no way it is adequate to the criteria which is proper of Homeopathic medicine"[384]. From this view, if an individual does not get sick (or not for too long) while being present in a "polluted" atmosphere (in a bacteriological sense), it is because the individual's being is in an "*indisposition*" to receive such disease[385]. It can be said that when the individual's order of being (the disposition) is *in a healthy position, it cannot be affected.*[386] When the individual gets sick, it is because he or she was in an order of being that was not favorable and sane, therefore it affected him or her; it defiled the body.[387] This follows the Homeopathic concept of disease, which is a "state of existence" and "a way of being of the living organism"[388], never an entity in itself.[389]

It can be deduced that the miasma is not a thing, but a process, not an element, but a movement, not a set of morbid cells that one ought to destroy and get rid off, but a living motion in which the individual is immersed and that needs to shift.[390] The miasma, from a depth psychological view, is the *psychic dynamism* that entangles the individual in relations that are sickening—and which defile the individual's way of being and loving. It is in principle an energetic atmosphere, and it can be perceived and observed in the symptomatic effects (corporeal manifestations) that follow and express the affectivity as experienced by the individual. It is not something that one can measure out through the usual means and devices of scientific materialism. Jung, in his early writings, when researching the so-called "mental diseases" realized that a "[s]cientifical materialism axiomatically refuses to acknowledge any other causal connection than the physical one"[391]; but he intuited a psychogenesis for such diseases, and he emphatically refused the organic explanations. Similarly Ortega, following Hahnemann, believes that all diseases, not just the so-called mental or psychological ones, have a miasmatic genesis.

In order to comprehend the miasma, one requires a different way of perceiving, a way which allows one to see into the psychic complexities and the energetic patterns. If the miasma is not an objective element that can be observed and measured with microscopes and scales, then a specific method is needed with which to see it and *see through it*. But the miasma is not to be seen as if it were a thing out there, displayed on the body or on the literal space, as if it were something that one ought to attack or defend from. The miasma, in this view, is the effect, due to the human vulnerability, of a dynamic which in principle is psychic—in other words, pertaining the movements of the soul. It would be a great mistake to confuse the bodily effects of such dynamic, observable in the molecules, cells, tissues, fluids, organs, and the functions of the organism in general, with the *dynamic and structural aspects of the psyche*.[392] One is the visible effect of the other.[393]

However, from the homeopathic medicinal research it was observed that aside from the eventual manifestations of disease, which would be due to the individual's disposition, there is a constitutional structure and dynamic of being, which determines the individuals' susceptibility to some kind of diseases and not to others. Hence Ortega, and others, wrote about the *chronic miasma*; its condition, he claimed, is "the answer to all our inquiries about the destructive, about what perturbs us, what we dislike, and what from our part hurts and attacks our fellow men"[394]. He even, quite boldly, saw in the miasmatic the origin of war[395] and *all chronic diseases*[396].[397]

The chronic miasma, claimed Ortega, is the result of thousands of generations that have suppressed the pathologies with treatments that fight and try to eradicate disease as if they were entities, that is, elements that are foreign to the body and that one needs to get rid off (*allo-pathy*); that has constituted the chronic condition.[398] Such constitutional pathology is in truth a *diathesis* that is inheritable, transmissible, and predisposing[399].[400] When speaking of pathologies one might think not just of organic pathologies, which of course indicate something, but also of psychic affections, which refer to issues that affect the psyche and not always in clearly observable organic symptoms. A sudden death in one's family might perturb the unfolding of the whole family system, even when not manifesting clear physical symptoms. The murder of a family member, for instance, can produce such a psychic atmosphere of unrest and vengeance in the family, that later family members, as grandchildren, great-grandchildren, or even further generations, might still feel the impact of the event—independent of them knowing where such a psychic situation comes from. Such condition of unrest or vengeance, most of the times being a perturbed psychic condition, might pass on from one generation to another, trying to reach someone who can do something about it. Most often the so-called, and wrongly named, hypersensitive individuals are the ones who get affected first.[401] It is as if the unrest and lack of peace of the murdered member were calling someone in the blood lineage to attend the issue—not for revenge and bloodshed, but for acknowledgement and peace.

The chronic miasma that is spoken about in Homeopathic medicine, also referred at times as a diathesis, is, as the last word suggests from its Greek origin *diatithenai*[402], the way one's psychic constitution is *"arranged"*—structured within a given positioning within the family (psycho-) system, and determining a constitutional organic disposition to the dynamics of life.[403]

Jung, for instance, in his early writings, when investigating the so-called "mental diseases," was already well aware that the "modern aetiological [*sic*] conception [was] no longer causalism but *conditionalism.*" And he affirmed that, "[u]ndoubtedly a psychological cause hardly ever produces insanity unless it is supported by some specific *predisposition* (italics added)"[404].[405] In such early view, Jung considered that most cases of dementia praecox[406] were "driven by their congenital predisposition into psychological conflicts," but he considered such conflicts as "not essentially pathological," many of them as "common human experiences"[407]. Without being a follower of Hahnemann, or even without mentioning much about Homeopathic medicine principles, Jung showed an insightful vision for seeing into psychopathology—a vision that nowadays clearly fits with Ortega's views on the miasmas.[408]

Hahnemann distinguished only three great morbid predispositions (miasmas), which Ortega corresponds to "the three only forms of initial alterations of the functions (*hipo*, *hyper* and *dis*) in physiology and anatomy-pathology"[409]. These three types of miasma are named: psoriasic (hipo), sycosic (hyper), and syphilitic (dis)—which do not refer to the usual use of the word in allopathic medicine. Although they were taken from diseases named as such (e.g. psoriasis, sycosis, and syphilis[410]), they rather refer to the structural constitution and metabolic complexion of the individuals.

Ortega, through Homeopathy, conceives only "three alterations of the cellular functions: the defect, the excess and the perversion"[411], that in terms of the nutritional functions of the cells affect the structure of the whole organism, and those three alterations correspond to the three miasmas, the psoriasic, the sycosic, and the syphilitic, respectively. The miasmas, in this view, are those which determine a lack of or inhibition, in the case of psoriasis, altering the rhythms of the cells and organs functions *to the less*[412]; an excess or acceleration, in the case of sycosis, altering the organism into *hyperplasia* or enlargement of its tissues and organs[413]; and destruction or perversions, in the case syphilis, which violently *degenerate* the organism[414]. The observed effects in the body due to each of the miasmas indicate an imbalance (*a lack of order*) that is not only organic, but, as Ortega clearly wrote, primarily psychic[415]. "The miasma is a disorder"[416].[417]

Hence, following Hahneman, Ortega considered chronic diseases as "a predisposing anomalous condition to suffering"[418], never a monstrous entity that one ought to fight or destroy. These three chronic dispositions, which he corresponds to the three main faults in the cellular functioning, determine "all conducts"[419] and "are the cause of all human unhappiness"[420]. The miasmas, it can be assumed, are not physical issues, but psychic ones, which originate in the dynamic aspect of the individual's life-force[421], determining not just physical afflictions but also psychological disturbances in the spheres of volition, intellection, and feeling—unfortunately, this is often oversimplified, misunderstood, and overlooked, in spite of its tremendous importance. Moreover, the miasmas, according to Ortega, even predispose the individuals to certain types of couple relationships, where catastrophic consequences happen if the miasmas are not attended[422]. The miasmas can be seen as the patterning of human affections, the pre-disposing energetic code that colors the type of life that the individual sees, desires, pursues, chooses, wills, and consequently lives.[423] He even claims how "in order for two persons to have a real harmonious correspondence, the relationship shall be established with miasmatic coincidence, continuity, and discontinuity"[424].

The miasmas, following Ortega, can be seen from a chromatic perspective, in which the psoriasic is blue, the sycosic is yellow, and the syphilitic is red, because the three of them compose the whole chromatic spectrum—as well as the whole spectrum of dispositions to any disease. He brilliantly proposed how, if one were to imagine the predisposition of an individual, it would fall inevitably in a certain tonality of color, which in fact is nothing but a combination of the three primary colors[425]. For him, the ways individuals experience feeling, conduct, and even the ways they relate, create, express, think, reflect, and understand,[426] are tinctured by such coloring.[427] Moreover, the miasmas tincture *all* perception, and because of this any life-event is literally seen and experienced differently by every person. An individual's worldview, including the sexual and immanent as well as the philosophical and transcendent, is first and foremost colored by the chronic miasma; and it is always reflected in his or her peculiar ways of expression, whether that happens in the arts, the humanities, politics, or in any given field of human interaction, and oftentimes even in the individual's spiritual path and religious observance.[428]

Therefore, Ortega alluded that any individual claiming himself or herself a serious physician should observe, explore, and cure the miasmas, in other words, the energetic situations in which the individual lives and loves, not merely curing symptoms and abandoning the psychic aspects of the human being[429],[430] He claimed that *just* the full understanding of the miasmas help treat disease integrally and can give a complete comprehension of Homeopathic medicine[431],[432]. The miasmatic is and occurs in the (psychic) dynamism[433], and it has to be treated there, and in such way, never from, and only for, the physical.

However, the miasmas are not merely individual phenomenon. Ortega emphasized the necessity of widely acknowledging the *taras* (*defects*) as constitutive of the miasmas[434]. *Tara* (singular) is a Spanish word which means: "a physical or psychical defect, mostly important, and of hereditary character"[435],[436] Ortega was clear in his insight and the chosen word for the individual origin of the miasma. They are not constituted by just usual individual's physical or psychological defects, or faults, but by psychical conditions (dynamic patterns) that are hereditable and transmissible. The very meaning of the word *tara* is implying something that flows along the blood lineage, something that one carries in one's constitution. One can even think that *the miasma is by default one's (faulty) dynamic psychic structure.* One comes into the world from a blood family and within a miasma, inevitably. No individual is ever isolated from the psychic family system (among other systems), so that the psychic atmosphere is inevitably about the blood family psychic situation—regardless of the individual having been given in adoption, moving far away, or not knowing about the previous generations. Just as no individual is ever free from the hereditary physical constitution, just so, no individual is ever free from the *hereditary psychic configuration.* "Inheritance includes the pathological of the man of before with the pathological of the man of today"[437]. Ortega wisely realizes that the *atavistic* is one of the greatest forces that determine man's existence[438]. It can openly be said that man and woman are by nature atavistic, in other words, ancestral. Atavism stems from the Latin *at* meaning "farther beyond," and *avus* meaning "grandfather"[439]. One's existence is influenced from far beyond one's grandfathers and grandmothers, and such influences determine the psychic situations that one is fated to face, to endure, to shift, to attend, and to live, prepared or unprepared, knowingly or not, and beyond one's will and decision.

The notion, idea, and image of the miasma, as it is described by Ortega, is *a medical view* of what Jung called the complex, and which can be constellated in the ways of Hellinger, and his followers (Hausner, Kutschera, and many others).[440] The miasma, also and very appropriately called *terrain*[441], can be imagined and displayed on a literal but limited physical place, as in a constellation—but never the totality of it, only an aspect. In such a display, the individual who suffers certain diseases, pains, or symptoms, can look at the positioning that he or she is in, and can also look at the relation that he or she has with the rest of the psychic contents (or persons).[442] It facilitates a way to see how one is standing in relation to other components of the psyche, and how's the affectivity of such circumstances. It is in a way a method with which one can see into the psychic dynamism that is configuring one's terrain of existence (one's life and one's body) and disease—because disease, in this view, is nothing but a "state of existence" due to a psychic disorder.[443] When one constellates a symptom, an illness, or a disease, one virtually displays a set of psychic interrelations through the representatives (who are visible), so that one can *perceive and observe* the dynamic affection in which one is involved, immersed, and intermingled—and therefore sick or ill.[444] In such a sense, any person interested in seeing the psychic affection and intrinsic movements of his or her pathological condition is able to perceive—sensing and feeling—the morbid relationship that affects his or her physicality, in order to find and embody a healing solution.[445] The persons helping as representatives, because they are within the psychic field of energy, also experience the healing, naturally, and one can assume that in some way they get an immunological effect.[446] It has been widely conjectured, by the inexperienced, that by participating as a representative in tough and painful constellations—those with perpetrators and dead victims—one could get infected by such disturbances, but that has not proved to be the case. On the contrary, individuals who participate in the resolution of difficult entanglements, by allowing themselves to momentarily sense and feel as persons within a disordered disposition, generally become psychologically stronger, more compassionate, and less judgmental.[447]

The word *terrain* for referring to the chronic miasma is a quite suitable allegory, because it offers an illustrative, even picturesque, view of it. One can imagine a literal terrain, where certain persons and elements dwell, even if unknown, and some others come through and where certain events happen. One's totality of the complex can be imagined as the whole terrain, which might be impossible to glimpse altogether—one can just see it a bit at a time; as when one constellates, one can just see an aspect or a fragment of it. One can imagine that such terrain (a territory) is peopled, with entities or presences with which one is in relation—the so-called psychic contents. The interrelations create a pattern of arrangement, a psychic organization that structures one's psychic atmosphere in which one has *to find oneself a place*—inevitably.[448] Such interrelations are not static and always the same, they are in constant change and movement, because of the dynamic nature of the psyche. So, when these relations are actual, as it is when one has a clear image of some content, they generate motion and force; and when they are potential, as it is when one has not seen them yet, they elicit a state, attitude, or condition. In both cases, they create an atmosphere of affections in which the individual inevitably lives; that constitutes what Jung called psychic energy.[449] The terrain, however, is not built or chosen at birth, but given by *inheritance*; it is one's psychic heir. One is born in it, and one does not choose at first who dwells in it, those who lived before in the lineage inhabit the terrain by priority. This should not be taken in a literal sense where one sibling (for instance) has some relatives in his terrain, and the other sibling has the rest of the relatives. Since the terrain is a metaphorical image of one's psychic space, the presences are not necessarily the literal persons, but a living image of them. In the same way that two siblings could have exactly the same photos of all their relatives, just so each one of them co-inhabits the psychic terrain with all the imaginal presences of their lineage.[450]

In one's terrain one is not supposed to fight those who were there before one came into life, but to befriend them, or at least to respect them and honor them. Pathologies, in such allegorical view, can be seen as the oblivion of a certain fragment of the terrain, a brutal disinfection to get rid of those who are there, a constant fight with such psychic persons, an overgrown piece of land that has not received attention, or maybe dead corpses from the lineage that have not received proper death rites, and that are disquietingly producing a bad smell (a miasma). In any case, the terrain is what one might call the physical body and one's actual circumstance—as if the circumstance were only an extension of the physical body.[451] Nietzsche's poetic insight is quite appropriate: "Body am I and through and through, and nothing besides, and soul is merely a word for something about the body"[452]. The terrain and its inhabitants are what ought to be cared, and cured, never attacked, destroyed, or bombed with medicines.[453] One's life happens on it; one can make it a pleasant garden in good relations with family, friends, allies, and even teachers and mentors; or an ugly and forgotten wasteland that pollutes one's air and where one does not even dare to look at.[454] Well-being from such view is not about treating and pampering the ego personality (the "I") into comfortableness, but about attending and carefully treating one's terrain and all that it encompasses—even at times when one *seems* healthy and strong.[455] The psychic situations that are given (by default) in the terrain, and which involve persons and presences that were there before one's birth, are one's psychic leitmotifs;[456] they are, as the etymology of the word suggests, the *leading motives and motivations*[457] in one's life. One can think that such 'motives' are latent conflicts and that they get active whenever a similar situation in life happens; but it might also be the other way around, where such 'motives' move the individual into life situations that present (and represent) the dynamism of the psychic structure. In this sense, the psychic situations of one's terrain, which can be thought of, and imagined, as archetypal patterns[458] of relations, are one's *life-motives* that one ought to consider, treat, care,[459] and cure;[460] or which one might just need to tend and attend.[461]

In the homeopathic view and treatment, as well as when departing from the complex or a constellation, one has to base the method on the individual (and the individual's family system and ancestral lineage), where no rules can be made out of plain generalizations from the collective, but only from the perception and observation of every case.[462] This principle, which Homeopathic medicine derives from the morbid individuality and which calls *medicament individuality*[463], might be useful for the consideration of the complex and the phenomenological display of a fragment of it (the constellation), where every situation requires a fresh look, not a perception coming from texts or clinical standards and statistics. Just as the miasmas, following the chromatic allegory, are the peculiar ways in which the individual lives, loves, sees, senses, and perceives life according to a specific tonality of color, just so the complex is the peculiar energetic situation in which the individual exists.[464] Illnesses and diseases are not random and capricious casualties of one's embodiment. Hence, just as in Homeopathic medicine every individual requires a specific and personalized *dosage*, which is potentially *dynamized* with extreme care[465], just so when dealing with the psychic complexities, every individual requires his or her particular look (dosage) and sensed-felt experience (dynamic) of his or her own complex—although there are clear exceptions in the Constellations work, as it is when an individual, by being a representative or even only an attentive observer, perceives and experiences the healing solution for a similar situation that he or she also embodies and suffers.[466] In both cases, the miasma and the complex, a *minimum dosage*[467] which accurately addresses the situation, as it is recommended in Homeopathic medicine[468], can have lasting effects and change the structural dynamic of the psyche—because it helps to restore the flow of life-force.[469] In the Constellations work, this minimum dosage is most of the times the verbal expression of a word or an empowering sentence between the representatives,[470] and it is widely observed that if it is appropriate and truthful it will generate an unprecedented reaction that moves the whole (family) system towards healing and reconciliation.[471] In some other times such a minimum dosage is even a slight touch, a caress, or a strong embrace, which, if comes from the right person, is felt quite deeply. In other words, it is not felt only superficially on the skin and muscles, but in some way that it can alter the course of life and unfold long lasting effects, changing the perception of existence in powerful and beautiful ways and helping the autonomous nervous system to self-regulate an soothe its functioning in an unprecedented manner.[472] And even when the person touching or being touched is a representative of the real person, the experience is sensed and felt in such a genuine way that it leaves no doubt that it was real and truthful. These remarks, however, are not insights but experiences, and only those who have been through them can attest their veracity.

Many people have doubted Homeopathic medicine, some of those because they do not follow Hahnemann's *unicist*[473] method[474], some others, maybe, because they have not been treated from the perspective that departs from the miasmas, and some others even without having tried. The constellations method, as developed by Hellinger, has also been subject to criticisms and doubts. In constellations, just as it is the case of homeopathy, it is *pure experimentation*[475] what allows the individual to shift the perception of experiences and begin a healing motion.[476] In Homeopathic Medicine this means that the observations of remedial effects have not been taken from sick individuals, dead corpses, or animals (as allopathic medicine would do), but from sane individuals.[477] In the work of Constellations, the basis for the healing insights—the orders of love—is a mature healthy individual (as much as possible), never the diseased, the apes, the computers' programming, or the infants.[478] The therapeutic aspect of the constellations insights strive for health, wholeness, happiness, and well-being to the most possible manner; it is not based only on the perceptions of a therapist or analyst—because it can be a sick or insane perspective, regardless of the long years of training and education (as it is in many cases).[479]

For example, Hellinger has criticized the strong emphasis that many of the Western so-called psychotherapists have put on the complaints for blaming, offending, and dishonoring the parents during the therapy sessions, and which has been the main theme for decades. He seriously considers such attitude and praxis more damaging than whatever the parents could have done[480]. It has been a serious sickly practice that has been widely popularized, widely accepted, and widely institutionalized and professionalized with very morbid and damaging effects in the physical, social, political, educational, medical, and many other domains of existence—particularly the ecological.[481]

In constellations, as in Homeopathic medicine, the therapeutic aim is to shift the dynamic aspects of the psyche, which is what structures the ways the individual perceives, acts, thinks, feels, behaves, and loves.[482] In Homepathic medicine this can *only* be done if the physician departs from the holistic *unicist* perspective (considering the disease as part of the totality of the individual) and aims to alter and eventually cure the miasmas[483].[484] Similarly, when considering the therapeutic aspect of the complex, the aim has to be to shift the psychic dynamism, which is always a transgenerational issue. If the therapy is limited to enhance better relations only with the living, to arrange couples problems, to elicit exalted states of mind, to produce hypnotic trances, to promote cathartic screams, to provide linguistic life-meaning constructions, or to any other technique that does not engage the *soul* and the *psychic* aspects and dynamics of life (which are transgenerational), then such therapy should not be called psycho-therapy but something else (i.e. conduct therapy, emotions therapy, linguistic therapy, etc.). In such cases, the important energetic aspects of the complex (which are of a psychic nature) remain foolishly neglected, unnoticed, and unattended, and are passed on to further generations—as it is the case when the miasma is not properly treated, and the individuals only continue passing on the *taras*[485].[486] It is noteworthy what Hausner said from his observations in the work of constellations: "disease should be considered bound to the transgenerational context of the family and it cannot be reduced to a personal happening of the patient"[487].[488]

This excursus is not a defense of Homeopathic medicine as the one and only healing method, but only a parameter of orientation; it is only a set of comments on the similarity of some principles that can enrich both views about the human phenomenon. The importance of the Homeopathic medicine perspective lies in the fact that it deals with diseases, illnesses, pains, and any kind of symptom in a truly holistic way, never considering such issues as something foreign to the individual.[489] There are many other practices and perspectives that claim to be holistic but which are at the most "integrative," that is, including several, or even all possible, spheres of the human being (the dietary, the anatomical, the emotional, the intellectual, the professional, the environmental, and so on) but still considering and treating diseases as something foreign that the individual needs to get rid off, that needs to fight, that needs to annihilate, or even kill and destroy. Such practices and perspectives cannot be holistic, not even if they try to tackle the issues through all the known fronts; at best, and with much effort, they can be integrative,[490] because such views still fragment reality into what the individual is and what happens to him or her. The word holistic stems from the Greek *hólo-s*, which means whole or entire[491], and a truly holistic view can just be that which sees and addresses what happens to the individual—including what makes him suffer and even die—as the individual himself (or herself).[492] However, as Hausner pointed out, such a view *ought to* include the patient's family and his or her relevant social environment[493]. One can read similar views in Jung's work, who claimed that, "the real point is the treatment of the whole psychic human being"[494], not only one or another symptom; "[i]t is, in fact, impossible to treat the psyche, and human personality in general, sectionally"[495].[496]

A story might illustrate the whole idea of the miasma, the chromatic view, and the concept of being human; it is titled: *Light, sight, and sunshine.*

Long time ago a young pupil in Greece asked a wise old philosopher what was to be human. The wise man turned his head to the sun and perceived its brilliant light that did not let him see it directly. Then, before he turned his head again towards the young man, he looked at the world in front and around him. He saw the mountains, the tall leafy trees, some flowers, and all the things that were displayed in the most varied range of colors. However, he also noted that those things under the shade were not seen as bright as those that directly under the sunrays, and right before seeing the young man again, he saw his shadow. Once facing the young man he said: "The human being is light happening." The young man remained perplexed for a bit, thinking that the wise man was going to say something else, but he didn't. The young man asked him what did that mean, and the wise man said: "To be human is to be lighted and delighted in the guise of the time and place that you occur." But the young man was still perplexed with the answer, so the wise man continued. "While being human one sees the world through the colored lenses that one was given, together with those that one has acquired. One is essentially light, but while being human one has to see colors, and one sees the other people colored, but colors are not the light, they are just the human way of seeing the world," and having said that, the wise man looked again into the open space. The young man did the same, and right before he was going to say something, the wise man continued: "To be human is to be light happening, light allowing to see the world, but the light is not the world, it is just that which lets the world be seen, in colors, naturally; and those who cannot perceive the light in other human beings are just too attached to their lenses, misperceiving the essence for the appearance, and they consequently think that the human beings are of certain definite colors. Moreover, those who do not realize the essence and the light confuse themselves with the colors in which they see themselves, and they attach strongly their views and thoughts to their perceptions, seeing just according to their lenses and conceiving the world only according to such ways of perceiving." And then he turned his gaze to the young man, and looked him straight in the eyes. The young man was not perplexed anymore, but delighted. He saw the brightness in the eyes of the wise man, and felt a pleasant sensation. After seeing each other, the wise man added: "You must also know that the most heinous person in the world is also light happening; such human being is also light, but the lenses with which such person sees the world do not let him realize that the world and his nature are not as he sees them, but both are just his light passing through his lenses." After hearing this, the young man asked promptly: "Are we supposed to get rid of our lenses?" But the man did not answer quickly; he remained silent and turned his gaze into the open again. After letting his vision see wide for a long moment he turned back to the young man and said: "While being human one sees a colored life, but if one realizes that it is light that which colors the world, and that it is light that which lets the other human beings see and understand their lives, and that they are actually light, then one has given up the lenses, but one remains with the colors." And having said this, he smiled and took a long breath. The wise man was about to walk away, but he stopped, looked at his shadow and said: "One last thing I have to tell you, light is not a thing, it is not an essence, it is not a something that one is, light allows the world and the things to be seen, but it is never a thing. In such a sense, man is light; and that which you see on the ground as your shadow is merely the projection that occurs when your body hinders the sunlight. This will remind you three things. First, that your body always casts a shadow. Second, that your body, and your seeing only from your body-lenses, can hinder the light. And third, that even when you can see your body, you never see your seeing, because seeing is the most 'sunlike' activity" And he added before he left: "Think of your soul as that which you see, and the spirit as the light which lets you see, and you will get a notion of what is to be human."[497]

There is still one question remaining regarding the miasmas, and which, in a sense, also applies to the complex: What is the primary origin of the miasma? It has been said that it is the determinant origin of diseases, and even, in Ortega's view, the origin of human unhappiness and destructiveness. It has been said that it is strongly inherited and that it determines a predisposition to certain affections, but that seems to be a secondary observation that does not deal with its primary origin. Ortega, departing from the Homeopathic principle of *vitalism*[498],[499], leaves it to an imbalance in the life-principle that comes from a *transgression* to the order of life that might come from long time ago.[500]

Jung, passed his sixth decade of life, when writing and commenting on schizophrenia, which he considered as the psychopathology that showed more clearly and with more force the *autonomous complexes*[501], thought on the possibility that it was a question of *atavism.*[502] He "seriously considered . . . that [an] amount of primitive psychology remains intact and does not become adapted to modern conditions"[503]. The human *terrain* is ancestral, and it might require ancestral honors and ancestral life-practices.[504] The question of what is the origin of the miasma or the complex is not answered, but Jung and Ortega, point the direction, which obviously is not in the ambient, not in the social or economic conditions, not in the educational or political affairs, not even in the diet and food quality, and most definitely not in one's personality traits and one's character formation.

The paradox lies in the fact that anything related to the chronic miasma, which is of an atavistic nature, is still active and actual in the psychic terrain; in other words, it is not only something that happened in a distant past, once upon a time, from which one is a passive consequence, and from which one tends to victimize oneself. Like Jung claimed, "*the cause of the pathogenic conflict lies mainly in the present moment*"[505].

Chapter 5
The Family: A Community of Fate

"Perhaps the great renewal of the world will consist of this, that man and woman, freed of all confused feelings and desires, shall no longer seek each other as opposites, but simply as members of a family and neighbors, and will unite as *human beings,* in order to simply, earnestly, patiently, and jointly bear the heavy responsibility of sexuality that has been entrusted to them."

Letters to a young poet[506]

One notion of "body" is the immediate physicality that in some ways follows one's desired movements and volition—and I mean in some ways, because in many other ways it is still autonomous, as if fragmented in independent parts, because I believe nobody willingly gets sick of cancer or hepatitis.[507] But there is a wider notion of this "body," that is not so immediate, and yet it is equally primal. This notion is family—*blood* family. Everything in the physical "body" comes, inevitably, from the parents and the ancestors, up to the point where one can say that nothing in one's body pertains originally to oneself; everything bodily is primarily *given.* One's physicality is crafted after one's family of origin, in semblance and resemblance. One's physical image is made after one's family and lineages. Just as one's face and physicality have been crafted after a given and certain community of people—say, one's ancestors—just so one's fate and *psychicality* are embedded and embodied in *a given community.* In a quite insightful way, Hellinger has observed how "all the members in a family are related between themselves through fate"[508], because "consequences are carried by the family as a unity, independently of how much other members were involved or how much they know about it"[509]. One cannot escape or avoid blood-family, no matter how much one distances from them, rejects them, ignores them, forgets them, or avoids them. One's fate is, in a big part, in relation to one's family and the ancestors. It does not imply that it is all predetermined, but that it is strongly bound to them. One's place of birth, one's family structure (size and organization) and dynamics, cultural and social conditions, economic and spiritual spheres, it all gives form to a fate that is not individually free-willed, but to a fate that is embedded and entwined with one's family and ancestors. In such a sense, just as the body (one's physicality) is not free-willed and chosen, but firstly given and from then on experienced and lived in whatever ways, so one's life is not merely free-willed, but given from determined conditions that predispose one's life to some circumstances. One's life and body are not entirely individualistic, but in a sense they both belong to a community, an interdependent community in fate. It is *as if* one's life and body were part of a bigger and wider being. On a first instance it is not necessarily meant to refer the Great Being, to which everything belongs, but to family and ancestors as this more extensive living system to which one ineluctably belongs.

These insights point to a more inclusive notion of existence, in which one's life and "body" are in inevitable relation to those other important people that made one's existence possible. It is a notion that includes all members of immediate family, and especially those to whom the individual comes after—into the realm of being. This extended notion of embodiment includes first of all the mother and the father, regardless of the individual having known them or not; and the siblings, whether *dead or alive*, given in adoption, aborted or miscarried[510]—and particularly all siblings that came first into the phenomenon of the world. It is important because it brings attention back to those who gave life, parents; they are those to whom everybody is in relation, even if it is a relation of rejection and oblivion. And it also brings attention back to those with whom the individual is immediately related in fate and its fatal conditions, siblings; one shares with them not just tragedy and luck, blessings and misfortunes, health and disease, but also *blood, psychic terrain, and fate.* It can be assured that one's family is the first conformation of one's fate, consciously or not-consciously.

However, there are more implications in the notion of family's fate. Hellinger has changed some of his views along the years, but for practical and therapeutic matters, the notion of who belongs to the family's fate has remained the same along the years. He emphatically includes: the children first, along with all of the siblings, as it was just explained, dead or alive, and of course the parents and all of their siblings, and all of the parents' previous partners,[511] even when already dead. Second, he includes the grandparents with their previous partners as well,[512] and rarely a grandparent's sibling. Not often, but circumstantially he includes a great-grandparent. However, he controversially includes also those on whose behalf our family might have obtained a benefit, or on whose health or life's behalf our family did better or got enriched—for example. He includes also all those who were victims of our family's violence, or those who were murdered by our family; and even those who murdered someone of our family, the murderers[513]. These insights, which have extended radically the views on families' fates, have also extended the notions and reach of our physicality, our "body," and our ways to heal the "body," because, as Hellinger clearly observed, "in the pathological symptoms are embodied concrete family happenings"[514]. By concrete events one can think, for example, of important happenings that altered the course of the family in a drastic way, as it could be migration, bankruptcy, war, separations, suicides, accidents, failures, frauds, slavery, sexual abuse, criminal acts, kidnappings, adoptions, chronic illnesses, physical disabilities, murders, people exploitation, financial crises, or many other variable situations.

This is not something to be overlooked, or something to be considered just as interesting; it is something groundbreaking in the fields and practices of healing. The fact that one's symptomatic embodiment is in relation to concrete family happenings opens a completely new way for dealing with one's family history and fate. The family is *a community united by fate*[515]. In this sense community is not meant as the wider social, economical, cultural and religious spheres where an individual is born, grows, develops, and lives; that is too conceptual and ambiguous. It rather refers to a clear idea and a more defined and factual image: blood family and their important implications and relations towards others and among themselves. This means that one's first community is one's family and ancestors, even if one does not know them because one was given in adoption, because they died, because one ran away, because one was kidnapped, or because some other reason. This is important because the physical "body" as we know it, is *always* in relation to the family's fate; it acts and reacts in correspondence to concrete events in one's family of origin. It is as if the physical "body" of a member of a family was an extension of *the family's body*, which goes beyond the physical notions of it, because it includes the psychic aspects and what one would call the fatal.[516] In this sense, the family, as a unity, as an embodiment of flesh with detachable members, is ensouled too, and guided too, by a common fate, in which the consequences are lived in community. Hellinger has claimed how "we are exposed to an incalculable fate, that independently of our goodness or evilness, decides over our life and death, salvation and disgrace, healing or ruin"[517]. Nobody before him has so clearly *discovered* (*un-covered*) and talked about the implications of how this fate is embodied in community.

In Hellinger's words, the family's trans-generational implications can be observed in the effects on family's members, as in severe diseases, psychoses, accidents, suicides, crimes, and even renunciation, expiation and incomprehensible fears due to an "unconscious conscience" that watches over its members[518]. By an unconscious conscience one can understand a not-known way of finding balance and orientation within the psychic terrain; however, it is not a personal function, but a function that includes all of its members, and as Hellinger claims, from several generations—maybe even from generations that we have not even imagined before, or thought about or known of.

In this view, "many symptoms, physical and psychical, as well as severe diseases, are a kind of systemic balance"[519]. A disease that might seem as a physical imbalance in one individual, as it is when departing from the medical standpoint, is considered a way to achieve psychical balance when looking the "body" as part of a bigger and wider, but nevertheless intelligent, and conscious, system[520]. The family is a system, a physical and psychic system, where every member is *like* an individual organ, and where all members together conform a dynamic and interconnected organism. In this view, one's life and body is always in relation to one's family, and, most importantly, to what happened before in the lineages. One is not detached from the events and deeds from the past in one's lineage just because one ignores them; those events are *actual* in one's psychic terrain, and they have a psychic influence that if not explored, remains out of the scope of one's individual consciousness—as autonomous unconscious forces. As Jung said, "[t]he past is terribly real and present, and it catches everyone who cannot save his skin with a satisfactory answer"[521]. The individual is part of a more encompassing conscience that guides the whole family, regardless of the individual's knowing or not. It is a family conscience that, if not known and explored, might unfold unexpected events for all of the members of the family, producing those kinds of shifts of destiny that one usually addresses as "sudden" tragedies or simply bad luck. But the family conscience, which is like a force binding all the members together, orients itself and moves accordingly within its own territory, within its own unconsciousness.

Hellinger has also observed that it is this unconscious conscience that "chooses innocent persons of further generations and in their suffering they represent those who suffered before . . . as a way to reestablish dignity, honor, and the balance of those who suffered before," in the past[522]. I believe he has been clear in such ideas, pointing out that many physical and psychical affections are *in relation to* trans-generational issues that pertain the whole family, not just to the member of the family who embodies it. It would be insane, for example, to blame the liver for getting sick, as if it had nothing to do with the rest of the organism and the totality of life of an individual. Some physicians might practice in such a way, but the perspective is blind to familial psychic aspects that the individual manifests bodily.

The notion of family as a community of fate, and as a wider embodiment of a community of soul to which our physical body belongs, allows one to explore physical affections from a wider perspective and allows also to have a different view on the so-called psychological disturbances. This view looks even to those so-called evil people in one's family and whom one might think have nothing to do with one's health and well-being—as it could be murderers, enslavers, or any kind of perpetrators. But as Hellinger observed, "just he [or she] who faces the dark forces and nods to them, finds himself united with his roots and with the fountain of its strength . . . attuned with something bigger, with depth and force"[523]. When one *actually looks* lovingly and courageously into one's own family's fate, including all those not-blood related but implicated by our family's deeds, then one cannot distinguish between good and evil anymore, and it does not even matter; family is *seen,* then, in its full display as a powerful movement of life, with all of its members required, with all of their deeds assumed, with all their fates honored, and with all of their lives well-loved[524].

The insightful views of Hellinger regarding the individual ask for a new way of conceiving and seeing man (in a generic sense, including man and woman); although it might actually be an old way of seeing him. After Hellinger's discoveries one cannot remain attached to the modern ways of conceiving the human being, where one thinks that every individual is born free and independent, as if a *tabula rasa.*[525]

One is always born within a family system, and one cannot escape that, it is inherent to life. And, as Hellinger once claimed, *one cannot escape one's parents,* even if one thinks that because one follows a spiritual path, and one assumes that one comes directly from God, or that one has detached from them[526]. Hellinger's views of the individual and his or her family do not limit the scope just to the nuclear family and just the parents. It rather points to other places where psychology and psychotherapy have not looked assuming that every individual life is a fresh start, and forgetting trans-generational issues that everyone carries and unconsciously deals with.

This view on how every individual is bound to his or her family system and ancestral lineages have harnessed the explorations of the psychic terrain, grounding them on that which is blood related. From this viewpoint, one avoids losing oneself on psychic speculations of every kind, where psychological disturbances can be related to demons, vampires, gods, goddesses, witches, or any sort of fantastical image. It does not categorically deny such approximations and cultural paradigms, but by remaining with what happened in the family one remains with what is essentially human.

One can say, then, that one's family of origin, with its peculiar communal fate, determines at first the dynamic of one's psychic structure. In other words, the psychic terrain where one stands and moves is already inhabited by the time one comes into the world, and in such terrain the inhabitants have an organization (a structure), and they move according to it, propitiating a dynamic. For example, a boy is born, and even when such a child is the first from his parents, he is the second from his mother, and the fourth from his father. Psychically, his terrain has members from his father's previous marriage, his older siblings (often called half-siblings), and members from his mother's previous partner, his older sister (also called half-sister). In the case of such a boy, for instance, his terrain shares some peculiarities with his sister, this being the whole mother lineage; but they do not share the psychic aspects from the father. The boy's terrain includes the father's first three children, which are of no importance to the boy's sister, psychically speaking, because there is no bounding by blood. Those three siblings, even when not known and not respected, are inevitably the boy's kin, they share the father and his psychic inheritance, which is completely unimportant to the boy's sister. However, it does not involve just father and mother, but a few more previous generations, at least. In the case of such a boy, his paternal lineage is entirely different from that of his sister, with entirely different people and presences, and so is the psychic terrain where he will move in his entire life. It is not the case that just because they shared the same household they share the same primordial psychic terrain. On a first basis, such psychic terrain is determined by one's family of origin, and then by one's household. In some cases it is the same, but in some others, as when there are divorces, second or more marriages, or simply second, third, or more families, it is not.

It can be said that one's psychic structure and dynamic is particular to one's psychic lineage, which is very much determined by the family's fate. But in spite of all individuals being born of mother and father, and all mothers and all fathers having been born from mother and father as well, and in spite of this genealogical structure being in principle the same for everybody, it is not as simple as just tracing back the grandparents, great-grandparents and so on, in order to *see* and know the dynamics of one's own structure. Every individual is a case in its own; and oftentimes the psychic dynamics are in such *disorder* that the structure is drastically disorganized, and disrupts what Hellinger called the *orders of love*—with very tragic consequences. In many of his transcribed seminars[527] one can read how Hellinger observed that many physical and psychological problems were because there was a rupture in the orders of love, oftentimes because the family had excluded someone, or because an individual was making him or herself responsible for something from the previous generations—almost always without knowing. This has also been said over the years by Hausner (among many others), who dealing mostly with symptomatic issues in constellations work, observed the perseverance that the children have for bearing themselves something, in representation of their parents and other close persons[528]. In many cases, it is such helping attitude, from the children to their parents, that breaks the orders of love, and damages the children. A brief story might help to illustrate such nuances, it is titled: *Father, where art thou?*

A married couple has three children, and they live together in the same household. The paternal grandfather died when the father was still a small boy, and the father never speaks about it, never mentions him, and does not show much interest in him. However, decades later, the eldest child perceives the sadness of his father and, without knowing why, tries to help his father bear his lack of father. The father, because of his young age at his own father's death, and because of the circumstances in which he was not taught how, could not nod to such an event. Therefore, he instinctively and unknowingly carries with such unresolved grief and misfortune. Regardless of his optimism, it is as if a deep issue hidden somewhere in his psyche, in his body tissues, as if it were there, but at the same time lost. Being older and already with children he thinks that it is a minor issue; but he does not know that one of his children will take upon his shoulders such grief and the responsibility for grieving the missing grandfather. The son does that without knowing, and without clear external manifestations; it is an unconscious drive that makes him take upon himself the unattended grief of his father. The son's attitude is mainly for helping his own father, but unknowingly he disrupts one of the orders of love, he displaces himself and gets disoriented in the order of life. This attitude makes him, at times, distracted at school, other times, inexplicably unhappy and miserable, and it even gives him physical symptoms. The son's disorientation is heavily determined by the lack of his grandfather's presence, which is the lack of the father for the father; but even when dead, he could be mentioned, remembered, honored, thanked. They do not know that the grandfather, in a way, is them (father and son), and yet it is missing in their lives. The un-acknowledgement of this makes them feel that they missed something, that they require something, or that they need something which they look incessantly in life, but which is hidden in nowhere else but in them.

Hellinger's constellation work is full of such cases and it would be redundant to quote them. The important aspect of such a view is that one's life is inherently affected and directed by what happened in one's family, but also affected by the attitude one shows to one's family history. Hausner, while treating many chronic symptoms, has observed how one's life, health, and happiness is marked by the attitude that one has adopted towards one's parents and one's family history[529].

In some sense this can be seen as a complimentary insight to Jung's view regarding the complex, where he knew that there were psychic autonomous contents with which one had to cope. However, if the view of the complex is harnessed by a systemic approach, and grounded first and foremost by that which happened in the family of origin, including several generations, then the complex theory gains weight and attains and attends very specific matters. In such a sense one does not get lost in speculations about mythological complexes or archetypal ways of being that are similar to fairy tale or fictional characters, but one gets really grounded into the systemic psyche, into blood issues and into issues with which one's embodiment is in inevitable relation. This allows one to explore the psychic dynamics and allows one to reestablish a healthy order to its structure. It is worth noticing Jung's observation, saying: "*The psyche, like the body, is an extremely historical structure*"[530]; therefore, one has to start psychological explorations with one's historical body: blood lineages and consanguine relations.[531]

There is a controversial issue in the constellations work, where often people, seeking for help regarding any kind of issue, are told that they are bearing something which does not correspond to them, but to previous generations, whether to the parents, grandparents, or even several generations before them. In such cases, it is as if such people were guilty of carrying something that they were not supposed to carry (in and through life), and because of that they suffer, either in a physical sense with a symptom or disease, or in a psychological sense with some kind of disturbance or hindrance. In any case, the fact is that individuals are entangled in a psychic situation which is in disorder, regardless of them having tried to fix it in an infantile way,[532] or them having been blindly involved—in a heroic or tragic sense—by their family and circumstance. What seems of great importance is that individuals are deeply affected by what happened to their family of origin in the past, and such a situation conforms an energetic complexity in which the individual psyche is immersed—the complex,[533]— and it severely affects any domain of human relationships, whether these occur in the familial, social, professional, or sexual and intimate spheres of life.[534]

This view, which could be radical and new from a Westerner's perspective, can be similar, in some sense, to old indigenous ways of living, where kinship was a very important aspect in one's life[535]. According to Deloria Jr., in the Sioux traditions it is known that "[m]any people, both vertically in ancestral time and horizontally in kinship space, are psychically injured if a family member acts wrongfully"[536]. It seems that such indigenous peoples knew that biological family relations were not just present in the physical inheritance (genetics), but also in the some kind of *psychic inheritance* (2009, p.135). Jung was very well aware of this, and in a very similar way he said that, "[p]sychic heredity does exist—that is to say, there is inheritance of psychic characteristics, special gifts, and so forth[,]" he even considered them as an "essential phenomena of life which express themselves, in the main, psychically, just as there are other inherited characteristics which express themselves, in the main, physiologically, on the physical level"[537].[538]

This view does not fall into the epistemological ways of the psychoanalytical traditions, where the individual's intricacies of fate are looked up in the developmental stages of life, as if important psychic issues were to be found in one's childhood, lactation, or even worse, at one's prenatal stages. Such ways for getting to know and understand life processes (epistemological views) find that the crucial psychic dynamics are to be found only between the person and his or her parents, or, at the most, only between the nuclear family. The usual psychoanalytic ways of knowing anything psychological, are bound to an ontological premise which is a hard to break nut in Western thought: the idea that the individual notion of psyche starts its conformation at the individual's birth, or, at the most, when such ideas pretend to be radical, at one's conception. In any case, such notion of psyche is individual, isolated, personalistic, and altogether detached from the rest, as if it were a phenomenon of its own and for its own, as if it could have an intrinsic independence;[539] and as if it were for its own wishes and its own sake, detached from the world.

Such narrow views only reflect an infantile idea of existence, where life is imagined to be for oneself, at any cost. I believe there is an imminent necessity to abandon such child-based views, and get oneself exposed to a greater domain of psyche.

The view of family as a more encompassing body of soul is rather a dynamic flow that moves along the generations; and actually moves the generations into circumstances that often reflect a psychic issue from the past. The father and the mother are not the only important psychic figures in one's life; nor are they the cause of one's psychological disturbances. There are many more factors playing a very important role than just the parents. The movements of life, in all its entanglements, encompass, as Hellinger has repeatedly observed, an extensive psychic domain—far wider than just the triad of child, mom, and dad. Jung, for instance, was very well aware of how "[t]he quality and disposition of the whole family and the ancestors lay a much greater role in the creation of the child's disposition than the individual's disposition of father and mother"[540].

Unfortunately, as Hillman claimed some time ago, "the most devastating effect of Western psychology is . . . its deliberate rupture of great chains of generations, which it has accomplished by means of its myths of individual development towards independence"[541], as if the individual could get completely detached from his origins, and is if the individual could live ignoring the many members from previous generations that passed on life, as if the individual could be independent of what made his or her life possible. In many of the psychotherapeutic methods of Western thought, because of their ontological premises, it has been given little attention to the fact that one's existence comes from a movement of life that stretches far "back" in time, including many people—and that life is always given under certain conditions and compromises.

It seems that the *disposition*[542] to be affected by certain situations, to suffer certain diseases, and to *pathologize* in certain ways, is strongly influenced,[543] in this view, by the dynamic flow of psychic energy—the movements of the soul. It is as if the individual, by the sole fact of having been born within a certain family, is already pre-positioned in a certain family configuration, which could be imagined and literally displayed phenomenologically on space, *as if occupying a terrain*; and therefore pre-disposed to certain psychic situations that convey affective atmospheres, and which are inherent to such circumstances. In this view, every individual is born within a certain, but dynamic, pattern of psychic arrangement. In simpler words, every individual is born already within a structuring family situation, which, if seen poetically, could be imagined and amplified with mythological motifs from any culture.[544] It can be said that the family situations in which one is born are archetypal in nature, *archaic types* of human ways of living, loving, lasting, dwelling, and dying.[545] Hillman, departing from archetypal psychology, claimed how "family is less a rational place than a mythical place"[546], arguing that it is less the result of computerized and programmed logical actions, conducts, and cybernetic ways of communication, but rather a scenario with dramas and dreams, epics and fantasies, tragedies and comedies, stories and fictions, as if unconsciously enacting old ways of being human,[547] so old that one can read such situations and human entanglements in antique folklore and mythologies.[548] It is interesting how Hillman considered family as a place, which if seen poetically is the first scenario of one's life-opus, and the family members as the main characters accompanying one's life-script and plot. However, family as place, as a setting, is also akin to the idea of terrain, as a territory that holds all of its members, even members that one might not know. As a place, family is more than just its members and their interrelations; it is also a psychic domain where family events and acts are kept, guarded, treasured, protected, remembered, retold, silenced, forgotten, or simply ignored, but always actual—in the act of having been and having happened. Family is actually the primal terrain into which one comes to life, and upon which one dwells and walks on Earth. It is one's first actuality, and in regard to the language, the customs and traditions, the morality and religion, the philosophies and ideologies, and the many aspects that the individual learns through and from life, family as a psychic place is prior to everything else. "Does not the world consist chiefly of parents and grandparents?"[549]

All individuals come into the world through a family. All individuals are such individuals, in principle, because of the peculiarities of their family. Family is one's entrance to the world, and in many ways it also conforms and influences one's psychological idiosyncrasy and tendencies. Idiosyncrasy stems from the Greek *ídios*, meaning "personal, peculiar;" *sún*, meaning "with;" and *krasis*, meaning "mixture"[550];[551] and indeed, one's inheritance in combination with the life experiences that one acquires (consciously and unconsciously) conforms a peculiar way of being in accordance to the psychic, visible and invisible, presences in one's family, depending on one's positioning and timing in such terrain—it is of an ontological importance.[552] It does not mean that personal circumstantial events and happenings do not mould one's character and destiny, or as if they were not important; but it is rather an acknowledgement of the priority of one's *given* psychic terrain (which in fact is one's psychic legacy and heir) over one's life situations. Hence, one can observe why Hellinger, in his many transcribed or video seminars, asked for the important events in the family of the individual seeking for help, not giving so much importance to the events that the individual per se was suffering or was enduring at the moment, or to all of his or her explanations, rationalizations, excuses, and justifications.[553] Of course this is not an absolute fixed rule of Hellinger, but a sharp insight that revealed that many issues and problems that individuals think and feel to be their own, as if belonging to their person and their intimate nature, as if pertaining only to them, are in relation to important events, crucial happenings and concrete and very specific events that previous generations in the family went through. Hellinger's claim is that "problems are the result of happenings, not of one's feelings, and very rarely are they the result of other's behavior, as from one's parents' behavior"[554]. It is indeed a radical way to display and attend to what is truly essential for the individuals; and when done so, many of the so-called life problems unexpectedly shift and take a different course—not being problems anymore.[555]

What has been astonishing is the fact that the ways in which many individuals behave, believing that it is because they have build up or conformed a character after their life experiences and their own ways to cope and to deal with life, are oftentimes similar, or in active or reactive relation, to the ways that previous members in their family behaved. It is as if one were repeating a pattern, without knowing, and, moreover, as if one were getting into the same kind of situations, problems, conditions, entanglements, and affairs, as those who lived before in one's lineages. In such a sense, it is as if one's life unfolding were a loyal repetition to the many life situations in which such previous family members were, but not as an exact replica (even though it happens) but in one's idiosyncratic ways—in one's own way of mixing the characteristics from one's antecessors.

This is also the interest of *psychogenealogy,*[556] which is a way of studying psychic and psychological phenomena from a genealogical standpoint, where it is not only important to trace back the names of one's ancestors and build up a genealogical tree, but to investigate the important events that such previous members suffered, endured, provoked, caused, went through, and had to live; "the decisive is the events, the happenings"[557]. Deloria Jr. said that for the Sioux, "much of the discussion was devoted to genealogies" and therefore "[p]eople kept track of everything"[558]; as if to lose something were like losing an aspect of one's soul.

Dumas, a French psychoanalyst who integrated some insights from shamanism and Taoism into his therapeutic practice, argued that Jungians do not have a theory of the functioning of the collective psyche, because, he suggests, they have not understood the trans-generational consciousness[559],[560] The ancestors and the trans-generational blood issues have been an overlooked aspect in some traditions of depth psychology; many therapists and theorists have jumped from the personal into the collective (as trying to speak for entire peoples, nations, religions, and so on) and even into the "world unconscious" without regarding any attention to the influence of the individuals who lived before in one's own lineages.

The insistence on the importance of exploring family issues in any therapeutic setting lies in the fact that many of these issues when seen only from a personal sphere and scheme of consciousness, reveal innumerable possibilities of explanations and attempts to solutions, from social, to medical, dietary, ideological, temperamental, circumstantial, financial, and even spiritual, but hardly ever address the autonomous psychical—as if the ontological premise were that the individual is detached from his family system, and as is the individual life had nothing to do with it.[561]

When intended to do something about family issues in a psychical sense, it is not meant to address and change the memories and experiences from childhood and young age, as common psychotherapies would do by just trying to find a better meaning for lived experiences, early traumas, and familial relationships; it is rather an intervention intended to alter the dynamics in one's psychic terrain—which is populated by autonomous presences and psychic figures. By an intervention one can think of a different way of looking into one's family, or even a few spoken words and actions that would start a psychic movement. This should not be confused with the literal understanding of ordinary movement, as it is conceived in the usual sense of the word, often implying mobility, as it is when one exercises, walks, travels, and even moves out to far away lands. One can move a lot on the physical landscapes of the world and even live far away from one's country and family of origin, and remain almost within the same psychic situation, as if there had been no change.

Psychic movement does not necessarily imply extreme physical movement, and it can be achieved in a small space with a few body movements, or even by means of imagination. It means a motion in the depths of psyche, an important shift of one's positioning in relation to the others in one's psychic terrain. At times, just by altering the attitude with which one looks at other persons or presences generates a drastic change in one's psychic configuration, and it becomes a movement of the soul. I dare say that it is only with psychic movements that one can completely change the dynamics of the psyche.

One's family is one's first and most important psychic configuration, it is the place where one comes into life, and its members are one's main figures in one's complex. The *family-terrain* provides a structure and set of psychic dynamics, which later develop into ways getting along among the family members and with other people in general; and if such structure breaks the orders of love, then, as Helllinger has observed, the dynamics of the psyche generate trouble—whether sicknesses, diseases, failures, misfortunes, losses, etc. But, as it has been explained, the notion of family is not reduced to the Western idea of a two generations family; it is rather something extended throughout time, and, as Hellinger has brilliantly shown, it includes even non-blood-related people throughout several generations, with which a community of fate is shared. This comes quite close to a Native American notion of family, which "might best be seen to be organized around the concept of several generations instead of a two-generation nuclear family[,]" including of course "personal parents, a kinship family, the extended community, a cultural collective and the living presence of the ancestors, all psychically present in powerful ways"[562].

What is very important and what one should not overlook when reflecting about the family is the observation made by Hellinger regarding the family conscience, which is that it is a force that binds the members together, regardless of them knowing or not, and that it is this conscience that watches over all of its members, keeping the orders of love through a principle of *compensation*[563],[564]. Hellinger considered it as a *participative conscience*[565], where the individuals are affected by what happens to the whole system. In such sense, it was revealed that whenever there is an exclusion from the family (which would be a rupture in the first order of love—denying someone the right to belong), as it is the case with illegitimate children, illegitimate wives, aborted, or so on, then someone in further generations will take its place, energetically speaking, and will suffer the consequences of such *dis-order* as a way to give back the right of belonging to such excluded member.[566] It is what has been called the principle of compensation, in which "innocent" members from later generations amend without knowing the ruptures from previous members, and re-establishes the balance in the family system.[567] Hellinger has warned that excluding someone just for being different, for instance, might have severe consequences in the young members of the family[568]. This is so, because "in the depths of the soul prevails a transgenerational eagerness to achieve equity and compensation"[569].[570]

From the constellations work it has become clear that fate is lived together as a family, and that not because one moves away, and physically separates from the family, does that mean that one is out of such sphere of conscience, as if physical distance could keep one's psychic inheritance away. It is as if one would always live within one's psychic terrain, somehow always in relation with one's family system—which creates a complex that constantly constellate any kind of situations in all the possible spheres of life: profession, vocation, work, couple situations, marriage, finances, health, etc.[571] It is not hard to deduce why Hellinger originally called his style and method as *Family Constellations*;[572] by it, he stayed in the mundane but always working with the essential—the life principle—, and he seemed to have offered a refined and fully empirical therapeutic way to deal with what Jung called the complex. A brief story, titled *Those Women!*, might illustrate and expand the vision on the influences of the family on the individual.

There was a woman who had two children, a girl first, and then a boy; and she always referred to herself as a single mom, and she constantly spoke of the father of her children as an irresponsible man who had left her with all the load. She was a hard-working woman, the kind of woman that some feminists would be proud of, not just because of her great capacity to do it all by herself, but also because of her immense disdain for men. She was the kind of woman that often thought that women can do it all on their own, without the need of a husband or a man; and she kept repeating to herself that she belonged to those so-called strong women around the globe who were self-sustainable, who needed no man around, who could live on her own, and who could even raise her children all by herself, carrying everything on her own, enduring all difficulties with a proud smile on her face, secretly revealing that she liked fate to be that way. She was not the kind of woman that would go on to those feminist reunions or public manifestations. She could carry the whole load of maternity and paternity by herself, in a camel-like way, and she could remain for long periods in such existential dryness, seeing life and the world, indeed, as a desert that ought to be endured.

Her kids were still young, but whenever she had any trouble with them, she would scold them and remind them that they were a team, that they were one for another, that they were a team of three in which they would have to keep an eye for one another. And in a so-seemingly lovely fashion she started to educate them, thinking that it was the right thing to do, and, moreover, a noble perspective that her children would have to be aware of her. In her naïf mind, they were a team of three meant to support one another, meant to live for one another, meant to care for one another; and even when the kids were barely eight and six, they were already worried whenever they saw her worried, they were sad whenever they saw her sad, and concerned whenever they saw her concerned. Such woman, in all her arrogance, did not see that she was relying on her children and giving them part of the load, rather than allow the children rely upon her.

The children started to get indeed infected by her psychic condition, it took almost no time for them to start helping her to carry the load of life, and they became camel-like as well, in other words, great carriers of others' burdens. Curiously, they did it out of love, out of childish love for their mom; and their mother felt proud of them, because her good children were becoming good support and good carriers, and they all conformed a great team, and the three of them were successfully enduring the arid dryness of such desert-like existence. She did not know, however, that when one is camel-like, the world seems endlessly a desert, no matter how much one works or walks, and no matter how much one tries to get away. In fact, she was working harder and harder every time, getting heavier and heavier loads of work, and she felt proud for her strength and stoic ways, but not seeing that life was just as dry as ever, and her hunchback more and more pronounced. In her mind, it could all be solved by harder work, and getting heavier loads of work.

What this woman did not know was that she was only repeating what had happened to her own mother; but in her blind womanish pride, she constantly convinced herself that it was because men were irresponsible, idiots, good for nothing, and that she had enough strength to do it all alone. She constantly thought that her own mother's life story and hers were completely different, because she repeatedly thought of herself as a woman of great capacity to do things on her own, unlike her mother who had have bad luck and had to raise the five children on her own because the man (her father) was lazy. She could not see that she was only repeating a pattern of her mother's life, and in all her brightness she could not see that she did not even cared for her own father either, just as her own children were taught to do, and in their loving obedience already starting to do. This woman could not see that her children were behaving like she and her siblings did, when they were themselves children, trying to help their mommy get through life on her own, also as a single mother, as a woman abandoned by her man.

Moreover, she could not see that she was plainly living a life quite similar to that of her own grandmother, who got pregnant of the first child, a daughter (the woman's mother), and had to raise her all by herself. Her familial idiosyncrasy did not allow her to see that her own grandfather, the man of her maternal grandmother, was never even mentioned, and never ever remembered.

Because of her great familial pride she did not realize either that her great-grandmother had also had great disdain for her own man, the great-grandfather (father of her maternal grandmother), and that the man's name was barely remembered, and hardly ever brought to the memory, because in fact she did not cared. And so it became impossible to realize that her great-great-grandmother, the grandmother of her maternal grandmother, had been a deeply sad woman living a miserable life, constantly oppressed and beaten by her husband, the great-great-grandfather. However, by some strange reason this man, the great-great-grandfather, was the only man remembered with much love by all these women in the mother's lineage. From her fathers' lineages she did not know or cared a pinch, just like her mother did and just like her grandmother did. Moreover, she behaved towards men, but particularly towards her man, the biological father of her children, in the exact same ways that that her mother had, and just like her grandmother and great-grandmother had.

Unfortunately, her stubborn ideology, which was nothing but a transitory and fashionable philosophy, kept her from realizing that she was only enacting a trans-generational pattern, that she was only repeating the life of the women in her mother's lineage; but because she was a good daughter and indeed very loyal to those women, she felt proud, she felt as one of them, and being a mother without a husband was the way to belong to "those women."

Even more unfortunate was the fact that the fate of her daughter, her first child, was being directed towards a quite similar pattern if some serious intervention was not done. In this woman's mind, it was all because of those lazy men, and with such firm convictions, there was no other way to live, but to show that women can do it alone, on their own, and that they can raise children without the men, and also without the actual father.

Of course she did not know why she behaved like this, her familial pride only taught her to be proactive in a one way, but not to be perceptive of unconscious ways of living and loving that she dragged from events or secrets from the past of her family. Naturally, she thought that her problems and life situations, and her lack of a man and her great way to carry the loads of life, was something justifiable from her personal life-story; she never ventured to look back and see that it was not something new in her family.

Jung was well aware, probably through his therapeutic practice, that one is bound to one's family in the most uncanny ways, not only because of the household situation, with its peculiar ways to handle economy, education, nutrition, spirituality, and so on, but bound to family in ways that are hidden, occult, or invisible.[573] Jung, when explaining a chapter of Nietzsche's Zarathustra[574] said that "it is surely a great truth that under certain favourable or unfavourable [*sic*] conditions, the son reveals the father's secret"[575]; and by such statement he makes one think that he knew of the inevitable bond that runs from father to son (or daughter), beyond the casualties of the child's awareness, which, by the way, "[o]f course is true for both parents"[576].

Jung did not fully explain how this happens, nor did he mean that the child reveals the secret in a literal way, but that the son (or the daughter) would be under the influence of such important event, and would reveal it in some way, either acting out and thinking that such enactment is deliberate, or through strange or compulsive ideas, or by getting ill, or even by killing or dying.[577] In any case, as Jung pointed out, "it really explains much in a human life which cannot be explained otherwise"[578], because those influences, even when *hidden*, remain within the family conscience (which directs the lives of the individuals, as Hellinger has observed). Jung also realized how "[t]he secrets of the parents have the most extraordinary influence upon the lives of the children, and nothing in the world will prevent the children from being influenced"[579]. By the fact of being born within a family, one is already born within a structure that might have hidden issues, often shameful or guilty events, that parents, grandparents, or even great-grandparents prefer not to speak about and which they keep as something unspoken, secret, and almost taboo—thinking that it will not affect further generations.[580] But, as Jung also observed, "[a] certain side of the secret consists in the inheritance of the body," which could be thought of as those unconscious psychic aspects that get embodied as "degenerate functions" and which "we hand on if we have children"[581]—*taras and miasmas*. Moreover, as Jung sharply pointed out: "we cannot help having secrets, secrets which we don't know ourselves"[582] secrets that rather have us and take us to their service—unconsciously—if we are not aware of their powerful influence.[583]

Some other aspects are not necessarily hidden as secrets, but remain *occult*, as it is the case when someone does not know much about the ancestors or when one does not even have a face, a name, and place for them. From the psyche point of view, it does not matter if the individual does not know what important events might have happened in his or her lineage; even if events are occult to all the members of the family, they are psychoactive nevertheless. One's ignorance and indifference does not save one from psychic inheritance. Just as one can often see how much a child physically resembles the parent that was excluded from the family, as it is the case (for example) with those "single" mothers that make their child forget, ignore, and reject any trace of the father because of a trouble between themselves as man and woman (a couple); in just the same way one can figure out things in the psychic sphere—it simply occurs beyond one's volition and without one's permission.[584]

It is as if many things and processes that happen to the individual, in a concrete physical way, as it could be an accident or a disease, or in a psychological way, as it is the case with intellectual tendencies, sexual preferences, professional activities, and even consequential events as economic and marital failures (just to name some examples), are influenced by *invisible* factors that one might not know and might never get to know with the usual ways of coping with life. The reason lies in the fact that the usual, normalized, ways of (Westernized) living have offered almost no *technique*, from the Greek *tékhnè*, meaning "art"[585], for seeing into the so-called unconscious, and for seeing through those life events that one considers as deeply personal.

So far, I can speak of two ways for doing this. One, inspired by Hillman's proposals is to recur to the "imagination" and one's fantasies, because by means of images one can *personify* and *see through* one's deep desires, longings, wishes, cravings, needs, and motivations.[586] Whether healthy or perverse, shameful or immoral, obscene, compulsive, criminal, or silly, fantasies reveal a psychic structure that might be moving the individual into some pattern of behavior, feeling, and thinking; but such fantasy, that the individual could rapidly think to be deeply personal, might belong to the whole psychic structure, in which all family members reside. By being truly aware of the fantasies that come to one's mind, and without any further analysis or interpretation, one can see the psychic contents (which require images) and then see through them, realizing what do those images want (treating them as if they were autonomous). When one's fantasies are not imagined as enacted always by the ego (the "I"),[587] then with such technique one can de-personalize feelings and thoughts, because by giving a face, a persona, and an image (different from oneself) to such fantasies, one realizes that such cravings might belong to someone else—as if one were only being called to remember something from them.[588] For Jung, for instance, "mental processes are occurrences or events…figures…[with] life of their own…and you suffer from [them] exactly as you suffer the effect of bad inheritance"[589]. This could be considered a phenomenology of imagination, in which all ideation (images and fictions) is not taken as produced but as perceived, and where one reaches into psychic matters by means of an acute awareness of one's fantasy.[590] If practiced honestly and without censorship, it is a way to reveal unconscious, most probably transgenerational issues.[591] Jung mentioned, when commenting on personifications, that, "one can train to such an extent that they become visible or audible also in a waking condition"[592]. The burden of this technique lies in the fact that one might not hit the essential, and one can become heavily delusional if one is not well grounded.[593]

The other way of which I can speak with certainty is the Constellations work, which is indeed a phenomenological method to reveal the psychic dynamics in the family, and even psychic dynamics in other domains. This technique lets one literally see the position and motion of the family members (including oneself) in relation to one another, and from such display one can re-arrange one's position in relation to them, and also one's disposition towards them, in order to find a better place in which to stand. This way of seeing into the psychic terrain and its peculiar movements is an embodied phenomenology that reveals the individual's "characterological disposition," which Jung mentioned "can be seen most easily in the relation of the patient to his [or her] parental family"[594].

In both cases, either by means of the imagination or by means of representatives (with the help of other individuals) one reaches into the phenomenology of hidden, occult, or invisible aspects of the psyche; and "the fact that the unconscious is personified means that it is inclined to collaborate . . . inclined to form a connection with [the individual] consciousness"[595]. If one does not explore one's psychic terrain, it remains unknown, out of one's individual consciousness, and one is fated to experience it throughout the casualties of daily life, blaming society, economy, politicians, the government, or even God, and thinking that its over with one's suffering.[596] But it might be worth remembering Heraclitus fragment saying: "The living, though they yearn for consummation of their fate, need rest, and in their turn leave children to fulfill their doom"[597].[598] However, one should never think that ones parents or one's grandparents or great-grandparents are to blame,[599] but one's ignorance or inability to cope with life issues, which if not attended, resolved, and redeemed, might be passed on to further generations.[600] Like Jung very well said: "[i]t is not . . . a question of the parents committing no faults"[601], but a matter of getting acquainted with one's unconsciousness, so to speak, those tendencies and inclinations, those desires and wishes, those thoughts and cravings, those attitudes and perspectives, those ideals and convictions, those ways of loving and living that even when consciously willed, and justifiably convinced that one wants them, might be as if imposed on one's (notion of) soul.[602]

Chapter 6

Honor: A Religiosity of Flesh, an Attunement with the World as it is

"Were one asked to characterize the life of religion in the broadest and most general terms possible, one might say that it consists of the belief that there is an unseen order, and that our supreme good lies in harmoniously adjusting ourselves thereto."

The varieties of religious experience[603]

When speaking about family lineages, and ancestors, one attitude and action should be remembered: to give honor. Hardly anyone has ever remarked or insisted upon it more than Hellinger.[604] He has observed how "in relation to the essential all parents are perfect, whole"[605]—where the "essential" means having received life from them. Such a sentence, brief and simple, can open up a life of deeply religious implications; but not a religious life towards a sort of deity, or (what one imagines to be) God, but a sense of religiosity towards life as it is, *just as it is.*[606] From this profound insight—that all parents are perfect—there can be a religiosity of flesh with profound impact and profound wisdom—but it is not easy to attain. Hellinger has claimed how "wherever someone demands something from his [or her] parents reduces the essential in himself. He [or she] becomes narrow, little, limited"[607]. An individual who complains about his or her childhood or his or her parents loses the strength to face the intricacies of fate, loses the gifts of such difficulties, remains psychologically infantile, with infantile desires and infantile thoughts, and seeks to fulfill those desires while letting those thoughts configure—*constellate*—the perception, embodiment, and sensed-felt notion of reality. When one is not content with one's parents, accepting them fully as they are, then one remains a child in one's heart, and, not strangely, the perception of the world is like that of a child. One can see how such childish individuals—even after their fifth or sixth decade of life—focus on how authoritative some people or some institutions are, or they focus on all the wrong things that their parents did and did not do and that they think they endured because of them, or they focus on how terrible their life and their jobs are because of their difficult childhood, and so they end up believing that their miseries and failures have to do with their first years of life.[608]

But these childlike perceptions, where one blames one's unhappiness upon childhood memories, lead also to an embodiment of such "fantasies." In other words, it affects the way the body unfolds and functions. By fantasies in this sense, it is meant the collection of imaginings (memories, feelings, thoughts, desires, beliefs, motivations, and sensations) about one's life-story, that is, one's psychological fiction; but, like Jung wisely observed, "fantasies can just be as traumatic in their effects as real traumata"[609]. Often it is not so much what actually happened during one's childhood that affects the body in adult life, but the way one remembers one's early life, and the way one stubbornly sticks to such perceptions—which drastically affect and configure one's corporeal, relational, and circumstantial existence.[610]

One can see, for example, how often young men who lack their father's presence and strength, because they disrespect him or because they have been denied such presence (most often because of their own angry mother's suggestions), lack also muscular weight—as if they had been denied that too, revealing a male force deficiency. One can also see how often women who have trouble accepting their mother's fate, or women who cannot stand their mother, often overeat and are frequently overweight. These are not unbreakable rules of psycho-physical development, but common observations that can lead to important insights. One's embodiment is also built and affected by one's perceptions of the essential; and what could be more essential than one's parents? Not only does one's "body" get affected; but also the way one senses and feels about oneself and about the world is directly affected by such perceptions. Often these child-like adults complain about the difficulties of life in similar ways that children would complain about anything; and also very often these kind of adults seek for pleasure in the ways that children would look for it, whether demanding it abruptly or without consideration for others involved, making tantrums or becoming obsessive and showing off, reacting angrily if they do not get it or behaving as martyrs, taking it without sharing or even abusing others for getting it, and so on[611]. The reason of this lies in the fact that psychological maturity does not always go along with biological maturity[612]—everybody grows old, but not everybody ripens into the sweetness of happiness. When seen psychologically, a lot of people still demand things from other people, from the government, the institutions, or even from the world and from God, in exactly the same way that an infant would demand something from his or her mother.[613] Oftentimes people who bitterly complain about their city, their government, their society, and so on, are people who deep inside do not appreciate, care, and value that they were given (through their parents) a mysterious gift called life.

This is not implying that one's development is *the* crucial issue for one's later years, but that the *perceptions*[614] that one has about one's family, and especially about one's parents, is crucial for any moment in life.[615] This argument is a categorical rejection of the developmental theories in psychology that emphasize the care and pampering of the so-called "inner child," and the therapeutic emphasis on one's childhood memories and environments.[616] This is rather a perspective that aims towards a very stout vision of the world, a vision that demands one to bow to life just the way it presented itself and came to oneself. If attained, it is a perspective that allows one to see the world with depth and power, and when one truly gains such view, one feels a notion of religiosity that might have not been felt before. It is a sensed-felt notion that does not require previous knowledge from the established religions, but it is felt with such certainty and infallibility that one can just call it a religiosity of flesh—with one's own flesh *in this life.*

A deep religiosity of flesh can just happen if one completely respects his or her parents, not wanting them to be better or different in any sense, not even in the tiniest way. For if one is discontent with his or her parents, then one disrespects them, and also one is also disrespecting the ways they had to face fate, in the fullest of its implications; and one cannot face one's life fully, because secretly one is wishing a few details to be different. But that is completely insane, sick, and silly, and perhaps no one has said it better than Nietzsche: "Did you ever say Yes to a single joy? Oh my friends, then you said Yes to *all* woe as well. All things are chained together, entwined, in love"[617].

Hence Hellinger has been quite firm on his stance towards parents, towards *all* parents. For the one thing they deserve the most from their children: honor! Because, in Hellinger's words, by honoring the parents one is taking all that came through them, but mostly one is *taking life!* This "taking", he claims, is a "humble realization" and it means, "a nodding to life and fate just as it comes through the parents"[618]. More properly speaking, I would say that, it is in no way an act of grabbing something that one feels that one deserves, but an act of *receiving* something that was given as the greatest gift. In this sense, one could think, nothing in life is for granted, only the possibility to *receive* the blessings—from the material and physical blessings, as health and prosperity, to the relational, intellectual, and spiritual blessings. The issue is that one does not take life (metaphorically speaking) in the same way that a thief takes something; a blessing cannot be stolen or taken arrogantly. Only by being humble is it that one can be open to receive it, and once having taken it one shares it. Hence the insistence on honoring the parents, because when one genuinely feels like doing so, one is ready to receive the force of life from them, and only then can one *take* it—for oneself and for sharing it with the world.

This insight has deeper sense-felt consequences, which can just be observed in their effects. It is, somehow, as if life-force was not given once, at one's birth, but as if it were flowing continuously from somewhere else, through them, to oneself—even after the parents' death. In some uncanny way, they seem to be a fountain of life-force—in a sort of psychical way. Biologically it is them who gave life *once*, but psychically it is as if they were *a constant source* from where a peculiar strength comes, a strength that is needed to face one's destiny—a most certain *resource*[619].

To some peoples and cultures, this might sound extremely obvious, to some other peoples and cultures it might sound strange, while some other peoples might even defend their posture and perspectives of not honoring their parents and even rejecting them with all kind of excuses, justifications, and sophistry. But the last sort of people seem to have a difficulty assuming the implications of this community of fate, where the tough and the terrible are part of the light and the bliss of the family and life. Hellinger has observed how common it is that people seeking for the so-called "self-realization" are nothing else than individuals who have not *honored* their parents fully, wholly, as they are, and therefore these individuals feel often "empty"[620]; oftentimes, there are plenty of individuals who seems to have achieved everything, i.e., money, success, properties, fame, etc., but who still feel a deep and severe lack.[621] Hence for Hellinger, honoring the parents is actually the most important principle in his method—Constellations—, and he has firmly taken it as the basic fundament of his work or any other kind of therapy[622]. For him, any person wanting to help others first has to honor his or her own parents[623]; otherwise, it is just pretentious and continues the folly, the childishness, and the diseases.[624]

There are several ways in which one can show honor—as one can also observe in some cultures, like the Japanese. Hellinger proposes, and, during his work asks for, a bow—a literal physical bow, as a profound gesture to give honor. During the Constellations work, this act is a kind of ritual, where one is actually bending down towards one's progenitors. There are several kinds of bows, and Hellinger seems to know them all; from inclining the head, to bending the upper half of the body, to kneeling down and placing one's forehead on the ground, to even the last act of surrender which is to lie down flat on one's belly facing the ground.[625] Hellinger explains that the bow to the parents is a gesture, a posture, and an attitude of "supreme humility" in which one accepts and takes life as it came from them, with all that it implies, with all that it might cost, and with all that might be required, and that such act is "*the* religious act"[626].[627]

This is an act of reverence and humility towards those who gave life, and in such a way towards life itself; it is an act of *reverence* because, as the etymology of the word suggests; it is a display of "deep respect"[628]. The word reverence stems from the Latin *vereri* with the prefix *re;* the later is used in the sense of a "response to a stimulus, of intensive force"[629], and *vereri,* which means "feel awe of"[630]. When one faces one's parents within a ritual setting (as it could be a Constellation) one literally feels the awe for something greater than anything else, one feels the awe towards something that came through them, something so powerful, incomprehensible, and mysterious, that one can only bow in gratitude. One bows in humility to the life that came *through them*, only through them. It is hence an act of *humility,* because, as its etymology clearly points out, it deeply "grounds" one to the human condition, it brings one down to "earth," the "*humus,*" which is cognate with *homō*—and related to *humanus*[631]. It is not meant in the sense of lowering the estimate of oneself, but in the sense of bringing one to a lower position in regard to one's parents; it is a *humble* act because through it one recognizes that one's parents have always been great. Only then is one capable of seeing the greatness of their life, the greatness of their way to face fate, endure life, and pass it on.[632]

Only those who revere their parents in full sincerity can come out of childish positions, childish philosophies, childish psychologies and childish psychotherapies that want the world and life to conform to their childish wishes and childish fantasies.[633] Hence this is a profound act of religiosity, but not based on an established dogmatic religion, not towards a divinity from a text-based religion, but towards life itself, and towards the world of flesh—and when this occurs something else happens unexpectedly. It seems that all true religiosity of flesh, and therefore a true religiosity attuned with the Earth, starts with the most honest bow to one's parents; just as *any* complaint, no matter how tiny, is infantile—moreover, it is a severe transgression to the life-principle.[634] Anything that an individual still cries about his or her childhood is only a complaint for how things did not match one's ideals. But Nietzsche said it quite clear when he rhetorically asked: "Is all weeping not a complaining? And all complaining not an accusing?"[635].

This idea has deeper consequences than one can glimpse at first sight. Often there are people who do not complain directly about their parents, but they complain about their education, about their neighborhood, about their country, about the current economic times, about politicians, and so on and so forth, complaining all the time about something in the world; those are in essence complaints about *this* world into which their parents brought them. And such complaints are nothing but a whining for having to be in *this* world.[636] Moaning about one's situation and about one's life is of no help; moreover, it is a secret accusation against one's progenitors for having brought oneself into *this* life and into these times of the world. Such complaints often secretly desire life to be different, in ways that one thinks life should be or ought to be; but the moaning keeps individuals in a position that is not attuned with the world as it is, as it has

been, and as it was given at one's birth. The moment that one feels entitled to complain for
not having gotten this or that, either from one's parents or from the world, one has dangerously
forgotten that, in principle, life is a powerful and beautiful gift. It is worth noticing Jung's
observation, saying that, "in the unconscious the mother always remains a powerful primordial
image, colouring [*sic*] and even determining throughout life our relations to woman, to society,
to the world of feeling and fact"[637]; she heavily tinctures one's perceptions. The father, on the
other hand, "determines our relationship to man, to the law and state, to reason and the spirit and
the dynamism of nature"[638]; he strongly frames one's perceptions. However, he observed, this
happens "in so subtle a way that, as a rule, there is no conscious perception of the process"[639].
Hence, in essence, accusations, and often accusations against God, against fate, or against the
Zeitgeist, are only disguised accusations against one's parents for having brought one into this life
that has it's own challenges.[640]

For if one resists the temptation to be lead astray by the limited perspectives and theories of some
generations of intellectual men and women—mostly psychotherapists—, then one can acquire a
position to see the world with an extensive perspective, with a vision that encompasses so many
generations that one will find no one to blame. Blaming is not possible when one stretches vision
and genuine compassion into the past. Nietzsche got it quite clear when he said: "One must learn
to *look away* from oneself in order to see *much*"[641]. One must learn to see life beyond the vision
of one's pettiness, in order to see the varieties and depths *in* this life. How different it is when
one faces existence just the way it is, and, despite the difficulties, one sees the gift of being alive
in this time, in this world, right now. One then grows ripe and stout—and only then might one
find true meaning and one's purpose. Jung mentioned that, "no matter how much parents and
grandparents may have sinned against the child, the man who is really adult will accept these sins
as his own condition which has to be reckoned with" (1952/1968, p.117). Only beyond blaming
others (and oneself) can one venture deep into the matters of destiny and soul.[642]

Unfortunately there are many out there trying to convince everybody, with their elegant theories
and therapies, to feel pity about those in suffering—as if their suffering were not already
sufficient. But, as Nietzsche rightly saw it, "all great love is above its pitying"[643]; because in
pitying, as he saw too, "[people] have no reverence for great misfortune, for great ugliness, for
great foundering"[644]. When pitying there is no respect for the others' fate, and even worse,
there is no respect for the others' dignity, and one behaves as if one could do better in their place,
as if one would know better. But verily, what can one know about their place, their situation,

and their suffering in this life? When one feels pity for the others' suffering, and especially one's parents suffering, then it seems as if their struggles would have been in vain, and, as Hellinger sharply noticed, one steals away their dignity.

These insights are not merely interesting but actually quite radical, and in fact they start to address *the philosophical* and *the moral* aspects of the Complex Theory. By means of a gaze into the complex—which can be only partly displayed—one can actually see that one's "individual" life is immersed in a river that flows from way back, as if one's life were but a tiny moment of the river, continuing what has happened, and continuing from what has been.

It opens a deeper philosophical dimension of being human because only when one sincerely honors one's parents, only when one truly acknowledges in one's heart, that they are great because our life passed through them, despite everything and despite anything, can one start to see life from a deeper dimension. "A look to what the parents *have done* (italics added) is focalized and limited[,]" because, as Hausner pointed out, "paternity is in itself much more[;]" and, as he well said, "respect is achieved when one looks at them as a whole and, beyond them, also their family and fate"[645]. Only then is one ready for the world; before this, one it still an infant in the heart. It is such a profound shift—of ontological dimensions—in one's way to see and live existence that everything in any sphere of life acquires a different brightness. It is as if suddenly one could see clearer, with less falsity, without the tinctures of one's infancy. Once this shift is felt, one even thinks that those who do not or cannot honor their parents should not be taken seriously; above all one might think that they should not teach or educate others, because they do not see clearly, and they still feel and see life like children[646]—and this, of course, would be worth taking into consideration with physicians, social workers, psychologists, and people helping others in general, like psychotherapist.[647]

However, this philosophical deepening is accompanied by a deepening into the moral aspects of the Complex Theory as well. In fact, that which allows one to perceive the greatness of one's parents in order to give them the honor they deserve, is an amoral perspective from which one can look at them beyond their acts, beyond any deed that could possibly accuse them.[648] It is indeed a difficult stance to achieve in some cases, especially in cases where children suffered—but what a great relief it is when they redeem the memory of their parents from their acts and still look at them gratefully for the life received. One can see that in such cases, if the individuals were not infected by the pitying of the therapists, they could obtain strength from all their suffering, and they could find a special strength in their fate that nothing else could have given it to them. One sees then how beautiful it is when they can still look at the greatness of their parents, and they can still redeem their own past from all complaints and accusations, and find something which only the heart can see—but which requires humility to be received and *courage* to be taken.[649]

It is worth saying that one does not redeem one's parents, or grandparents or some other antecessor, from their deeds, as if one were the redeemer of their "sins" and "bad" acts, because that makes one feel superior in relation to them, as if better than them, as if knowing what should have been done, as if being a better person or a better human being; that only disrespects their life, their fate, and their ways they had to face and endure struggles. One only redeems oneself from one's judgments about them; one redeems one's ideas and feelings of them from one's own morality and stupidity—nothing else. In this sense there is no place for the concept of dysfunctional family, only families with tougher, rougher, and harder fates; "the notion of dysfunctional condemns what it's dealing with"[650], and it has become urgent to get rid of such label, because only by getting rid of it can all families, and all members of such families, be respected as being an embodiment of soul—all required, all needed, all included, all loved. It seems that the concept of functionality, if dictated by human ideas and clinical standards (according to the times and place), might exclude great parts of the human population, but if considered from the perspectives of the soul it is always functional to fulfill its own purposes. What has been called dysfunctional[651] (in families) is probably only a misunderstanding of the depths of the soul.

It is a paradox that the moral aspect that was still required to be discovered and seen in the Complex Theory, was the *amorality*, and specially towards one's parents, one's family, and one's antecessors. It is not meant to say that one can deliberately behave like a brute, a criminal, or a pervert, as some people often imagine when they listen or read the word amoral, but that one is not in a position in which one can judge the deeds of those who lived before in one's lineages—and especially never in a position to judge one's parents. Just as one was born within a certain energetic configuration, just so they were, and when people and events are seen within a bigger context, one realizes that moral judgments are only based on a lack of an extensive vision, a sick heart, and a narrow consciousness. The acknowledgement, display, and attention to the complexities of one's psychic life allow one to see that one's existence came into the world only because many other events happened, and more importantly, because many other people did what they did—just the way they did, and not in some other "better" way.

This acknowledgement of one's psychic history suddenly connects the individual to the strength that comes through many generations; but it does so in such a way that it is not a matter of blaming, but a matter of reverence, as a gesture of deep respect towards them for having lived what fate presented to them, and still pass on life. One feels suddenly connected to the origins, to the force of life that came through many people, many more than one can even count or imagine. But if the contrary happens, as it is "[w]hen we refuse the historical aspect in our complexes" then, as Hillman blatantly said it, "we create orphans[;]" we create psychic orphans and "we abandon our complexes to the power of the child archetype"[652]. And such is the *position* in which one thinks and firmly believes that life has nothing to do with the rest of the family clan, the rest of the system, or with the ancestors; and once in such a stance, bereft of the force and gifts of one's origin, which is nothing but a sickly psychic *disposition,* it is just a matter of time in order to feel oneself in the right side for judging or blaming them[653] —like often children would do.[654]

When the historical perspective of the complex is lost, then one is at the mercy of psychologies that look at the individual on his own and for his own (or on her own and for her own)—without any systemic sight or insight of the situation. In this sense, it seems that even Archetypal psychology, in all its elusiveness, has fallen short in realizing that all individuals of the same family share an inevitable and crucial bond, and, more importantly, that all individuals belong[655] not just to a family system, but also to given blood streams that run throughout the generations. It seems that most of the varied perspectives of Archetypal psychology still remained ontologically attached to the Western (by this it is meant West European) paradigm of personal individuality; one's life for oneself—as if it has nothing to do with the rest of the family, the antecessors, and the ancestors, and not foreseeing how one's life and one's attitude towards one's progenitors will influence further generations.[656]

It is no simple thing *seeing into* one's lineages. Oftentimes the mere display of representatives for several previous generations (as it can be the case in a Constellation) gives one the opportunity of an experience probably never felt before; one suddenly knows that one is connected to many lives before, one suddenly has an absolute and total bodily certainty that one's life comes from all of them and that it is somehow in an inevitable psychic relation to all of them. But most importantly, one feels small when one is standing in front of the representatives for one's ancestors, and even without having actually known them in physical life, one feels the absolute certainty that one is in front of them;[657] their mere psychic presence fills their physical absence.

It is such an important acknowledgement, because life then acquires an entirely different sense and direction, and one opens oneself to the experience of belonging to a wide community of presences that dwell in an invisible domain—a realm that one cannot see through ordinary sight, but only by means of ritual or through seeing into the imaginal. Life problems also acquire a different perspective, and some issues that one would have thought to be very personal when seen through a perspective that considers many of those who lived before seem suddenly not so personal. Life, and all its struggles, is perceived then as something more than only an individual vanity, as something more than only "me and my problems;" life acquires a sort of cosmological dimension,[658] where one's existence is the continuation of many lives and many fates before, and one's individual fate and life challenges can then be perceived with the strength from all those who lived, did well, endured, and passed on the force and gift of life regardless of anything else.[659]

Nietzsche, in his beautiful little paragraph titled "Historia abscondita," opened in a poetic way, yet philosophical, a reflection about the past, where he claimed that "[p]erhaps the past is still essentially undiscovered!"[660], needing a "retroactive force" in order to bring "thousands of secrets from the past . . . into [one's] sunshine" (p.104). And possibly such retroactive force is nothing but the courage *to look back*, and *look again*—as the etymology of the Latin word *respectus* suggests[661]—into one's past before one was even born. Perhaps it is only this retroactive attitude of respect that is needed in order to claim the force from one's still undiscovered history[662]—a history that reaches into many generations of one's past, but which is nevertheless actual in the psyche and from which one is the latest embodiment.[663] However, the main problem is that, "[w]hen looking behind before moving ahead, our usual mistake lies in not looking back far enough"[664]; that is, getting one's thoughts trapped and one's feelings entangled only with what immediate antecessors did, and forsaking the strength from the past. Most certainly, like Jung said: "our body is history"[665].[666] To negate the historical roots of the complexes makes one an orphan, believing that there's nothing behind[667], it makes one a renegade of one's own psychological condition, and quite blind to the unfolding of one's corporeal life. "History, one might say, is written in the *blood* (italics added)"[668] and the body is affected by the psychic dynamism of historical events.[669]

The first and crucial step in any respectful acknowledgement of one's past, starts indubitably with one's parents—otherwise it is only a dangerous farce. The parents are the gateway to re-connect with the force that flows from far "back" in time. This ought not to be taken only as a commandment that one has to follow blindly, without involving one's heart and vision; the honoring of one's parents also releases one from psychic issues that might not correspond to one's destiny, and opens a greater understanding of one's life. This is so, because one's parents are essential members of one's psychic terrain, and oneself is configured—constellated—in relation to them in such a terrain.[670] It is clear that the parents are an undeniable truth, even if dead, far away, or unknown. One comes into the world because of them, and only through them—they constitute, conform, and configure one's first notion of psychic actuality. At first, one is everything, if anything at all, because of *both* of them—and because of that they deserve one's honor.

But honoring one's parents might have more difficulties than one might simply think of. To many people it is a hard process to achieve, and to genuinely feel, because many of those think, and can argument with all sort of defensive ideas, that their parents did them wrong, or raised them in incorrect, painful, severe, or whatever ways, always positioning themselves as better or superior human beings than their own parents; and it is not until such individuals realize that they as well as their parents are involved in a psychic motion that is flowing along the generations, that they can start feeling the force and meaning of their fate—as well as of the fate of their parents, grandparents, and so on. But this is not the only difficulty for honoring one's parents, there is another one, and a very common one, which is more subtle, and harder to see. Due to Hellinger's insightful comprehensions, it has been revealed that oftentimes the children are willing to help their parents in their suffering, as if trying to help them carry a burden, or as if trying to help them grieve for someone, or as if trying to keep them out of the fate that they are supposed to endure. And it has been observed that even when the children have become grown-ups, adults, they still try to help their parents endure their fate. But such an attitude towards one's parents, even when seeming noble, loving, and helpful, is a rupture in the orders of love, because parents came first into the world, and that is an unchangeable truth. They gave life, and it flowed from them, and one has to respect the ways they endured and faced *their* fate. If one tries to help them carry their fate, Hellinger observed, one is then behaving as if one could know better, as if one could do better than them if one were in their position, and such attitude is an arrogation that steals away their dignity out of a kind love that is blind to their greatness.

Such "blind love in the son [or daughter] towards his [or her] parents, that love which potentially is capable of sickening, is oriented towards himself [or herself] and not towards the parents"[671]; it is a selfish love that cannot resist one's parents peculiar ways of enduring *their* fate, and hence wants to do something about it out of love, but out of a childish way of loving—a way of loving without respect, and more so, without honor towards them. During the Constellations work, this has been observed to be a very common situation, where the phenomenological display of the psychic dynamic reveals that individuals are willing to take over some difficulty in representation of their own parents, as if they could help them endure it; but such arrogation has been observed to be, in fact, a dishonor.[672]

It seems no easy thing to honor one's parents; one has to have enough resistance and temperance in order not to feel bad for them and in order not to feel unhappy for them, even when they are going through very hard, even miserable, times. To suffer for them or with them, by claiming their suffering as proper or shared, without any reason, is only, like Hellinger has warned, *double suffering*—and it helps nobody;[673] he has stated that "the only valid suffering is that which fate brings, not that which we look for"[674]. Unfortunately there is a widespread idea that has been popularized as kind, noble and compassionate, in which individuals feel like "good persons" if they feel as bad as their parents—and they call that empathy. To honor one's parents requires a mature way of loving, a way which can respect their great suffering and great misfortune.[675]

Nietzsche suggested that *love has to be learned*[676], but one also needs to learn *how to love*—otherwise, even when one loves boldly, one might still love in childish (sickening) ways.[677] And it seems that even hate, is nothing but the result of an infantile way of love, still stuck to images, ideas, conceptions, and perceptions of how people and the world (and even God[678]) should be, and where one is still incapable of loving life wholly and to the fullest.

In a similar way one can read Jung's advice, who wrote in his early mid-life that, for achieving a "whole-hearted dedication to life" then "[a]ll the libido that was tied up in family bonds must be withdrawn from the narrower circle into the larger one[,]" towards a wider community, so to speak[679]. He knew quite well that to "remain fixed in the endogamous unconscious relationship to the parents[,]" as it could be when one keeps one's psychic energy devoted to complain and moan about them, or to fight with them, or even for wanting to improve them, then one "seriously hamper[s] . . . [one's] freedom"[680].[681] He observed that if one allowed "libido to get stuck in a childish milieu . . . one falls under the spell of unconscious compulsion . . . at the mercy of [one's] affects"[682]. Of course, "[a]s you know, by libido . . . [is meant] 'psychic energy'"[683].[684]

A brief story, titled *Two mules*, might illustrate these insights.

A bit more than seventy years ago, there used to be two young peasants in a small and rural town in Mexico who had been given a mule each, by their father. They were told that such animal would help them do their work in the fields, planting and harvesting, and even for traveling to sell their produce in the market, rather than doing it all on their own and by foot. Both discovered that even when the mules were useful, they needed a lot of effort to make them walk and work. Weeks passed and one of them, while being on the fields under the blazing sun told the other: "I am going to leave this place, I am tired of this, I will make the mule take me to the city, and see what I can do there." But the one who listened just laughed and pushed him to try to do it. The one who wanted to leave started to spur on the animal so that it would go further than its usual ways, but the mule would hardly move more than a few steps from its known paths and territory. The man, then smacked it on the back, but the mule barely did anything else than a braying. He hit it hard with a stick, but the mule just brayed louder. The other peasant, who was watching, just laughed at the whole thing, and said: "I told you, these mules do not go far, they are meant for working, they know their home better than us, and they will not leave this place."

The man who wanted to leave replied nothing and feeling frustrated directed his gaze towards the open, far into the wide open, and he stared at the immensity. Days later he sold his mule, and he did not get a lot from it, but with the money from it he bought a bus ticket to the closest city and some provisions. Finally the day came when he left, and his family and friends, and especially the other young peasant, thought that he did not know what he was doing. But he left anyway. Once in the city he got a job, and a place to stay. He worked there and learned new things, met knew people, and even when not earning much he started to save a little bit of money. Months later he decided to go venture into another city and bought a train ticket and went there. It was not easy, but he found his way to settle there and he learned more things and met more new people. Years passed, and he would move on and on, seeing new places, learning from different people, and meeting all kind of customs and traditions. And even when he did not have money for transportation tickets, he would find some joy in the long distance walks from town to town, at times for several days or weeks.

The other peasant, the one that had stayed, was still working on his piece of field. He was convinced that because he had been born in such place, having lived childhood there, that was meant to be his fate. One day, while trying to make the mule go to the city so that he would make some business, he beat it very strongly without making it move more than a few steps from its usual ways. The mule, after a lot of braying and hits, started to bleed, and it suddenly moved around and gave a kick in the man's face. From that kick he got severely injured, he lost the sight of one eye, and became a very ugly man. A few days later, the man, enraged with his animal, tied the mule to a tree, and beat it to death in front of everybody. He had not just become ugly but even mad. His father, knowing what had happened and seeing his deep unhappiness, gave him a horse as a gift, thinking that with it he would be able to go to the city. But the man took the horse for a mule and tied it to the same tree and beat it to death too. The father did not understood and thought that maybe he needed a better animal, so he gave him a stud, but the man also tied it to the tree and beat it to death while cursing those mule-like animals. The man got pretty mad, and would go on the streets warning about the dangers of the mules, not realizing that most people had horses. Years passed by, and he still worked his field, never leaving the vicinities of his parents, and complaining at all times of mule-like beasts.

Life went by like that for decades, and one day the man who had gone away remembered his old days as a peasant and remembered his father's gift, the mule. He remembered also many places of the world to which he traveled, and the people that he met, and all kind of pleasurable and painful experiences that he had, all the adventures and sorrows that he went through. He was happy for having experienced the world, and even for having experienced deep suffering; he realized suddenly that he had become a traveler, and smilingly and thankful he thought since then: "this mule really brought me very far."

To honor one's parents has deeper consequences than one can imagine if one only thinks or arguments about it without actually doing it. Father and mother (*pater* and *mater*) are not only etymologically related to patrimony and matrimony, but also energetically, as the givers of blessings for such issues[685]—if one is willing to receive them, of course.[686] Honoring one's parents is in fact *the* act of honoring life; and the effect of doing so extends to the totality of existence, to all domains.[687] Just like Hellinger has pointed out, it might even be considered as *the* religious act, where one attunes oneself with the world as it is, and with the existence as it was given.[688] It is a truthful religiosity of flesh that strives not for the otherworld or the afterlife; as Nietzsche well said: "we do not want to enter the Kingdom of Heaven at all: we have become men—and *so we want the Kingdom of Earth*"[689].[690] It is a kind of religiosity that looks at the world of flesh as noble, looks at life as a gift, looks at other humans as brethren, and ultimately looks at Earth as numinous.[691] Actually, the word numinous, which is related to the Latin *numen*, and which refers to a "divine will" or "divinity," originally stems from the Greek *neúein*, that means "nod, incline the head"[692]; and it is only a reminding concept of the *mysterium tremendum et fascinosum* that is felt when presently experiencing the overwhelming power of a *living-force*[693]. Curiously, when one nods to one's parents, and to their fate, and their families' fate, one is nodding also to all life itself, and to the great force that gave them life, that took them at its service, and that came through them. One experiences something very similar to Otto's words when describing the numinous as "the emotion of a creature, submerged and overwhelmed by its own nothingness in contrast to that which is supreme above all creatures"[694]. By the act of sincerely nodding to the ways in which life was given to oneself, and to those from whom life came through, one is not just inclining one's head (to the front, as in a bow), but one is also letting one's petty judgments and rationalizations incline in submission to something mysterious, which is in fact *tremendous*, *majestic*, and *forceful*[695]. It is mysterious in the sense of being "perhaps the most striking expression of the 'wholly other'"[696], inspiring awe and wonder, fascination and stupor, and giving a state of astonishment and uncanniness.

The nod of honor to one's parents is in fact a nod to everything that happened before them; it is a nod to one's ancestors, and to what they did and did not do, to what they left and did not leave, and to all that they passed on.[697] Such simple but humble act opens a profound experience of joy and bliss in *this* life, as if unexpectedly experiencing a "*numen praesens*"[698].[699] Hence Hellinger has said that, "the yearning we feel for Heaven might be answered here on Earth"[700]; and one might feel then a deep affirmation for life, a profound "yes" to existence, an attunement to the world as it is,[701] which would be in itself a religiosity of flesh.[702]

Chapter 7

Siblinghood: A Brief Note on Brothers, Sisters, Psychosis and Insanity

"… it is important to envision community and family as a bunch of souls who are holding hands and heading towards the precipice, if one person makes a deal to get there first, is gonna be deadly, if everybody hold hands and jump together is gonna be exhilarating…"

Ancestralization[703]

In the exploration of the importance, influence, and impact of ancestry, one cannot omit siblinghood. In the case of one's siblings, it is because one shares their fate with them; but as Hellinger sharply discovered, also one's parents' and occasionally grandparents' siblings belong to the community of fate where one is immersed. Not because one is not a direct offspring from them (as children, grandchildren, great-grandchildren and so on), should one forget to consider them when regarding ancestry.

There have been plenty of things said about brothers, sisters, brotherhood and sisterhood in general; but mostly from perspectives that study everything from the conscious and the known sides of life. Mostly from perspectives that observe and over-observe the attitudes, the behaviors, the tendencies, the inclinations, the likes and dislikes, the capacities and incapacities, the gifts and the defects of the siblings, but often without any insight into the trans-generational stream of un-consciousness—which is strongly conformed and configured by important and concrete *events* that the family members went through. Such stream of psychic energy uses some of its members for some things and for some events, for some pathologies, and some catastrophes, and some others of its members for some other things, and entirely different events. For example, one sibling could be severely and physically affected by the unresolved pain of a murdered antecessor that he or she did not even know about, while the rest of the siblings show no relation to such an issue. From a perspective like the one presented in this work—which aims to see into the domains of psyche—one can see through the issues of brotherhood and sisterhood with a completely different attitude, comprehension, and compassion.

It is foolish to say that because two brothers or two sisters grew up in the exactly same environment, with the same parents, and with kind of the same education, and kind of the same support, are they meant to be equally or fairly equally successful, sane, productive, or balanced in general. People who say that lack a vision towards the unconscious aspects of life, aspects that affect one member of the "immediate" family and not the rest of them. Theories that pretend to say things about siblings based on studies that have not developed a way of knowing that reaches into the psychic aspects of life, are doomed to remain as theories of the obvious with a very narrow paradigm of life. Such theories argue, pretend, and behave as if trying to improve the shapes of the shadows by putting their attention, their intentions, their intelligence, and their hands-on-work on the projected shadows, never on that which causes the projections, and many theories even cover the shadows in order to pretend that they are not there—because most of such theories and (social and clinical) practices lack an epistemological device to look into the deep actualities of the psyche.[704]

Psychic aspects of life are the crucial aspects of existence, those are the depths of life, those are, even when so seemingly immaterial and invisible, the true matters of psyche; that is what matters to the soul, that is the *Wirklichkeit der Seele* (the reality of the soul) *and where the soul is effectively at work.*[705]

For this reason the issues related to siblinghood, when observed through a trans-generational lens, acquire a deeper dimension of understanding. In the Constellations work, for instance, it is a frequent fact that one sibling carries something for the rest of the family; where "carrying" is not meant in the material sense of the word, but in the psychic sense, and where it is nevertheless felt as a load that weights on the physical body, as if it were a heaviness that burdens such an individual for doing other things and for living in a freer and happier way. It has also been a frequent observation that some siblings are deeply affected by some psychic issues, and those siblings are vulnerable to get severely ill, more prone to get into accidents, or even to become psychologically insane or suicidal, while the rest of the siblings might not even get a headache. Jung, for instance, was very well aware of the huge difference that there is between the usual "neurotic" individual, who often suffers from issues mostly related to his or her life and circumstantial actuality, or the life of the parents and the grandparents; and the "psychotic" (or potentially psychotic) individual, who is vulnerable to extremely deep psychic issues, issues that require a so-called hyper-sensitive individual[706] to see them and to attend them.[707]

This insightful distinction, which was crucial for Jung throughout *all his professional life*, and to which he always returned in order to understand any psychological trouble or issue, has been overlooked, and hardly ever explored or mentioned.[708] This basic view of individuals is not similar, not even a little bit, to the usual ways of describing and distinguishing neurotics from psychotics from the (Freudian) psychoanalytic standpoint, where the psychotic, or potentially psychotic, is someone stuck or fixed in the psychological developmental stages, and because of that, so they claim, the individual ends up with a kind of clumsy psychic structure or a kind of *schwaches Ich* (a weak ego) vulnerable to the many varieties of psychosis. Jung's arguments are not based on a child's developmental stages, and also are not based on Freudian theories of sexual development[709] and its regressions.[710] Definitely psychosis is also not conceived as mere misunderstandings of the ambiguous communicative activities within the family, like Bateson, Watzlawick, and many others proposed. Those views have been extremely complicated, highly sophisticated, and with a kind of mathematic rhetoric that tries to explain the psyche and everything psychological as if it were a cybernetic programmable machine; they have been applauded by intellectuals and theories-addicts, but they have had so little healing impact that one would do well in questioning if they are not indeed all useless and wrong—is it not a sign of madness to keep thinking within a paradigm that has proven to be ineffective?

Jung's view clearly arguments that it is a hyper-sensitiveness, as if it were an openness that makes them experience psychic issues *that are already there,*[711] never with the idea that such psychic issues are the outcome of personal impulses, sexual drives, or personal unattended remnants from one's development, childhood, lactation, or the so-called traumas from the moment of birth.[712] Jung argued that "it is the affective concomitants of the complex that form the symptom specific for schizophrenia"[713], and this would apply for all those psychopathologies that many clinicians and institutions would label under the category of psychosis in general.[714] It is an entirely different approach when one realizes that potentially psychotic individuals have an extremely, out of the ordinary, *gifted sensitivity,* rather than thinking that they are maladapted, psychologically underdeveloped, sexually fixated, ego-wise dumb, or even psychologically weak.[715] Maybe academic researches and healing institutions and clinics are maladapted to the *real* necessities of soul, while they seem underdeveloped to attend psychosocial calamities that are expanding rapidly. In many cases, such places are fixated with old useless Victorian and Vienesse ideas and practices, foolish when trying to address issues that prior to be chemical and about the brain are psychical and about the psyche, and certainly quite weak in all their *theoria* and *praxis* as for being a real and adequate solution to psychoses. It might be that psychotics are not the only ones who have problems with *reality,*[716] but also those professionals who pretend to be helping them, not *realizing* that the borders of the psyche go much deeper than they have speculated, perceived, observed, and imagined.[717] The greatest problem with people trying to heal psychosis is the almost complete lack of understanding of anything psychic, and a very common aversion to the word soul (psyche), because they feel it to be unscientific, un-intellectual, superstitious, and retrograde.[718] In most educated and psychiatric circles, like Jung said, "psychic reality . . . is regarded as a miserable vapour [*sic*] exhaled, as it were, from the albuminous scheme of things"[719].

Many theoreticians and practitioners from many disciplines, including medicine, psychiatry, psychology, and social work, have overlooked the fact that those hyper-sensitive individuals suffer—*pathologize*—issues that might require attention, solution, or redemption; in other words, that they require not just help for themselves, but that through their affections they are pointing to something else (or someone else) that needs help.[720] Unfortunately, there is a generalized blindness towards the depths of the soul, and many such individuals become schizophrenic and they only get treated with drugs, their sensitivity becomes severely anaesthetized, and the pending issues remain unattended, unresolved, and unredeemed—to everyone's misfortune.[721]

At least for the last hundred years (and more actually) psychiatry has been numbing the best potential healers with powerful chemicals, and even with electroshocks, and it has kept them isolated in madhouses, farms, prisons, or right on the sidewalks (as many homeless) where no one cares for them. Treating psychotics with those allopathic drugs that anaesthetize them is only a palliative and a temporary stabilizer that ends up being a great lie, a powerful farce; it does not acknowledge or cure anything psychic. Indeed such treatment is useless (as Ortega claims) because it leaves the *taras* and the miasmas unexplored—passing on the disposition to disease to the next generations. Rather than being a discipline for *healing souls*, as the etymology of its name suggests, stemming from the Greek word *psyche* and *hiatrós*[722], psychiatry has become the great life-dulling practice, dozing off the capacities to feel and sense the great psychic distress that humanity is currently experiencing in the communities and in the natural world. It has only become a tool of the industrial fantasies that in fact are directed by the corporations' mentality, including the pharmaceutical industries, aiming for a society in which all individuals fit the Westernized "normality" standard of production and consumption, and work, or are slaves of, the so-called progress and its unending greedy desires, while the natural world is being severely devastated with catastrophic ecological disasters. In actuality psychiatry, if its epistemological methods remain as an offspring of rationalism and scientific materialism, definitely makes all understanding of the psychological disturbances quite opaque, and possibly absurd and erratic. It would be worth noting that physicians with great understanding of the effects and reactions of the chemicals in the brain and the body in general do not necessarily "cure souls;" they can be indeed completely blind, deaf, and anesthetized to psychic motions and to the movements and necessities of the psyche. As a proof of this, one just has to look into the so-called developed countries and realize the brutally increasing number of psychotic and addicted individuals, and even those homeless people living in misery, despite all the powerful chemicals with which they pretend to treat them.

It seems to me that the approach and the attitude ought to be entirely different, even when the path might resemble similarities to some actual methods currently used. This seems to be a very weak spot even for some people practicing and facilitating Constellations work (for instance), where often there is no depth of vision to issues that go beyond the limits of what is known in the family. Because of a lack of ability to distinguish between people who suffer "neurotically" and people who suffer "psychotically," individuals get therapeutically treated in the same common way, as if they were suffering from the same sort of disturbances as the "neurotics." As a result, it is common to see individuals who suffer from literally unknown issues, from issues that are deeply unconscious but nevertheless powerfully actual and active, been treated through the ordinary techniques of a nuclear family Constellation, for example, as if their issues were only something they were doing wrong in their way of life and love—such therapies are becoming a regression to the family therapies of the nineteenth seventies and eighties, with a complete lack of *in-sight and vision* into the psychic depths. If the approaches for healing remain with two, three, or four generations at the most, they are doomed to remain as the kind of therapy without much social, community, and ecological impact.

There might be exceptions out there (in the world), but certainly one of them is Hellinger himself, who has developed some of the original Family Constellations techniques to a point where he has powerfully, radically, and controversially overcome them—currently naming them as *multidimensional Constellations*, and for which he has even been rejected and banned by many of his original followers. Despite his followers' disagreements, if one observes the ways some siblings deeply suffer in life, the ways they pass that tremendous suffering to their children (if they get any), and the ways they are trying to get healed, there is a new paradigm coming into the existence—which in fact is an old indigenous paradigm.

The current, usual, and modern paradigm is that some individuals, or some siblings, for instance, are just made that way, that they are merely psychologically prone to be imbalanced, that they have some kind of brain secretion or hormonal malfunctioning,[723] that they did not develop a strong enough ego with which to maintain the boundaries of what psychiatrists narrowly call "reality," that they suffered some kind of sexual fixation (as Freudians and psychoanalysts would say[724]), or that they are somehow breaking the orders of love (as many ultraorthodox

Constellations facilitators would claim, with evident arrogance). But there seems to be something else that cannot be seen clearly under the burden of these static theoretical lenses and their fixed practices[725], if one has not enough boldness to perceive beyond them.[726]

The interesting issues, which I believe Jung would have asked too, are: What if those individuals are telling us something through their suffering? What does the suffering of a sibling inform us about? What if that suffering is not produced by them, but only felt by them? If one is deeply connected with the siblings, and if one shares an ineludible community of fate with them, would it not be one truly important if one could get to know what is affecting them, regardless of whether one is being affected by it or not? The answer, from a trans-generational approach, is yes; not because one does not suffer from it, does it save one's children or grandchildren from suffering from it—as Hellinger has observed frequently through the Constellations phenomenology. This might be one of the very important reasons for being aware of the lives and important events of one's parents siblings, and even one's grandparent's siblings—they constitute, conform, and configure one's community of fate. But the importance of the suffering of siblings, might go even deeper than that, because a psychotic suffering might point to layers of the psyche which one cannot reach with the usual mundane literality, as it is the case when trying to explain everything according to the factuality of one's known family history. Jung considered that, in schizophrenia, for instance, "the unconscious almost entirely suppresses the functions of the conscious mind and supplants it"[727]; and this could be similar in most other psychoses, where that which caused it is not-known (not-conscious), and not even by the family—as if it were a trans-generational secret, or even something of greater dimensions, something that is so overwhelming for the rational mind to grasp that it literally suspends it[728].

The issue that is arising is that some individuals might be pointing out something else that needs to be done in regard to psychic matters and the depths of the soul. In fact, in some cases, their hallucinogenic visions or voices, rare dreams, or fantastical daydreams, indeed directly point to unavoidable *psychic issues that matter,*[729] which of course they cannot avoid seeing or hearing and which make them clinically crazy or socially mad.[730] In his last years, Jung wrote: "I could never be satisfied with the idea that all the patients produced, especially the schizophrenics, was nonsense and chaotic gibberish"[731]. In other words, he realized that the condition that had fallen, as if by chance, upon the insane was symptomatic[732] of their psychic autonomous actuality—a *virtual* notion of reality. One can think that the symptoms that fall upon schizophrenic individuals, by fate, bring together something that the psyche cannot afford to lose—maybe a trans-generational, trans-personal, or even an other-than-human acknowledgement.

The traditional psychological perspective, on the other hand, has argued that these individuals are not well-adapted to family, society, and current civilization, and that their psychologically chaotic and imbalanced life is due to some sort of personal error—in other words, they suffer because they are doing something wrong, as if it were blatantly their own fault—or because something was done or not done to them and they could not recover psychologically from it. But the paradigm is quite personalistic;[733] it is usually thought that it is only them who are wrong.[734] But, what if there were a serious massive psychic disorder to which they are vulnerable, and which indeed they have the capacity to see, and, moreover, to heal? What if they were hyper-sensitive and susceptible to psychic phenomena that others could not perceive? Would not that be an entirely different psychiatric approach to schizophrenia and psychosis, like Jung foresaw?[735]

The issues and explanations of siblinghood cannot avoid the trans-generational approach, seeing that all members pertain to a family system that shares a sort of psychic terrain with unknown, but active, contents. From this view of life, accidents, allergies, diseases, and even failures, lack of productivity, lack of life-meaning, confusion, depression, suicidal thoughts and attempts, schizophrenia and the varieties of psychoses among many other issues, acquire a different vista and a much deeper understanding; much deeper than trying to explain and solve everything through behaviorism, through optimism-oriented therapies, through "mental" techniques, through helping them socialize and communicate better, through an Oedipal theory for everything, or even through drugs—all of those therapies are indeed a grave insult to the real needs of such individuals.[736] "We've gotta get into the unconscious, so we know what the hell's going on"[737],[738].

All these issues were mentioned in this chapter of siblinghood because nowhere else can one see how some individuals are terribly affected by such issues—hard, heavy issues—as if they would have been raised in an entirely different home, while others of the exact same blood family only see these individuals from a distance, almost as if belonging to a different kin. The observations from Hellinger's insights are actually redeeming for the individuals who suffer from such deep unconscious issues, because, as he has pointed out, such siblings are in fact dealing with something that pertains to the whole family, something that had to be experienced and dealt with inevitably, by one member of the family or by the other. And it is such a huge different way to look at your brother or sister and see that he or she is doing a service for the whole family system, that he or she is actually leaving the path without so many burdens for you, that he or she is maybe struggling with something so overwhelming that you could not even imagine how you could face it, that he might be coping with psychic presences that would have come to hunt you otherwise.[739] One gets an entirely different attitude towards such sibling, when one acknowledges that he or she saved you from something tough, possibly from craziness.[740] How different it is when one sees the suffering sibling and one thinks: "it could have been me;" and if one were not frivolous and silly one would not feel lucky, one might only realize that it was impossible for him or her to escape his or her own multidimensional and all-too-powerful sensitivity.[741]

When siblinghood is seen in this way one can look at one's brother or sister with genuine compassion and deep understanding, not only with that banal understanding which often says: "he is like that," or "God made her that way." When one glimpses into the psyche and realizes that maybe it was the other one, one's sibling, the one dealing with some very important issue of the blood lineages, then one can only bow in recognition, maybe even in gratitude and pride; and such gesture and attitude gives honor and dignity to such sibling, and, unexpectedly, a deeper connection with him or her occurs—even without one having to say or do something directly to him or her. It is an entirely different feeling and sensation when one sees one's sibling, who suffered (or suffers) deeply, and one recognizes his or her role in the community of fate.[742] When one can do so, all those standard measurements and normalizing ideas about what an individual should do, how should the individual achieve it, and what to expect from him or her, are utterly useless—rubbish. It does not matter then if he or she failed according to the social, educational, professional, or even (those so-called) spiritual ways of life; when speaking of, and from, psyche—the soul—nobody fails.[743] *Psyche makes no mistakes;*[744] just like Hillman claims, "[t]here is no mediocrity of soul"[745].

A brief story titled *Dear Brother* will illustrate these insights:

An old man got ill and had to stay in bed for a few weeks, which was unusual for him, because he had been a healthy man most of his life. During his time in bed he unexpectedly remembered his older brother, and he remembered how different their lives had been, which was in fact a reason of their separation and distance. First he remembered that his brother had been the one prone to sicknesses when they were very young, and that his brother always had a lot of trouble at school. He recalled that when they reached young adulthood, it was his brother the one who experienced great distress and suicidal attempts, and when taken to the doctor it was his brother the one diagnosed psychotic.

He also remembered that while he had a smoother transition into his vocational and professional life, his brother had in the meantime wandered around aimlessly, drawing the strangest kind of pictures and figures, and living an incomprehensible life.

While being in bed, this man suddenly felt that his older brother had lived tougher experiences in life for something, not just for nothing, not just for randomness, as if his brother had carried the heaviest burdens of the family, as if he had left him a lighter and smoother way to walk. One of those nights, while being in bed he missed his brother deeply because he somehow realized that it was just true, his brother had lived harder things and that had taken some of the family load away. That night he realized too that because his brother lived such harder experiences, he had been freer to do enjoyable things, to study, to travel widely, and many more things that his brother simply could not, as if his brother would have been too busy all the time figuring out his psychological life. The next morning he woke up with some clear words from a dream, those were: "Dear brother," but the moment he murmured them he immediately started to cry because he did not know if those words were his previous night's wish to get close to his brother again, as when children, or if it had been his older brother attitude during his whole life, taking care of him, protecting him, saying silently all the time to him even when in pain and desperation: "Dear brother…"

Chapter 8
The Dead: Those who are having been

"The experiences that one calls "ghosts," the entire spirit world, death, all these related things have been forced out of life through daily resistance to such an extent that the senses with which we could grasp them have become atrophied. And this is not even considering the question of God."

Letters to a young poet[746]

When exploring and researching about ancestry, one has to carefully acknowledge the realm of the dead. *Ancestors are by definition dead.* But speaking, or writing in this case, of the dead is quite complicated; it is an issue seriously complex. The topic seems very difficult to understand, and to elaborate it with words seems even more difficult. Jung—who has been a guide for this work—wrote scarcely of it;[747] Hillman wrote a few insights; and Hellinger—the other chiefly guide for this work—seems to have seen the importance of the topic, and worked it through in his Constellations, but also with reserved words. In order to get more clarity and to achieve a deeper understanding of it, a leading authority from an ancient tradition is needed—whose words and wisdom, in fact, will deepen also the understanding of the whole work. This is Somé, an elder, diviner, and shaman from a Dagara village in West Africa, born in what is called today Burkina Faso. His perspective is quite valuable for this work because the things that he has spoken or written about are not elucidations from some sort of highly elaborated rhetoric, nor are they just some elusive insights about this or that issue, nor are they the result of a privileged higher education, but his actual vocation in this world, his actual life purpose—which is to share ancient knowledge to the so-called Western cultures (since that is the reason of his painful exile from his natal village). So, it is important to keep present that his perspectives of the topics and issues are not only *his*, but also the perspective of an ancient, but still living, tradition.[748] In a certain sense he is an authority on the topic, but not because he has authored a few books, but because he has been guided and authorized to share and disclose the importance of the whole issue.[749] The intentions of his aim, however, were not to establish a kind of foreign cult, religion, or a new spirituality with the people he shared such knowledge with, as it has happened with many Yogis, Buddhists, and some other Easterners that have traveled to Europe and the Americas. This, in his words, "is not yet another one of those compendium of ancestral ancient spirituality that you need to know about"[750]. The aim, as he presented it, is to re-connect with one's *deep past*[751]. Therefore, it is not about embracing an exotic religion, in this case an African one,[752] but about re-connecting with one's own *deep legacy,* with one's ancestors—in order to reclaim one's *deep wisdom.*[753] The issues of the dead require therefore to be explored;[754] and one can ponder their importance with Jung's rhetorical question: "Was there a time when there were no dead?"[755].

For Somé, as it is also for some other indigenous and autochthonous traditions, there is an important difference between the dead and the ancestors; so to speak, not all dead have become ancestors. For this, he claims, one "need[s] to understand ancestry differently"[756], because one way, as he said, is the kind of Biblical genealogy in which one is linked up to those who lived before, up to where imagination and memory allow. But, he claimed, such is only a way that resembles a sort of "gene pool that seems to self-replicate"[757], and with such an understanding there is really no difference between one thing and the other. Another way, he said, is by acknowledging that there is something else, something that ought to be done for the dead, in order to help them "cross over" and become ancestors[758],[759]. If this is not done, then, those dead do not reach the destination that they were supposed to, and, Somé said, they end up "trapped between worlds" and "feeling an increasing sense of homelessness"[760].[761] Moreover, he continued, such situation produces that those "loved ones or the ones they left behind," who remain in the continuity of life, "experience [a] similar sense of lostness, disorientation, confusion, and utter sadness about the way things are"[762]. He firmly relates much of the worldly struggles, mundane difficulties, and, paradoxically, most of life problems, to the dead.[763]

This view of such things is indeed quite similar to some of Hellinger's observations, who said that, "many of the problems . . . have to do with the dead"[764]; and I believe that all those experienced in Constellations work would agree unanimously.[765] For example, Hellinger has noted how often a diagnosed "difficult child" (and one can think of the type of child that is problematic at school, aggressive, rude, or violent, only to name some kind of symptomatic behaviors), *looks* at someone who is excluded, oftentimes being someone dead to whom he or she looks at[766]. By "looking" Hellinger has not meant an actual physical view of the excluded dead person, who might have been buried or burned to ashes, but, I would say, an unconscious *psychic look*, as if it were a pull of the child's psychic attention and intention (psychic energy) towards a member that the child's family does not *re-member*, willingly or unwillingly, and that the family does not consider important.[767] In a situation like this, it is as if the child, in his or her entire vulnerability, has to respond, without knowing and without warning, to the oblivion of an important member of the family's fate. It is an inevitable *instinctual* pull; but it is not a drive towards death, like psychoanalysis would stubbornly observe, but a drive towards the dead, towards persons who require something. Most of the times, unfortunately, the automatic response of the child is a difficult attitude, a psychological disturbance, as could be a psychosis, a disease or symptomatic illness, or even a *fatal* accident—because he or she does not know about those dead ones in the lineage. This observation is not an interpretation produced by some sort of refined ideation during consultancy room psychotherapy, as if trying to convince people of something. This has been repeatedly observed and bodily proved by people who participate in a Constellation due to its phenomenological display, the emotional reactions, and the accuracy of its healing effects, as controversial as it may sound—because of that, in fact, Hellinger's work has been called a radical empiricism.[768]

Many things can be said about the realm of the dead, and there seem to be no materialistic logic ways to prove any, yet; but this has happened because oftentimes, like Jung said, one thinks that "it is much simpler to suppose that what we do not understand does not exist"[769], as if we were out of the influence of the dead just because we do not hear them or see them. However, the effects of releasing issues pertaining the dead have proved to be beneficial, reconciliatory, healing, and peaceful to many people through the work of Constellations[770]. Thus, under a *psychic logic* it is not only interesting and possible, but even necessary and obvious. The dead are among us when something has not been solved, producing some kind of disturbance or some sort of suffering—in the Greek sense of *pathos*[771]—whether psychological or physical. The dead dwell in our psychic *terrain*, and create a deadly atmosphere (miasmas) if they do not reach peace and become ancestors. This might be the reason why Jung called the unconscious *the land of the dead*[772],[773], because, as he said, "the unconscious is fate . . . There are the roots, and whatever your roots are, is what you will get"[774].

There are discussions about what to do about those dead that might not be yet at peace, and especially in the cases of inter-racial or international conflicts, from reparation to restorative justice and even forgiveness to all sort of *all-too-human* desires; but, from the Constellations work, what has been observed to help the most, even in cases of murder, violence, abuse, and perpetration, is *grief*—on both sides, the descendants of victims and perpetrators. Hellinger has firmly suggested that grief without reclamation precedes any reconciliation, *just mourning with sorrow*[775].[776] Hence, from vast experience, he claimed: "[t]he dead are reconciled through our pain when we weep in front of them"[777].

There are, unfortunately, many unjustifiable taboos and beliefs about the dead, and a lot of people would rather not speak about the topic, or they would rather avoid anything having to do with the mere fact and act of *re-membering* them[778]. The dead, however, in this sense and under these views, are not to be feared but recognized, honored, and released. Often, like Hellinger has noted, we cling to the dead, as it is when one remains angry and with rancor towards them[779]; or simply because we cannot stop on our own the instinctual pull—out of blind love—that brings us to them and keeps us looking only at them and not at life and the living.

How can one willingly stop looking at the dead, if by principle one does not even know if one is (psychically) looking at them? The dead are present in the psychic terrain, but invisibly to the naked eye, and they configure one's energetic situation without one's permission. Hence, it is not only about not looking at them, as if one could suddenly turn the head and vanish them. There might be something more than just "us" clinging to them, something more that, like Somé claims, one is required to do for them.[780] These reflections could be pondered in relation to some lines by Rilke, who wrote:

Lord, we are poorer than beasts,

which, though unaware, at least can die;

for we can only die halfway.[781]

More than often, in Hellinger's views, what is required is a look and an act of *gratitude* towards them[782]; especially in the case of family members and persons implicated with them in fate, because then we can accept what they left under the conditions that they left it, and we can give them honor by respecting the ways they lived—whatever those ways were. This, when engaged courageously and with the thought of the heart, in some kind of symbolic ritual (as a Constellation, for instance), seems to bring, most times, a resolution to a psychic situation that might have been disturbing for the living, but which in principle and in origin had to do with the dead. Oftentimes, a chronic tendency to brutal anger or rage (which would correspond a syphilitic miasma) is the feeling of revenge that an individual experiences without knowing why, but which is psychically directed to a murderer of some family member back in the lineage—as if the impulse for vendetta were the feelings between the long-time-dead victim and perpetrator, which the living individual experiences in his or her psychic terrain, not only years after the event, but sometimes a few generations later.[783] Therefore, in an uncanny way, with symbolic acts of gratitude and honor, the pending issues from persons of the past are psychically dissolved, and one keeps only their gifts and strength in powerful ways.[784]

Hellinger, throughout his work observed and was bold enough to say that, "the dead influence us, and us, maybe, them as well"[785]. He realized, from the effects sensed, felt, and observed in his phenomenological work, that there is something that one can do for the dead—and it might be something, indeed, that one *ought* to do, if one wants to remain healthy and sane, with purpose, and a deep, even wordless, sensed meaning in life. Because, as Somé claims, "unless the dead have been allowed to complete their journey home, we are homeless too"[786]. By homeless he did not mean the literal lack of a concrete house (although that can happen too), but maybe a more tragic sense of homelessness, which is in fact a sense of being lost in the mundane of modernity, distracted by the technologies of materiality, with entertainment for all and on demand, and aiming for all kind of things that give immediate and ephemeral satisfaction but which are unimportant for the matters and technologies of the soul.

Somé *knows* and has told clearly what is needed: to grieve the dead ones. From his knowledge, "grief is seen as food for the psyche[,]" because "[j]ust as the body needs food, the psyche needs grief to maintain its own healthy balance"[787]. Strangely, maybe, to some Westernized customs, "[i]t is the presence of community that validates the expression of grief. This means that a singular expression of grief is an incomplete expression of grief"[788],[789]. Contrary to some modern Western ideas, the issues with the dead affect several individuals and even several generations, not only one person; and so the ways to release the dead involve also many people.[790] In some sense it comes very close to the practices of Constellations (which occur in large groups), where one, by looking and acknowledging the presence of past members of one's community of fate (through the representatives), suddenly feels a genuine need to weep, to grieve for them at least for a brief moment, in order to release them and let them finally go. And one feels as if they were waiting for the tears of recognition—almost like redemption.[791] Weeping in this context is different from the kind of circumstantial weeping that is an accusation; under a ritual setting, the tears, like Somé said, "produce a flood capable of washing the dead to the realm of the ancestors" and, actually, "refraining from weeping wrongs the dead"[792].

One has to keep always present, however, that the dead have been and have lived, but they still *are,* having been; *they are already having been*[793]. Hence all regret of how things could have been, should have been, or how things were not, can be tremendously sick and dangerous. One has to be fully aware that one cannot change a single detail of the lives of those dead, they are already having been, and just because they lived so, in pleasure and pain, tragedy and joy, health and wealth, poverty and disease, with longevity or without it, it is that one became what one is. Realizing without fear what it cost them to live such a fate—even if it was a tremendously terrible or horrible fate—and still endure it and pass on life, gives them honor and dignity back, and it gives one a specially powerful strength and soothing sense of relief and peace.[794]

What one definitely requires is the courage—from the French *cour*: heart—to participate, and perform symbolic acts in which one can look at one's own family's fate and to the dead ones in one's lineages, in order to look at them in their totality, including all those not-blood related who importantly partook in their lives, and then give them a reverence to honor their life and fate. Such acts of remembering might elicit grief, but, as Somé explained, "it is terrible to suppress one's grief . . . [and in fact] the dead have the right to collect their share of tears"[795]. It is, somehow, also a way of re-membering oneself with them, re-membering oneself with the life-force that surpasses the notions of individuality.[796] When the excluded, said Hellinger, or in this case the dead, regain their right of belonging, then they stop being frightening, and one experiences peace; moreover, he said, if one gives them the place they deserve in one's (individual notion of) soul, one is at peace with them, and one feels complete and whole[797], or at least more complete and more whole than one has ever felt before.[798]

There is, however, one requisite to experience deeper notions of peace, in order to feel more at ease bodily, this requisite is "to leave behind the ideal of innocence"[799], where one often feels that one has done nothing wrong and nothing evil, and therefore one finds out constantly how many other people do all the wrong things in, and to, the world—whether politically, ecologically, economically, professionally, emotionally, and so on. If one cannot leave the ideal of innocence behind, then, as Hellinger claimed, one prefers to remain as a child rather than to grow up[800]. Then one does not acquire enough restrain in one's own heart to face what one's own past family members have done, because to do so might mean to share the guilt, the responsibility, and face what, or whom, they might have damaged,[801] and then one is not innocent anymore.[802] If one faces one's family's past, one might not remain feeling innocent and virginal, but certainly one becomes stronger and more compassionate. For instance, if one boldly, but without judgment, faces and looks at the dead that one's family members in the past have murdered (as it can be done in a Constellation), then one gets a deeper sense of what was needed in the unfolding of life and fate in order for one to be here now, and one assumes that on behalf of others' suffering and others' existence, it was possible for oneself to come into *this* life.[803] Often, when this happens, one stops complaining and one takes life as a beautiful and magnificent gift. Innocence then loses its fairy tale charm, and one feels mature, ripe, stark, and ready for the world of men and women; and, curiously, an instinctual need for repairing the damages of the past often arises—often a need for restoration that can have wide impact in communities and ecology.[804]

The importance of awareness to the dead lies also in the fact, as Hellinger has pointed out, that they belong to the "family net"[805], which is just another way to name the family system; they are, undeniably, part of the family's biological realm, which compromises the "body" (and the psychic *terrain*) of those who carry their semblance and resemblance. They belong to also to the continuity of the family's fate, which can be observed in the psychic entanglements and psychological lives. The family's net's span, as Hellinger mentioned, includes the living *and* the dead[806] of several generations—most probably many more generations than one could trace literally and get acquainted with factually. Therefore a literal approach might just hinder the process, and only an *imaginal* (not imaginary) or ritual approach might reveal its intricacies and entanglements[807]. In the modern Western cultures one can hardly trace back more than four or five generations, and even in those cases, facts are often incomplete. Hence, a symbolic approach is needed, as it is through ritual or imaginal sensibility, a way of addressing issues from the past, and a way of seeing into other realms, in which one can transcend the limits of literal factuality (the few facts that one is sure about).[808]

Van Kampenhout, who has written about the similarities of Constellations and shamanism—particularly from Native American and Siberian practices—has noted that in psychotherapeutic language, usually, the dead are only a memory, and they are considered to exist only as an image without life or influence; but, he said, such is "a limited perception of them"[809]. It is probably such assumption in the psychotherapeutic circles, of all kinds, which has done more damage to the psyche of the individuals, making people believe that the issues with the dead are fictional (in a pejorative sense) or unimportant, or at the most of an imaginary nature, as if only they were products of their reminiscences in their personal memory.[810] Indeed such perceptions are flawed and narrow, and they kill the opportunity to see extensively and with vision, they kill the chances to heal and regain deeper notions of oneself; and nothing of what the past members of a family might have done could be more wrong than to deny them the opportunity to reach peace in the land of the dead.[811] But this of course, is hardly ever important under the sophistication of the modern culture ways, and all the *psychotherapeutic maladies*, where perceptions are limited by a tremendous lack of knowledge—by blatant ignorance.[812] Chief Seattle once said, while signing a famous Treaty, in 1854: "Our dead never forget the beautiful world that gave them being . . . . [Moreover] the dead are not powerless . . . There is no death, only change of worlds"[813].

The dead are not only self-produced images that one retains from those who once lived, nor are they only memories of persons who *are not* anymore. The dead are *actual* in one's psychological configuration and in one's psychic terrain—as one can attest through Constellations, for instance.[814] Many problems that individuals think and overthink to be deeply personal, as if produced or generated in one's life, are, in fact and act, issues that have to do with the dead; one's *actuality* is permeated and interpenetrated by other domains of reality.[815] Somé's views are clear, "unresolved errors are passed on to the surviving relatives"[816], and "[u]nless the relationship between the living and the dead is in balance, chaos results"[817].[818] The perceptions of the physical material world can be expanded to a refined qualitative degree in which one has no doubt that the world is a great inter-relational field that contains all the past—and, naturally, the future.[819]

When one allows oneself to open the possibilities of perception—as if opening the doors of perception—into other domains that have been denied by academicians and professors, by school education and modernity; then one agrees with Hellinger, who said that, "[w]e are all connected to one another in a larger sense . . . We walk among the dead, who surround us. We aren't aware of them, but they have an effect nonetheless"[820]. Most certainly, just like Somé has encouraged, one can and ought to do something for those dead. It is not surprising from this view what at least Hellinger has also done with, and for, the dead, while saying that throughout his work: "[one] bring[s] the dead and the excluded back into the system"[821].[822] This might be a way to re-structure the orders of love, in order not to lose someone important, in order to keep him or her in the heart, and in order to help him or her journey to the land of the dead.[823]

One might fairly ask: what can one do for the dead, if they are already gone? Hellinger, through his simple but profound ways might have pointed the way: bring the dead back into the system, do not let them be lost in the limbo of oblivion and disdain. In other words, first acknowledge them in order to re-member them in the soul, because they might be lost and not-yet-at-peace.[824] Curiously, besides grief, often it has been observed too (in the phenomenological work of Constellations) that what the dead need is just gratitude for having passed life or for having helped in some important way to sustain life, or to maintain the movement of life throughout the generations. However, when remembering the dead, genuine gratitude seems to be preceded by grief—and both displays of emotionality can hardly be separated, especially at first. It is not through an intellectual speech, or some kind of sophisticated discourse that one expresses grief and gratitude, nor necessarily with expensive funerals and statues, but through tears and emotion. Most certainly, like Somé warns, "[a]n adult who cannot weep is a dangerous person who has forgotten the place emotion holds in a person's life"[825].[826] It might be "through emotion . . . [that we can] encounter . . . the grace and might of the spirit"[827].[828]

This way one gives due honor to the dead, helps them travel into the dead land, and nourishes peace for the living, and those who will come after. It gives respect for *those who are having lived*, and eventually joy of life for those still living. Paradoxically, those who do not grieve and let themselves be taken through the sorrow of letting a loved one depart from this world, risk themselves to become severely unhappy or sick in later years, and if not them, someone in further generations.[829]

Somé is clear with the claim that only when the dead have reached "the land of the dead" is it then that "they become entitled to be referred to as ancestors"[830]; not before. Prior to this, they are "between here and there, with some limited capacity to be [positively] active in our life, but with no capacity to journey by themselves to their final destination"[831]. So, if the dead have not been able to leave this world, then they are homeless and are not-yet-at-ease, and those who stay in this world might get into trouble, confusion, or dis-ease, because in principle "their feeling is our feeling too"[832].[833]

Hence, Somé came up with an English term that refers to the process of helping those deceased walk to the realm of the dead; he called it "ancestralization." The process, as presented by him, is a ritual that follows some African ways, and basically "consists in accompanying the dead to their realm, and therefore allowing them to become ancestors"[834]. "If you push this [insight] carefully," like Somé quite boldly and firmly said, "you will realize that there is a profound implication in there"[835].[836]

One might think at this point that one does not know the African ways of ritual, that one does not know how to walk them to the realm of the dead, or that one is merely ignorant of such matters; and one could suddenly feel discouraged to do it. But the point is quite the opposite; the moment one acknowledges one's ignorance is also the moment that one starts to grieve the loss of knowledge, and one is already on the right track—as if crying out for spiritual help. The work of Constellations, if not plagued by psychotherapists and psychologists[837] who interpret everything as *only* a mental image or as only a product of the personal unconscious (in the popularized Freudian sense), can be seen as an intuitive and organic kind of ritual, without drums and chants, but equally powerful, respectful, and even sacred.[838]

It is interesting to note that Somé's description of the process of *ancestralization*—based on the Dagara practices—is basically a ritual designed with a kind of choreography through which one walks the dead to the otherworld;[839] and for which one literally needs to see the dead bodies in order to mourn them and "remember that they are well on their way to becoming an ancestor"[840]. Similarly, but in a modern, maybe minimalistic, fashion, through the Constellations work one literally enacts and performs the movements of seeing the dead (by seeing a representative lying on the ground), and usually one cannot avoid mourning and weeping for him or her (although briefly), in order to finally let the dead close his or her eyes or help him or her do it, so that the dead can really leave this world.[841] The Constellations work, in cases related to the dead, can be seen as a symbolic response to a psychic necessity (or even duty) that ought to be fulfilled, even years or decades after the person has died.[842] Only when the dead have reached peace can one *see* them differently, not as dead people but as sources of strength, guidance, and wisdom.[843] Somé explained that once the ancestors get healed, "[they] will bring health, prosperity, and a sense of intimate connection that is unparalleled"[844].[845]

Therefore, by acknowledging those who have lived and by helping them achieve peace, one becomes aware of something else that is invisible; one becomes aware of the profound dimension that embraces and contains human life on Earth.

Hillman claimed that, "the first community are the dead, the ancestors, the community of souls"[846]. At first, maybe, the acknowledgement might be only through photos, memories, places, or objects, but in any case, if done through the eye and thought of the heart, all that opens the door to images—which are images of the soul, and images that in fact speak and one can listen.[847] By this, I mean images that one does not produce, but that one receives; images from figures that in fact visit one, that come to one, as in dreams.[848] Hence those are called *autonomous images* (or figures), which in fact are so essential to one's life that it could be said that they energetically configure one's mundane actuality—they are the dwellers of one's psychic terrain, the native inhabitants of one's (notion of) psyche.[849]

But, like Hillman argued, if "you lose that sense of the essential images, then instinct is off and you build ugly buildings, and you overeat, you become obese, and your whole structure is disoriented"[850]. If so happens, one easily displaces oneself, one easily distorts reality in order to make it fit one's petty wishes and goals—like capricious children. Then one convinces oneself that life is to be lived to satisfy only one's desires, everyone on and for his or her own, without the strength from the past and without care for the future. Existence is then considered an individual journey, an individual task, an individualizing process of salvation and no notion of genuine community can go along with it. Even the concepts of disease and healing become individualized too,[851] and one can easily be convinced through the professionalism of all sorts,[852] that one's ailments and suffering are merely one's fault, one's problems are only one's stupidity, one's failures are one's incapacities, and finally one's existence is merely considered as one's personal whim.[853] This loss of contact and communication with such images[854] is equivalent to a loss of one's deep instinctual nature—which is communal.[855] "This loss of instinct is largely responsible for the pathological condition of our contemporary culture"[856], where one can see extreme poverty right next to millionaires, extreme scarcity and starvation tolerated by abundance and financial prosperity, extreme degradation of the natural world and extinction of species happening along with highly sophisticated cybernetic and virtual technologies. Like Jung wisely said: "once a man is cut off from the nourishing root of instinct, he becomes the shuttlecock of every wind that blows. He is then no better than a sick animal, a demoralized and degenerate, and nothing short of a catastrophe can bring him back to health"[857]. Once the unity with the ancestors is lost, the notion of genuine *comm-unity* is forgotten, and then no communication is established or sought, one is at the mercy of not remembering what one's deep purpose on Earth is (which is of course community oriented), and one gets lost in the delusions of materiality, seeking fulfillment in all kind of entertainment possibilities and technological gadgets—like children do. All genuine communities have to start with the ancestors—otherwise, they are doomed to fail.[858]

Jung knew that "[t]he soul of the dead ancestors are especially significant" for the continuity of life; and it makes one think that he truly meant ancestors, not the dead-not-yet-at-peace, because he even ventured to comment and advise that, "any important new events must be immediately reported to them"[859], just as one would hear from the Dagara through the voice of Somé. The ancestors, once they have reached the "otherworld," become a source of guidance to whom one can ask council and strength, and whom, in fact, "need to be notified of a situation that needs instant attention"[860].[861]

These remarks are not for the sake of commenting about something interesting, but because they indeed disclose a groundbreaking notion of reality—which had not been talked about much in academic circles. If for a moment one stops thinking as usual and refrains from the kind of intellectualism that dismisses anything for the sake of rhetoric, and if one reflects on what this topic involves, one might discover that Somé's statement that this is "a new perspective of life"[862] is quite accurate and radical.[863] This—which is rather an old view of life presented as new—brings a powerful ontological shift that would inevitably propitiate a new epistemology, and ultimately also entirely different ways (methods) to address clinical issues and how to achieve them (methodologies).

The premise is that if one is physically and psychically affected by the realm of those invisible and dead-not-yet-at-peace, then the study of one's ways of being, of one's very primal and ultimate nature of dwelling on Earth, is severely at risk of being incomplete, or even quite wrong—although this might be hard to accept for some highly educated people. After these implications, the study of being and the nature of "reality" cannot stop only at the limits imposed by the academic philosophical scrutiny, with its semantic labyrinths, linguistic and conceptual delimitations.[864] Existential philosophy, for example, with all its well-articulated discourses is indeed dreadful because it departs only from the personal notion of life—as if one's birth were one's beginning, and one's soul (or mind) a tabula rasa; with such philosophies, while one unknowingly carries the issues of the dead on one's shoulders, one believes life problems to be deeply personal, and failures, diseases, and misfortunes are experienced as one's personal punishment or errors. What an existential nausea, indeed![865]

Moreover, these revelations imply also a drastic shift in the ways that one claims to know things, especially pertaining psychology, psychiatry, social sciences, and related fields. For example, in the communication studies and theories, it is not that Habermas, Bateson, Watzlawick, and even Bandler and Grinder, are completely wrong, nor is it that it is all vain; but such studies are stuck with the superficial, seeing narrowly and without depth.[866] The communication and behavior problems in a family or in a couple relationship, for instance, can be exhaustively observed, categorized, measured, stimulated, corrected, controlled, measured again and changed without ever getting close to issues that are in relation to the dead, and which might be at the depths of their actuality; it is as if the dead were calling the living through problems, while waiting to be attended.[867] Jung wrote: "We are a blinded race . . . We roughly accept with the past in that we do not accept the dead"[868].[869] It is unfortunate that most of the disciplines in humanities and social sciences lack the psychic technologies to investigate what all indigenous cultures speak about—it truly makes one think that the epistemology of such disciplines is vague and useless, indeed erratic, despite the sophistication of their jargon, the proliferation of journals, and the hyper-specialization of their methods that have only obscured perception, vision, and understanding.[870]

The so-called clinical practices, and particularly those of psychology, psychotherapy, psychiatry, and some related fields, like social work, cannot be ever the same after having acknowledged that there are pending issues, in need of attention and resolution, which individuals might be dragging from previous generations—very close to the idea of dragging issues from previous lives.[871] Suicide, depression, addictions, manias, phobias, obsessions, compulsions, perversions, schizophrenias, and psychoses, and all other diagnosed psychopathologies and even physical diseases acquire a very different understanding when seen through a perspective that contemplates the past and the present deeply intermingled.[872] How different that discipline called healing of the soul—*psychiatry*—would be, if it would re-vision and see psychic matters beyond the brain and neurons, beyond materialism and literalism, and especially beyond the paradigm that family, community, and social contexts, refer only to the living.[873] This could also be thought in relation to a fragment by Heraclitus, saying: "It makes no difference which is present: living and dead, sleeping and waking, young and old. For these changed around are those and those changed around are again these"[874].[875]

Even the ways of doing things in the educational, communal, and political spheres of life (as only naming few examples) would be changed, and several ways of envisioning knowing perspectives would be drastically challenged. For instance, there are places where there have been thousands of assassinations by the hands of mafias, drug cartels, criminal organizations, security squad groups, or the military, and aside from the implemented well-intentioned policies by the government and institutions, something is required to be done for those murdered, suddenly dead and not-at-peace, whether they had been drug dealers, political rebels, or civilians—in many cases they are thrown in mass graves, without even knowing the identity of those who passed away, generating a powerful *civilization's discontent,* psychically speaking[876]. In such situations, oftentimes a lot of people get out to the streets, march for hours, and demand and claim for peace for those still living, asking their governments for solutions and better life conditions, but hardly anyone does anything to bring peace for those murdered.[877] Unfortunately one cannot read the powerful tone of voice in which Somé quite boldly asked to "forget this whole process that walking on the street and expressing your discontent is gonna make any difference"[878], realizing the uselessness of all those social marches and manifestations that address no *real* powers. Like he wisely said: "Walk in ritual space! Express you discontent there!" How different the results would be if for extinguishing the fires one would pour water on the flames and not on the smoke![879]

The problems of the present might rather be seen as *states of being* that embrace the hanging issues from the past, and which are at the same time the best attempts of solutions to issues that might require a new order of loving and living, one which allows perceiving extensively—by means of unconscious processes, like Jung; by means of the imaginal, like Hillman; by means of systemic phenomenology, like Hellinger; by means of ritual, like Somé, van Kampenhout, and many more indigenous peoples; or by other means not yet discovered, or not yet shared.[880] The psychic complex—one's energetic configuration through which one inevitably always lives and loves at the core—is seriously affected by the unresolved issues of those who have died; the dead constellate one's psychic atmosphere until they are in peace.[881]

The perspectives of life are radically different when one realizes that existence is some sort of psychic continuity, with psychic responsibilities. The ways to address and try to solve social and community issues and conflicts are entirely different if one departs from an ontological position that is able to sense and feel the calling of the unconscious (Jung[882]), the needs of the invisibles (Hillman), the pending issues in the families' consciences (Hellinger), or, in simpler words, the requirements of those not yet at peace. Jung clearly acknowledged that: "Great is the need of the dead"[883].[884] Maybe the following story, titled *Farewell* and which was told to me by an elder, will illustrate these insights.

A long, long, time ago, in a time before most men can remember, there used to be a community of people that lived in several villages right in the middle of two rivers. Because of the proximity to the water, the villages were prosperous and had abundance. The land was so well irrigated naturally that people just had to work a few hours a day, and still they would get plenty of food from the land. The community was not perfect by any means, but they had what they needed to live a good life on Earth. For uncountable generations the people lived in such community, passing on the gifts of life to the next generations, and maintaining a balanced relationship with the land that had fed them since time immemorial. Back then they did not have any laws, because those were not needed, they just had some rules that they were supposed to keep in order to live harmoniously. But of course not everybody kept all of the rules, and every now and then they had to amend the ruptures in order to rebalance the community, and this had to involve all the community, not only the individuals who broke the rules. There was, however, one single rule that was the most important one and which no one could avoid following for the sake of all the peoples. Because the rule was in fact the next step after someone had died, it was often not seen or considered as a rule, but more like a kind of farewell gathering to which all were invited to assist. Paradoxically, while the other rules that were not so important could have been twisted, bended, or even broken from time to time, and amended later of course, the rule of the farewell gathering was adamant and unbreakable, and there was a reason for this that not everyone knew.

The people in this community lived for such a long time that no one remembered how many generations had walked on Earth; but that was not relevant for their well-being as long as they maintained the first rule, which was more like a feast, but in a sad and tearful way. However, one day an event changed the fate of such community. While two men were toughly playing on the fields, one of them hit the other one on the head with a stick and immediately killed him. The murderer was the kind of man that wanted to do everything well and perfect, and rather than going back to the village to tell the people about the accident, out of shame he carried the body to the riverbank, threw it there, and let it drown.

When he went back to the village and was asked about the other man, he simply lied with a true fact and said that he had returned on his own from the field, and that the other man had remained longer. By night there was concern in the village, and they sought the missing man everywhere, thinking he could be harmed or even dead, but they did not find him. The people of the village told members of other villages nearby, and so the message that he was missing spread out all over the community, and they all sought him, but none found him.

After three days, there was great concern about him, and the man who had killed him told another lie, but this time cloaked with greatness. He told the people that in fact he had seen him being hit by the hand of the creator and had been taken away through the tears of the Earth to the otherworld, and that in fact he had been probably chosen to have departed from the Earth in such a way. And strangely most of the people believed him, and they thought that indeed this missing man had been chosen. From that moment on a split began in the community, and some thought that the missing man was the most special man for having departed in such a way, and they started believing that those who acknowledge his specialness were also chosen ones; but since there was no such concept as creator in the community, the others thought simply that it was not possible, and that it was only mysterious.

In any case, a little after that happened, the village started to experience a series of misfortunes, although not completely out of the ordinary. But after a longer time, there was another disappearance that they could not solve either. And time went by, and generations went through with a drastic consequence. Since then, there were several murdering, which were not new in the community, but which were addressed and thought of as disappearances from then on. And life continued on, through out the generations, and more and more persons who were killed were missing their farewell gathering.

Life continued, but the community of villages was not what it had been, and after several generations the conditions of life were somehow tougher, and the disappearances were more and more frequent in this one village. And one day all the fish from one of the rivers died because of the pollution in the waters form dead bodies, but since the people could not see the corpses that were lying at the bottom, they simply thought it had been a natural event. Some time after, the fish of the other river also died, and they thought it was really a tough moment of history. But those polluted rivers were the ones irrigating the land, and in a short time all the fields were contaminated too, and the trees and plants started to get very ill, and the legged animals started to die too. By this time there were disappearances in almost all the villages of the community, the chosen ones were assuring themselves that the times were only a test of the creator, and the farewell gatherings were dismissed as old superstitious beliefs.

Once the waters were severely polluted, and the lands also at risk of growing nothing, with fewer produce and fewer food for the animals, the peoples started to worry about the state of affairs, and decided to produce some artificial fertilizers with which to cure the land, and also artificial cleansers with which to purify the waters. And so the scientific endeavors achieved the highest esteem, and people had the expectations of getting better by such means. But in the meantime more and more people had been disappearing into the rivers or even dumped underground.

After only a few years, the community of villages was excessively pestilent, but most people thought is was the aftermath of their civilization and the inevitable progress, like a kind of sacrifice for their way of living, which by the way they referred to as the pinnacle of development and intelligence. The fact is that the conditions of the lands and the waters had never been that bad, not even ever imagined to be in such deplorable state, but the people kept convincing themselves that those artificial products were going to clean all the mess.

By the time that the human community was almost at a catastrophic moment, an old wise man from one of the smallest villages was asked by a young pioneer who happened to met him, what to do in such times of chaos and pollution. And he answered simply the least expected: "Discord and lack of grief have given birth to the calamities. Make farewell gatherings for all the disappeared ones who have not been able to leave from Earth, because only then are we going to drink clean water, breathe fresh air, and get again the gifts of the land."

This story, which even children can understand, reveals a great understanding of the human cosmos, its nature, and the ways to maintain its well-being; "[o]nly recently have men begun to forget the dead and to think that they have now begun real life, sending them into a frenzy"[885]. There is a mocking remark by Jung, which is quite suitable for those who think that all valuable wisdom started with the old Greeks: "[t]hose who are particularly brilliant even discover that the fundamental concepts can be traced back to Heraclitus or someone even earlier"[886], and even when Jung could have not been aware of Kingsley's[887] bold research and critique to the Western intellectual traditions, he anticipated him and dared to say: "[l]et me confide to these knowing folk that the fundamental concepts employed in the constructive method go beyond all historical philosophy to the dynamistic ideas of primitive peoples"[888], the knowledge of shamans and tribal people—like Somé, in fact[889].

Even when the Dagara's insistence on the dead could be hard to understand for some (so-called) well-educated people, one can reflect that this is not at all different from some insights by Jung which say: "Your darkness, which you did not suspect since it was dead, will come to life and you will feel the crush of total evil and the conflicts of life that now lie buried in the matter of your body"[890],[891]

At the same time all these remarks can be easily criticized, rejected without experience, and denied as unscientific from certain current views (although science, in its many disciplines, is changing its assumptions faster than most ordinary people can). Moreover, there will be people who will enjoy making fun of these insights, and who will feast on their thoughts, excuses, and jokes, "[making] noise in order not to hear the truth"[892]; this is the case of people who have never been in a constellation, but who attack the idea of releasing and helping the dead with any kind of sophistry at hand—they rather make intellectual noise, than experiencing an embodied truth. But certainly, like Socrates claimed, "[t]he fear is not of being laughed at, for that is childish, but, lest, missing the truth" (1989, p.690).[893] Jung was well aware that there are a lot of people who are "incapable of thinking psychologically and can operate only with rational concepts, which must on no account savour [*sic*] of metaphysics, for the latter is taboo"[894]; and the same applies today, more than fifty years later in the so-called sophisticated and educated circles.[895] It is worth noticing and remarking that he realized that there could be very rational people, even extremely gifted for such kind of thinking and speaking, who were at the same time completely and shamefully incapable for any in-depth psychological insight; these kind of people dismiss what their logic cannot understand.[896] It seems quite veritable that if one is only capable of rational thoughts and rational ideas, one is doomed to live in psychological darkness, at the mercy of the unconscious. Jung noticed that all those people with severe "[r]esistances against the psychological standpoint, which regards psychic processes as facts . . . [do] not understand the empirical nature of the psyche"[897], and of course those skeptical people[898] end up labeling such insights as belonging to spiritualistic or mediumnistic circles, as metaphysical rubbish, or even as plain irrational madness without ever turning their head and glimpsing that there is more than what reason can give them.[899] In any case it has been well-known, since twenty three centuries ago, that most people prefer to discuss about the shadows at the bottom of the cave (because they see nothing else), than venturing into the open, into the fresh air, into the light, and into the bliss[900]—in any case, one could honestly ask, like Empedocles: "why to attack them as though one were achieving something great?"[901]

Chapter 9

Destiny: Fate, Blood, Daimon, and Zeitgeist

"Destiny itself is like a wonderful wide tapestry in which every thread is guided by an unspeakably tender hand, placed beside another thread, and held and carried by a hundred others."

Letters to a young poet[902]

When exploring ancestry, one inevitably confronts issues that appear to be destined in one's path, in one's journey of existence and not always are these issues happy or lucky ones. But often one feels that there are certain events which one is fated to live, as if one could have not escaped them, and when one honestly observes one's life or even the unfolding in other lives, one realizes that many, so-called misfortunes, failures,[903] and fatalities, are indeed life-shifters, life-guiders, or even life-enhancers.[904]

Destiny is a very complex word; hypothetically it stems from the Latin *stanare* following the prefix *de,* the latter meaning "down to the bottom or dregs . . . completely, thouroughly[,]" while *stanare,* that means "settle" or "fix," is related to the Greek *stanúein* that means place, and to the Sanskrit *sthanam,* which also means place[905]. In its original sense, the word denotes not only a meaning but also an image, maybe an ambiguous notion of getting thoroughly to one's place, for which one has to move and find a way. An individual must figure out what it can possibly mean, maybe *a deep motion down to one's place on Earth,* or a thorough motion to one's fixed destination, or something else; but, quite like Hellinger claimed, it is advisable and humble to realize that it is not me who determines destiny, but destiny what determines me[906].[907]

It is indeed an unfathomable word which some prefer not to mention, and some others, with little vision of psychic issues, prefer not to believe in—as if it were a matter of belief—and so they keep convincing themselves that life is created everyday anew—of course, with such vision of life, cancer, accidents, sudden deaths, or some other terrible event, are happenings of mere chance.[908]

I will deliberately use the word "destiny" to encompass the profound mystery that guides every individual. In addition, I will explore four dimensions of that word which involve the concepts of *fate, blood issues, daimon,* and *Zeitgeist.* By *fate* I mean those situations and circumstances that are felt as superimposed upon one's life. *Blood issues* I define as those traits, attitudes, or behaviors that one inherits or unconsciously assumes from one's family and clan. Those aspects which seem to be very personal, as if they were one's mission, one's duty, or one's gift, can be thought of in relation to the notion of *daimon*; while those aspects that one inevitably shares circumstantially in the public sphere and which constitute the spirit of the times, can be understood as the *Zeitgeist*. This arbitrary perspective of mine is only to facilitate the understanding of destiny in relation to one's ancestry, because in one's life, this fourfold division is not clear. Moreover, many could possibly feel and coherently argue that it is non-existent; others could say that one lives them (fate, blood issues, daimon, Zeitgeist) altogether throughout the years; and some people might not even distinguish between them even if they wish so. Hence, it is frequent to hear people conceive and speak of any of these four aspects merely as plain and simple destiny. Hence, there is the popular idea that what one lives through is that which was destined to be experienced, including that which would often be thought of as cruel, painful, or terrible and also that which would be thought of as fortunate, joyful, and blessed. However, without intending to make a fixed and unchangeable idea of what destiny is, by considering and reflecting upon these four different aspects, one can deepen the views of one's being, and one might acquire a very different *vision*, yet quite personal, of what is life about. The assumption of this, of course, is that a written text, whether ancient or new, cannot tell anyone what is life about. In simpler words, one has to discover it, or, like traditional cultures claim, one has to *remember it*.[909] In such a sense, the following insights will not try to establish a "this is it" attitude of what is the purpose of being on Earth. They will rather offer a view of life that explores the notion of destiny from four crucial aspects, in order to see life differently and to acquire a new dimension when considering the importance, influence, and impact of ancestry.

Jung fully realized that every individual carries something throughout his or her life which indeed constitutes something of utter importance for the sense of fulfillment of one's earthly existence. When saying that one carries something, it is not meant in a literal sense, but only as an allegory in order to give an image of an aspect of life that feels as if one in fact would need to support and hold. As Jung mentioned that, "every carrier is charged with an individual destiny and destination, and the realization of these alone makes sense of life"[910]. It is as if one is invested with this primordial load and it is the keeper of one's profound sense of purpose, meaning, and identity. But, fortunately this cannot be read in an old book, not even in a very old sacred one, or bought as if it were a consumable product that one can suddenly choose. Nor can one receive this realization from professors, teachers, mentors, masters, or gurus—some of whom often show or point to a specific path and affirm that to be the only correct one.[911]

Many of these guides are often blind to the fact that they behave as if their path were the best, the highest, the most sublime, and the most spiritual, and as if the others would have not been chosen[912]—as if the other cultures required spiritual salvation, as in the times of the Inquisition, but disguised by modern media, trendy concepts, monopolistic ideas, and some exotic sacred words and chants.[913] "Like ancient Rome, we today are once more importing every form of exotic superstition in the hope of finding the right remedy for our sickness"[914]; but all this happens because we have deceived ourselves with the claim that those unending studies in "psychology" will help to heal us, or will help us to gain balance and peace, and we have not realized that we have completely lost contact with our ancestors.[915]

Hence, when speaking about destiny in relation to one's ancestry, one is speaking about one's roots, and aiming to encourage every individual to search for his or her own source of wisdom, to grow down his or her roots deep enough in order to reach the waters that can nourish his or her tree of life.[916] The roots of others, like Jung claimed, will not give what one needs; one requires growing deep into the Earth in order to reach Heaven. Unfortunately there is a lot of confusion about what one's roots are, and many individuals, because of fears, failures, or unfortunate events, end up adopting some kind of foreign cult, foreign ideas, foreign languages, and even foreign practices, in the search for life's meaning.[917]

Therefore, in order to expand the sense of destiny, it is quite advisable to explore the notion of fate, and what seems to have been fated in one's life, as if it would have been an inescapable situation, like many of those inexplicable life events that were felt way beyond any personal influence but which shifted the course of one's existence. The word fate stems from the Latin *fatum*, which was originally used in the sense of "sentence or doom," but was also used later as an equivalent of the Greek *moîra,* which meant "portion" or "lot", "but came to express the impersonal power by which events are determined"[918].

Fate, therefore, is not only a personal issue, it is, like Hellinger claims, something lived, endured, and suffered in community. It is something that binds people, first of all, all the members of the family, but also, not family-related people with whom one shared important life events, especially in what is frequently referred to as terrible, cruel, abusive, horrendous, perverse, murderous, or "inhuman", but also in those events which one would consider of extreme and vital importance, as well as the happenings that change the course of a whole region, a nation, or a country—like catastrophes. Fate seen in this way is an uncanny agent that organizes the unfolding of life, for what one usually refers to as "good" and for all those aspects too that one refers to as "not-so-good;" moreover, "[it] behaves irrationally, and the energy of life inconveniently demands a gradient agreeable to itself; otherwise it simply gets damned up and gets destructive"[919].

Somehow fate is a notion beyond the personal, and even when one could strongly relate it and correlate it to family deeds, misdeeds, problems, and the family context in general, it is a collective situation that often surpasses the mere image of one's living or historical family, involving at times the land, the nation, and the country. Jung, for instance, seems to have been well acquainted with similar ideas, and he wrote: "I have seen how the roots of the psyche and of fate go deeper than the 'family romance,' and that not only the children but the parents, too, are merely branches of one great tree"[920]. A brief story, titled *Aftermath*, will illustrate these insights.

Not long ago, in a Latin American country, there was a civil war, called the revolution. It occurred at a time when the people were not happy with their current lifestyle, when they wanted political things to be different, and when they wanted a change in the ways the country was unfolding; yet, without really knowing how did it come to be an event of such magnitude, it simply occurred. Suddenly, what had started as a social conflict became an intrinsic war, one main group of people with similar ideas against little groups of people with sort of ideas contrary to those of the main group.

What is important to mention, is that people had to live in such situation, as if by fate, whether they were conservative politicians, active soldiers, audacious rebels, bold revolutionaries, housewives staying at home, physicians attending at hospitals, women helping the wounded ones, priests giving funeral masses, children hiding, or whatsoever. But, important to mention too is that every individual lived the revolution in his or her peculiar way.

In this war, for instance, there was a man named Xavier, who was a young soldier at the time. He, however, was part of the revolutionaries, one of those bold men who wanted things to be different, and in such state of events, his participation was bloody. The war lasted for several years, and for all those years he was an active member of the rebellious movement, having to kill many people almost face to face, and having to kill hundreds through other means. One could say that the times of such nation required in such human ways, and he, as thousands of other men from either side of the situation, had to become a perpetrator, a killer.

When the war ended, he was one of those alive, and the nation started to gain peace again. A little time later he got a job, and soon after he also got married and begot children; he knew that life had to keep on going despite what had happened. The state of affairs in the nation was still changing, and each individual and each family was accommodating to what had been lost and to the new situations; and just as in the years of war, each person was living the situation in his or her peculiar way.

However, there were some who had been perpetrators, and some others who had not, some who had lost many family members, and some who had not. Every family was different. Xavier, for instance, had killed many, not because he had been a mean man, but because it had been times of war; and so, his life and the life of his new family, wife and children, was on behalf of all those dead individuals who had died because of him, and even on behalf of the suffering of all those families that had lost dear ones because of his deeds.

His children, without ever knowing how many people he killed, shared a fate with him, one that bound them to all those dead ones. So, even when they did not know about the war, they were alive and living as part of the effects of it, and directly in relation to the aftermath. Not all the people in such country shared their fate, every family had lived it in its own way, but Xavier's children, even when they did not want to do anything with the military and weapons, with revolutions and civil movements, were part of a fate that they shared with their father. In spite of them having been good children, having eaten healthy, and having been well-educated, they were affected by such an event and by their peculiar way to be in relation to the aftermath of the event: all those dead ones.

The aftermath is not something that they willed. It was simply something that was part of their community of fate. The affection was inevitable. For one of the children it was in one way, and for another in some other way. But the event was there, in their past, and even the grandchildren were severely affected by it, as if it had been a psychic cry of lament vibrating all the way down through the lineages.

A situation like this, which to historians could see often only as a socio-political-economical movement, is also a major psychic event whose aftermath can last centuries and several generations. Many events, such as wars, important social movements, migrations, natural catastrophes, or the like, are lived in community and affect the whole family system, in one way or another; and, most often, these kind of events are inevitable, one has to go through them or perish. However, it is not so well known that very frequently the aftermath of this kind of situations is still felt several generations after, as if a dynamic flow of psychic affections were reaching family members who do not even know much about such events.

Fate, therefore, is something lived and endured in community; but not only within the actual living community with which an individual shares the immediate experience, but also with further generations that somehow are affected, without knowing what happened in the previous ones. It is as if the suffering (the *pathos*) from what happens in one generation is still psycho-active in the psychic terrain of later generations and it indeed becomes pathogenic if nothing is done about it. Quite accurately van Kampenhout has observed that, "we, the living, are the body of our ancestors and we carry in our bodies the tears that they could not cry during the course of their lives"[921].

A lot of pathologies can be seen in this way, from those one thinks to be hereditary, to those which are congenital, acquired, or even accidental. It is not a trans-generational point of view based on genetics, but based on the dynamism of psychic events and psychic happenings that flow throughout the communities of fate, and which includes people who are not blood-related. It can be a very insightful way to look through the chronic miasmas.

For instance, that which could be thought of as highly destructive attitude (a syphilitic chronic miasma) could be in relation to an event or series of events in which there were perpetrators and victims, so that the murderous impulse and even the desire for revenge that happened in past generations was flowing psychically to an individual who has not been in such a situation, but who nevertheless feels such an impulse, as if by fate. Such a statement should not be interpreted as a deterministic view of the human being, implying that we, as individuals, share an unchangeable nature. Rather I merely wish to point that many attitudes and inclinations, and many ways of behaving, feeling, thinking, and even loving, are in relation to deeper aspects than those of a strictly personal nature.

Hence, fate, besides being transpersonal, is also the way in which an individual fulfills psychic necessities, the needs of the soul. However, it is not meant to be thought with the image of a savior, as if suddenly an individual were the redeemer for the whole family's tragedies. This view rather points that some issues that individuals do not deliberately choose to live, but which nonetheless affect them, physically or psychologically, can be healed and resolved if one sees them not as only bad luck, but as issues for which one was fated *to do* something.[922] It is important to mention that some issues might not be possible to heal completely in a physical sense, as in the case of irreversible damages caused by accidents, but certainly, when seen in this way, such issues acquire a deeper dimension for having to be lived, as if one's *fatal* suffering had not been in vain.[923]

Fated aspects of life are inevitable, either in one's life or in the life of those who lived before. Somehow these fated events have to be endured as there is still something to be solved. One is a participant of them, in relation to them, or an aftermath of them, whether one desires this or not. This realization does not imply that one must live fatally, because things can be done about them, but it is particular of situations in which one feels to be moved and chosen by a strange necessity, as if decided by the *Fates*.[924] One does not choose, not in the mundane sense of choosing, to be the grandson of a general who killed hundreds of persons, including women and children, because of a war situation. Neither does one choose to be the granddaughter of someone who cruelly exploited miners for the sake of money, and from whom one is comfortably wealthy and without financial stress. Serious events such as these are simply there, and one lives with them, and in many cases because of them or because of a direct benefit given by them. However, oftentimes one is merely, and not-knowingly, affected by such issues, but not because an individual did something wrong or because one loves like a child (breaking the orders of love), but rather because such issues need to be attended to, or compensated for.

Many times fated issues have to do with dead-not-yet-in-peace who require to be ancestralized. It is as if those issues were one's psychic "portion" for which one ought to do something about, and frequently people know about these issues only because they feel distressed, disturbed, or because they suddenly get a disease.[925]

However, one can think of other facets of destiny that have to do specifically with one's family interrelations, independently of the fate of the collective times. Such aspects are what can be thought of as *blood issues*.[926] In a way those aspects are not so tough or difficult because one can acknowledge them in order not to live and endure them. One cannot choose not to live the war, if it happens, one is fated. Or, if one's parents left their country and migrated to another, having lived with the feeling of displacement and nostalgia, then such an event remains in the community of fate that made one's life possible, and one is, trans-generationally speaking, displaced too. But there are other aspects in the unfolding of life, which one could naïvely think to be one's destiny because they are shared with other family members, but which one can choose not to manifest. For example, there are individuals who think and say: "That's how my grandfather was," in order to excuse themselves of a certain attitude or behavior; and there are others who do not even know that they are exactly like their grandparents or great-grandparents. These issues, however, are not strictly fated, only assumed, imitated, arrogated, blindly copied, or unconsciously transferred from one's family of origin.[927]

By blood issues it is not meant to refer to the literal red blood in its chemical sense. It is rather used as an allegory for all those issues that run in one's blood because they belong to one's kin, all those qualities (vices and virtues[928]) that come from one's progenitors, from one's blood lineages, and from one's family conscience. In some ways this notion is quite difficult to separate from fate, but one slight difference can be made, and even when it could seem only as a theoretical distinction, it can be very important for the sake of deepening the notion of destiny.

Blood issues are those aspects that are not inevitable, and even when members from previous generations had them or presented them, or when suddenly one has them or one starts to manifest them, one can simply shift them, leave them, or decide not to keep them or not to actively present them. Those are not issues for which one has to do something actively, one does not have to attend or compensate them, one only has to be aware of them and respectfully decide to leave them, if one dares.[929]

In this sense, when speaking of blood issues, one can think of many of the so-called characterological aspects and traits. However, it is important not to relate this idea with that of physical traits and genetics, because it can hinder the reflection. While many physical traits are not changeable, blood issues are, through psychic means. The premise lies in the fact that many personality qualities are not personal; in other words, one carries them in the blood, but one can decide not to make them manifest, not to present them, or, if one has them already one can decide suddenly to leave them, to get rid of them.

So, a person who is prone to anger, and who might think of himself as "being that way," can explore such aspect through a trans-generational view and discover that it might not be his way of being, and that the anger was the way of being of someone back in the lineage, either a man or a woman—that is ultimately not important. This would be what Hellinger has called *identification*[930];[931] it is a situation in which one is affected (even possessed[932]) by the energy of a previous member, and because one does not know that one is identified, then one simply feels, behaves, and even thinks as such a person from the past, as if adopting his or her essential views but in a different place and time, even when one might have not known such a person face to face, or if one might not know that a such person ever existed.

The explanation for this kind of blood issue is clear from Jung's notion of the complex, where one is not born within a sanitized, pure, and empty psychic environment, but already within a psychic context that is highly charged with relational patterns (archetypal situations). It could be thought that one's embodiment is not the isolated entity that externally ends up with the skin cover, but a circumstantial biotic being that is related to psychic presences, some alive and some already dead, all living on the psychic terrain on which the ego—what the person conceives as the "I"—is merely one more among many. It becomes clear then, that the notion of "the body" is not separated from its psychic past or from family presences, even if one were far away, as when abroad or in exile, for example. "The body," conceived as such, is a relational field within a field, but at the same time it is the whole field—it is a *holo-field*, a micro of the macro.[933] But, most importantly, by some uncanny reason, this field is also intelligent, as if directed and guided for being organized, and following a certain *order of being*—and the force that keeps it all organized is the psyche. Hence, when one disrupts the organizing psychic structure one is in fact creating a disorder in one's imaginal field of being (one's terrain), and that will inevitably create distress or even disease in one's actuality.[934]

This insight is not meant to equate the field with the perceived phenomenal public shared space upon which one walks, works, eats, and so forth, but with the psychic terrain, where one is inevitably in relation to essential contents, even when one might not factually know them in the physical actuality, or even if one has no direct contact with them. Such essential contents are those from whom one's body came from, blood family; therefore, they are also the essential configurations of the complex. This field, which, on the one hand, is explained through the allegorical image of an extensive terrain in which presences dwell, is, when seen only from the biology of anatomy, non-existent. If seen imaginally, it is one's most essential place,[935] and where one must find oneself one's correct place, but, paradoxically, it is not an actual physical place; however, such field affects mundane existence and everyday relations, somehow altering ordinary public life. It can be observed that a shift in the relational patterns in this field can not only drastically change actuality, but can also generate a powerful lasting effect upon it[936].

These insights require imagination and the *thought of the heart,*[937] because if one meticulously scopes the literal body organs or the physical environment around an individual, one will find bacteria, viruses, and such things, but not important patterns of interrelation; moreover, in many cases, some people even argue that the circumstantial relational field is not of much importance for the embodiment of an individual or for his or her health and their process of healing.[938] However, if one aims to see the psychic dynamism, one has to display an imaginal terrain where the important contents will show their autonomous motion and emotion (a constellation), and where one can intentionally alter the inherited patterns and what could seem as the inevitable implications—that is, the invisible loyalties[939]. This way of seeing through an individual's condition reveals the most crucial movements (dynamics) within his or her psychic field, which if not attended to could indeed unfold a psychological uneasiness or a physical disease.[940]

Hence, the importance of looking into blood issues relies on the fact that when one is aware of such contents one can then realize that they influence the atmospheric affectivity of one's terrain (the chronic miasma), and that they directly affect one's integral way of being, from the various conducts, compulsions, and cravings to the moments of reflection, rest, and relaxation. But if one dares to, one can deliberately move out of their psychic space of influence. If one is not aware of those contents being foreign to oneself, one cannot objectify them (realize the *objective psyche*[941]), and therefore one cannot discover that they are the resultants of a psychic dynamism in which one is entangled and possibly fixated and stuck. However, if one sees them as separate from oneself, one can then take some distance and get out (propitiating motion) of an affective stagnation that one might have believed to be of the most intimate and personal nature.[942] A brief story, titled *In the name of the father,* will illustrate these insights.

In a city like any other, a man got together with a woman, they married, and begot several children, but after a few years they disliked each other heavily and, like many other couples, split. They liked to think that the separation had been because of a difference in the idea of work, shared expenses, and living conditions, but that had only been the surface of the conflict, because deep down there had been other issues that had to do with her femininity and his masculinity.

The thing is that the woman had decided to keep the children, believing herself to be more capable and more responsible to raise them to become productive and good. She was indeed a hard-working woman and quite laborious, but she did not know that all her love for her children was not sufficient for them. She did not know that she could not replace their father. She did not realize that even when she could afford to buy them things that he could not, or give them a life that he could never dream of, she was taking away a strength that only their father could give them, even in all his laziness.

The children, then, three women and two men, grew up with their mother, and constantly heard that their father had just been serviceable for procreating but almost a good-for-nothing. She, a woman who had grown up without a father, and who had become well educated and a professional on her own, thought that she needed nothing else to raise them. By the time that her children were young adults, some of them had finished their studies, and others had not. Some had a poorly paid job, and the others did not even had a job. In general, they were closer to being good-for-nothing, like their father, than laborious, like their mother.

Unfortunately, the issue did not end up there. One of the sons, being still young, got into a sexual affair with a woman and got her pregnant. They decided to live together, without being married, but after a little while, when the child was still very young, they decided to split. He was behaving just like his own parents. However, not only was he was circumstantially behaving like his own progenitors, his own son was suddenly living a very similar situation, being raised by the mother only, and separated and distant from the father.

Of course these people had only academic education. Thus, they thought their problems were due to emotional ruptures, sexual failures, social conditions, couple's misunderstandings, differences of opinions, money troubles, lifestyles discrepancies, and so forth. In fact, they never realized that their issues could have something to do with their family of origin, as if it would have been something that was running in the blood.

The grandson strongly believed that his father abandoned him and left him to be with his mother. He convinced himself that he could live without his father, and ended up lacking the strength and psychic force that only his father could give him. Without knowing and without willing it, he lived the same misery as his own father, childishly blaming his father and his mother and thus perpetuating old situations that ran through the psychic blood.

A man like the grandson of the story would probably inherit, from his own father, who inherited from his own mother (the grandmother), a condition of insufficiency, psychically speaking, because of the absent father in the grandmother's life, which would correspond, for instance, to the psoriasic miasma, indicating an important *lack of*. Many conditions correspond to this chronic miasma, which is considered to be a basic one in homeopathic medicine where the lack of an essential family figure, and, more importantly, the lack of recognition and honor towards such figure, ends up manifesting an evident imbalance in the psychic life of further generations, with ongoing consequences until something is done in order to heal such an atavistic condition.

The importance of blood issues is that even when they might be thought of as being inherited, they can be avoided. One is born within a psychic terrain (a field) in which one is influenced by the relational patterns of those who brought one into life and who gave one's physical semblance, but one is not *destined* to be like them.[943] If one does not know their history, one might live such situations unconsciously, and one might end up caught up in circumstances that are almost magically the same.[944] Just as one repeats their physical features in one's embodiment, at times it is as if one were plainly repeating their life situations and struggles, as if psychic patterns and psychic *maladies* were also running in one's blood, and with the possibility of passing them on to one's offspring without one being conscious of it.[945]

But such situations, in most cases, are due to what Hellinger calls *good conscience,* which is a way of being loyal and keeping with the ways of the family, so that one feels that one belongs and therefore one feels innocent. In this sense, "[l]oyalty is love"[946], a kind of love; but there are other ways of love. So, what in a lot of situations could be thought of as a sort of casualty, excusing oneself with this or that argument that suits a completely logical theory of why things went wrong, could be indeed an issue that pertains to the family, and which runs in one's blood, until one looks at it and chooses to do something about it—it is something that one decides.[947]

The way to get rid of such blood issues, as Hellinger has pointed out clearly, is by being disloyal, in other words, by not being loyal to the family conscience.[948] It is important to mention that this does not mean a lack of honor; quite the contrary, it is only achieved through it. Moreover, it seems that the deepest experience for honoring one's family and origin would imply the capacity to be disloyal to one's family's beliefs, convictions, behaviors, tendencies, inclinations, judgments, ideals, customs, and so forth, and having the courage to be oneself, living and loving freely, and perceiving without the tinctures and frames of one's family, including their traditions, their religion, and, in some cases, their images of God or the divine.[949]

In this context, being disloyal, as used by Hellinger, means daring to have enough *bad conscience* in order not to follow the paths of one's family. It implies being aware of one's family history, one's family suffering, one's family ways of doing anything, and deliberately, but respectfully, stepping away from it, stepping away from such psychic influence, almost as if one were stepping out of their sphere of belonging.[950] That is the reason why one feels bad; one feels guilty for not being like the rest of the family and one feels that one will not belong anymore.[951] The fact is that one will still belong but one will also be free of issues that one does not like to have present, manifest, embody, face, or endure. It is as if one were changing the psychic DNA, the psychic code, the psychic arrangement—the *diathesis* (miasma).[952]

These insights point towards the clear need of a new biology, a new study (logos) of life (bios) that acknowledges the psyche in it.[953] This is because one can observe that an individual, who is primarily a living entity, reacts more powerfully to contents and relations of his or her psychic terrain than to the contents and relations of his or her physical setting.[954] One can observe this in people who live in conditions that could be considered bacteriologically polluted, infectious, or harmful, but who nevertheless are more or less healthy, in comparison to individuals who in spite of being in sanitized rooms, do not get healed. Of course this would not deny the importance of clean hospitals and clinics, with sterilized instruments and careful doctors, but that there are issues that have not been studied in-depth (or maybe not disclosed widely enough) within the medical research and practices.[955] This might open reflections and new understandings in health studies and in that which can powerfully generate a healing effect.

The assumption behind this is the *holo-field*.[956] Every cell of the body, for example, can be conceived as a *holo-field* itself, and all the cells conform together the "body" that moves, lives, loves, and relates with others; and it is with such notion of embodiment that one participates in a psychic terrain, in which others also dwell and live.[957] But paradoxically, this terrain is a reflection of one's *holo-field;* when *seen* like this it is clear that a slight change in the psychic terrain will also shift the nutritional dynamism of the cells—and consequently the miasma.[958] Therefore, when dealing with such so-called blood issues, which could be dismissed as only of a psychological nature (in the popular misuse of the term), one is actually altering, shifting, and moving the energetic functioning of the whole living organism[959].

However, when speaking of destiny it is not all about fated and blood issues that come from the community of fate and from blood family, there are aspects that indeed are felt very personal, and which could be related to one's most intimate nature. In order to make this clear, Hillman rescued an old notion and explained it with contemporary and popular examples, while he kept the original word for it: *daimon.* The word stems from the old Greek language and traditions, translated as *dæmon* in Latin and from which the word demon derivates, but, unlike the latter one, it does not necessarily have a bad, evil, or malignant connotation. *Daímon* originally means divinity or genius[960]; and it is in such a sense that Hillman referred to it. He clearly stated that, "your daimon is the carrier of your destiny"[961], considering the idea that "each of us is given a unique daimon before we are born"[962].

This insight about the particularities and uniqueness of destiny is not only a concept, but also a living and powerful image. Hillman claimed that, the idea of the daimon can be best understood as if it were a *guardian angel* or indeed a *genius* or even a *paradeigma* which is an "accompanying image . . . [and] the bearer of fate and fortune"[963].[964] It is as if such a notion were what indeed overcomes fated situations which at times seem unbearable, extremely painful, or almost impossible.[965] But the daimon, in any case, has to be embodied; in other words, it lives within a family setting and circumstance that has its peculiar blood issues. So, in spite of the daimon being a very personal notion of destiny, as if a gifted quality, it has to be born from a human family that has already an atmosphere of psychic issues (miasmas), and it has to exist within a community of fate, enduring life as human—for the time being. Because of this, it is hard to distinguish between one's deep purpose in life and the earthly social, familial, and cultural conditions that made one's life possible, and which many people believe that to be their true and only identity.[966]

Jung, in fact, was also well aware of such a notion, and he also mentioned that "[i]f we normal people examine our lives, we too perceive how a mighty hand guides us without fail to our destiny, and not always is this hand a kindly one"[967].[968] One can assume that Jung was referring to the same idea, as if it were a powerful presence that moves one to certain places, closer to certain persons, in the correct time and at the adequate momentum, sometimes confidently and other times in opportunistic ways, but always in order to fulfill something that only after a while will prove to have been destined. This might be the reason why, for Jung, this notion was indeed strongly felt in one's vocation, which in fact stems from the Latin *vocatio,* that means call[969].[970] But one's *calling,* in this sense, is not to be misunderstood with one's election of the field of studies, with one's career, with one's profession, or with one's way to earn money and a living; it rather aims to a deeper sense-felt notion of one's being on Earth.[971] Hence, Hillman said: "Your calling is your psyche's first nourishment"[972].

But it is very important to mention that although Hillman and others refer to such a notion as if it were another being, or an essential personal substance, this might only be a metaphor just for the sake of a clearer explanation. It might come close to being a pre-essence that directs one's life, which could be imagined as a presence, but which is paradoxically inexistent—because it is not other but oneself.[973] Hillman has also referred to it as "your soul's portion in the world order, and your place on earth, all compacted into a pattern that has been selected"[974]; this is quite similar to the idea of the "body" being a moment of the world-soul moving in any of its human tonalities of love. Rather than meaning an entity in itself, Hillman seemed to be using the image to describe the whole individual paradigm in which every person lives, loves, laughs, lasts, and leaves—and, yet, it also harbors a deeper identity that one could not possibly explain.

However, one has to be careful when speaking about what is the daimon. Like Hillman warns, even when it is always embodied within a family environment, and socially contextualized, the daimon cannot be reduced to the outcome of the experiences of one's personal life, or, what would be more terrible, to consider it to be the result of one's parental milieu[975].[976] When Hillman describes it like an angel,[977] one sees that he speaks of it as an other-worldly agent. It is a way to name something which is invisible, mysterious, and powerful. Hillman clearly claims that the daimon is one's connection to the spirit world, and that one should not conceive it with *an all-too-human concreteness*[978].[979] Therefore, even when some portion of one's destiny is biologically structured, humanly patterned, familially configured, and archetypally governed, there is another portion of it that is not the outcome of any of that, and which is considered divine.[980] Because of this, it would be a grave mistake to suddenly equate the literal family's past with one's *deep* purpose, meaning, or identity on Earth.[981] If it so happens, then the next step is to equate ancestors with mere humanoid biological predecessors, and then, like Hillman sharply warned, "biogenetics replaces the spirit world"[982],[983]; and once this has occurred one is fully divested of one's utmost spiritual origin, and one ends up believing in a God that is elsewhere[984] or that the divine could not be oneself.[985] Ancestors, when thought of only from the mundane point of view, are nothing but those who happened to live before and those to whom one physically resembles, in a kind of Darwinian view—where one almost fits that zoological theory of man being a very evolved and "naked ape"—; but when thought of from the vision and image of the daimon, they are those with whom one is most spiritually related,[986] those who watch over one's life,[987] as in the Dagara view.[988] In this sense, Somé's insistence acquires an entirely different tone, when saying that *the relationship of the ancestors has to be revived, and brought back to the center of attention in everyday living*[989]. He was obviously not meaning the ancestors as those dead long time ago or those human individuals from whom one happens to be like, that is a quite opaque view of ancestry due to scientifical biology and minimalistic philosophies.[990] It seems clear that he rather encouraged a spiritual view on ancestry based on psychical biology.[991] Instead of conceiving ancestors as mere physical antecessors, they ought to be seen as daimonia who walked upon Earth in a human form and left.[992] There is an urge to develop spiritual thinking, feeling, loving, and living, beyond the categories imposed by the dominant religions—Abrahamic, Vedic, Buddhistic, or their derivates[993]—in order to avoid the nihilistic fundamentalism[994] that stems out of the academic philosophy and which has seriously impoverished and devastated life.[995] In the Dagara view of life, for instance, "[t]he illness is a physical manifestation of a spiritual decay"[996], and the corollary is that healing requires a spiritual dynamism.

The daimon in this sense could sound as something invented, as a mere fiction that elicits believing in something more than the mundane.[997] But, unlike many spiritual traditions that stress upon the idea of a certain path to be followed, a clear aim to be achieved, and a certain moral way that is the correct one, the notion of daimon is open, accessible, and attainable for everyone, whether he or she speaks of it or not, whether he or she considers himself (or herself) "spiritual" or not. Hillman, therefore, argued that "it is not a moral instructor or to be confused with conscience"[998]. It is rather a notion that one discovers, that one remembers: who or what was I before this life? But the answer is not necessarily another human reincarnation from a previous past, a remote time, or a foreign land.[999] The answer seems to require much more effort, even a breakdown of one's rationality,[1000] and, most certainly, a deep longing[1001]—or a genuine expression of grief.[1002] Perhaps, like Rilke suggested, if the spiritual value of grieving were known, "we would endure our griefs [*sic*] even with greater trust than our joys"[1003].[1004]

Jung too, surprisingly, considered this insights to be quite sane; he claimed that "[t]he tendency to live in illusion and to believe in a fiction of oneself—in the good sense or in the bad—is almost insuperably great"[1005].[1006] One can attest this with the paintings and writings from his *Red Book*[1007], which in fact revealed profound experiences,[1008] imaginal dialogues,[1009] revelatory visions,[1010] and an exquisite wisdom of an other-worldly nature.[1011] Maybe, this might be the reason why Heraclitus claimed that, "[t]he habit of knowledge is not human but divine"[1012].[1013]

This, which could, of course, sound excessively mad for the rationally oriented people and philosophies, is, in fact, the core of Jung's knowledge.[1014] He asked rhetorically: "What is it, then, that inexorably tips the scales in favour [*sic*] of the *extraordinary*?" And in his case, besides his bright intellect, his sharp analytical eye, or his acute intuition,[1015] one finds, like Hillman suggested, that there was *something else*.[1016] Jung boldly answered: "It is what is commonly called vocation: an irrational factor that destines man to emancipate from the herd and well-worn paths"[1017]; in other words, something so out of one's capacity for rationalizing,[1018] that one might well call it the daimon.[1019] It might be wise remembering Rilke's observation, especially during difficult times, who said to a young poet: "You must believe that something is happening to you, that life has not forgotten you . . . It shall not let you fall"[1020]. A brief story, titled *I see you,* might illustrate these insights.

If you are reading this, it is because it has come to completion; but this written work was the work of many people, not me alone who happened to put the words into sentences along with a variety of references. This work was possible only through the great help of my family, but also many friends, colleagues, classmates, professors, strangers, and even some uncanny moments that felt as if some powerful agents would have been watching over me.

To set a beginning is awkward, because it is indeed very hard to define; somehow it felt as if the work had always been there waiting, claiming its due, and requiring me to give it part of my life, and bring it into life. By no means does this imply that this work is important for others, as if it were groundbreaking or transcendent; it is rather an acknowledgement of the mysterious ways in which it came to be.

By the time I finished university studies in psychology, in Mexico City, I was solidly certain that I was going to enroll at the C.G. Jung Institute in Zürich, which I had in mind since eight years before, and for which I had solicited admission. I was asked to go there to be interviewed, and so I did.

I knew Zürich from a previous trip, in which I had stayed for a few days, but this time it was different. I felt as if I had lived there before for a long time, and so it was enchanting even in plain winter, but I also knew that I was not going to stay there for long, I knew since I arrived and stepped on the streets of the old town that I was not going to move there for studies. Six interviews occurred with different analysts, I met students, professors, the people from admissions, strangers, and I even visited, without having it planned, almost by pure chance, Jung's grave. I breathed Küsnacht's air, put my hands into the Zürich's lake water, enjoyed a few solitary days in town, and a day before the last day I met a Mexican man who was a Jungian analyst, and who had been very close to Marie-Louise von Franz. He was not only fluent in Nahuatl, and knew Mayan, which is extremely rare, but told me that there was something about the old Mexican cultures that he wished he could study more. He said to me that if he had more life, he would inquire more about those "old ways;" his desire seemed almost a suggestion, which was rare to me, especially coming from a man who moved to Zürich after university studies, never to go back to his natal Mexico.

Weeks later, being back home, I received the notification of having been accepted, but somehow, by a very strange reason, I did not enroll. It was a decision that surpassed all my reasoning; I just allowed it to happen, and submerged in absolute confusion, professional disorientation, and deep uncertainty.

A year and a half later, I solicited admission to Pacifica, which was an almost crazy decision because there were many things against, but mostly the financial issue. In simple words, I had no money with which to enroll. Nevertheless, I found a way to enroll and decided to move to California. Just a few days before moving I received the news that the Mexican man in Zürich died about three months after my visit—I remembered, at the time, that he had told me that he was very ill and expecting death, but it felt as if he had waited for me. I kept thinking about his words and the way he expressed them for several months.

The decision about the studies in California also surpassed all rational arguments, and, in fact, there were factors that could compromise security, health, and other personal aspects. However, by the time that I arrived to California, things occurred in unexpected but favorable ways, by deeds of strangers and people without whom I would have never achieved the long process required prior to write this. At my arrival, a very kind family, without having ever met me, gave me accommodation and help for a week; a woman of eighty-seven years of age helped me for several months with a cheap deal for accommodation; some classmates gave me books, and others gave me money to buy them; a friend helped me in numerous occasions with a place to stay; some professors also helped me in almost impossible ways; and many more helped me in various ways. But the help was not just financial; there were also unexpected encounters that seemed to have directed me, without me knowing it.

During that time, in the span of a year and a half, I did a training in Constellations work, without really having planned it, with a couple who helped me incredibly, I heard Malidoma Somé on a public talk, then I also attended several public events by James Hillman, and I met him and talked to him personally. In addition, I attended three international training seminars by Bert Hellinger, and met Somé again but face to face. Also, at some point, Mary Watkins, who had just published a scholarly book on Psychologies of Liberation, asked me with genuine inquiry: "What is psychology like, in Mexico?" And I mumbled that it was only an imitation of the European ways, and mostly American psychology. That moment I thought that psychology in Mexico was only a caricature of what other countries were doing, but I also realized that the native, the local, the autochthonous, and the indigenous ways had not been explored sufficiently, aside from the usual ethnocentric studies, i.e., anthropology, sociology, and the like.

Somehow, even with scarce resources, destiny was moving me through something important about ancestry, not just for me, but also important for other peoples. I suddenly realized that rather than teaching and studying psychology in any of its branches, and rather than developing techniques that aim to be therapeutic in any of their modalities, it is rather an awareness and attention to ancestry what is deeply needed. But I would have never achieved it without the help, deeds, support, and good intentions of my family and all these people. To all these people I bow in gratitude. I lack the capacity to express how it felt to be helped unexpectedly in moments of great need and desperation, great confusion and uncertainty, as if destined not to fail. I felt constantly as if somewhere deep in them knew and saw something I did not know and did not see, as if their daimon were helping mine. To all of you: "Gracias."

In discussing one's personal destiny, one has to consider also such a notion as that of *Zeitgeist*, which literally means the spirit (*Geist*) of the times (*Zeit*). However, in doing so, something has to be clarified for the German word *Geist* is dynamic. Hence, when thoroughly going to the bottom of destiny, one inescapably has to embody it within the world context that one is meant to live, both, globally and locally, personally and trans-personally, humanly and other-than-humanly.[1021] The spirit of the times is in a way that which dresses up the fated and blood issues with contemporary forms and patterns; it is that which gives them the current image with which one will face them, endure them, and possibly perceive them, acknowledge them, and overcome them.

This can be easily perceived when observing family situations; most of them, if not all of them, are mythical.[1022] That is not meant to say that the gods provoked them, or that families worship gods or goddesses in the literal Western religious sense, but that they are structured in ways that resemble very old stories, and which can be explained by imagining governing forces that give them such patterns: archetypes[1023]. So, if one examines the problems and conflicts within families, one realizes that such issues are in fact similar to issues that families have lived before, in other times, even very old times, and other places, even very remote places. Jung observed that "[m]ythological motifs frequently appear, but clothed in modern dress"[1024]. It is only the spirit of the times that covers them with post-modernity, high-technology, cybernetic problems, electronic devices, sophisticated philosophies, trendy theories, highly complicated explanations, and lifestyles that obey the *empire of the ephemeral.*[1025]

Jung, of course, being a scholar of the old ways of seeing and explaining things, was also well aware of this. He encouraged his readers to ground themselves to their roots, to go down to one's dregs, to explore one's traditions, to get to the bottom of things, and to search for one's psychic past, in order to find one's correct and most suitable place. Without this awareness, Jung warned, "[t]he man who is unconscious of the historical context and lets slip his link with the past is in constant danger of succumbing to the crazes and delusions engendered by all novelties"[1026].[1027] If this happens, one could say then that one is at the mercy of the Zeitgeist, craving any interesting or equally absurd thing that it might demand, and almost at any cost: celerity, fast food, faster communications, accelerated reading, fast-paced rhythms, better gadgets, hyper-productivity, multitasking, instant messaging, virtual chats, virtual seminars, greater social networking, stimulants, more money, always more money, sleeping pills, or whatever else.[1028]

One has to be aware that although one's fated and blood issues are disguised and contextualized with current conflicts and situations, and even when one's daimon tends to believe that such is everything there is, as if one's purpose in life were only meant to serve the Zeitgeist, there is yet a deeper truth.[1029] Just like kabbalists would claim that the physical world that one perceives represents only one percent of reality,[1030] just so the Zeitgeist seems to be only a fragment of a much greater reality.[1031]

The spirit of the times is only the surface, it is only the movement upon which most people live, in which most people get entangled, implicated, worried, concerned, preoccupied, alienated, and trapped. The Zeitgeist is only the custom with which one sees the world-soul and its stream of being.[1032] Yet, there seems to be another dynamism of the spirit worth considering, one that indeed moves the Zeitgest; Jung called it the *spirit of the depths*.[1033] While the spirit of the times "like[s] to hear of use and value . . . and changes with the generations[,]" the spirit of the depths, which "possesses greater power[,] . . . [might force one] down to the last and simplest things"[1034], as if it, indeed, would bring one to the dregs of the Earth. Jung wrote that the spirit of the depths placed his understanding and knowledge "at the service of the inexplicable and the paradoxical . . . [in a] melting together of sense and nonsense, which produces supreme meaning"[1035],[1036]; in fact, not in the service of the utilitarian or productive view of life, but *on the service of the soul*, as he wrote, which would require of him to "waken the dead"[1037].[1038] One has to be careful, because if one takes Jung's words literally, or too narrowly, it could easily be thought of as some kind of fascination with death, a thanatophilia, as some sort of attachment to the dead which burdens life, a necrophilia, or even as kind of cultish, obscurantist, pagan, or devil-worship idea. But taken symbolically, it might in fact be a call for those dead in peace, a call for the ancestors[1039]—and then one might dangerously and apologetically claim with Socrates that, indeed, "these geniuses [daimonia] . . . are wise in a wisdom that is more than human"[1040].[1041] The following story will illustrate these insights, it is titled: *A forbidden story waiting to be told.*

Once upon a time, there was great concern for the way to the ultimate truth, and there was a lot of confusion and consternation. It was a time of conflict and war, and the scarcity and poverty were not only material but also of the spirit. Some people were afraid, some others were merely thinking that it was the end of the planet, and few others agreed and decided to pay a visit to a so-called wise man, who was famous for his profound insights, revelations, and prophecies.

People representing many countries and many corners of the Earth gathered, and traveled for several days in order to see him. Once they reached his sojourning place, some argued that such was the East because they had to travel in such a direction, but others argued that such was the West, and, of course, others argued that it was a bit North, while others claimed that it was South. In reality, such was the impossible center, the very place that is felt as the very core of the manifested universe once the space is set for it, but only for the time it is designed to be so. So, aside from their childish disagreements of what Cardinal spot was that, once they were all settled on the beginning of the day, which was right after dusk, they started a three day gathering, in order to find out the most truthful path and the most sacred language with which to pray.

That first night they all sat by the warming fire waiting for the acclaimed and unknown wise man, who had not yet appeared. They were all commenting calmly about their views, and what similarities and differences they shared, and it all seemed peaceful, as if they were not in the need of someone to tell them which was the path to the great truth. When the wise man arrived they got quiet and very surprised because he was riding a beige, lean donkey, rather than the majestic white horse that everybody expected.

Once the wise man, whose eyes shimmered like a starry sky, settled sternly with them, around the fire, the people started to ask very specific questions. The man with the black hat asked if the holiest language was indeed his, claiming that it was the oldest, but before the wise man could even blink, a man on an orange robe was already on his feet arguing that the language of his people was holier because it came from the mountains of his country, the highest visible peaks. The wise man slightly smiled, and he asked them if there was another question, something of more value, but right away, without even letting the echo of the question disappear, several of them started to speak loudly and it felt like a marketplace. They were shouting that there could be no other more important question than knowing, which was the most sacred of the sacred languages. The wise man was hearing nothing intelligible, until, somehow, a silent moment let a bald monk's voice stood out from the rest, saying: "we need to know in what language shall we pray!" And right after that the donkey brayed: "Yea-ah! Yea –ah! Yea-ah!" The wise man looked at them smilingly, stood up, and right before leaving for the night, he said: "the donkey has spoken." All those people remained perplexed for an instant, and went on with their discussion for the rest of the dark hours.

By the second night, also by the fire, the people were already disgusted with one another, and there were alliances among them. The wise man arrived again on his donkey, and after he settled with them, they started such a loud atmosphere that he could barely understand what they wanted to ask. It remained so for a while, until they got quiet and a man in a white long tunic stood up and said: "As long as you pray to the real God, it does not matter if it is the right language, he will understand!" The donkey brayed: "Yea-ah!" But the rest of the people howled in horror, and in full rage attacked his suggestion, because that would have meant that their secret sacredness would have been vain. The wise man stood up, they got silenced, and while looking at them he could not avoid it and he brayed "Yea-ah!" louder than the donkey. But some of them got so enraged with such an exclamation, that they were almost about to start a fight if it would have been not for those who preferred peace to sacred languages and holy letters.

By the third night there was already a great disagreement among them, and they thought that it all had been in vain. The wise man appeared one more time on his donkey, and after he settled, knowing that it was going to be the last day, they started to raise all kind of imprudent questions. But this time he asked them for silence, and he said that he was going to tell them an old, forbidden, story.

He said: "In the old times, our ancestors knew that the Earth besides being first and foremost a place, has always been soil, in a spiritual way. They knew well that it was a suitable environment to plant and grow things, as if it were a terrain that one could care and make into a garden. The Earth, however, had been there, before them, and rather than bothering who or what had made it, they saw that they could get into it, and grow themselves into its being. Several ancestors did this, and so they planted men and women, who they cultivated into groups and societies, until they had well-developed cultures. This was the way of Earth for a long time, and the differences that existed between peoples were due to the different seeds of consciousness that had been planted, at different eons, with different purposes. Because of this they spoke very different languages, had different body structures, and ultimately different ways of developing. In the old times, the people on Earth did not bother to argue who or what was God, because such concept was not only not-conceivable, but even absurdly impossible. They rather concerned themselves with the ancestor who had planted them, which, in many cases, had been a flow of actual persons embodying the force and intention of the ancestor, and because of this they were thought of as one spirit who had taken many forms on Earth. Life on Earth was a flourishing variety in those old times. Every ancestor was the guiding spirit for his cultivated beingness, and the Earth was the garden where it was blooming as beings and, in some cases, fruitfully developing. Actually, they are called "ancestors" because they were once on Earth; and because of that they are the genesis and genetic spirit of their culture. As you can see, there were many origins, not only one. However, by some uncanny reason, in several of the cultivated crops, people started to argue about their origin and about their ancestor, and some claimed their ancestor as the ancestor of everything on Earth, and even of the Earth itself. A disagreement that started with a clever monologic idea, all of a sudden transformed into our actual conflicts that aim to dominate the ways of the Earth. Since then, peoples and cultures have been trying to impose their ancestor on the others, claiming such an ancestor to be even the one who planted everything. They even call it the creator of all. Of course, the problem of language, scriptures, prayers, and traditions, is reducible to what culture you belong to, but, unfortunately, you will still think that your ancestor created mine. As I told you, this is a forbidden story, waiting to be told." The old wise man looked at them, silently, while they, in turn, looked angrier than the day before. The donkey brayed again:

"Yea-ah!" Nasrudin, who had been very attentive to the animal, brayed too: "Yea-aaaaa!" but Baal, his friend, told him: "there is a silent 'ha' in the end, it should be 'Yeah-aah!"

The man with the black hat, however, was the first to stand up and shouted while pointing at him: "You are a pagan! A polytheist!" and the man in the white tunic followed, saying: "You fool! You buffoon!" And another man in a white tunic exclaimed: "You are a clown in the most detrimental sense!" Others also stood up in great discontent and anger, and they shouted: "He is only a old fool!" A guru exclaimed: "If you don't know the primal creator, why would you believe such stories!" And a man in a red tunic, the peaceful one, said: "You charlatan, you are a deceiver, a creator of illusions!" A man in a long purple tunic, who had been quiet, cried: "You devil! Your beliefs are inferior and primitive! And his companion Benito shouted: "Apage, Satanás!" Some others hurled all possible insults, feeling that he was devaluing "the creator" to a mere pagan deity; and several of them started to mock him. But not all of them were against him. Lao shouted with great gusto: "Ching! Ching! Ching!" and his companion, The Confused one, barked in agreement, while Greco smilingly whispered: "Akea!" An old chief loudly expressed: "Ho!" And a man who was almost naked looked up and said: "Aljira." Many of the rest only observed the enraged ones who were already throwing at him torches and things, and who were already starting to fight among themselves, and encouraging the rest in order to burn him.

They would have probably killed him if it were not for a very unexpected incident. Suddenly, right in the middle of such a riot, a half naked woman appeared. They stopped all their shameful arguments and a powerful silence was felt. She, who was very beautiful, crossed the rabble and walked towards the wise man, while he told the rest of the people: "She has many names, but I call her Aletheia. She has all the answers." But the man with the black hat, indignant, exclaimed: "How can a woman have any answer!" and he covered his eyes with his hands in order not to see her nakedness, which was strictly forbidden to him. The man in a purple tunic kneeled down and put his forehead on the ground thinking that she was a prostitute. The man in the orange robe started chanting for having seen such a creature, and the one in the red tunic turned around with eyes closed in order to see no more, not wanting to desire such apparition. Some others were about to throw stones at her for being naked, but suddenly an old man in the crowd, named Rising Owl shouted: "Hetchetou aloh." And unexpectedly, the long-time disappeared one, Falling Eagle, who had been quiet all those days, echoed him, although he did not know what the words meant, because they were not from the same culture. Standing Dear, who had been serious the whole time, growled in deep agreement, and Lame Bear danced joyfully all around.

The wise man, fearing that they would get stoned, helped his woman to ride the donkey and then he climbed on it too, right behind her, but as he did this one of his sandals fell on the ground. He looked back to the crowd once more, and said: "May you reach the great sunshine someday!" and the donkey prayed: "Yea-Ha!" He grabbed Aletheia around his arms and they galloped gaily towards the East, where the sun was beginning to rise. Curiously, with the first rays of light the donkey's fur started to look golden, and Apuleio thought that such an animal had been a great ass, and that the whole meeting had been like an ass-festival. Anton, who was next to him, was the only one to notice that the sandal on the ground was made out of bronze, and he picked it up and kept it. The rest of them, unable to see them because of the powerful sunlight, decided to leave. As they started to walk away their shadows also started to grow longer, but they did not notice; they were fully convinced that it had been all in vain, and that they had been cheated by very wise foolery.[1042]

It might not be literal, but not in vain either, that Rumi wrote in his poem titled *Put this design in your carpet:* "Spiritual experience is a modest woman/ who looks lovingly at only one man"[1043].

Chapter 10
Soul: Psychic-Riverrunning

"So let me be thy choir, and make a moan

Upon the midnight hours;

Thy voice, thy lute, thy pipe, thy incense sweet

From swingèd censed teeming:

Thy shrine, thy grove, thy oracle, thy heat

Of pale mouth'd prophet dreaming..."

Ode to Psyche[1044]

The awareness to the presence of the ancestors is inevitably bound to, and even contained by, the soul; but unfortunately the soul has been popularly conceived and it is generally spoken of as something that belongs to the "me." Hillman, however, already in his old age and after several decades of dedicated scholarly writings and varied clinical work on psychology, wrote that, "[the] core issue for all psychology [is:] *Where is the 'me'? Where does the 'me' begin'? Where does the 'me' stop? Where does the 'other' begin?*"[1045]. This, in fact, seems to be a very important inquiry, and rather than generating a fast answer, it elicits reflection, doubt, uncertainty, irrationality, even incomprehension, and after much effort, possibly, just like with a Zen koan, satori. The idea of ancestry presented throughout this written work can open unspoken dimensions into the visions of soul and a re-vision of ideas in disciplines interested in it; and with such views the notion of the 'me' might be experienced and explored differently, possibly extended, expanded, and conceived also as extroverted, unlike some psychological paradigms that consider the 'me' as the internal world of the "I."

The notion of soul, however, is quite difficult to explain—since time immemorial. To ask, "what is the soul?" is to begin erratically because it already demands a definition, and it presupposes a "thing;" such a question *thingnifies* the soul, and maybe it is rather a process, a loving dynamic, a perspective, a way of seeing, and a way of knowing.[1046] There seems certainly to be a personal notion of it, a personal grasp of it that is felt as owned, but such is a limited perception of it.[1047]

Soul has been conceived also as covering all places, at all times. Soul, as Hellinger pointed out, is extended not just through space, but through time too[1048]. Soul, in such a way, is like a field of happenings, yet it is not a "thing" but the whole life-flow; it is like water through the river: running. This stream of life is not moved by isolated divisions of water (how ridiculous!), it seems to be all moved by a greater force; one could take this as that which Hellinger called "the Great Soul"[1049].[1050] This mysterious notion was beautifully expressed by Rumi, who wrote in the poem titled *A dove in the eaves*:

Day and night I guarded the pearl of my soul.

Now in this ocean of pearling currents,

I've lost track of which was mine.[1051]

Maybe it is just that it is *all* interrelated in an interminable interdependent *flux*, but since one is utterly incapable of knowing it *all*, which includes realms other-than human, then one might just as well call it the Great Soul. In any case, the image of a flow is only that, a metaphor that helps understanding; and Hellinger has also mentioned that, "the soul is like a river"[1052]. But, what is the phenomenology of the river? What makes a river, a river? The water? The furrow? Is soul, then, the movement of the river? A few lines from a beautiful passage by Rumi, in the poem titled *The long string*, might help:

Soul of my soul of the soul of a hundred universes,

be water in this now-river, so jasmine flowers

will lift on the brim, and someone far off

can notice the flower-colors and know

there's water here...[1053]

Entertaining and following the metaphor of the river, for the sake of this written work, will keep the idea of soul being a watery force; as in the case of the river, it is both the water and its movement on Earth, and yet something else, without which it would not be a river. Just so, *soul* is *riverrunning*—on a riverbed of course.[1054]

Soul, conceived as that, is extended not only at the place where one perceives that it moves, but back to the past form where it comes and further towards the future to where it runs, flowing always through its different currents, at times fast and furiously, other times slow and calmly, at times with high potent waves, and other times with smooth and suave rhythms. In such a movement it involves all, it keeps all within the stream of life—whether good ones or bad ones, terrible or noble ones, cursed or blessed ones, and even the animal, mineral, imaginal, and the whole natural spectrum of life; all are included.

This idea brings an even wider sphere of soul from the one that could be felt as "personal" or the one described as pertaining to the family and the community of fate.[1055] This notion of soul, extended into *everyone, everything, everywhere, everywhen, everyhow* and *everywhat*, allows one to deepen the inquiries, reflections, and wonderings into the experiences of this force—because a force could be conceived as the interrelations between the elements happening on a field, but the elements can also be conceived as forces themselves, which are also the result of other interrelations, so that every element is also a field within the great unfathomable field. Particularly, it is in these extended domains of soul where one can challenge some notions of time, and step into that which *is having been* (in the past) in order to feel the present flow easier, smoother, or simply to attune with its current. This notion allows us to develop a technology (like a ritual art) with which one is capable of looking at the dead, for example, even when dead for a long time, the aborted, the abandoned, the forgotten, the given in adoption, or any other presence that one wants to look at even if it is not physically "present." In other words, this is what allows one to look at all the psychic presences that also belong to the phenomena of life, whether they are dead and (physically) gone, far away and (physically) apart, or even unknown and (physically) invisible.[1056] Certainly, when one looks into this extended notion and allows consciously "the Movements of the Soul," as Hellinger called them for a time, then "new dimensions open up for help"[1057]. Unfortunately, it seems to be that some followers of Hellinger have not clearly acknowledged that the principal agent that propitiates the powerful healings, insightful observations, and movements of reconciliation and resolution during the Constellations work is the soul. That which seems to be really important during the constellations are not the communicative actions, the linguistic jargon, the hypnotic wording, the theoretical assumptions, the clinical experience, educational biases, or the "good intentions" of the persons facilitating them, but a respectful, humble, sincere, and yet fearless acknowledgement of the soul at its depths—which is an *intelligent principle,* as if *moved by something else.* Therefore, when one allows the movements of the soul, even without words, as in Hellinger silent constellations, strong but succinct emotions take place, propitiating resolutions, reconciliations, and healing. But such movements are not controlled, directed, or guided in any sense by the facilitators, they are often felt as motions from the depths of life—the *autochthnonous* psyche.

The Great Soul, in this sense, is literally and virtually anything and everything; it experiences itself through beings and persons of all kinds—whether monks or madmen, police or criminals, prostitutes or priests, saints or sinners. Therefore, as Hellinger wrote in a brief tale, called *Margen de movimiento* (Margin of movement), it can allow itself to replace its members without effort, just as Nature[1058], as if no one were indispensable or irreplaceable. He meant that there is not one single individual who is the most important for the totality of the psyche, even if it is a so-called "good man;" but there are not unimportant individuals either. His work recognizes the right of belonging and right of existence to those who are often considered as the scum of society, the murderers, the addicts, the perverts, the prisoners, the thieves, the criminals, the terrorists, and all kind of wrong-doers. It is a powerful acknowledgement and integration of what many cultures in humanity have labeled and categorized as evil, embodied, for example, in the mythic figure of Cain and his descendants.[1059]

Hence, Hellinger observed and insisted repeatedly that everything belongs, and, moreover, everybody belongs to the community of mankind—also the outcast, the bad ones, the perpetrators of all kind of victims, the psychopaths, the mad and insane, the terrorists, and all the dead. He observed, through many workshops, that the inclusion of the excluded, in *whatever* condition they were excluded, brought reconciliation, healing, and peace to individuals and families[1060]. This act of integration and inclusion is not for the sake of a moral duty, or because some sacred scriptures command it, but because one indeed feels that one strives towards wholeness, that one is becoming more complete. This happens because one is including in one's heart that which one rejects in others—and suddenly, without even thinking about it, one realizes, and somehow embodies, the actuality and power of the Great Soul. In a sense, it is a deep movement of psychic reconciliation with what had been separated, fragmented, isolated, kept apart, casted out, rejected, or even forgotten.[1061] One realizes that oneself is like everybody else, without distinction between superiors and inferiors, better ones and worse ones, good ones and bad ones.

However, it is important to mention that Hellinger claimed how in the Constellations work, any "reconciliation starts in the soul of the individual and in the family's"[1062], not as a puritanical commandment, a philosophical abstraction, a political cliché, or a dogmatic statement to be preached. What Hellinger emphasized is that prior to trying to help other countries and other peoples, prior to going to a mission afar into a conflictive land or signing with peace organizations that aim to save the world from struggle, war, and divisiveness, one has first to integrate all the lost aspects form one's personal and family soul—otherwise, it seems quite a dangerous farce.[1063] Sometimes one's psychic situation is just like the lines that Rumi wrote in his poem *Childhood Friends:* "Your stream water may look clean,/ but there's unstirred matter on the bottom"[1064], maybe dead stinking corpses, that have not found peace for centuries, and that have polluted your terrain (your "body" and circumstance).

This is crucial, because, as Hellinger has observed, "excluding certain members of the family [and the community of fate] or being ashamed of them … atrophies and isolates the family"[1065] with severe consequences for further generations; in simpler words, it literally sickens the family and the next generations—it enhances and strengthens the chronic miasmas. Rather than getting rid of the so-called bad people, one needs, first of all, to get rid of one's ways of excluding them from one's family, from one's hearts, from one's terrain, and from one's holistic notion and motion of soul.[1066] But in order to achieve that one need to let go the feeling of being a "good" one.

By means of this extended and fluid notion of the psyche, it is possible to comprehend that we are all embedded and entwined in the mysterious phenomena of life, the arcane of Earth's actuality, all accomplishing a destiny that is entangled to unfathomable dimensions that in fact go beyond the pettiness of all morality and rationality.

Therefore, realizing and looking into this notion offers the extraordinary capacities to heal and bring peace to tough problems, such as those intergenerational victims-perpetrators conflicts which have dragged on through the centuries involving many peoples, cultures, religions, and countries, where, in most cases, it is obvious that none of them could be considered "the bad" one, and where it is extremely delicate to judge morally anyone—even those who might have killed "innocents." It is not for nothing that Hellinger was considered a candidate for achieving the Peace Nobel Prize (in 2011).

These insights are quite crucial because no one is born in a blank psychic context, everyone appears as a member of a soul that is flowing throughout the generations; one could say, following Jung, that, "[w]e have no reason to suppose that the specific structure of the psyche is the only thing in the world that has no history outside its individual manifestations"[1067]. He considered, quite reservedly, that "[e]ven the conscious mind cannot be denied a history reaching back at least five thousand years"[1068]; in other words, the human affairs and human conflicts, i.e., familial, educational, social, political, or economical, happening either in local and domestic situations, within nations, internationally, or as ecological calamities, have a relation to the ways of consciousness that have been ontologically planted at the beginnings of every culture, and which are ingrained with certain ways of knowing that have not been fully explored and developed, that have been forgotten, or that have been parodied as superstitious, retrograde, and primitive.[1069] However, the direct results of the actual underdeveloped—and even atrophied—ways of consciousness are the tragedies that humanity traverses at the beginning of the twentieth first century—mostly a massive un-acknowledgement of anything related to the unconscious (autonomous) psyche and the ancestors.[1070] This is so, because, as Jung claimed, "we remain ignorant of whether our ancestral components find an elementary gratification in our lives, or whether they are repelled"[1071]. This could be thought of as a great blindness; or as a general, politicized and institutionalized, incapacity to see into and see through the everyday pathological phenomena that is primarily of a psychic order—individually or collectively, socially or systemically, personally or politically, interpersonally or internationally, humanly or ecologically.[1072]

The main and radical assumption, ontologically speaking, is that "[t]he unconscious psyche is not only immensely old, it is also capable of growing into an equally remote future"[1073]. Such view of life assumes that actuality has grown out of old ontological seeds and intentions, and that the current ways and movement of soul could be thought of as a consequence of that which grew out and occurred—for good or for worse. In simpler words, the world in which one exists today could be thought of as the offspring of the conscious and unconscious ways of life by hundreds of generations before, all the way back to Ancient Egypt, Ancient Persia, Ancient Greece, Ancient Judea, Ancient India, Ancient China, the Ancient Americas, and many other ancient ontological orchards.[1074] This does not imply any childish call to blame the past; on the contrary, it is an attitude that realizes the challenges of the spirit, both the *Zeitgeist* and the *Tiefengeist* (the spirit of the depths), and encourages responsibility and pro-activeness towards profound and fundamental issues. However, it also recognizes that life on Earth requires a powerful shift in its living dynamics; there is a need of a different way to see the world—to begin with—, maybe *a soulful worldview,* which seems indeed to be ingrained in the origin of many cultures. The aim, naturally, consists in the maintenance of life in its widest possible diversity and richness, and, possibly, in the planting of intentions that will sprout in the future, maybe a remote future many generations after, maybe dozens of generations later, who will enjoy, appreciate, and be thankful that they were already present in the intentionality and imagination of their predecessors.[1075]

Somehow, it is as if that which is most required is the need to remember the ways of the past, the origins of culture and the original ways of dwelling and walking on Earth. It seems quite certain that the conscious life is only a little piece, a very tiny fragment, an almost insignificant moment of the psyche that particularly moves according to the place and the times—through the individuals' lives. "The unconscious, on the other hand," and according to Jung, "is universal: it not only binds individuals together into one nation or race, but unites them with the men of the past and with their psychology"[1076]. However, he did not only mean the practical ways of life, like hunting, working, traveling, selling, buying, warring, and so on, nor the obvious physical necessities, like eating, mating, sleeping, and all those inevitabilities that some people and scientists could claim that are the origins of civilization, but profound ontological intentions along with ways of knowing (epistemological devises) that after hundreds of years grew into the actualities of consciousness, according to specific *cultural consciences.*[1077]

It seems probable that that what we call nowadays "science" (developed and enhanced by the Westernized minds) is only one kind among many other possibilities of doing and making sciences that would pertain to other consciences—old consciences that are powerful, multidimensional, and less grotesque and less polluting. Hence, like Jung observed, "the unconscious is the prime object of any real psychology that claims to be more than psychophysics"[1078]. It becomes clear for him that the unconscious is not the sack of one's personal unfulfilled desires, pleasurable reminiscences, life memories, forgotten experiences, infantile cravings, childhood conditionings, and unknown fantasies, but the matrix of humanity, and, more importantly, the foundational ways of being and knowing of every human individual. The unconscious in this sense is not information and sensory and emotional stimuli recorded in the brain and the neural pathways; it might rather be the ontological archives of every culture that are coded in the bones—particularly in the marrow,[1079] but also in the sinews, the heart and blood, and the flesh of every man and every woman.[1080]

A good example of this could be the Jewish people, alleged descendants of the mythic *Sem*—therefore Semites. They follow a kind of conscience, developed throughout four millennia (approximately), illustrated, transmitted, and sustained by their mythical stories of origin, that dictates what to do, how to do it, when to do it, where to do it, and why. One could think, that, according to such a worldview, Abraham planted some ontological intentions that were developed further by Isaac, Jacob, Moses, Aaron, Joseph, and David—as it can be read in some Kabbalistic writings[1081], and wisely maintained by their people until today, in order not to lose them, and in order not to lose themselves in mundane and *dark chaos.*

It would be interesting to inquire and reflect if their names of God, and the Hebrew letters (images of God), are not in fact their spiritual archive and code, which is their divine origin, intention, purpose, and aim—and it is reasonable to question whether they are universal and unique, because other cultures and peoples have spoken and narrated similar insights, realms, powers, and experiences, without having known Hebrew, Aramaic, the Israelite mythic stories of origin, or their secret rituals.[1082] In any case, their ways of being—when they follow the paths of their culture—clearly manifest an attunement with their ontological origins, that is, with their story of creation (their cosmogony); hence, the festivities, the prayers, the holy days, and all the organization of their activities and ways of life, follow the cosmic cyclical rhythm of their recorded and codified myths. The teachings of the Kabbalah (alleged by some as Jewish mysticism) reveal a cosmic understanding with which they structure their life events, according to an astrological Sun-Lunar time cycle, and in which their living myths take place,[1083] and which they embody symbolically year after year. Hence, their religious observations and duties in Purim, Pesach, Shavuot, Rosh Hashanah, Yom Kippur, Sukkot, and Hanukah, for example, are marked and designed by the happenings that their people went through in the alleged cosmic and historical times—their mythic origin, often referred to as stories that took place during the Biblical times. In simpler words, their religiosity unfolded and developed throughout all those generations that embodied and pertain to such an ethnic conscience. It has not been the same since Abraham, it has been and still is in-the-making, striving to achieve a Messianic conscience with the aid of spiritual technologies.[1084]

This kind of religiosity, based on an ethnic cosmogony and specific spiritual technologies, can also be found in some other indigenous cultures, although with a different astrological language; and it reveals both a mystical description of Earth and the universe, and also a cosmic participation in the world. The etymological origin of the word cosmic, actually, stems from the Greek *kósmos* and it does not denote a realm in the outer space, but it rather means an "order"[1085], presumably to be followed.[1086] In such a sense, religiosity might mean a harmonious way of living that knows the power of one's cosmogonic stories. Deloria Jr. acknowledged that the Sioux people, for example, knew that "[p]ersonal development involves the reconciliation of the ancestral with the present, and social systems—including family, kinship, and institutions—play a key role in such harmonization"[1087]. The reconciliation with the ancestral, however, is not merely meant in a biological, socio-political, and historical sense, but mainly in a spiritual sense;[1088] in other words, with one's ontological origin and conscience.[1089]

Jung rhetorically asked: "Aren't we the carriers of the entire history of mankind?" And in his conception of the notion of being human, he realized that, "[w]hen man is fifty years old, only one part of his being has existed for half a century. The other part, which also lives in his psyche, may be millions old . . . None of us knows what we know"[1090]. It could be thought that he really glimpsed deeply into the human being, being aware of other kinds of conscience which had been planted also on Earth—long ago, in times prior to any written language—and in which people have kept a continuity, like some black Africans. That may be the reason why he wrote that, "[t]he unconscious is the written history of mankind from time unrecorded"[1091]. One can attest to these ideas when reading about the tribal Dagara[1092], who would be considered illiterate and *savage* according to the pedantic Westernized worldview, or even according to the Middle-Eastern religions, because they have no writing or any kind of scripture, nor even a tiny interest in it, but who have ways of knowing that are still unimaginable and unthinkable for the Westerners—as if their knowledge were not recorded with letters in books, but in their own embodiment, ways of living, ways of loving, in their spiritual technologies, and in the stories that have been passed on orally since long time ago.

Hence, the vision that, "the unconscious psyche must consist of inherited instincts, functions, and forms that are peculiar to the ancestral psyche"[1093], should be conceived out of the Darwininan evolutionary biological basis, and more in tune with the spiritual nature of each culture, which could be thought of as a kind of psychic code with knowing possibilities and potentialities. This has to be seen, of course, "in accordance with phylogenetic law," from which, Jung observed, "we still recapitulate in childhood reminiscences of the prehistory of race and of mankind in general"[1094].[1095]

Phylogeny might have a broader and deeper meaning, if seen beyond only physiological genetics. The word stems from two Greek words, *phulé*, that means "race," and *génos*, used in the sense of "kind" or "class"[1096]; following its etymological sense, it speaks for the differences and diversity among humans, according to their racial origin and history. This, however, is not an undervaluing and negative attitude of racism, but rather an acknowledgment of its actuality, diversity, and potential of knowing.[1097]

The idea of phylogeny aims not to enhance divisiveness and confrontations among cultures and peoples, as if one were better, or, what could be worse, chosen, but a tolerance of diversity in what seems to be a pluralistic universe.[1098] This also opens up reflections on "cultural" characteristics that are peculiar to certain ethnic groups, regardless of their actual practice of religion, modern lifestyle, epistemological certainties, and ontological premises. In this light, the black peoples' powerful and dimensional ways of knowing can be understood differently, whether it occurs in Africa, Brazil, the United States, or the Caribbean[1099]; just as some other indigenous common ways of knowledge and ways of science, particular of the many Native American tribes, and what is left of the ethnic groups that dwelled in Mesoamerica, and South America, can be appreciated and valued.[1100] This can be observed, for example, in the fascination for yoga and its *psychic hygiene*, or in Buddhism and its mental and meditational trainings aimed at *spiritual enhancement and liberation*, or in the wide range of *divination* practices among indigenous peoples, or in the many kind of *limpias* practiced throughout the Americas (particularly from Mexico to South America), or in the increasing popular interest for Kabbalah, and its *conscience attunement,* or even in the inexplicable, but much commented, shamanic *archaic techniques of ecstasy.*

Pondering these reflections, one can pair with Jung, who quite obscurely mentioned that, "[i]t does not seem to have occurred to people that when we say 'psyche' we are alluding to the densest darkness it is possible to imagine"[1101], in simpler words, to very profound visions of the dimensionalities of one's domain of being—it is not vain and superficial that Jung conceived *esse in anima*[1102], Being in Soul, one's being in the psyche, one's existence a psychic but very profound flow: a living river running deep. Therefore, he claimed quite paradoxically, "[t]he ethics of the researcher require him to admit where his knowledge comes to an end[,]" because, he might be quite right, "[t]his end is the beginning of true wisdom"[1103]. It is as if the end of one's certainties and beliefs that help sustain a fixed, concrete, material, linear, time-based, and cause-effect worldview, could be suspended, in order for a new dimension of being to be born[1104]—maybe an *übermenschliche* way of being, maybe an old way of being that happened already, in the cyclical past that is returning, as if humanity and humanness were only a stage of being that can be, and *ought to be*, transcended.[1105] Like Eliade wrote, "[i]n modern terms, we could say that this sacred knowledge no longer belongs to an ontology but to a mythical history"[1106].[1107]

When entertaining a deep and extensive view of the soul, it could be thought then, that, "[o]ur souls as well as our bodies are composed of individual elements which were present in the ranks of our ancestors"[1108]; but not only in an anatomical and genetic sense, including the phenotype and genotype, shaping one's countenance, conforming one's physical structure, and giving material actuality to some of their characteristics, but in a spiritual and ontic sense too, including the conscious and unconscious ways, shaping one's fate, coding one's destiny, conforming one's psychical terrain, and giving potential ways of knowing Earth through them—because an individual is their living continuity.

However, one might agree with Jung, in that, "[s]uch a continuity can only exist if we assume a certain unconscious condition carried on by biological inheritance"[1109]. In other words, this continuity is carried on in the body itself, in the bones, organs, nerves, teeth, blood, and fluids—because the living organism is, somehow, the depositary of a millions of years old intelligence and wisdom, as if the body were, indeed, the actuality of ancient beings and the dormant potential of their capacities.[1110] This could be the reason why Standing Bear, a Sioux Chief, when commenting on the ways of the Native Americans, said: "Men must be born and reborn to belong. Their bodies must be formed of the dust of their forefathers' bones"[1111]; as if it were an imperious necessity to reclaim one's ancestry, in order to make the best of one's inheritance, and get the best of one's spiritual legacy.

However, these insights could be quite difficult to grasp, to *know deeply*; one can easily discuss them, find them interesting, or discard them and avoid them, as if the *notion* of psychic issues were philosophical constructs (quite fashionable among post-modern thinkers), or even some kind of semiotic game with which one tries to explain things, processes, events, and life in general.[1112] But, just like Jung said: "What most people overlook or seem unable to understand is the fact that I regard the psyche as real"[1113]; and, moreover, it might be considered the basis of any knowing, the condition that allows one to know what one claims to know.

Therefore, in this sense, it seems quite correct to say that, "[t]he unconscious [psyche] is the root of all experience of oneness . . . the matrix of all archetypes or structural patterns . . . and the *conditio sine qua non* of the phenomenal world"[1114]; the way one *knows* the world is rooted in one's consciousness, but that seems to obey a cultural conscience that was planted purposively on Earth, and which has a potential of knowing that has not been yet claimed.[1115] In simpler words, the *notion* of what is a human being can change drastically if one could actualize the spiritual gifts of one's culture, which seems to be, in the most cases, unconscious, because of a terrible un-acknowledgment of one's roots—due to shame, colonization, slavery, ethnic annihilation, religious repression, political domination, financial interests, etc.[1116]

The value of these arguments, insights, and visions, in relation to ancestry is of the highest importance. It is clear that an individual's life is affected, as if immersed, in a psychic complex, which can be constellated, in order to be perceived and be seen. This psychic condition is related, on a first and primal instance, to family, especially the parents, and the ways in which one honors or dishonors them; but also to the issues related to the siblings, and one's antecessors' siblings, as well as issues with the dead, the aborted, lost souls, and excluded members—most of whose issues could be verified or speculated factually. But the psychic flow, as Jung was well aware, is connected to deeper currents, and one's consciousness is only aware of a tiny fragment of the psyche; and yet, "somewhere you are also a spirit—somewhere you have the secret of your particular pattern"[1117], the secret of your daimon, of your divinity.[1118] Therefore it seems that Heraclitus was right when he said: *ethos anthropos daimon.*[1119] Moreover, the whole doctrine of *eudaemonism*, the old Greek "system of ethics having happiness for its end"[1120], would require a new revision under the perspectives and living practices of ancestry.[1121]

However, in many people, consciousness has been framed and tinctured in certain limiting ways, according to the Zeitgeist, and, therefore, it allows some things to be perceived and some processes to be thought of as possible, while it cancels other ideas, prohibits certain images, lets other things go unnoticed, and firmly claims many processes to be blatantly impossible.[1122] Scientific discoveries sometimes become a hindrance and burden severely the individual's notion of actuality, as it is the case when a specialized physician tells a person that he or she has an incurable disease—the doctor kills the opportunity for the unexpected. But some other times, science enhances one to wonder on fantastical and almost magical ideas, dreaming of ways to achieve impossibilities, kindling the crave for the wonders of the old times—like those of the Native American medicine men[1123]. This is so because every individual's consciousness has emerged from the psychic *riverrunning,* which, in fact, relates him or her to very ancient times, where the worldviews were quite different[1124]—hence one can claim with Hughes:

I've known rivers ancient as the world and older than the

flow of human blood in veins.

My soul has grown deep like the rivers.[1125],[1126]

In other times, the ways of being and seeing allowed and elicited powerful and uncanny possibilities to occur, like healing someone who is physically far away—today people call such things miracles. In some ways, this is similar to some rarities that quantum physicists are claiming nowadays, without always being able to come close to plausible scientific explanations.

Why do people believe in, and use, telephones, televisions, telecommunications, and some other interesting gadgets? The answer is clear, because it is not a belief, but a technology, a scientific art that has arisen from the development of a specific and powerful conscience—but it is only one among other ancient consciences. It is only after having rejected other ways of knowledge for centuries that Western science has come to realize that telepathy, telekinesis, distance vision (television), teletransportation, time travel, hands-on-healing, shape-shifting, and many other quantum dreams are miraculously possible—like magic.[1127] Such powerful and prodigious acts are not possible because Westernized science has enhanced them, invented them, or imagined them as possible; it has only discovered something already old and, for other cultures, well known. However, the difference is that Westernized people often gimmick and want to show off such discoveries, while other peoples keep them secret and reserved for important spiritual practices, which can only be performed for certain purposes.

From a depth psychological view, this is deeply connected to every individual's ancestry, so to speak, to every individual's original nature, or, as it could also be thought too, to every individual's spiritual origin.[1128] In this sense, the psychic riverrunning in which one is a "conscious" notion is indeed the movement of thousands of generations that flow throughout the illusion of time, or more properly, the illusion of being in time.[1129]

Seeing this in a strictly ontological sense, one is not flowing through the river of time, as if one were moving forwards and distancing oneself from the first watery spring, but only enduring the paradox of being conscious of a moment of the riverrunning, while, in fact, one represents the original intention of the ancestor who conceived this kind of human life on Earth.[1130] Hence, when speaking of ancestry, from this view, one is not merely thinking on those humanoid antecessors that populated Earth and that some scientists argue to be the origins of all actual human cultures, consciences, and ways of consciousness, following an inevitable straight line of time in forward development and movement. The ancestral origin, in the sense presented throughout this work, is more akin to the indigenous idea of a place out of the spell of time.[1131] Therefore, what separates an Israelite from Shimon Bar Yojai and the Israelite original people, or some kinds of Mexican from Pakal and the ancient Mayans, for instance, is not the many human generations in between, but the lack of psychic technologies, the lack of a scientific art that would reconnect the individual with his or her spiritual conscience, ontological origin, and

Earthly purpose.[1132] One can be connected and attuned with the wisdom of a great ancestor. But, like Jung warned regarding these capacities, "[o]ur rationalism simply cannot understand naturally how it is possible but it does work"[1133], and all this is often denied as superstition or primitivism.[1134] Jung knew well that, "[o]ur mania for rational explanations obviously has its roots in our fear of metaphysics"[1135]; the direct consequence of such maniacal attitude is an ontological poverty of catastrophic dimensions—the actual condition of the natural world is a proof of that.

Therefore, when saying that it is of extreme importance to revive the relation with the ancestors, it is not meant in that vulgar sense of imagining the cavemen, but as a longing for a place to which one is connected, as if it were the deep hidden well—a *hypokeimene hyleg*—from which one sprang out into the river of life.[1136] After all, like Corbin inquired: "Where is the future of a river? Is it at its mouth where it begins to lose itself in the ocean, or is it rather at its source? May our human sciences not forget this"[1137],[1138] In the meantime, while one lasts and endures the movements of the psychic currents, it is one's capacity to flow and even navigate throughout what keeps one safe in order not to drown. But at the same time, paradoxically, one can say along with Jung that: "if you are in the river of life you are joyful, and are lifted up by the river"[1139], enjoying the stream of being soulful,[1140] while being indeed in the act of what Hillman called *soul-making*[1141],[1142] In such a sense, it could be rather appropriate to say that "a human life is actually a personification of the soul, a projection of it, contained by it"[1143], like an image flowing through the psychic riverrunning. In this sense, like Hillman suggested, "making soul" means "putting events through an imaginal process . . . an imaginative work"[1144]. In other words, imagining that all "[e]vents are related first and foremost to soul rather that to theology of God, science of nature, or humanistic disciplines of language, poetics, and history"[1145], as if existence were not a human whim, but a movement of the soul—psychic motion and emotion, divine influxes throughout the river of life. Like Hillman boldly and dangerously claimed: "Soul-making means dehumanizing"[1146], which should never be though of as something inhumane. Such a premise rather strives to acknowledge the need "to dehumanize, depersonalize, and demoralize the psyche in order to deepen the meaning of its human experiences beyond the measure of man"[1147],[1148] that is, realize experiences and powers beyond the human—acknowledging the numinous quality of existence.

When life and the world are seen only from the human, all-too-human, perspectives, existence becomes the narrow and petty caprice in the search for meaning, money, and minuscule pleasures, and even many philosophical explanations, based on the human as a measure (e.g. the economic, the social, the political, the moral, etc.) fall on such a spell—with all kind of delusions of grandiosity, success, prosperity, and happiness.[1149] However when life is perceived in terms of *something else*—which is not necessarily God—, incorporating a sense of *daimonic* ancestry, then it acquires a deeper notion of sense, duty, direction, purpose, identity, commitment, and, ultimately, destiny.[1150] It is as if one would not only require philosophy but *phylosophy*, and not only knowledge of physicality and genetics but the *genius* of one's genesis too—one's spiritual roots.[1151]

The main idea behind these insights can be expressed in many ways, even with Shakespearean words, saying that the world is a stage, and that it is the scenery for one's *opus*; with Hesse's imagination, conceiving life as the magic theater; or in de la Barca's view, saying that life is dream, and that dreams are just dreams.[1152] In any case, Hillman wrote something similar when he suggested that we should conceive "ourselves as metaphors and images made by soul"[1153], and through our living making-soul.[1154] These insights could shatter, for good, for all, and maybe forever, what Hillman named as "the naturalistic and humanistic fallacies . . . [which have tried] to shore up and solidify our frailty"[1155], so to speak, our fragile certainties, our weak premises, our childish beliefs, and mostly our futile and silly philosophies that have tried to make sense of death.[1156]

Nietzsche conceived that, "every philosophy may be viewed as a remedy and an aid in the service of growing and struggling life . . . presuppos[ing] suffering and sufferers." But, as he suggested, there are "those who suffer from the *over-fullness of life* . . . and then those who suffer from the *impoverishment of life*"[1157]. The first kind, he named Dionysian, the second romantics. In any case, those are only names, but what he expressed, however, is quite profound. There is a striking difference. Romantics often conceive this world as mere appearance, as an illusion, something dreamlike, and this life as transient, ephemeral, and subject to death, while striving throughout their life for some other place (salvation, Nirvana, Heaven, or any of its other names); the Dionysian kind, instead, conceive the world and life just as apparent and transient too, but aim for more of it, bravely saying: "This is a dream, I want to dream on"[1158].[1159]

Hence, Nietzsche said that such a human being "must first of all 'overcome' this time in himself . . . and consequently not only his time but also his prior aversion and contradiction *against* this time, his suffering from this time, his un-timeliness, his *romanticism*"[1160]. Hillman, who took these insights further and gave them his particular twist, argued that there is therefore the need to develop a *Dionysian consciousness,* which could be conceived as the awareness of "the divine force of living nature and the taming of that nature"[1161], which would elicit an almost overwhelming mystical experience, an ambivalent joy in spite of suffering, and a zest for life in spite of death—as if it were a happiness for existence in spite of it being a psychic flow of images that end in Hades.[1162]

Therefore, one could say, just like Rilke wrote, that, "the greatest miracle is knowing that still *all life is lived*"[1163]; but it is worth inquiring, as he sensibly asked: "Who lives really? Is it you, God?"[1164]—maybe, a lowly God, an ancestor? One might even inquire honestly, like Paz who questioned: "life, when was it really ours?"[1165], and possibly, if one were humble enough as to put the forehead on the ground and kiss the soil, feeling the mud on the palm of the hands, and not being able to lower oneself anymore, then one could conceive and describe existence like him, saying that:

never is life ours, it's of the others,

life is of nobody, are we all

life? Bread of sun for the others,

all the others that we are?

I am the other when I am, my acts

are more mine if they are of everybody,

so that I can be of another being,

getting out of me, looking myself out among the others,

the others are not if I exist not,

the others that give me full existence,

I am not, there's no I, it's always we,

life is something else, always there, further,

outside of you, of me, always horizon,

life that lives us incessantly out of ourselves,

that invents us a face and later wears it out,

hunger of being, oh death, bread of all.

Piedra de Sol[1166]

From these visions altogether, one might realize that it is not psychology as a theoretical discipline and clinical practice what *really* matters or what will provide the deep consciousness shift that might open up a multidimensional paradigm, nor all those psychological studies, researches, and jargon, not even all those clinical observations and experiments that have followed only one kind of science and conscience, and which have severely obscured perception and seriously fooled and ridiculed all other cultures, but ancestry—that *something else* which gave us countenance and lives us through, that *someone other* to which we give semblance with our resemblance.[1167]

There is a clear, yet quite profound and visionary, insight that Jung wrote in his last book, which is of course an anticipation of a systemic view of family and the trans-generational psychic flow. But, if seen under the light of the issues just presented, it takes a quite different direction; moreover, it can be an *orientation* for one's spirit.[1168] He wrote:

I became aware of the fateful links between me and my ancestors. I feel very strongly that I am under the influence of things or questions that were left incomplete and unanswered by my parents and grandparents and more distant ancestors. It often seems as if there were an impersonal karma within a family, which is passed from parents to children. It has always seemed to me that I had to answer questions which fate had posed my forefathers, and which had not yet been answered, or as if I had to complete, or perhaps continue, things which previous ages had left unfinished . . . the cause of disturbance is, therefore, not to be sought in the personal surroundings, but rather in the collective situation. Psychotherapy has taken this matter far too little into account.[1169]

These lines by Jung could be read as a clear awareness of what could be called psychogenealogy, but that would not challenge or change any ontological and spiritual premises, and, if not read along with the rest of Jung's large works, then one could easily fall into the spell and error of many family therapists, believing that all existential meaning, purpose, and identity relies on one's earthly biological predecessors and their social contexts—such would be a very cheap reading of Jung and a great misunderstanding.[1170]

The paradox is that one has to start with the family of origin and the parents or grandparents, inevitably. Jung seemed to have been well aware of this, since he wrote that, "[a]mong all possible spirits the spirits of the parents are in practice the most important; hence the universal practice of the ancestor cult"[1171]. However, this insight hides something quite powerful, not disclosed by Jung, which could shatter some Westernized certainties, beliefs, creeds, and paradigms. The ancestor cult is not an idolatry of one's earthly predecessors, or a kind of worship for those persons who lived before in one's lineage. This type of misunderstanding could jeopardize the whole ontological basis that needs to be experienced, or else render it beyond our grasp.

The issue is rather close to what Somé explained to be the Dagara cosmological view of life—which is shared too by other indigenous Africans. He mentioned that, while his father was still living, it was the presence of his long time dead grandfather the leading and protective spiritual figure with which he had contact, but once his father passed away, and got ancestralized, his own father supplanted the grandfather, and he became then the luminous connection to the spirit world, guiding, protecting, giving council, advise, instructions, and intuitions.[1172] The assumption is that if all predecessors in one's lineage have been ancestralized, then one's connection to the spirit world and its great powers and legacy, or what could be conceived the divine, are unburdened.[1173] This explains, in a way, why such cultures do not bother to pray to (an image of) God, or have intermediaries, or maintain sacred scriptures, or go around the globe preaching the "truth";[1174] they rather claim a direct and clear spiritual communication[1175] that allows them to propitiate and keep the continuity of family and community on Earth in the healthiest possible ways.[1176] Moreover, it elicits an inquiring reflection upon which some religions might call *The Father* and the *Patriarchs*.[1177] This notion could be conceived, although with careful and sensible considerations, as a kind of adoration and veneration, in their strictest etymological sense, not to be confused with their popular connotations and usage by institutionalized religions, which are often stained with purity and sanctity. Adoration, stems from the Latin *ad* and *ōrāre*, and implies *to speak to*, in the sense of "expressing divine honors"[1178], while veneration, that stems from the Latin *venerāri*, implies "worthy of being revered," and is cognate to reverence[1179]—not far at all from bowing as a gesture and posture for showing deep respect and giving due honor.[1180] Even the action of prayer would be tinctured by a different hue and it would become extremely personal and genuine; and it would be closer, in some way, to its etymological root, the Latin *precāri,* that means entreat[1181]. To entreat, in the sense of "imploring," stems from "treat" and means to "deal *with*"[1182]. Hence, when praying to the ancestors, one implores them to treat some issues, one asks them to deal with things that are much greater, too difficult, painful, or simply overwhelming and problematic; and one beseeches them to be present while one also requests for their help, vision, and guidance. From this view, praying is not merely repeating a given set of so-called sacred sentences like a parrot—even if those are in ancient languages. A prayer is a very specific petition that will *draw*[1183] into this world a powerful intervention from the realm of the ancestors—an otherworldly force that will bring assistance and solutions to issues with which one struggles. Praying in this sense is not only helpful but also humbling; it is even an act of intimacy.[1184] It brings the ancestors—and their blessings—into one's life. However, praying is not merely a petition from a disempowered place, it is rather a demand that requests their intervention.[1185] One only needs to invoke them, give them a place, see their face, and feel their gaze—even if one never met them in life and if one has no photos of them.[1186] Therefore, one could claim along with Rilke:

Then there's room for another face

for a light that's never been there before,

and your story begins anew...[1187],[1188]

Therefore, a deeper understanding of Jung's psychological vision and *Weltanschauung* (worldview) would necessarily have to consider what he referred, in his personal private life, as "the old man" or "the ancient," who he experienced since a child as "personality No.2"[1189],[1190] and which indeed is similar to the notion of *the ancestor*—the Great Man.[1191] Maybe one can pray along with Rilke, who wrote:

You are the Ancient One, whose hair

is marred by soot and signed by flame;

you are the utmost indistinct;

you are the blacksmith, song of years,

who by his anvil stands...[1192],[1193]

One might possibly understand why it is that Jung wrote, in his *Red Book*: "*He who sleeps in the grave of millennia dreams a wonderful dream*"[1194]. Hence, close to the end of his life, when he answered about what to do with the chthonic and instinctual nature in man, he advised his students saying: "Go to bed. Think of your problems. See what you dream. Perhaps the two million-year-old-man will speak . . . . [he] may know something"[1195]. And if you do not know him, be solid-rock certain that *he knows you*. A last story, titled *Feathered Serpent*, will illustrate these insights:

A young man, desperate for acquiring knowledge, started a journey to foreign lands, where he aimed to learn the secret of life. He traveled to the Yellow Land, and he began to learn the yellowesque language and its customs. Some parts of his body became stained with yellow, but he realized that his nature was not compatible with the original Yellowness. He decided to keep searching, and traveled to the Red Land, where he immediately started the learning of the Red language and its practices. His body also acquired some red stains, but after a while, he realized how absurd it is to follow the Red lifestyle, so incompatible with him. He moved on and visited the Blue Land, thinking that with mixture of the Yellow and the Red with the Blue he could attain the promised White. He learned also all the Blueness that he could, but he failed too, and went back home. Once there, desperate again, he took a smoked mirror and looked at his face. He cried. That moment he decided to visit an old magician. He waited for the new Moon night and full of doubt walked through the forest all the way to the top of the mountain, where the old man was already waiting for him. As he arrived, the old man smiled, and gestured him to keep quiet and to sit. The old man said that he would sing a very old story, which could only be sang at a pitch black night, when colors do not matter and do not distract one's attention. Before beginning he told him: "First and foremost, remember that 'this tale is true and formative.' Then, while looking towards the dark night, he sang:

"Once, there was a Falcon, a beautiful, strong, and majestic Falcon that flew through the air at the speed of thought. It was perceived to be always here and there, but had never actually existed, grown, or aged. The Falcon was, in a way, an eternal presence, and never disappeared, for it was, as if, everywhere and nowhere at once. All one had to do was call for it and it would arrive with the immediacy of one's thought, for it had been always here and everywhere, within the invisible. In its ingenuity, the Falcon did not know good or evil; to it there was no difference, and it did not matter. It simply acted spontaneously, which was why sometimes it incurred in irreparable acts. It did not care

about anything, for it escaped morality by acting purely at will, never becoming compromised. All it cared about was obtaining more power; every one of its acts was done because it gave it greater power in allowing it the freedom of choosing it, and with every one of these acts its wings became stronger and their feathers brighter. The more power it obtained the faster it became, and this allowed it to be as if everywhere and nowhere at once, for like thought itself it was always here, now, and it was never noticed until it was asked to stop, otherwise it was only motion, creating itself. The Falcon enjoyed playing and going into strange places. When it had not been summoned it flew wherever its whim took it; and it was while traveling through the infinity of the imaginable that it unexpectedly met the Black Serpent.

"The Serpent had scaled skin whose color was impossible to define, as it reflected that with which it is associated at the moment in which it was seen. This was why sometimes it was hard to tell what color it was. Some referred to it simply as iridescent, while others said it was in fact black, absent of all color and that it only filtered the light, which made it looked colored. There were long discussions trying to define it. But there was no possible way to do so, for these were all vague beliefs that were justified by the judgment passed on her transitory appearance, which was always determined and limited by the interpretation of what was at that moment perceived. Like her gleaming and alluring skin, her eyes were seductive and hypnotizing, and whoever looked directly at them was consumed by desire to possess her. It had been said that whoever fed on her would obtain profound understanding, and although it was still unknown what kind, it is assumed that it is an understanding of the entire universe and all things created, so that true and eternal knowledge would be thus obtained.

"In her allure and permanent seduction, the Serpent was constantly pursued, for whoever laid his eyes upon her tried by all means to capture her, and in order to defend herself she would bit with a pair of fangs, sinking them deep into their body while she injected them with the spell of truth, which lulled her pursuers in a sea of imaginings, a play of words that is the poison of wisdom. It was said, that he who had been poisoned by the Serpent believed to have eaten her and to carry her powerful knowledge in his veins.

"The Falcon, however, knew little about her, and as soon as it saw her it was desperate to hunt her, aiming to eat her. It was irrepressibly fascinated, it watched her, and it could not keep its eyes off her. It observed her carefully, followed her stealthily, and suddenly hunted her with the total desire for her flesh. Once it had her twisting and writhing in its mouth, it tasted the enchanting flavor of an unknown pleasure, something not yet known by it, and it pressed its strong beak around her to prevent her from getting away while it immersed itself in the feeling of an unexplainable doubt. However, the desire was already too strong and it ate her, devouring her completely, and it felt satisfied about it.

Strangely, the Falcon felt too a new desire, something it had not experienced until then: the desire to sleep.

"The Falcon, ever-present in the eternal flow of its insatiable will, fell under the desire to dream, generated by the ingestion of the Serpent's flesh. It laid down—it was all he wanted at such a moment—and closed its eyes for the first time," and the old man closed his eyes too, smiled, took a deep breath, and made a long pause.

Then, the magician explained the young man that such story would open his awareness towards something else, but he said nothing more. The old man said, before walking away, that it was already quite late in such a dark and silent hour, close to midnight, and told him to stay until the sun appeared.

The young man piled up some leaves to make a kind of bed, laid watching the stars, and not long after closed his eyes and fell in a deep dream. As he dreamt, he became aware of his sleep, and he realized that the Falcon, during its deep sleep, had dreamed of him, the human being, but he realized that the Serpent was also the dream of the Falcon, who, in its dreaming, saw a black Serpent that it hunted and devoured, and which produced the whole story of the Falcon itself—like a dream within the dream, out from which he appeared as human. However, as he became conscious of him being the Falcon and his whole human historical past as only the dream-effect of having devoured the Serpent, he also noticed that even the possibility of having seen the Serpent, was because, as a Falcon, it was already dreaming, as if it would have been dreaming of its own origin, dreaming of a beginning, when in fact there had been none; there had been no separation, no distinction. He was the man, his father and his mother, his predecessors, and all his imaginable human lineages, and yet the Falcon, and the Serpent, and none of them.

The Last Word for This Opus

"His destiny was to be elusive of social or religious orders. The wisdom of the priest's appeal did not touch him to the quick. He was destined to learn his own wisdom apart from others or to learn the wisdom of others himself wandering among the snares of the world."

A portrait of the artist as a young man[1196]

Jung, in 1907, while still a young man, professionally speaking, wrote the essay titled: *The feeling-tone complex and its general effect on the psyche*[1197], which became a foundational notion and structuring image for his further observations and praxis— although it is not considered one of his major works. Its importance might not rely on the wording of the essay and the discourse itself, but in the deep psychological vision that it opened. He knew that it was only the beginning of something that he would develop further, and it seems too that he knew that he would not even live to see it complete—and he confirmed that in 1934, when he mentioned, in the review, that *The Complex Theory* still awaited discussion. In the same sense, this work on ancestry is very far from complete, it is only a beginning; moreover, it is only an *opusculum* (a small work) that lacks solid arguments as a conclusion. I can even say safely, along with Jung, that, "I have made it easy for the critics: my work has many weak spots and gaps, for which I crave the reader indulgence . . . Somebody, after all, had to take it on himself to start the ball rolling"[1198].

When I was repeatedly asked by professors, colleagues, and people in general, why was I writing on ancestry, the answer was always clear: "There are few writings about it, if anything at all, from a perspective considering an extended and multidimensional notion of soul." Therefore, the contribution of this work seems quite obvious in a first instance, it is not anything new or anything not-yet-said, but something not yet integrated in this way. However, it does not aim to be one more work in psychology, whether in the domain of Jungian, Archetypal, or Depth Psychology, but a beginning in the studies, visions, *knowings,* and practices of *Ancestry.* I am offering no fixed conclusions, but a starting point. Hence I claim and suggest, just as Hillman did long ago, when young too, that, "[i]nstead of explanatory hypothesis being treated with the *maximum* skepticism when they are new, and the *minumum* when they are *old,* a reversal of this policy might be profitable"[1199].

The aim of this work was clear since the beginning, the introduction; it wanted to open reflections regarding the main inquiry: "how are we living in relation to our ancestry?" Everybody has antecessors, and everybody has ancestors, but not everybody acknowledges them, nor their impact, influence, and importance. Rather than fixed conclusions about how one is affected or not, influenced or not influenced by them, this work aimed to elicit more inquiries, insisting on the importance of every individual's way of being, and one's individual ways of loving and relating—which are often in regard to the invisible ancestors. This insistence, of course, requires an attitude of supreme humility, because one is nothing without them, and an attitude of magnified responsibility, because one has to do something with what they left—whether one *feels* that it was very little, or very much. If, for example, someone is born with a great inheritance, not just in terms of money and properties, but also in regard to health, education, relationships, and so on, the question is: What will he or she do to transform such heir into blessings? Socrates was right, when he said: "to a man who has any self-respect, nothing is more dishonorable than to be honored, not for his own sake, but on account of the reputation of his ancestors"[1200].[1201]

The insights and theories of Jung, who was a visionary physician and an alienist,[1202] but also considered an alchemist and a Gnostic,[1203] along with the imaginings of Hillman, who was a great scholar, a neoplatonist philosopher, and a radical re-visionist, along with the sharp observations and practical work by Hellinger, who was for a time a priest, but who is also a great, if not the greatest, therapist, and ultimately a mystic,[1204] along with the comprehensions and understandings of Somé, who is a tribal elder, diviner, and shaman, weave the colorful worldview —as if it were a mythic magical mat woven to aim for the impossible. Actually, the word *complex*—which was the leading psychological notion of the work—stems from the Latin *complexus*, composed of the prefix *com*, that means "with," and *plexus*, that means "woven"[1205].

The obvious theme of this work was ancestry, but it engaged other important topics—quite relevant for a practical deepening into its nuances. In this sense, one could say that the first chapter was not only about the psychic complex, but also about consciousness, perception, attention, affectivity, and their role in human relationships. The second chapter weaved the Complex Theory with the Constellations work, but also the value of a phenomenological approach in order to broaden experiences beyond the known, the factual, and the chronological, aiming to open a multidimensional awareness. The third chapter delved into the body, but also into the process of healing, the somatized unconscious, and some reflections on the ideas of disease, health, and medicine. Hence, the fourth chapter, mainly about homeopathic medicine, presented a holistic approach, a practice of healing, and some insights about the psychic inheritance that runs through the biological embodiment. The fifth chapter, which was about the family per se, implied the affections generated by human interaction, interrelation, and interdependence through the notion of what has been called the "community of fate."

The sixth chapter was mostly about honor to the parents, and I cannot raise my voice enough in order to exclaim its groundbreaking importance. Honor is not something that one can pretend to achieve, it is not possible to fake it; either one genuinely feels it in one's body or it is something feigned. Hence, the chapter also involved a specific notion of religiosity and acquaintance with the numinous as a direct outcome of having bowed in reverence towards one's progenitors.

The seventh chapter was a brief note on insanity and psychoses, but also a suggestion for a new way for addressing disturbances that are powerfully psychoactive, but unconscious, systemic, and transgenerational in spite of seeming personal. The eighth chapter, which was about the dead, aimed to open reflections on death rites, rituals, suicide, and murdering, but pointed to a wider view of life, in which the ways of being, the ways of knowing, and the ways of doing virtually anything could be radically enriched. The ninth chapter presented a fourfold idea of destiny, engaging the notion of familial loyalty, conscience, and blood, but it also implied a personal, transpersonal, and yet trans-human notion of spirituality, rescuing the power and value of imagination, the importance and awareness of the imaginal realm, and hinted the notion of gift and purpose. The tenth chapter offered finally an image of soul and its dynamism, but it also invited reflections on philosophical inquiries regarding the human phenomenon and the diversity of its potential ways of science, knowledge, and divinity. In any case, all these ideas, images, and insights, followed Rumi's lines from his poem *Of being woven*, saying: "Rushes and reeds must be woven/ to be useful as a mat. If they weren't interlaced,/ the wind would blow them away"[1206].

I would say, following Jung, that "[m]uch has still to be learned about the psyche, and our especial need today is liberation from outworn ideas which have seriously restricted our view of the psyche as a whole"[1207]. Therefore, it would be a grave error to conceive it as a mere written work on psychology, or even worse, on psychotherapy. The first has been too broad, too Westernized, too scientific, too sophisticated, with excessive rhetoric, and in the majority of cases, without psyche; the second has been, mostly, an offspring of the first; and not one of them seems to have addressed any insight regarding ancestry beyond the biological or familial genealogy.[1208] Jung, claimed critically: "Psychotherapy today, it seems to me, still has a vast amount to unlearn and relearn if it is to do even rough justice to its subject, the full range of the human psyche"[1209]; and more than half a century later this is still the case. However, this is not a written work in Constellations either; nor this is a work only about an African perspective, and even less is this an anthropological or autoethnographic account.[1210] More so, it is not a work on ancientry, as if it were only a research and study of the ways "of times long past" (*ante-ānus*), like the etymology of the word suggests[1211], but a remembrance of those who came, walked, passed on life, and left (*ante-cedere*)—the ancestors.

Romanyshyn, a clinical psychologist and, once upon a time, one of those close collaborators of Hillman, humbly acknowledged that, "[m]aybe psychology needs a quantum revolution analogous to the one in physics which moved that discipline beyond its Newtonian phase"[1212]; I would say, one which can move psychology beyond behaviorism, social categories, humanism, and clinical standards altogether, but also beyond personalism and the huge egotistical notion of the "me," beyond only conceiving the physical world as real, beyond the dualistic categories of inside-outside, external-internal, you-me, and beyond the splits between matter and spirit, man and the world, humanity and the divine.[1213] This work, in such a sense, could be considered an acknowledgement of that which is yet to come, which Romanyshyn foresaw as "a discipline in service to soul beyond psychology . . . a way of knowing and being that is yet to be"[1214],[1215], and mostly a way of loving that will elicit a kind of *invincible happiness* and *victorious joy* that have not been imagined yet.[1216]

The best way to conceive this work would be as a proposal for the participative enhancement of a practical study, practical vision, and practical knowing of the dimensionalities of ancestry. This is so, because, from the perspectives presented, our human reality could be conceived as an *ancestreality*—a word compound of ancestry and reality, both unfathomable, both mysterious, both arcane, and both conforming actually the same thing: this world; but potentially, an old world that is coming, and to which we are re-turning. Hence, it is not only one's sophistry and intellect that is compromised when studying this "topic," but one's essential ways of dwelling and walking on Earth, as well as one's ways of loving, lasting, and leaving, which directly influence, impact, and are important for, health, relationships, environment, prosperity, happiness, and well-being—individually and in community.[1217]

Moreover, I began by saying that it was going to seem like a work of hermeneutics, but that it was going to be, properly speaking, a *psychologizing*, which means a re-vision of ancestry seen through psyche. But it was only till the last chapter that psyche got poetically described—not exactly defined.[1218] Therefore, if the way I presented this work was not always clear and straight, is because just by the end did it come full circle, almost inviting the reader to begin with the end; hence, I would ask you, like Rumi once did, to "excuse my wandering," because indeed, "[s]ometimes organization/ and computation become absurd"[1219]. In addition, if I incurred in repeating certain issues or in being overly redundant, I pledge consideration, like Socrates, "for they say that it is good to repeat and examine twice and once again what is good"[1220],[1221]. More so, if the text is ambiguous, and allows different perspectives, it is not in all cases a mistake or a failure, but an asset; even though, like Thoreau mentioned a while ago, "in this part of the world it is considered a ground for complaint if a man's writing admit of more than one interpretation"[1222].

Ultimately, the deepening into the notion of ancestry is not for the sake of it being just interesting, as if it were the work of a meticulous historian investigating the remote past; it is not either for the sake of documenting exotic anthropological practices, as if they were sacred relics; it is not either for the sake of understanding other communities and human populations, as if it were a cross-cultural sociological research; definitely not as one more academic philosophy study, aiming hopelessly for scholar recognition and elegant rhetoric; it is genuinely and humbly for the sake of affirming and maintaining the rich diversity of life in well-being, aiming to enhance the notions of *deep* community and compassion. It is a profound "yes" to existence, aiming also to keep the continuity of what was once planted on Earth, making the forest of life grow stronger, taller, healthier, wiser, more fruitful, and more abundant.

The time seems fertile, and humanity ripe enough, for the prophetic motto to be powerfully actualized in every region of Earth, so that every individual can acknowledge and claim: "*por mi raza hablará el espíritu*[1223]"—without feeling inferior, un-chosen, cursed, worse, denigrated, or feeling obliged or in the need to embrace someone else's cult.[1224] The word cult, in fact, stems from the Latin *cultus*, in the sense of worship, devotion, or homage, and it is cognate with culture and cultivate[1225]—as if conscience and human existence would have not been just dreadfully thrown *in-the-world*, but deliberately, intentionally, purposively, meaningfully, and spiritually *planted on Earth.*[1226] It is of utter importance to realize that, "for archaic societies, culture is not a human product, its origin is supernatural"[1227].

A brief story, titled *Quechelah,* will give the last word to this work. (*Quechelah* is a Mayan word for forest.)[1228]

On a mild spring day with clear sunlight and cool wind, a man and a woman, who were in love with each other, went for a walk in the forest. It was the first time that they were in that region of such a land. Both were foreigners, and therefore unfamiliar to the place, but both found it astounding. None of them had seen that variety of trees in such splendor, but there was a special kind of tree to which they were very attracted to, as if those trees were moving, and seeing them and calling them in an almost human way. The whole forest was enchanting, and the more they were walking into it, the more their fascination for these trees grew. Somehow, they felt that these trees were akin to them, as if they could speak to and converse with them, but they had never done such a thing before, and it would have felt rare and even clumsy and clownish to do something uncertain and rare.

As they walked more through it, the man became quite sure that he could just talk to such beings, those trees that seemed like people. He stepped a little away from the woman and he got close to a tree and spoke to it. The tree, at first, did not answer, but the man felt a noticeable change in his perception, and suddenly, as he turned around to see where the woman was, he could feel that the trees were indeed like people, although quite big. Actually they were more like giants. He was seeing them in a tree-like form, but he was feeling them as people. So, he talked to the tree again, and he felt quite certain that the tree said something, but he did not hear anything. Somehow, it was as if he had comprehended the tree but without having heard any spoken word or sound. He looked to the treetop, stepped back a bit, and smiled to it. Then, he went towards the woman, but did not say anything.

However, his vision of the trees and the forest had changed. They did not appear to him as woody and leafy green things, but as powerful wise people in a movement that was so slow and solemn that it was difficult to notice any motion. The woman saw his great astonishment in his face, and she asked what had happened, and why was he in such weird state, but the man, unable to explain rationally, simply said smilingly that the trees were talking to him. The woman, of course, laughed at him, and demanded to know what was the real reason of his secret enjoyment. He repeated his reason, but this time he said it seriously and with a quite peaceful tone of voice. The woman looked at him and said nothing at first, then, she looked towards some big trees that the man was looking at, and turned back to the man and asked how was he doing it. He simply said that it was a matter of listening to them. She grabbed his left hand, and they both glanced the living forest.

They sat, and for a while they contemplated some huge trees. They did not utter a single word. The air felt full and fiery, the presence of the trees occupied the whole forest, and even the rock where they sat felt like a living entity. They enjoyed the fullness of silence, and perceived the unfathomable dimension that was open in such a place, among the trees, as if ancient times, old times, recent times, and even times to come were converging in that present moment. They breathed eternity, listened infinity, and glimpsed the end of space when they laid their backs to the trunk of a tree. As they did this they felt embraced, but not by the tree, but by something flowing through the tree that was felt whole, holy, powerful, almost other-worldly, and yet watery and earthly. They somehow acknowledged that the saying, that everything was connected or interdependent was quite wrong, because in fact everything that they could see was the forest, and nothing else. And yet it was also felt as the presence and wisdom *of every single tree. They somehow knew that the unending light of the universe was emanating from that spot in the forest.*

They did not know, but such a tree, where they were lying, was a very old Sequoia that was rooted deep down in the earth and with a tall, leafy top where many kinds of birds nested, and whose singing made the tree grow taller, wider, and greener. This was so because the birds and their songs, and even the worms, insects, weed, and all other beings, were merely extensions of the trees, and all the trees together were the living forest: Quechelah. Without them knowing rationally, the tree blessed them; and suddenly they looked at each other and smiled without any reason or knowing why. The time they spent sit on the ground and lying by the tree, listening to the songs of the birds, and imagining the unfolding of their lives together as man and woman with a lineage of uncountable generations of descendants, was later thought to have been a little while, as if only a brief moment, but it had been indeed—infinite.

List of References

Abram, D. (1995). The ecology of magic. In Roszak, T., Gomes, M.E., & Kanner, A.D., (Eds.). *Ecopsychology: Restoring the Earth, healing the mind*. New York, NY: Sierra Club Books.

Addas, C. (1993). *Quest for the red sulphur*. In P. Kingsley (Trans.). Chicago, IL: Independent Publishers Group. (Original work published 1989)

Aizenstat, S. (2009). *Dreamtending*. New Orleans, LA: Spring Journal Books.

Arden, N. (1996). *African spirit speaks: A white woman's journey into the healing tradition of the sangoma*. Rochester, VT: Destiny Books.

Ariès, P. (2007). *Morir en Occidente: Desde la Edad Media hasta nuestros días*. In V. Goldstein (Trans.). Buenos Aires: Adriana Hidalgo. (Original work published in 1975)

Barnes, J. (Ed.). (2001). *Early Greek philosophy*. In J. Barnes (Trans.). London, England: Penguin Books.

Bateson, G. & Ruesch, J. (2009). *Communication: The social matrix of psychiatry*. New Brunswick, NJ: Transaction Publishers. (Original work published in 1951)

Berg, M. (Ed.). (2001). *The zohar* (Vols. 1-23). In M. Berg (Trans.). New York, NY: The Kabbalah Centre International Inc.

Berg, M. (2010). Chukat, *The Kabbalah Centre*, https://kabbalah.com/en/online-courses/lessons/3627-chukat-disconnecting-from-darkness-creating-miracles/

Berg, M. (2011). Korach, *The Kabbalah Centre*, https://kabbalah.com/en/online-courses/lessons/5312-korach-the-beauty-of-korachs-idea/

Berg, M. (2012). Emor, *The Kabbalah Centre*, https://kabbalah.com/en/online-courses/lessons/3793-emor-limitations-are-an-illusion/

Berg, M. (2013). Tzav, *The Kabbalah Centre*, https://kabbalah.com/en/online-courses/lessons/3833-tzav-structuring-our-souls-journey/

Berg, M. (2014). Metzora, *The Kabbalah Centre,* https://kabbalah.com/en/online-courses/lessons/5858-metzora-elevating-sparks-of-light/

Berg, M. (2014b). Shmini, *The Kabbalah Centre,* https://kabbalah.com/en/online-courses/lessons/6284-shmini-love-and-appreciation/

Berg, M. (2016). Metzora, *The Kabbalah Centre,* https://kabbalah.com/en/online-courses/lessons/6712-metzora-removing-the-effects-of-evil-speech/

Berg, M. (2017). Korach, *The Kabbalah Centre,* https://kabbalah.com/en/online-courses/lessons/7288-korach-humility-in-thought-and-action/

Berg, P.S. (1986). *Iniciación a la Cabalá: Una guía a la conciencia cósmica.* In M. Yanai, (Trans.). U.S.A.: Imprenta del centro de investigación de la Cabalá.

Berg, P.S. (1989). *La conexión astral: La ciencia de la astrología judáica.* New York, NY: Centro de Investigación de la Cabalá. (Original work published in 1986)

Berg, P.S. (2005). *Days of power: Part one.* New York, NY: Kabbalah Centre International.

Berg, P.S. (2006). *Days of power: Part two.* New York, NY: Kabbalah Centre International.

Black Elk, W. & Lyon, W.S. (1990). *Black Elk: The sacred ways of a Lakota.* New York, NY: Harper One.

Bly, R., Hillman, J., & Meade, M. (Eds.). (1992). *The rag and bone shop of the heart: A poetry anthology.* New York, NY: Harper Perennial.

Boszomrenyi-Nagy, I. & Spark, G.M. (2012). *Lealtades invisibles: Reciprocidad en terapia familiar integeneracional.* In I. Pardal, (Trans.). Buenos Aires, Argentina: Amorrortu. (Original work published 1973)

Budnik, D. & Johnson, S. (1994). *The book of elders: The life stories & wisdom of great American Indians.* New York, NY: Harper Collins.

Bührman, V. (1984). *Living in two worlds.* Cape Town, South Africa: Human & Rousseau.

Carpa, F. (1975). *The Tao of physics.* NY: Bantam Books, Inc.

Casement, A. & Tacey, D. (Eds.). (2006). *The idea of the numinous: Contemporary Jungian and psychoanalytic perspectives.* New York, NY: Routledge.

Casey, E.S. (1985). Reflections on ritual. In *Spring 1985: An annual of Archetypal Psychology and Jungian thought.* Dallas, TX: Spring Publications.

Casey, E.S. (2004). *Spirit and Soul: Essays in philosophical psychology.* Putnam, CT: Spring Publications.

Castaneda, C. (1999). *El lado activo del infinito.* In B. Scott (Trans.). Barcelona, España: Ediciones B.

Castaneda, C. (2000). *Las enseñanzas de Don Juan: Una forma yaqui de conocimiento.* In J. Tovar (Trans.). México D.F.: Fondo de Cultura Económica. (Original work published in 1968)

Changaris, M. (2015). *Touch: The neurobiology of health, healing and human connection.* Mendocino, CA: LifeRhythm

Corbin, H. (1972). Mundus Imaginalis or the imaginary and the imaginal. In R. Hornie (Trans.). *Spring Journal,* pp. 1-19. Zürich: Spring Journal.

Corbin, H. (1975). The imago templis and secular norms. In *Spring 1975: An annual of archetypal psychology and Jungian thought.* New York, NY: Spring Publications.

Corbin, H. (1980). Eyes of flesh eyes of fire: Science and gnosis. *Material for thought 8,* pp.5-10. San Francisco, CA: Far West institute.

Corbin, H. (1981). *The concept of comparative philosophy.* In P. Russel (Trans.). Ipswich, England: Golgonooza Press.

Corbin, H. (1983). *Cyclical Time and Ismaili Gnosis.* (R. Manheim & J.W. Morris, Trans.). In H. Landolt (Ed.). London, England: Kegan Paul International & Islamic Publications.

Corbin, H. (1987). The theory of visionary knowledge in Islamic philosophy. In. L. Sherrard (Trans.). *Temenos 8.* Ashford, Kent: Temenos Academy Review.

Corbin, H. (1994). *Man of light in Iranian Sufism* (N. Pearson, Trans.). New Lebanon, NY: Omega Publications. (Original work published in 1972).

Corbin, H. (1998). *Alone with the alone: Creative imagination in the Sufism of Ibn 'Arabī* (H. Bloom, Trans.). Princeton, NJ: Princeton University Press. (Original work published in 1969).

Corbin, H. (1998). *The voyage and the messenger: Iran and philosophy* (J. Rowe, Trans.). Berkeley, CA: North Atlantic Books. (Original work published in 1990).

Dalai Lama, The. (1999). *Ethics for the new millennium.* New York, NY: Riverhead Books.

Dalai Lama, The. (2005). *The universe in a single atom.* New York, NY: Broadway Books.

Dalai Lama, The. (2005b). *Essence of the heart sutra* (G. Thupten Jimpa, Trans.). Boston, MA: Wisdom Publications.

Damasio, A. (1999). *The Feeling of what happens: Body and emotion in the making of consciousness.* New York, NY: Harcourt Inc.

Deloria Jr., Vine. (2002). *Evolution, creationism, and other modern myths: A critical inquiry.* Golden, CO: Fulcrum Publishing.

Deloria, Jr., Vine. (2003). *God is red: A native view of religion.* Golden, CO: Fulcrum Publishing.

Deloria Jr., Vine. (2006). *The world we use to live in: Remembering the powers of the medicine men.* Golden, CO: Fulcrum Publishing.

Deloria Jr., Vine. (2009). *C.G. Jung and the Sioux traditions: Dreams, visions, nature, and the primitive.* New Orleans, LA: Spring Journal.

Deren, M. (1983). *Divine horsemen: The living gods of Haiti.* Kingston, NY: McPherson & Company. (Original work published 1953)

Diathesis. (n.d.). *Oxford dictionaries.* Retrieved, November 24th, 2010, from: http://oxforddictionaries.com/view/entry/m_en_us1240143#m_en_us1240143

Dodds, E.R. (1951). *The Greeks and the irrational.* Berkeley, CA: University of California Press.

Durand, G. (1976). The image of man in the occulted tradition of Western culture. In *Spring 1976: An annual of archetypal psychology and Jungian thought.* New York, NY: Spring Publications.

Duress. (n.d.). *Oxford dictionaries.* Retrieved, November 8th, 2010, from: http://oxforddictionaries.com/view/entry/m_en_us1242565#m_en_us1242565

Eliade, M. (1973). *Australian religions: An introduction.* Ithaca, NY: Cornell Universty.

Eliade, M. (2005). *Rites and symbols of initiation: The mysteries of birth and rebirth.* (W.R. Task, Trans.). Putnam, CT: Spring Publications. (Original work published in 1958)

Ellenberger, H.F. (1970). *The discovery of the unconscious: The history and evolution of dynamic psychiatry.* USA: Basic Books.

Franke-Gricksch, M. (2006). *Eres uno de nosotros: Miradas y soluciones sistémicas para docentes, alumnos y padres.* Buenos Aires: Alma Lepik (Original work published in 2002)

Gendlin, E. (1978). *Focusing.* New York, NY: Bantam Books.

Giegerich, W. (1998). Is the soul "deep?": Entering and following the logical movement of Heraclitus' "fragment 45." In *Spring 64: The journal of archetype and culture.* Putnam, CT: Spring Journal.

Gieser, S. (2005). *The innermost kernel: Depth psychology and quantum physics. Wolfgang Pauli's dialogue with C.G. Jung.* Germany: Springer.

Grinberg-Zylberbaum, J. (1994). *Curaciones chamánicas: Pachita, el milagro de México.* Madrid, España: Editorial América Ibérica.

Grinberg-Zylberbaum, J. (n.d.). Misticismo indígena. In *Los chamanes de México* (Vol. 2). México: Alpa Corral-Henri C. Bergonzi B.

Guggenbühl-Craig, A. (1980). *The emptied soul: On the nature of the psychopath.* Putnam, Connecticut, USA: Spring.

Guggenbühl-Craig. A. (1995). *From the wrong side: A paradoxical approach to psychology.* In G.V. Hartman (Ed.). (G.V. Hartman, Trans.). Woodstock, CT: Spring Publications.

Hafiz. (2003). *The subject tonight is love: 60 Wild and sweet poems of Hafiz* (In D. Landinsky, Trans.). New York, NY: Penguin Compass.

Hafiz. (2006). *I heard God laughing: Poems of hope and joy, renderings of Hafiz* (In D. Landinsky, Trans.). New York, NY: Penguin Books.

Hahnemann, S. (2009). *Organon of medicine.* (R.E. Dudgeon, Trans.). USA: Merchant Books. (Original work published in 1833)

Hahnemann, S. (2014). *The chronic diseases, their specific nature and their homeopathic treatment.* (Ch.J. Hempel, Trans.). USA: Michigan Historical Reprint Series. (Original work published in 1845)

Hamer, R.G. (2005). *Resumen de la nueva medicina: La nueva medicina germánica* (A. Pena, Trans.). Málaga, España: Ediciones de la Nueva Medicina. (Original work published in 1994)

Hausner, S. (2009). *Aunque me cueste le vida: Constelaciones sistémicas en casos de enfermedades y síntomas crónicos* (R. Steudel, Trans.). Buenos Aires: Alma Lepik. (Original work published in 2008)

Heidegger, M. (1962). *Being and time* (J. Macquarrie & E. Robinson, Trans.). New York, NY: Harper Perennial. (Original work published in 1926)

Hellinger, B. & ten Hövel, G. (1999). *Acknowledging what is: Conversations with Bert Hellinger* (C. Beaumont, Trans.). Phoenix, AZ: Zeig, Tucker & Co.

Hellinger, B. (2001). *Órdenes del amor: Cursos seleccionados de Bert Hellinger* (S. Gomez-Pedra, Trans.). Barcelona: Herder. (Original work published in 2000)

Hellinger, B. (2001b). *Religión, psicoterapia y cura de almas: Textos recopilados* (S. Kabelka, Trans.). Barcelona: Herder. (Original work published in 2000)

Hellinger, B. (2001c). *Supporting love: How love works in couple relationships.* In J. Neuhauser (Ed.), (C. Beaumont, Trans.). Phoenix, AZ: Zeig, Tucker & Theisen, Inc.

Hellinger, B. (2002). *El centro se distingue por su levedad* (S. Gómez Pedra, Trans.). Barcelona: Herder. (Original work published in 1996)

Hellinger, B. (2002b). *On life and other paradoxes: Aphorisms and other stories by Bert Hellinger* (R. Metzner, Trans.). Phoenix, AZ: Zeig, Tucker & Theisen Inc.

Hellinger, B. (2003). *Growth takes root in a past laid to rest: Bert Hellinger teaching seminars on soul work* (5 DVD set), by www.HellingerDC.com

Hellinger, B. (2003). *Farewell: Family constellations with descendants of victims and perpetrators* (C. Beaumont, Trans.). Heidelberg: Carl-Auer-Systeme Verlag. (Original work published in 1998).

Hellinger, B. (2006). *Los órdenes de la ayuda* (S. Kabelka, Trans.). Buenos Aires: Alma Lepik. (Original work published in 2003)

Hellinger, B. (2007). *Family constellations and their contribution to health: Bert and Sophie Hellinger teaching seminars on soul work* (4 DVD set), by www.HellingerDC.com

Hellinger, B. (2007). *La paz inicia en el alma* (V. Bassini, Trans.). México: Herder. (Original work published in 2003)

Hellinger, B. (2007). *Raquel solloza por sus hijos* (V. Bassini, Trans.). México: Herder. (Original work published in 2006)

Hellinger, B. (2007d). *Viajes interiores.* (P. Behrens-Dacak, E. Behrens-Dacak, et.al. Trans.). Buenos Aires, Argentina: Alma Lepik (Original work published in 2007)

Hellinger, B. (2008). *El manantial no tiene que preguntar por el camino.* (R. Steudel, Trans.). Buenos Aires, Argentina: Alma Lepik. (Original work published in 2001)

Hellinger, B. (2008b). *La verdad en movimiento* (R. Steudel, Trans.). Buenos Aires, Argentina: Alma Lepik. (Original work published in 2005)

Hellinger, B. (2008c). *Mística cotidiana* (P. Behrens-Dacak, E. Behrens-Dacak, et.al. Trans.). Buenos Aires, Argentina: Alma Lepik. (Original work published in 2008).

Hellinger, B. (2009). *El amor del espíritu: Un estado del ser* (U. Stutz, Trans.). Barcelona: Rigden-Institut Gestalt. (Original work published in 2008)

Hellinger, B. (2009b). *Success in life success in business: How they succeed together* (A. Schenk, Trans.). Bischofweisen, Germany: Hellinger Publications.

Hellinger, B. & Prekop, J. (2004). Si supieran cuánto los amo. (C. Cabrera, Trans.). México: Herder (Original work published in 1998)

Heraclitus. (2001). Fragments (B. Haxton, Trans.). New York, NY: Penguin Books.

Hillman, J. (1970). Why 'archetypal' psychology? In *Spring 1970: An annual of archetypal psychology and Jungian thought.* New York, NY: Spring Publications.

Hillman, J. (1972). *Emotion: A comprehensive phenomenology of theories and their meanings for therapy.* Evanston, IL: Northwestern University Press.

Hillman, J. (1976). Peaks and vales: The soul/spirit distinction as basis for the differences between psychotherapy and spiritual discipline. In J. Needleman & D. Lewis (Eds.). In *On the way to self-knowledge* (pp.114-147). New York, NY: Knopf.

Hillman, J. (1976b). Some early background to Jung's ideas: Notes on C.G. Jung's Medium by Stephanie Zumstein-Preiswerk. In *Spring 1976: An annual of Archetypal Psychology and Jungian thought*. Dallas, TX: Spring Publications.

Hillman, J. (1979). *The dream and the underworld*. New York, NY: Harper and Row.

Hillman, J. (1983). *Healing fiction*. Putnam, CT: Spring Publications.

Hillman, J. (1991). *A blue fire: Selected writings by James Hillman*. In T. Moore (Ed.). New York: Harper Perennial.

Hillman, J. (1992). *Re-visioning psychology*. New York, NY: Harper Perennial.

Hillman, J. (1992b). *The myth of analysis*. Evanston, IL: Northwestern University Press.

Hillman, J. (1992c). *The thought of the heart and the soul of the world*. Putnam, CT: Spring Publications.

Hillman, J. (1995). *Insearch: Psychology and religion*. Woodstock, CT: Spring Publications.

Hillman, J. (1995b). A psyche the size of the Earth: A psychological foreword. In Roszak, T., Gomes, M.E., & Kanner, A.D., (Eds.). *Ecopsychology: Restoring the Earth, healing the mind*. New York, NY: Sierra Club Books.

Hillman, J. (1996). *The soul's code: In search for character and calling*. New York, NY: Warner Books.

Hillman, J. (1997). *Suicide and the soul*. New York, NY: Spring Publications.

Hillman, J. (1998). Abandoning the child. In *Spring 63: A journal of archetype and culture*. Putnam, CT: Spring Journal.

Hillman, J. (2005). *Senex and puer*. Putnam, CT: Spring Publications.

Hillman, J. (2006). *City and soul*. Putnam, CT: Spring Publications.

Hillman, J. (2007). *Mythic figures*. Putnam, CT: Spring Publications.

Hillman, J. (2007b). *Pan and the nightmare.* Putnam, CT: Spring Publications.

Hillman, J. (Speaker). (n.d.). *Myths of the family, Part 1 & 2* (Cassette recording). Carpinteria, CA: Pacifica Graduate Institute Library.

Hillman, J. & Pozzo, L. (1983). *Inter views: Conversations with Laura Pozzo on psychotherapy, biography, love, soul, dreams, work, imagination, and the state of culture.* New York, NY: Harper & Row.

Hillman, J. & Shamdasani, S. (2013). *Lament of the dead: Psychology after Jung's Red Book.* London, Great Britain: W.W. Norton & Company.

Hillman, J. & Ventura, M. (1993). *We've had a hundred years of psychotherapy and the world's getting worse.* New York, NY: Harper Collins.

Jaffé, A. (1984). Details about C.G. Jung's family. In *Spring 1984: An annual of Archetypal Psychology and Jungian thought.* Dallas, TX: Spring Publications.

Jalāl al-Din Rumi, M. (1995). *The essential Rumi* (C. Barks, Trans.). New York, NY: Harper Collins.

Jalāl al-Din Rumi, M. (2003). *Rumi: The book of love* (C. Barks, Trans.). New York, NY: Harper Collins.

James, W. (1997). *The Varieties of religious experience: A study in human nature.* New York, NY: Touchstone.

Jodorowsky, A. (2005). *Psicomagia.* México: Random House Mondadori.

Joyce, J. (2003). *A portrait of the artist as a young man.* New York, NY: Penguin.

Jung, C.G. (1933). *Modern man in the search of a soul.* (W.S. Dell & C.F. Baynes, Trans.). Orlando, FL: Harvest Book.

Jung, C.G. (1957). Psychiatric studies. In H. Read, M. Fordham, G. Adler, & W. McGuire (Eds.), *The collected works of C.G. Jung* (R. F. C. Hull, Trans.) (Vol. 1). London, Great Britain: Routledge and Kegan Paul.

Jung, C.G. (1954). The development of personality. In H. Read, M. Fordham, G. Adler, & W. McGuire (Eds.), *The collected works of C.G. Jung* (R. F. C. Hull, Trans.) (Vol. 17). London, Great Britain: Routledge and Kegan Paul.

Jung, C.G. (1954b). The practice of psychotherapy: Essays on the psychology of the transference and other subjects. In H. Read, M. Fordham, G. Adler, & W. McGuire (Eds.), *The collected works of C.G. Jung* (R. F. C. Hull, Trans.) (Vol. 16). London, Great Britain: Routledge and Kegan Paul.

Jung, C.G. (1955). The symbolic life: Miscellaneous writings. In H. Read, M. Fordham, G. Adler, & W. McGuire (Eds.), *The collected works of C.G. Jung* (R. F. C. Hull, Trans.) (Vol. 18). Princeton, NJ: Princeton University Press. (Original work published in 1950)

Jung, C.G. (1958). Psychology and Religion: West and East. In H. Read, M. Fordham, G. Adler, & W. McGuire (Eds.), *The collected works of C.G. Jung* (R. F. C. Hull, Trans.) (Vol. 11). London, Great Britain: Routledge and Kegan Paul.

Jung, C.G. (1959). Aion: Researches into the phenomenology of the self. In H. Read, M. Fordham, G. Adler, & W. McGuire (Eds.), *The collected works of C.G. Jung* (R. F. C. Hull, Trans.) (Vol. 9 Part II). London, Great Britain: Routledge and Kegan Paul. (Original work published in 1951)

Jung, C.G. (1959b). The archetypes and the collective unconscious. In H. Read, M. Fordham, G. Adler, & W. McGuire (Eds.), *The collected works of C.G. Jung* (R. F. C. Hull, Trans.) (Vol. 9 Part I). New York, NY: Pantheon Books.

Jung, C.G. (1960). The psychogenesis of mental disease. In H. Read, M. Fordham, G. Adler, & W. McGuire (Eds.), *The collected works of C.G. Jung* (R. F. C. Hull, Trans.) (Vol. 3). London, Great Britain: Routledge and Kegan Paul.

Jung, C.G. (1961). Freud and psychoanalysis. In H. Read, M. Fordham, G. Adler, & W. McGuire (Eds.), *The collected works of C.G. Jung* (R. F. C. Hull, Trans.) (Vol. 4). London, Great Britain: Routledge and Kegan Paul.

Jung, C.G. (1963). Mysterium coniunctionis: An inquiry into the separation and synthesis of psychic opposites in alchemy. In H. Read, M. Fordham, G. Adler, & W.

McGuire (Eds.), *The collected works of C.G. Jung* (R. F. C. Hull, Trans.) (Vol. 14). London, Great Britain: Routledge and Kegan Paul.

Jung, C.G. (Ed.).(1964). *Man and his symbols.* USA: Dell Publishing.

Jung, C.G. (1964b). Civilization in transition. In H. Read, M. Fordham, G. Adler, & W. McGuire (Eds.), *The collected works of C.G. Jung* (R. F. C. Hull, Trans.) (Vol. 10). New York, NY: Random House.

Jung, C.G. (1965). *Memories, dreams and reflections.* In Aniela Jaffé. (Ed.). (R. & C. Winston, Trans.). New York, NY: Vintage Books. (Original work published in 1961)

Jung, C.G. (1966). *The psychology of transference.* (R. F. C. Hull, Trans.). Princeton, NJ: Princeton University Press. (Original work published 1954)

Jung, C.G. (1966b). *Psychology and religion.* Binghamton, NY: The Vail-Ballou Press. (Original work published in 1938)

Jung, C.G. (1966c). The spirit in man, art, and literature. In H. Read, M. Fordham, G. Adler, & W. McGuire (Eds.), *The collected works of C.G. Jung* (R. F. C. Hull, Trans.) (Vol. 15). Princeton, NJ: Princeton University Press.

Jung, C.G. (1967). Symbols of transformation. In H. Read, M. Fordham, G. Adler, & W. McGuire (Eds.), *The collected works of C.G. Jung* (R. F. C. Hull, Trans.) (2nd ed., Vol. 5). Princeton, NJ: Princeton University Press. (Original work published in 1952)

Jung, C.G. (1968). Psychology and Alchemy. In H. Read, M. Fordham, G. Adler, & W. McGuire (Eds.), *The collected works of C.G. Jung* (R. F. C. Hull, Trans.) (2nd ed., Vol. 12). Princeton, NJ: Princeton University Press. (Original work published in 1952)

Jung, C.G. (1969). The structures and dynamics of the psyche. In H. Read, M. Fordham, G. Adler, & W. McGuire (Eds.), *The collected works of C.G. Jung* (R. F. C. Hull, Trans.) (2nd ed., Vol. 8). Princeton, NJ: Princeton University Press. (Original work published in 1960)

Jung, C.G. (1970). Fragments from a talk with students. In *Spring 1970: An annual of archetypal psychology and Jungian thought.* New York, NY: Spring Publications.

Jung, C.G. (1971). *Two essays on analytical psychology,* (R. F. C. Hull, Trans.). New York, NY: The World Publishing Company. (Original work published in 1953)

Jung, C.G. (1971b). Psychological types. In H. Read, M. Fordham, G. Adler, & W. McGuire (Eds.), *The collected works of C.G. Jung* (R. F. C. Hull, Trans.) (Vol. 6). Princeton, NJ: Princeton University Press. (Original work published in 1921)

Jung, C.G. (1973). Experimental researches. In H. Read, M. Fordham, G. Adler, & W. McGuire (Eds.), *The collected works of C.G. Jung* (R. F. C. Hull, Trans.) (Vol. 2). Princeton, NJ: Princeton University Press.

Jung, C.G. (1976). The symbolic life: Miscellaneous writings. In H. Read, M. Fordham, G. Adler, & W. McGuire (Eds.), *The collected works of C.G. Jung* (R. F. C. Hull, Trans.) (Vol. 18). Princeton, NJ: Princeton University Press.

Jung, C.G. (1983). In A. Storr (Ed.). *The essential Jung,* (R. F. C. Hull, Trans.). Princeton, NJ: Princeton University Press.

Jung, C.G. (1984). *Dream analysis: Notes of the seminar given in 1928-1930.* In William McGuire (Ed.). Princeton, NJ: Princeton University Press.

Jung, C.G. (1988). *Nietzsche's Zarathustra: Notes of the seminar given in 1934-1939.* In James L. Jarret (Ed.). Princeton, NJ: Princeton University Press.

Jung, C.G. (1996). *The psychology of Kundalini Yoga: Notes of the seminar given in 1932 by C.G. Jung.* In S. Shamdasani (Ed.). Princeton, NJ: Princeton University Press.

Jung, C.G. (2002). In M. Sabini (Ed.). *The Earth has a soul: Nature writings of C.G. Jung.* Berkeley, CA: North Atlantic Books.

Jung, C.G. (2009). La vida simbólica. *Obras completas volumen 18/2* (J. Navarro Pérez, Trans.). Madrid: Trotta. (Original work published in 1954)

Jung, C.G. (2009b). *The red book: Liber novus.* In S. Shamdasani (Ed.), (M. Kyburz, J. Peck, & S. Shamdasani Trans.). New York, NY: Norton & Company.

Kerényi, C. (1967). The problem of evil in mythology. In *Evil*. In The Curatorium of the C.G. Jung Institute; Zürich (Eds.). Evanston, IL: Northwestern University Press. (Original work published in 1961)

Kerényi, C. (1976). *Dionysus: Archetypal image of indestructible life.* In R. Mainheim (Trans.). Princeton, NJ: Princeton University Press.

Kilpatrick, A. (1997). *The night has a naked soul: Witchcraft and sorcery among the Western Cherokee.* Syracuse, NY: Syracuse University Press.

Kingsley, M. & Kinglsey, P. (2006). As far as longing can reach. *Parabola* vol. XXXI/2, Summer 2006, pp. 56-59.

Kingsley, P. (1996). *Ancient philosophy, mystery and magic: Empedocles and the Pythagorean tradition.* New York, NY: Oxford University Press.

Kingsley, P. (1999). *In the dark places of wisdom.* Point Reyes, CA: The Golden Sufi Center.

Kingsley, P. (2003). *Reality.* Point Reyes, CA: The Golden Sufi Center.

Kingsley, P. (2010). *A story waiting to pierce you: Mongolia, Tibet and the destiny of the Western world.* Point Reyes, CA: The Golden Sufi Center.

Kutschera, I. & Schäffler, Ch. (2006). *La enfermedad que sana* (L. E. Fernández & M. Sommersguter, Trans.). Buenos Aires: Alma Lepik. (Original work published in 2002)

Lazlo, E. (2014). *The self-actualizing cosmos: The akasha revolution in science and human consciousness.* Rochester, VT: Inner Traditions.

Leitmotif. (2010). *Oxford dictionaries.* Retrieved, November 27th, 2010, from: http://oxforddictionaries.com/view/entry/m_en_us1262897#m_en_us1262897

Levine, P.A. (2010). *In an unspoken voice: How the body releases trauma and restores goodness.* Berkeley, CA: North Atlantic Books.

Levine, P.A. (2015). *Trauma and memory: Brain and body in a search for the living past.* Berkeley, CA: North Atlantic Books.

Liedloff, J. (1975). *The continuum concept: In search of happiness lost.* USA: Da Capo Press.

Marohn, S. (2003). *The natural medicine guide to schizophrenia.* Charlottesville, VA: Hampton Roads.

Mason Boring, F. (2012). *Connecting to our ancestral past: Healing through family constellations, ceremony, and ritual.* Berkeley, CA: North Atlantic Books.

Merleau-Ponty, M. (2003). *Phenomenology of Perception* (C. Smith, Trans.). New York: Routledge. (Original work published 1945)

Miasma. (n.d.). *Oxford Dictionaries.* Retrieved, November 23th, 2010, from: http://oxforddictionaries.com/view/entry/m_en_us1267636#m_en_us1267636

Narby, J. (1997). *La serpiente cósmica: El AND y los orígenes del saber* (A. Chirif, Trans.). Lima, Perú: Takiwasi y Racimos de Unguahui. (Original work published in 1995)

Neihardt, J. (2008). *Black Elk speaks: Being the life story of a holy man of the Oglala Sioux as told through John G. Neihardt (Flaming Rainbow).* Albany, NY: State university Press. (Original work published in 1932)

Neumann, E. (1969). *Depth Psychology and a new ethic* (E. Rolfe, Trans.). Boston, MA: Shambhala Publications.

Nietzsche, F. (1974). *The gay science* (W. Kaufmann, Trans.). New York, NY: Vintage Books. (Original work publishes in 1887)

Nietzsche, F. (1996). *On the genealogy of morals* (D. Smith, Trans.). New York, NY: Oxford University Press. (Original work published in 1967)

Nietzsche, F. (1998). *Beyond good and evil: Prelude to a philosophy of the future* (M. Faber, Trans.). New York, NY: Oxford University Press. (Original work published in 1886).

Nietzsche, F. (2000). *The birth of tragedy* (D. Smith, Trans.). New York, NY: Oxford University Press. (Original work published in 1967)

Nietzsche, F. (2005). *Thus spoke Zarathustra* (G. Parkes, Trans.). New York, NY: Oxford University Press. (Original work published in 1894)

Onions, C.T. (1996). (Ed.). *Oxford dictionary of English etymology*. New York, NY: Oxford University Press.

Ortega, P.S. (1992). *Introducción a la medicina homeopática: Teoría y técnica*. México, D.F.: Biblioteca de Homeopatía de México.

Ortega, P.S. (1999). *Apuntes sobre los miasmas o enfermedades crónicas de Hahnemann*. México, D.F.: Biblioteca de Homeopatía de México.

Otto, R. (1958). *The idea of the holy* (J.W. Harvey, Trans.). New York, NY: Oxford University Press. (Original work published in 1923)

Paz, O. (1997). Obras poética I (1935-1970). In *Obras completas: Edición del autor* (Vol. 11). México D.F.: Fondo de Cultura Económica.

Plato. (1989). *The collected dialogues*. In E. Hamilton & H. Cairns (Ed.). Princeton, NJ: Princeton University Press.

Quiller-Couch, S.A. (Ed.). (1955). *The Oxford book of English verse: 1250-1918*. New York, NY: Oxford University Press.

Ray, R.A. (2014). *Touching enlightenment: Finding realization in the body*. Boulder, CO: Sounds True. (Original work published in 2008)

Rilke, R.M. (1998). *Duino elegies: A bilingual Edition*. In S. Cohn (Trans.). Evanston, IL: Northwestern University Press.

Rilke, R.M. (2000). *Letters to a young poet*. In J.M. Burnham (Trans.). Novato, CA: New World Library.

Rikle, R.M. (2001). *The book of hours: Prayers to a lowly God*. In A.S. Kidder (Trans.). Evanston, IL: Northwestern University Press.

Russell, D. (2014). *My mysterious son: A life changing passage between schizophrenia and shamanism*. New York, NY: Skyhorse Publishing.

Romanyshyn, R.D. (2007). *The wounded researcher: Research with soul in mind*. New Orleans, LA: Spring Journal Books.

Sardello, R. (2004). *Facing the world with soul: The reimagination of modern life*. Great Barringtone, MA: Lindisfarne Press.

Sheldrake, R. (2009). *Morphic resonance: The nature of formative causation*. Rochester, VT: Park Street Press.

Sheldrake, R. (2012). *Morphic resonance & the presence of the past: The memory of nature*. Rochester, VT: Park Street Press.

Sheldrake, R. (2012b). *Science set free: 10 paths to new discovery*. New York, NY: Deepak Chopra Books.

Silko, L.M. (2006). *Ceremony*. New York, NY: Penguin.

Sophocles. (1984). *Three Theban plays: Antigone, Oedipus King, Oedipus at Colonus*. In R. Fagles (Trans.). New York, NY: Penguin.

Somé, M. P. (1993). *Ritual: Power, healing and community*. Portland, OR: Swan Raven.

Somé, M.P. (1995). *Of water and the spirit: Ritual, magic, and initiation in the life of an African shaman*. New York, NY: Arkana.

Somé, M.P. (1999). *The healing wisdom of Africa: Finding life purpose through nature, ritual, and community*. New York, NY: J.P. Tarcher/Putnam.

Somé, M. P. (Speaker). (2005). *Ancestralization: What do we owe the death?* (CD Recording, Produced by Malidoma & Associates. Recorded, mastered and designed by Eternal Voice).

Somé, M.P. (Speaker). (n.d.). *Creating a sense of home: The tribal community of the heart* (Tape Recording, Produced by Oral Tradition Archives).

Sohravardî, S. Y. (2002). *El encuentro con el ángel*. In H. Corbin (Ed.), (A. López Tobajas, Trans.). Madrid, España: Editorial Trotta. (Original work published in 1976)

St. Just, A. (2012). *Trauma: Time, space and fractals: A systemic perspective on individual, social and global trauma.* San Bernardino, CA: CreateSpace Independent Publishing Platform

Suzuki, D.T. (1956). *Zen Buddhism: Selected writings of D.T. Suzuki.* In William Barrett (Ed.). Garden City, NY: Doubleday & Company.

Tara. (n.d.). *Real Academia Española.* Retrieved: November 23th, 2010, from: http://buscon.rae.es/draeI/SrvltConsulta?TIPO_BUS=3&LEMA=tara

Torres, R. & Reig, E. (2018). *La curación verdadera a través de principios homeopáticos: Análisis y actualización del arte de curar.* España: Arcopress.

Van der Kolk, B. (2014). *The body keeps the score: Brain, mind, and body in the healing of trauma.* New York, NY: Penguin Books.

Van der Post, L. (1975). *Jung and the story of our time.* New York, NY: Pantheon House.

Van Eersel, P. & Mailard, C. (2004). *Mis antepasados me duelen* (M. T. Loriente, Trans.). Barcelona, España: Ediciones Obelisco.

van Kampenhout, D. (2007). *Las lágrimas de los ancestros: La memoria de víctimas y perpetradores del alma tribal* (L. Fernández, Trans.). Buenos Aires: Alma Lepik.

van Kampenhout, D. (2007b). *La sanación viene desde afuera: Chamanismo y constelaciones familiares* (A. Mirelman & N. Garassino, Trans.). Buenos Aires: Alma Lepik.

Von Franz, M.L. (1980). *Projection and re-collection of Jungian psychology*: *Reflections of the soul.* Peru, Ill: Open Court.

Waterfield, R. (Ed.). (2000). *The first philosophers: The Presocratics and the* Sophists. In R. Waterfield (Trans.). New York, NY: Oxford University Press.

Watkins, M. (2000). *Invisible guests: The development of imaginal dialogues.* Putnam, CT: Spring Publications.

Weber, G. (Ed.). (1999). *Felicidad dual: Bert Helllinger y sus psicoterapia sistémica* (S. Gomez-Pedra, Trans.). España: Herder.

Wilhelm, R. (1962). Death and renewal. In J. A. Pratt (Trans.). On *Spring 1962: A magazine of Jungian thought.* New York, NY: Analytical Psychology Club of New York.

Wilson, J. (2009). *Mourning the unborn dead: A Buddhist ritual comes to America.* New York, NY: Oxford University Press.

Wolff, R. (2001). *Original Wisdom: Stories of an ancient way of knowing.* Rochester, VT: Inner Traditions.

Woodman, M. (1993). *Leaving my father's house: A journey to conscious femininity.* Boston, MA: Shambhala Publications.

Zavala, J.F. (1977). *Die psychische Entwicklung in altmexikanischer Symbolik: Dargestellt an einem altmexikanische Gesang im Lichte der Psychologie C.G. Jungs.* Stuttgart: Verlag Adolf Bonz.

[1] Hillman, in his first writings, acknowledged the dangers by "[t]he gradual replacement of 'soul' by 'psyche' in this century [the XX century] and the consequent professionalism in dealing with its troubles are beginning to do as much damage as did the ignorance and moralisms [*sic*] about the psyche in the last century [the XIX century]" (1995, p.7); therefore, following Hillman's insight and warning, soul will be at the center of this work, and, even when at times it could be referred with the word psyche, it will mean always soul.

[2] Hillman, for instance, described the soul as "a deliberately ambiguous concept resisting all definition in the same manner as do ultimate symbols which provide the root metaphors for the systems of human thought" (1997, p.46).

[3] Most fields of mainstream psychology do not study, consider, or even mention the soul; however, "the search for soul leads always into the 'depths'" (Hillman, 1997, p.45), hence *depth psychology*. It is in a sense tautological, because the word "psychology" etymologically implies the study of soul, but the name is required in order to distinguish itself from the kind of psychology that does not even mention the word soul.

[4] Jung, 1953/1971, 1988, 1952/1968, 1960/1969.

[5] Jung, 1954/2009, p.31.

[6] 1960/1969, p. 96.

[7] Jung, 1960/1969, p. 15.

[8] Jung, 1988.

[9] Jung, 1988, p. 877.

[10] Hillman did a training in Analytical Psychology, popularly known as Jungian psychology, but I refer to him as a "self-defined" Jungian, because he often commented that he was, despite his radical psychological re-visioning, a Jungian.

[11] Hillman, 1992.

[12] Hillman, 1992.

[13] Hillman, 1992b, 2007.

[14] Hillman, 1992b.

[15] Hillman, 1996.

[16] Hellinger 2001.

[17] Weber, 1999.

[18] Hellinger, 2000/2001.

[19] Hellinger, 2003/2006.

[20] Hellinger, 2001b/2000.

[21] Hellinger, 1996/2002.

[22] Helllinger, 1996/2002, 2006/2007.

[23] Hellinger, 2009.

[24] Van Kampenhout, 2007 & 2007b.

[25] Hausner 2008/2009.

[26] Somé, 1993.

[27] Somé, 1999, p.22

[28] Somé, 1999.

[29] Somé, 1999, p.17.

[30] Somé, 2005.

[31] Somé, 2005.

[32] Corbin, 1969/1998, p.221

[33] Compare it to an old verse in the book of splendor: "...with your eyes you are not able to see the inhabitants of the world to come, nor angels, certainly not the Holy One, blessed be He, nor His Shechinah, but with the wisdom of your heart you can see everything..." (in M. Berg, Zohar, vol 10, p.484).

[34] Dalai Lama, 2005, p.4

[35] 1977, pp.20-22

[36] This story was inspired, and it is very similar to those used, by Hellinger, who frequently asked the representatives of a constellation to repeat very specific "empowering sentences." See: *On Life and Other Paradoxes* (Hellinger 2006b, pp.61-79).

[37] Hillman, 1992.

[38] Hillman, 1992, p.121

[39] Hillman, 1992c.

[40] Nietzsche, 1967/1996, p. 98

[41] Nietzsche, 1967/1996, p.10

[42] Hillman, 1992, p. 138

[43] Peter Levine, who has vastly and profoundly enriched the body-oriented therapies, remarked that, "[r]ather than trying to help patients make new meanings or *understand* their problems, body therapy creates a space for the 'body story' to unfold and complete" (2010, p.169 footnote). Just so, when dealing with an affection, one can track it throughout the body in emotion and sensation, and eventually new images and words will arise, words and images that give soul to existence. "When this occurs, new meanings and insights emerge spontaneously, generated by the patients themselves, as an integral part of this process" (ibid).

[44] Nietzsche, 1894/2005, p. 35

[45] Gieser, 2005, p.71

[46] 1957, p.219

[47] Jung, 1973, p.10

[48] Ibid.

[49] Jung, 1973, p.601

[50] The phrases feeling-tone or feeling-toned, in Jung's references, are not meant to designate only the rational "feeling function" that is characteristic of his psychological typology, but a more generalized sense of it (from the German *Gefühlston*), which could also be translated as *emotionality* (Editors, in Jung, 1957, p.97 footnote). "The feeling-tone is an affective state accompanied by somatic innervations" (Jung, 1960, p.40). This concept is close to what many decades later Gendlin would coin as *felt-sense* (1978), and which served Peter Levine to frame his understanding for psychobiological resolution of trauma.

[51] Jung, 1973.

[52] Jung, through this, discovered that the association tests and free-word associations (quite usual and basic in psychoanalysis) were not getting into the depths; he observed that "[t]he laws of association play a very insignificant role compared with the all-powerful emotional constellation, just as in real life the logic of thought is nothing compared with the logic of feeling" (1960, p.28 footnote). Nowadays we would even consider that thought is nothing compared with the logic of sensation, which governs those complexed somatic innervations that Jung clearly observed.

[53] Jung, 1973, p.599

[54] From now on, whenever *the complex,* as an idea, an image, a concept, or as a noun, is mentioned, it will be in reference to Jung's Complex Theory.

[55] Jung, 1960/1969.

[56] However, in 1935, at the Tavistock Lectures, when Jung was already sixty years old, he still mentioned: "the association tests . . . are really the foundation of certain conceptions" (1950/1955, p.71).

[57] Jung, 1960/1969, p.96

[58] Jung mentioned that, "as a matter of fact, everything thought, felt, or perceived is a psychic image, and the world itself exists only so far as we are able to produce an image of it" (1958, p.479).

[59] "The 'merely conscious' man who is all ego is a mere fragment, in so far as he seems to exist apart from the unconscious" (Jung, 1958, p.163); and it is worth noticing that Jung once wrote: "For me the unconscious is a collective *psychic disposition* (italics added)" (1958, p.537). Hence, to rely only on (the personal notion of) consciousness, and on what one might get to know through it, one becomes completely unaware of the other psychic contents with which one interacts and with which one is in relation—it becomes impossible, then, to see one's *psychic position* and *how is one disposed into life.* Jung mentioned: "By consciousness I understand the relation of psychic contents to the *ego* [the "I"], in so far as this relation is perceived as such by the ego. Relations to the ego that are not perceived as such are unconscious" (1921/1971b, p.421). "Consciousness[,]" like Nietzsche very well realized, "gives rise to countless errors that lead an animal or man to perish sooner than necessary" (1887/1974, p.84); one requires to get acquainted with that which is beyond the personal consciousness. Durand rendered Jung an honor, when he claimed: "It has taken all the discoveries of contemporary depth psychology to bring the *ego* back to this modest pluralism, to show that behind its triumphant consciousness the unconscious proliferates disquieteningly [*sic*]" (1976, p.89).

[60] 1960/1969, p.123

[61] It is interesting to note how Damasio, the great neuroscientist, many decades later after Jung, would consider that, "consciousness begins as the feeling of what happens when we see or hear or touch . . . it is a feeling that accompanies the making of any kind of image—visual, auditory, tactile, visceral—within our living organism" (1999, p.26). However, Damasio's point of departure is the brain interacting with the physical world through *the feeling of what happens*; Jung's was the soul interacting within the objective psyche through the sensing of what's perceived—physical or imaginal, archetypal or literal, tangible or dreamed.

[62] "You can define consciousness as a relation of psychic facts to the ego" (Jung, 1950/1955, p.11); and the ego as "a general awareness of your body, of your existence, and . . . your memory data . . . Therefore you can call the ego a complex of psychic facts" (p.11).

[63] "It is a system of orientation which concerns my dealing with external facts given to me by the function of my senses . . . [and] a system of relationship between the contents of consciousness and postulated processes in the unconscious" (Jung, 1950/1955, p.12).

[64] This might be the reason why Heraclitus affirmed that: "Eyes and ears are bad witnesses for men if they have souls which cannot understand their language" (2001, p.40), from the fragment B107 in the Diels-Kranz numeration, also rendered as: "Bad witnesses are the eyes and ears of those who have foreign souls" (in Barnes, 2001, p.69); which could be thought of as a distorted perception because of the unawareness of psychic contents—one's own foreign psyche. Jung, therefore, mentioned: "we always start with the idea that our consciousness is perfect. It never occurs to us that it could be dim, or that it might develop . . . [moreover,] that our consciousness is at fault" (1988, p.1289).

[65] 1887/1974, p.85

[66] Jung mentioned, in a poetic as much as in a truthful sense: "Gleaming islands, indeed whole continents, can still add themselves to our modern consciousness" (1960/1969, pp.189-190). But Nietzsche had already written about it: "A thousand paths there are that have never been trodden; a thousand healths and hidden islands of life. Unexhausted and undiscovered are the human and human earth even now" (1894/2005, p.67).

[67] Nietzsche wrote in the late nineteenth century: "what we call consciousness constitutes only one state of our spiritual and psychic world (perhaps a pathological state) and *not by any means the whole of it*. The profundity of this idea has not been exhausted to this day" (1887/1974, p.305). Jung, possibly, answered this better than anyone else, because, unlike Freud, he realized the spiritual dimension of the psyche and consciousness. He said: "The supposed vacuum of a merely subjective psychic space becomes filled with objective figures, having wills of their own, and is seen to be a cosmos that conforms to law, and among these figures the ego takes its place in transfigured form. This tremendous experience means a shattering of foundations, an overturning of our arrogant world of consciousness, a cosmic shift of perspective" (Jung, 1950/1955, p.763).

[68] 1992, p.84

[69] "People think themselves magicians who can conjure the psyche hither and thither and fashion it to suit their mood. In the meantime they have forgotten the essential point, which is that only the tiniest fraction of the psyche is identical with the conscious mind and its box of magic tricks" (Jung, 1954, p.177). This is alluding, of course, to the force of the will that stems from the "I," the ego, the persona. Hence, Jung said: "I regard the will as the amount of psychic energy at the disposal of consciousness . . . A psychic process, therefore, that is conditioned by unconscious motivation I would not include under the concept of the will" (1921/1971b, p.486). Hence, Rumi wrote: "In complete control, pretending control,/ with dignified authority, we are charlatans" (Jalāl al-Din Rumi, 2003, p.165).

[70] 1960/1969, p.96

[71] 1960/1969, p.96

[72] "Blind" because oftentimes one lacks the epistemological methods and techniques to look into psychic issues, and because human vision, in any case, always has a blind-spot.

[73] 1960/1969, p.96

[74] Jung insisted throughout his life that "[t]he complex is not under the control of the will and for this reason it possesses the quality of psychic autonomy" (1954b, p.131); and this indeed has been frequently overlooked, where people pretend to get better only by means of will-power, or when people naïvely claim to be "working" on their complexes, as if it were only a matter thinking positively or being more optimistic.

[75] Jung wrote in 1934: "This idea of the independence of the unconscious, which distinguishes my views so radically from those of Freud, came to me as far back as 1902, when I engaged in studying the psychic history of a young girl somnambulist" (1953/1971, p.133)—which became his doctoral dissertation, see *Psychiatric Studies* (Jung, 1957). Ellenberger claimed, in fact, that, "[t]he germinal cell of Jung's analytical psychology is to be found . . . in his experiments with his young medium cousin, Hélène Preiswerk[,]" the above mentioned somnambulist (1970, p.687). Hillman, in his essay titled *Some early background to Jung's ideas* (1976b, pp.123-136), explored these arguments further, arguing Jung's acquaintance with, and knowledge of, spiritism, because of his mother's interest and the séances that were taking place in his house. During a séance concerning Nietzsche, Hélène spoke the voice of Jung's grandfather (Samuel Preiswerk) warning "Carl" against Nietzsche's teaching (p.128). In any case, Jung got well acquainted with Nietzsche's philosophy, and he mentioned: "I had the great advantage over both Freud and Adler of not having grown up within the narrow confines of a psychology of the neuroses; rather, I approached from the side of psychiatry, well prepared for modern psychology by Nietzsche" (1953/1971, p.128).

[76] Jung, 1960/1969, p.4

[77] Ibid.

[78] Jung was clear in *his* use of the notion of "unconscious," which he said could have two ways of being understood, one physiological and another psychological; he referred to it in the second sense. He "define[d] the unconscious as the sum of all those psychic events which are not apperceived, and so are unconscious [not-known]" (1960, p.203). "It is therefore difficult to understand how people today can still doubt the existence of a collective unconscious. After all, nobody would dream of regarding the instincts or human morphology as personal acquisitions or personal caprices. The unconscious is the universal mediator among men" (Jung, 1958, p.277).

[79] 1960/1969, p.96

[80] Oxford Dictionaries.

[81] Onions, 1996.

[82] 1960/1969, p.96

[83] 1938/1966b, p.13

[84] 1960, p.38

[85] The "Freudocentric legend . . . which viewed Freud and psychoanalysis as the principal source for Jung's work . . . has led to a complete mislocation of his work . . . Freud and Jung clearly came form quite different intellectual traditions" (Shamdasani in Jung, 2009b, p.196), and, naturally, not just the psychological views have a different

epistemological standpoint, but the conclusions are also radically different. In principle, it is not only a difference of technique, jargon, or style—as if it depended on the use of a divan or a chair—as most people would think, but a major difference in the conceptual notion of the human *being*—a marked and irreconcilable difference in their ontological premises.

[86] Hillman has also warned about this mistake; "[b]y giving over any complex to a single archetype, we condemn it to a single view, a diagnosis made too often . . . When we fix a complex to one archetype, only one sort of insight can arise" (2005, pp.132-133).

[87] Jung, 1952/1968, p.301

[88] One could think that this is the reason why Jung mentioned that, "[i]f you identify with only one aspect of yourself you are merely an autonomous function, an autonomous aspect of yourself . . . [and] you are naturally up against the unconscious" (1988, p.562); meaning that other aspects remain severely unseen, unknown, and with a mighty effect on one's life.

[89] 1952/1968, p.481

[90] Jung mentioned: "To cave the honour [*sic*] of the objective psyche, which contemporary hypertrophy of consciousness has done so much to depreciate, I must again emphasize that without the psyche we could not establish the existence of any world at all, let alone know it" (1958, p.289). By objective psyche he referred to the totality of factors that are not subjective, nor subjected to one's judgment, decision, opinion, or thought; in other words, autonomous factors that are there, independently of the subject who is affected by them.

[91] 1952/1968, p.483

[92] Hellinger, through a story, gave an example of a physician who examined his sister, found nothing wrong, but told her to go see another physician. She went there and gave birth to a child. She and her brother were not allowed to perceive pregnancies in their own family (Weber, 1999, p.44). This is an excellent illustration of how perception can be flawed by the family conscience, allowing certain things to be sensed and perceived, while others are misperceived and unnoticed because they are avoided, denied, rejected, prohibited, or taboo.

[93] Jung commented that, "when people complain that whenever they try to do this or that, they have an attack of such-and-such a nature, it means that a complex comes in-between. And they cannot deal with it, it deals with *them*" (1988, p.939).

[94] Jung commented that, besides the Oedipus complex, "[t]here are also other typical patterns which regulate the relation of father to son, mother to daughter, parents to children, brothers and sisters to each other, and so on . . . Mythology, folklore, dreams, and psychoses do not fall short in this respect" (1950/1955, p.535).

[95] Hence, Jung, when commenting on Freud's Oedipal perspective, said: "Every time you accept that explanation you lose your soul. You have not helped your soul; you have replaced your soul by an explanation, a theory" (1950/1955, p.277).

[96] Affection is used in its original sense, from the Latin root, which means disposition or inclination (Onions, 1996, p.17). In this sense it rather refers to Aristotle's *paschein*. See also Aristotle's *Peri Psyché*, Book II, Ch. V. Affection, in such sense, comes close to Heidegger's notion of *Befindlichkeit*, which is often translated as state-of mind, but rather connotes *how does one find oneself*. See Heidegger's *Being and Time*, Part one, Division one, Ch. V. This notion, in the way Heidegger used it, reveals how does one stand in the world (and one could think in relation to what or whom), so that one's affective disposition is *"prior to all* cognition and volition". . . . and, moreover, it "discloses the 'there' more primordially, but correspondingly it *closes* it *off* more stubbornly than any *not*-preceiving" (Heidegger, 1926/1962, p.175). It seems that what one perceives or fails to perceive is in relation to one's affective disposition, which in German is *Stimmung*, and which has the colloquial meaning of *seelische Zustand* (Soul's disposition). It seems that one's affectivity is determined *by the position* of one's personal notion of psyche in relation to other psychic contents—which generate an atmosphere (*Stimmung*) and configure the Soul's disposition. This also suggests a different route when exploring "states of mind," known in Spanish as *estados de ánimo*, which, in fact, could be translated as *seelische Zustände*. Therefore, Heidegger wrote: *"Existentially, a state-of-mind* [*Stimmung*] *implies a disclosive* [*sic*] *submission to the world, out of which we can encounter something that matter to us"* (p.177). In other words, the soul's disposition implies an openness out of which one faces and glances the psychic contents that matter and that affect one's embodiment *and* circumstance—whether one sees them physically or not. This notion is very close to what in Tibetan is called *kun long,* "understood as that which drives or inspires our actions—both those we intend directly and those which are in a sense involuntary. It therefore denotes the individual's overall state of mind and heart" (Dalai Lama, 1999, p.30). The Dalai Lama commented that *kun long* could be translated also as "disposition," but, "although it comes quite close, [it] lacks the active sense of the Tibetan" (p.30). It is no coincidence that in his book *Ethics for the new millennium*, in the chapter titled: *No magic, No mystery,* when presenting the idea of a "spiritual revolution" (not to be confused with a religious revolution), he claimed that, "[t]he aim of spiritual and, therefore, ethical practice is thus to transform and perfect the individual's *kun long.* This is how we become better human beings" (p.32).

[97] This is close to what is called "morbid individuality" in homeopathic medicine, meaning that every individual suffers (the affections of life) according to one's individual way. "Every individual suffers according to his species and within his species according to his own nature" (Ortega, 1992, p.177 free translation).

[98] There are exceptions though, as when collective or cultural issues or complexes are explored through a phenomenological procedure, like a constellation. Hellinger, of course, explored cultural complexes in this way, vastly. However, St. Just, first a clinical traumatologist who worked together with Peter Levine, and then a constellations facilitator, developed a way of attending cultural and collective complexes within an individual paradigm. She wrote a book where she gives several examples of cultural complexes repeating traumatic events throughout time, as in a fractal movement, see: *Time, space and fractals* (2012).

[99] 1960/1969, p.98

[100] 1973, p.602

[101] 1954b, p.87

[102] Jung, 1958, p.163 footnote

[103] "Possession[,]" Jung ventured to say, "is indeed quite natural; it is, one could say, the original condition of mankind . . . Man is always a bit possessed" (1988, p.1265), as well as the women, of course. He realized too, that, "in his modern naïvité, [man] has entirely failed to notice that he is as much possessed by his pathological states as any witch or witch-hunter in the darkest Middle Ages" (1964b, p.146). Therefore, "[p]ossession, though old-fashion, has by no means become obsolete; only the name has changed. Formerly they spoke of 'evil spirits,' now we call them 'neuroses' or 'unconscious complexes'" (Jung, 1950/1955, p.599).

[104] 1952/1968, p.279

[105] Heraclitus, 2001, p.45

[106] This corresponds to fragment B45 in the Diels-Kranz translation, also rendered as: "You will not be able to discover the limits of soul on your journey, even if you walk every path; so deep is the principle it contains" (Waterfield, 2000, p.44). Also rendered as: "You will not find the limits of the soul although you travel all the path—so deep is its account [logos]" (in Barnes, 2001, p.54). Giegerich wrote a very interesting essay regarding this fragment, from a rigorous depth *psycho-logical* perspective (1998, pp.1-32).

[107] 1960/1969, p.101

[108] It is worth noticing that while Freud consider the dream as the royal road (*via regia*) to the unconscious, Jung saw much deeper and wider and claimed that, "[i]t is the feeling-tone complex that determines the meaning of the dream, both dynamically and also in regards its content" (1960, p.269).

[109] 1960/1969, p.4

[110] Jung, 1960/1969, p.101

[111] 1960/1969, p.104

[112] Hillman, 1992.

[113] 1992, p.12

[114] "From this basic fact of the psychic realism and autonomy of the image vis-à-vis the autonomy of the sense perception springs the belief in spirits . . . thought is visionary and auditory, hence it also has the character of revelation . . . Primitive superstition surprises us only because we have largely succeeded in de-sensualizing the psychic image" (Jung, 1921/1971, p.30). (Primitive in this context is not degrading and pejorative, but in the sense of primal, the first of its kind, *primus.)*

[115] Jung clearly stated that through his work he was "not dealing with categories of reason but with categories of the *imagination*[,]" which he said: "I call them 'archetypes' . . . . [and] *dominants* of the unconscious" (1958, pp.518-519). Jung knew that "[i]magination itself is a psychic process" (1958, p.544); therefore, dealing with images is a way to address psychological issues—and even issues that are thought to be only physical.

[116] Hillman, 1992, p.82

[117] 1992, p.110

[118] Ibid.

[119] Ibid, p.127

[120] Ibid, p.149

[121] Ibid, p.117

[122] Ibid, p.149

[123] Ibid, p.154

[124] Hillman, 1992, p.175

[125] Ibid, p.177

[126] Ibid, p.174

[127] Ibid, p.175

[128] Ibid, p.180

[129] Jeremy Narby, for example, after being exposed to shamanic practices, also addressed the urgent need to move away from anthropocentric views. That, he claimed, is the basis of many indigenous peoples; and that became his motivation for the book *La Serpiente Cósmica, el AND y los orígenes del saber* (Le Serpent Cosmique—l'ADN et les origenes du savoir) (1995/1997).

[130] This term, *imaginal*, was coined by Corbin in order to distinguish it and differentiate it from the undervalued and popularized term: imaginary. "[I]n current and non-premeditated usage, the term imaginary is equated with *unreal*, with something that is outside the framework of being and existing, in brief, with something utopian" . . . "I had to find a new expression to avoid misleading the Western reader . . . in order to awaken him to another order of things" (Corbin, 1972, pp.1-2). Bamford, when writing about Corbin, mentioned that, "the Imaginal World . . . is also *the world of the soul and of the dead* (italics added) . . . [it] is a place of union, of holy reciprocity . . . . [it] is not an end in itself but a stage, an isthmus or intermediary realm . . . it is purely psychic . . . [a] world of metaphysical images, the active mirror (or *speculum*) wherein spirit takes form and matter is immaterialized" (in Corbin, 1990/1998, p.XX). Hillman, who borrowed Corbin's term and used it as a touchstone of Archetypal Psychology, considered that the notion and concept of the "unconscious" was in direct relation to the loss of awareness and recognition of the imaginal realm. Hillman suggested, from this, that the term "unconscious" could be left behind, as a symptom of twentieth century psychology, only if this other (autonomous) realm were acknowledged—because we inevitably interact with in, and most possibly in it too (1992b, p.8). Bamford claimed that through imagination, "[w]hat

was interior, hidden, invisible, suddenly becomes unhidden, environing, phenomenal" (in Corbin, 1990/1998, p.XXIII). It can be assured, like Rumi wrote in the poem titled *The cat and the meat*: "Invisible, visible, the world does not work without both" (Jalāl al-Din Rumi, 1995, p.217).

[131] Jung remarked that to explain psychic processes only with concepts is "[a] rupture of the link with the unconscious and our submission to the tyranny of words have one great disadvantage: the conscious mind becomes more and more the victim of its own discriminating activity" (1958, p.290), as it happens with existential psychologists and philosophers who reduce themselves and the richness of their lives to their abstractions and concepts—mere words. "It is amazing how people get caught in words. They always imagine that the name postulates the thing" (Jung, 1964b, p.147).

[132] Hillman's insistence on the importance of images and the imaginal, resonates with, and even responds to, Deloria Jr.'s critique of ethics, who wrote: "Ethical systems are notorious for having the ability to relate concepts and doctrines to every abstract consideration except the practical situations with which we become involved. Ethics seem to involve an abstract individual making clear, objective decisions that involve principles but no people" (2003, p.72). (Moreover, ethics is something that could also be enriched with Hellinger's constellations work.)

[133] It has to be made clear, that for Jung, as well as for Hillman who learned it from him, "[e]very psychic process is an image and an imagining" (Jung, 1958, p.544). Therefore, it seems right and wise to claim that "[i]magining better describes the method for engaging the repressed than analyzing into meaning or moralizing into positive or negative" (Hillman, 2007, p.279); it reveals that (or those) for which one did not have a face before. Imagining offers a way of seeing and seeing through, enhancing compassion, comprehension, dialogue, responsibility, participation, and inclusion; rather than a way of judging and condemning which only promote divisiveness, exclusion, separation, superiority, distancing, and alienation.

[134] There are some profound lines by Rumi expressing just this nuance; he wrote: "If you want what visible reality can give,/ you're an employee./ If you want the unseen world,/ you're not living your truth" (Jalāl al-Din Rumi, 2003, p.13).

[135] 1960/1969, p.104

[136] When referring to Jung, the mentioning, the idea, and/or image of a "constellation" or being "constellated," came directly or indirectly from his texts, and it is in relation to his work, reflections and investigations. In his early work, Jung originally used the word "constellation" to designate the *psychic atmosphere* that the linguistic reactions from the word-associations brought into the individual's consciousness (Jung, 1973, p.80 footnote). Such connotation is not related to Hellinger, who was born fifty years after Jung. Later in the book, when Hellinger's work, method, and views, are fully introduced and described, both notions of a "constellation" will be merged.

[137] 1960/1969, p.94

[138] When founding the C.G. Jung Institute in Zürich, in 1948, Jung mentioned some possibilities for furthering the research of the "complex psychology;" and he said: "For instance, the question of periodic renewal of the

emotional tone complex-stimulators is still unanswered; the problem of familial patterns of association has remained stuck in its beginnings, promising though these were; and so has the investigation of the physiological concomitants of the complex" (1950/1955, p.475). Jung not only knew the huge importance and tremendous weight of the familial patterns for the individual's life and fate, but he realized too that they had physical consequences.

[139] Jung was well aware that "the complex exerts the strongest 'constellating" force,' . . . [they] appear as the chief components of the psychological disposition in every psychic structure" (1961, p.26); hence, important life events get powerfully influenced, as if moved, accommodated, and disposed, by the complex itself. He knew too that, "problems of which people are unconscious can give rise to exteriorization phenomena, because constellated unconscious contents often have a tendency to manifest themselves outwardly somehow or other" (1950/1955, p.322). Somé, for instance, claimed that, "[t]he indigenous does not believe in coincidence or in accidents . . . the indigenous address events, illness, natural disasters as if they were living entities" (1999, p.211); this view of life considers them almost as if they were autonomous psychic contents.

[140] Jung observed that, "the spontaneous utterances of the unconscious do after all reveal a psyche which is not identical with consciousness and which is, at times, greatly at variance with it . . . The manifestation of the unconscious is therefore a revelation of the unknown in man" (1958, p.289); at times, such revelations occur through abrupt shifts in the course of destiny, accidents, misfortunes, calamities, or even fatalities. Jung, since he was quite young, observed that, "[b]y far the greater part of psychic elements in us is unconscious" (1957, p.98). Jung's consideration was that "in the actual functioning of the psyche, it does not matter whether you do a thing or whether it happens to you . . . fate moves through yourself and outside circumstances equally" (1988, p.896), for which he said that "it does not matter whether you are the cause of the misfortune or whether the misfortune comes to you .. . you are miserable and that is all that counts" (p.896).

[141] Since his early investigations and writings Jung was well aware that his method could shorten Freud's psychoanalysis, and that the psychic and physical symptoms were "nothing but symbolic manifestations of the pathogenic complexes" (Jung, 1973, p.317).

[142] 2009b, p.211

[143] The name and trademark *Hellinger Sciencia* inevitably reminds me of Nietzsche's bold book *"la gaya scienza,"* (The Gay Science) where he ends with powerful statements about *The great health,* saying: "Being new, nameless, hard to understand, we premature births of an yet unproven future need for a new goal also a new means—namely, a new health, stronger, more seasoned, tougher, more audacious, and gayer than any previous health" (1887/1974, p.346). Hellinger, through the Constellations, has been mostly focused on health and happiness, promoting and offering a new path, a repeatedly proven means to a greater enjoyment of life—indeed a *gay science.*

[144] Castaneda, 1968/2000, p.293, free translation

[145] Merleau-Ponty already expressed that, "[p]henomenology is only accessible through a phenomenological method" (1945/2003, p.viii), which "is a matter of describing, not explaining or analyzing" (p.ix); in this sense , it might be the careful attention to what is displayed, without aiming to comprehend it through a given theoretical assumption, but with the sole comprehension that that which is happening is a piece of the world, and "I" [by destiny and fate,] for the sole act of being there, happen to be part of it. Hellinger once said: "it means subjecting myself

to larger contexts and connection, without needing to understand them . . . I submit without fear to what might arise" (1999, p.22). Corbin when explaining the phenomenological method, wrote that, it is "to hold and unveil consciousness just as it reveals itself in the object it reveals" (1990/1998, p.24), and he claimed, "this revelation of *itself* is also its exit, its exodus *out of* itself[;]" therefore, "[i]ts revelation to itself turns out to be a return to oneself, a 'knowing oneself'" (p.24). The phenomenological approach offers a "presence-oriented understanding, or science of presence, [that] is not structured along the lines of a *deductive* science, an explanation by genetic reduction, nor a reconstruction based on a pattern of material causes" (p.25).

[146] Hellinger, 2006/2007, p.11, free translation

[147] It seems to me that it is a grave mistake to consider the Constellations work similar to Augusto Boal's *Theater of the oppressed*, to Jacob Moreno's *Psychodrama*, to Alejandro Jodorowsky's *Panic Theater,* Enrique Pardo's *Pantheater*, or to any kind of psychotherapeutic group-dynamic.

[148] I use the word "represent" and "representative," because those are Hellinger's; but I suggest very careful considerations about them. In the essay *Reflections on Ritual*, Casey gave a clear notion of the connotation that I intend, that is, "by 'represent' we mean . . . [to] stand in for, be the human representative of . . . or . . . [being] the manifest expression of" (1985, pp.102-103). In this sense, a constellation is *not* an allegorical representation, but rather a ritual, because "it is the ritual action per se that matters, not what it represents via allegory" (p.103). "Seen in this light . . . they do not merely copy or represent but are absolutely real; they are so woven into the reality of action as to form an indispensable part of it" (Cassier in Casey, 1985, p.103). So, in a constellation, an individual "representing" another man's father is not faking or pretending to be the father, the representative does not need to act like or imitate the man's father; in such a setting he *is* his father—and, therefore, he *feels* like the father he represents.

[149] in Barnes, 2001, p.51

[150] This corresponds to fragment B55 by Diels-Kranz, translated also as: "The things I rate highly are those which are accessible to sight, hearing, apprehension" (Waterfield, 2000, p.41).

[151] These insights point to a notion (and a theory) of perception that resonate with a saying of Empedocles, in fragment B3 of the Diels-Kranz numeration, where he suggested: "come, observe with every device in the way in which each thing is clear:/ neither hold sight in more trust than hearing/ nor resounding hearing above the clarities of the tongue/ nor let any of the other limbs by which there is a passage/ for thinking/ be deprived of trust, but think in the way in which each/ thing is clear" (in Barnes, 2001, pp.118-119). In simpler words, Empedocles claimed that by clearing the channels of thought (the five senses, or devices, as he called them) and by integrating them with one another, one would get to perceive as it is. And, therefore, one would get knowledge and clarity of understanding. Hence, it has also been translated as: "Think not that sight is ever more reliable than what comes to hearing, nor rate echoing above the pores of the tongue, nor keep your trust from any of the organs by which there is a channel for understanding, but use whatever it takes to make things clear to the mind" (Waterfield, 2000, p.143). Kingsley's book *Reality* (2003) explains thoroughly this kind of perception, where he boldly and sharply claimed: "we don't know how to look or listen. Our problem is not that we see and hear. It's that we don't" (p.121).

[152] Hellinger, 1999, p.23

[153] Jung, with the help of the Nobel Prize physicist W. Pauli, conceived "a conception of reality that takes account of the uncontrollable effects the observer has upon the system observed, the result being that reality forfeits something of its objective character and that a subjective element attaches to the physicist picture of the world" (1960/1969, p.229). This conception is not only the well-known discovery that the observer affects the observed, but something even further. Jung stated that "every 'observation of the unconscious,' i.e., every conscious realization of unconscious contents, has an uncontrollable reactive effect on these same contents . . . [and] this uncontrollable reactive effect of the observing subject on the unconscious limits the objective character of the latter's reality and lends it at the same time a certain subjectivity" (p.229 footnote). In simpler prose, by observing an unconscious and autonomous psychic content, it not only becomes visible and determined to the observer (getting an image of such a content or situation rather than leaving it undefined), but it also becomes *friendly* towards the observer; in other words, it becomes less threatening, less aggressive, less disturbing, less annoying, and so on. See also *The innermost kernel: Depth psychology and quantum physics. Wolfgang Pauli's dialogue with C.G. Jung* (Gieser, 2005).

[154] A systemic view for family therapy and communication studies was originally developed, in theory, by Bateson and Ruesch (Bateson, G. & Ruesch, J. 1951/2009).

[155] Weber, 1999

[156] Hellinger said: "Through a constellation, I suddenly have access to a reality that is not accessible to me through thought processes" (1999, p.64). He mentioned that, "through this process, [the constellation,] things come to light that would never have been possible from a personal description" (p.71). This is possible, he said, because "phenomenology . . . is not dialectical thinking" (p.26). There are some lines by Rumi, saying: "There is a way between voice and presence/ where information flows./ In disciplined silence it opens./ With wandering talk it closes" (Jalāl al-Din Rumi, 1995, p.32). If talk therapies remain only as introspective therapies, not only they might remain blind to deep aspects of the human cosmos, there is also a great danger; Peter Levine acknowledged this, and remarked: "introspective examination can become pathological, contributing to increased rumination, inhibition, self-consciousness and excessive self-criticism" (2010, p.289).

[157] By being a representative in numerous occasions, having to embody a wide variety of presences, in many different kind of positions, and freely allowing the perception of sensations, feelings, and even thoughts, postures and gestures of those one represents, one comes close to the idea of a being philosopher in the sense stated by Nietzsche. He wrote: "the true philosopher may require that he himself once pass through all stages . . . so that he can traverse the range of human values and value-feelings and *be able* to look with many kind of eyes and consciences from the heights into every distance, from the depths into every height, from the corners into wide expanse" (1886/1998, p.104). He claims that a philosopher "needs to have been a critic and a sceptic [*sic*] and a dogmatist and a historian, and in addition a poet and a collector, a traveler and puzzle solver and a moralist and a seer and 'free spirit' and nearly all things" (p.104); and so it is, actually, when one has been many times a representative, one time one represents a father, another an aborted or a son, a killer, a rapist, a husband or a lover, a soldier, a victim or a perpetrator, or whatever is needed in the psychic field, and indeed one traverses the field of being human, and, most importantly, one literally acquires vivid experiences from the others' standpoints—from where it is *in fact* impossible to judge them. Quite wisely, Nietzsche asked: "Don't philosophers like these *have* to exist?" (p.105) This idea is very similar to what Van der Post wrote from what Jung told him. According to him, "[w]hen he [Jung] saw a frown or other expression appear on their faces, [people faces] or even just an unwarranted gesture accomplished with their hands,

he would repeat as best he could the expression and gesture himself, trying to think at the same time of the first thing his act of imitation brought to mind" (1975, p.114). Such a procedure is not only phenomenological but requires, like Nietzsche suggested, a true philosopher.

[158] This is so, because, as Jung observed, "[e]very great experience in life, every profound conflict, evokes the accumulated treasure of these images and brings about their inner constellation" (1921/1971b, p.221), even if that great experience happened before one's parents were conceived.

[159] Weber, 1999, p.203, free translation

[160] Daring to perceive clearly is the key for understanding in depth. That might be the reason for Empedocles saying, in fragment B108 from the Diels-Kranz numeration: "For men's wit grow in relation to what is present" (in Barnes, 2001, p.156). Hence, rather than analytical or dialogical, the procedure has to be purely phenomenological—perceiving without tinctures (i.e. judgments, ideas, assumptions, preconceptions, fears, etc.)—when one aims for truth. Phenomenology, Corbin claimed, is "a call towards light, a progressive *transparence* of the phenomenon" (1990/1998, p.25), which "is why phenomenologists characterize it as *hermeneutic* . . . [in the sense of] 'understanding'." This was made clearer with Corbin's saying: "your mode of understanding reveals your mode of being, and that the significance revealed in your manner of understanding is *dependent* on your mode of being" (p.25), which is indeed the hermeneutic circle.

[161] Hellinger has explained how important it has been for him "not trying to save the other," and "comprehending that a person can act by mere presence," by means of "a concentrated force that acts by non-doing" (Weber, 1999, p.206, free translations); which, by the way, is described in the Tao Te King. But, "non-doing" should not be confused with "doing nothing" (Jung, 1921/1971b, p.217), that would be a grave error. This premise is not far from Jung's peculiar idea and way of doing psychotherapy, where he said that "[t]he therapist is no longer the agent of treatment but a fellow participant in a process of individual development" (1954b, p.8), psychically affecting and being affected by the patient. It is indeed an idea that presupposes a psychic balance and psychic force from the therapist, facilitator, or person doing the healing. Jung said that "a suitable explanation or a comforting word to the patient can have something like a healing effect which may influence the glandular secretions [and even other metabolic functions] . . . their special quality is due to a particular psychic state in the doctor" (1958, pp.329-330). One can assume that in such view the most powerful healing agent, is the psychic atmosphere of the therapist, facilitator, or healer, "the attitude of the psychotherapist is infinitely more important than the theories and methods of psychotherapy, and that is why I was particularly concerned to make this attitude known" (Jung, 1958, p.346); and maybe this is in principle what Hellinger has done, taking such idea to its last consequences, where it becomes clear, as in his silent Constellations, that it is not even the words what heal, but something else—while *he* is present. Quite wisely, as Weber mentioned, Hellinger said prior to the first book of Constellations, which he was indeed reluctant to write: *the best cannot be said, and the next best will be misunderstood* (Weber, 1999, p.18).

[162] Hellinger in Weber, 1999, p.203, free translation

[163] Ibid, p.216, free translation

[164] This, indeed, was explained by the French phenomenologist, when he wrote that, "looking for the world's essence . . . is looking for what it is as a fact for us, before any thematization" (Merleau-Ponty, 1945/2003, p. xvii).

[165] Jung, 1964b, p.466

[166] There are some lines by Empedocles, from the fragment B2 by Diels Kranz, stating the dangers of not seeing vastly; he said: "In their lives they see a meager portion of life, and then,/ Doomed to a swift death, like smoke they fly away on high,/ Trusting only in whatever each has encountered as he was driven/ Here and there; yet he falsely claims to have discovered the whole" (Waterfield, 2000, p.143); therefore, he said too: "Think not that sight is ever more reliable that what comes to hearing/ Nor rate echoing hearing above the pores of the tongue, nor keep/ Your trust from any of the organs by which there is a channel/ For your understanding, but use whatever it takes to make things clear to the mind" (p.143).

[167] Weber, 1999, p.165

[168] Weber, 1999, p.363

[169] Ibid, p.363

[170] Ibid, p.166

[171] Ibid, p.167-168

[172] The fourth order is in fact very close to a saying by Jung, who mentioned: "Life . . . is essentially a comedy . . . nothing is quite true and even that is not quite true; and by such insight you slowly begin to step out of life without risking a neurosis" (1988, p.1454). However, this idea is also very close to something that, according to Castaneda, *Don Juan Matus* said: shamans have someone whispering that everything is ephemeral, that whisperer is the death (Castaneda, 1999, p.165); the relation to Castaneda's work is not awkward at all. In the passage that Hellinger refers to the fourth order of love, as life being ephemeral, he in fact mentions Castaneda's insistence of getting rid of one's personal history (Weber, 1999, p.168). Castaneda's books and the figure of Don Juan played an important role for Hellinger, as it is well known from his eighty-fifth birthday public celebration in December 2010.

[173] Jung, for instance, was very much aware of the fact that, "in modern times people cannot easily grasp the reality of a psychic event, unless it is concrete at the same time" (1950/1955, p.696); the constellations work, on the other hand, offer a very concrete and sensuous experience, which leave no doubt of its insights and perspectives.

[174] Jung wrote, in 1906, for a psychiatric literature review which included the book of his mentor, Eugen Bleuler, *Affectivität, Suggestibilität, Paranoia*: "Affectivity . . . is an inclusive concept which covers all non-intellectual psychic process such as volition, feeling, suggestibility, attention, etc. It is a psychic factor that exerts as much influence on the psyche as on the body." Therefore, he concluded: "Affectivity is of the greatest imaginable importance in psychopathology" (1950/1955, p.375). Jung, later in life, was also well aware of how affects or "*affectio*" (as in the Latin text from Albertus Magnus) are what play the most important role in what he called synchronistic events (1960/1969, p.448).

[175] Jung, 1960/1969, p.11 footnote

[176] 1957, p.181

[177] Bleuler in Jung, 1969, p.40 footnote

[178] Jung, in 1909, wrote an abstract for Bleuler's book (*Affectivität...*), saying: "The conception of attention and suggestibility as special instances or partial manifestations of affectivity is a pleasing simplification of the Babylonian confusion of tongues and concepts prevailing in psychology and psychiatry today" (1950/1955, p.399). And he concluded saying: "We could easily wait for a hundred years until we got anything of this kind from experimental psychology" (p.400)—one hundred years have passed, and the Constellations work has offered an empirical demonstration of Bleuler's bright insight and Jung's insistence. Hellinger has commented that, much of what has been said about "free will," "self-responsibility," "man's autonomy," "man's thought and volition" has been challenged after the Family Constellations (2005/2008b, p.26)—just like Jung foresaw.

[179] "Affects always have a disturbing influence on consciousness, as they place undue emphasis on feeling-toned thought-processes and thus obscure any others that may be present" (Jung, 1957, p.203). Jung also mentioned that, "disturbances caused by affects are known technically as *phenomena of dissociation*, and are indicative of a psychic split" (1964b, p.139), allowing, therefore, dynamic states of possession. He acknowledged that, the indigenous notion and concept of "loss of soul and possession . . . [describe] exactly the symptoms which today are called of dissociation or schizoid states . . . [which] are found just as much in normal people. They may take the form of fluctuations in the general feeling of well-being, irrational changes of mood, inertia, and so on" (p.139).

[180] Jung, for instance, described some situations where one thinks and feels to be in love as an "obsessional complex" (1960, p.48). Hellinger also said, without wanting to make it a fixed statement and considering it as a speculation, that when "falling in love" one might awaken child necessities (Weber, 1999, p.125); which, if seen through Jung's theory, would naturally be necessities in relation to one's complex. Moreover, such necessities, if seen under Helllinger's view, could also obey the family's conscience, in order to compensate some psychic event form the past; that would be quite similar to Jung's view, who knew that, "where [personal] conscience seems to play no role, it appears indirectly in the form of compulsions or obsessions" (1964b, p.447). In such a sense, it is as if conscience were directing the motion of psychic energy towards something or someone in particular, without one even being conscious; some naïve people could consider falling deeply in love as an outburst of passionate emotion, often present in obsessional love, but in fact it would rather seem as if one were an instrument of such conscience spectrum.

[181] Jung, 1960, p.38

[182] It is important to notice, following Jung, that "[a]ffects lower the level of the relationships and bring it closer to the common instinctual basis, which no longer has anything individual about it. Very often the relationships run its course heedless of its human performers, who afterwards do not know what happened to them" (1951/1959, p.16).

[183] Jung, 1960/1969, p.12 footnote

[184] 1960/1969, p.11

[185] Jung, 1960/1969, p.12

[186] 1960/1969, p.121

[187] Jung, 1988, p.991

[188] 1999, p.45

[189] When founding the C.G. Jung Institute in Zürich, in 1948, Jung mentioned some possibilities for furthering the "complex psychology;" and he said: "In normal psychology, [that is, applied to the average individual,] the most important subject for research would be the psychic structure of the family in relation to heredity, the compensatory character of marriage and of emotional relationships in general" (1950/1955, pp.475-476). The work of Hellinger is indubitably an answer to such a suggestion.

[190] 1938/1966b, p.1

[191] Hillman, 1992.

[192] "This re-visioning of archetypal implies that the more accurate term for our psychology in its *operational* definition is *re-visioning*. In what we do we are more re-visionists than archetypalists" (Hillman, 1991, p.27); in other words, seeing, looking, gazing, glimpsing, glancing, and seeing through more than anything else.

[193] This is not at all a new way of knowing, and *seeing*, but a very old one. Jung was well aware of how "we have that tendency of personifying everything since the days of ancient Greece" (1988, p.852). Hillman advocated strongly for the greater clarity and transparency of personifying over conceptualizing, because, he said, "[o]nce you're engaged with a personified figure the emotion is there, love is there, dislike, all kind of emotional activity" (Hillman & Shamdsani, 2013, p.32).

[194] Corbin claimed that, "the *imaginal* space . . . [is] where the active Imagination freely manifests its visions and its epics" (1990/1998, p.168). He made clear that, "[t]he *mundus imaginalis* is not the world of phantoms shown on the cinema screen, but the world of 'subtle bodies' in the world of sensible-spiritual" (1987, p.230). Therefore, he stated that such is "the world where the corporeal is spiritualised [*sic*] and the spiritual takes on body" (p.230).

[195] Jung said: "When a thing is personified it has autonomy and you can talk to it" (1988, p.1259); but such technique is not like that of Pearls and the Gestaltians, where one imagines a thing or a person and imagines childishly what he, she, or it would say. This view of psychic issues rather acknowledges their *real* autonomy, therefore they are *imaginal* and not simply imaginary.

[196] Jung commented: "if a patient in analysis feels obsessed, it is the task of the analyst to dispossess him . . . and in such a case one turns him around and says, 'Now look at the thing.' And in that moment it gets off him. He can objectify it. That is the reason why we should objectify unconscious figures . . . they occur as if they were really in one's system" (1988, p.1265)—and one might think of both the physical and the familial system.

[197] Even though a (family) constellation is referred to as an *Aufstellung* in German (Hellinger's original therapeutic coinage), the sense of it is to "figure things out" by placing (*aufstellen*) representatives in relation to one another, as if it were a positioning of people (*Montage*).

[198] Hillman, 1992.

[199] 1992, p.3

[200] Ibid, p.57

[201] Hellinger has expressed a similar idea saying: "it is curious that in certain diseases it is not that we are going through a bad time, but that the soul needs them [the diseases], so that through them it achieves something that through another path would be impossible" (Hellinger, 2000/2001b, p.59, free translation).

[202] 1992, p.71

[203] 1992, p.89

[204] Rumi wrote in his poem, *Childhood friends*: "Whoever sees clearly what's diseased in himself/ begins to gallop on the way" (Jalāl al-Din Rumi, 1995, p.141).

[205] 1992, p.110

[206] Hillman wrote it quite clear: "By *pathologizing* I mean the psyche's autonomous ability to create illness, morbidity, disorder, abnormality, and suffering in any aspect of its behavior and to experience and imagine life through this deformed and afflicted perspective" (1976, p.141); that which he did not explain so clearly was the teleological function of pathologizing. Jung, on the other hand, prior to him and regarding psychological disturbances, considered that, when "[a] man is ill . . . the illness is nature's attempt to heal him" (p.170), and such insight can be thought and applied for almost all physical diseases as well.

[207] The late constellations method, also known as the "new family constellations" has been developed, and named as such, by Hellinger since 2005, approximately, and it has kept on developing.

[208] Weber, 1999.

[209] Weber, 1999, p.43, Hellinger, 2008/2009, p.27

[210] Weber, 1999, p.43

[211] Bleuler, from whom Jung learned the importance of affectivity, mentioned: "It is likely that we act only under the influence of pleasure/unpleasure feelings; our logical reflections get their power only from the affects associated with them." In other words, the conscience of right and wrong seems to be directed by the feelings of pleasure or displeasure—not different at all from Hellinger's explanation of the *personal conscience*. "Thus affectivity, much more than reflection, is the driving force behind all our actions and omissions" (Bleuler in Jung, p.38 footnote).

[212] Weber, 1999, p.170, free translations

[213] Weber, 1999, p.170, free translations

[214] Previously explained.

[215] 2008/2009, p.32

[216] It is worth reading Jung's brief essay: *A psychological view of conscience* (1964b, pp.437-455), where he claimed that, "[c]onscience is, in itself, an autonomous psychic factor" (p.446). For him, it could be considered a "phenomenon consisting on the one hand in an elementary act of will, or in an impulse to act for which no conscious reason can be given, and on the other hand in a judgment grounded on rational feeling . . . [which] reveals the subjective point of reference" (p.437); as if it were something that pushes an individual to act in a certain way, according to the way he or she feels—quite close to what Hellinger discovered later, indeed. In his view, "[c]onscience may appear as an act of conscious reflection which anticipates, accompanies, or follows certain *psychic events* (italics added), or as a mere emotional concomitant of them, in which case its moral character is not immediately evident" (p.437). It is as if conscience, for Jung, were that which conditions the feeling values of every event or anything in the individual's life—produced and enhanced by the feeling-tone complex. However, he considered that, "the moral evaluation of an action, which expresses itself in the feeling-tone of the accompanying ideas, *is not always dependent on consciousness but may function without it* (italics added)" (p.438); in other words, one may not be aware of its influence, and one might follow one's conscience without one even knowing! That is crucial, because it would mean "that the ego has been replaced by an unconscious personality who performs the necessary act of conscience" (p.439), as if one were possessed or too identified with a certain psychic content or psychic event that dwells in one's conscience—which is of a communal nature. Therefore, Jung claimed, "[c]onscience as an ethical authority extends only as far as consciousness extends" (1950/1955, p.811), but as a psychic autonomous influence conscience extends as far as one's lineages.

[217] This is similar to Jung's view of conscience as containing "'collective representations' which almost invariably govern the prescribed mode of behaviour [*sic*]" (1964b, p.443), maintaining the actions of the people who belong to that group within a notion of what is perceived and believed to be good. Moreover, Jung, following observations and insights from the so-called "primitive peoples" (which could be thought in the sense of primal peoples) suggested that, "everything that we would call pure chance [or accidental, could be] understood to be intentional[,]" as if fate and fatalities were directed by such autonomous psychic phenomenon (conscience), which often, in such a context, is "regarded as a magical influence" (p.443). This observation, although not so detailed, is not different from Hellinger's notion of the family's and group's conscience.

[218] Nietzsche saw, for example, how "war" could be a "detour to suicide, but a detour with a good conscience" (1887/1974, p.270); in other words, following what the group supports to be good, even if one dies for it. In his peculiar hammering way he had already spoken about a "group consciousness" that "does not really belong to man's individual existence but rather to his social or herd nature . . . [where] consequently . . . 'to know ourselves', each of us will always succeed in becoming conscious only of what is not individual but 'average'" (p.299). Jung also knew very well "the inescapable grip of the collective" and knew that rarely a man (or woman) "has succeeded in extricating himself form that fatal identity with the group psyche" (1954, p.178). For Jung, "[c]ollective ideas always have a religious character, and a philosophical idea becomes collective when it expresses a primordial image" (1921/1972b, p.220); hence, he considered that, "the great problems of life, including of course sex, are always related to the primordial images of the collective unconscious" (p.220), like God, creation, the genesis, humans' origins, Heaven, Hell, salvation, liberation, redemption, resurrection, karma, and so on and so forth.

[219] 2008/2009, p.58

[220] Hellinger, 2008/2009, p.63, free translation

[221] Hellinger & ten Hövel, 1999.

[222] Weber, 1999, p.171, free translation

[223] Hillman, referring to a work by C.S. Lewis, was aware that, "'[c]onscious' once meant in English 'a knowing together,' or a together-knowing, shared like a secret between those let in on it." From such connotation, he argued further that, "consciousness itself has an erotic, Dionysian component that points to participation" (1992b, pp.295-296), and, one could say, to community. It is worth noticing that Jung emphatically mentioned that, "the so-called unity of consciousness is an illusion . . . We like to think that we are one; but we are not, most decidedly not" (1950/1955, p.73). In simpler words, an individual's consciousness, even when he or she thinks is very personal, is influenced by autonomous psychic contents; it is indivisible from his or her family history, community, and group conscience—it is, like Hillman claimed, a "knowing together."

[224] Weber, 1999, p.171, free translation

[225] Jung observed that "[i]t is safe to assume that what the East calls 'mind' has more to do with our 'unconscious' than with mind as we understand it, which is more or less identical with consciousness" (1958, p.484); and he ventured to say that "there is no evidence that the unconscious contents are related to an unconscious centre analogous to the ego; in fact there are good reasons why such a centre is not even probable" (p.485). In other words, the vast unconscious is not egotistical, it is not a personal issue, it is not an outcome of one's life; of course, this is a whole different notion and conception of the unconscious from that of Freud, Freudians, and Freudo-centric philosophies and studies. If this distinction were taken more seriously, one could not say that the work of Jung is similar to that of Freud; the ontological point of departure from each view is entirely different, it would be a grave error to see them alike—a most common error, unfortunately.

[226] Dalai Lama, 2005, p.122

[227] Kilpatrick, 1997, p.46

[228] 2009b, p.211

[229] Within such circumstances, one indeed feels like Rilke wrote: "It seems as if I were at once/ child, boy, and man, and more/ I know the cycle is only complete/ as each element returns" (2001, p.87). Kingsley, basing his arguments on Old Greek philosophy and a serious study of mystical traditions saw this clear, and he mentioned it with profound words: "we're not just twenty or forty or seventy years old. That's only appearance. *We're ancient, incredibly ancient* (italics added). We hold the history of the stars in our pockets" (1999, p.9).

[230] Hellinger did multidimensional constellations during his last International seminars (after 2006, ca.), but I have not come across a book explaining them. Later, possibly, the videos will be available.

[231] There are some lines by Rumi, from his poem *Where everything is music*, saying: "Stop the words now./ Open the window in the center of your chest,/ and let the spirits fly in and out" (Jalāl al-Din Rumi, 1995, p.35). Most

probably, like the Narby realized after spending some time with the indigenous and a few *sheripiari* (shamans) from the Amazon, *practice is the most advanced form of theory* (1995/ 1997, p.41).

[232] 2006, p.195

[233] Mason Boring has suggested that a constellation can be facilitated and seen as an indigenous "ceremony" (2012, pp.31-37), but it is a difficult word because "many associate the word 'ceremony' with their own personal experience with harmful zealous religiosity or theological insult" (p.36). Similarly, Nicky Arden, a woman who went through a transformational process, in South Africa, in order to become a *sangoma* (a diviner and healer), wrote, in regards to her process of healing, when listening to the spirits: "It is as though I have become connected to some deep energy, or perhaps some deep energy field" (1996, p.145). It can be thought that the "deep energy field," which can be accessed through divination or ceremonies, can also be accessed through constellations.

[234] Corbin acknowledged similar insights, and he referred the work of Nicholas Oresme, a XIV century French thinker, saying: "He considers the corporeal quality as being made up of a double corporeality. There is the one resulting from the extension of the subject in the three dimensions of space, and there is another which is only imaged (*imaginée*) and which results from the intensity of the quality multiplied by the multiplicity of surfaces which one can detect in the inner nature of a subject. I have just spoken of this as an intuition of Genius because from it it emerges that the whole notion of corporeality, from the very fact that it supposes a fourth dimension, completes itself in the *mundus imaginalis*" (1981, p.12).

[235] Dalai Lama, 2005, p.13

[236] Hellinger, 2008, p.25, free translation

[237] Hellinger once said that "[t]o some extent, the constellations have a liturgical quality and are healing rites" (Hellinger & ten Hövel, 1999, p.8), but constellations are never the same, they are like "a rite that is adapted to the specific situation . . . [it] arises from the configuration of the moment, and it's not repeatable" (p.69).

[238] Rumi wrote in his poem titled *Someone digging in the ground:* "Mysteries are not to be solved. The eye goes blind/ when it only wants to see *why*" (Jalāl al-Din Rumi, 1995, p.107). In this respect, Hellinger commented that a constellation is "an occurrence in multiple levels and if one does not interpret it then it has more opportunities to act" (2001/2008, p.262, free translation). More so, he continued, "In relation to subatomic particles it has been proved in physics that by observing thoroughly certain characteristics others go unnoticed . . . So, when one observes something thoroughly or defines it or interprets it, one takes away the openness and possibility to continue developing. For this reason diagnostics in psychotherapy are sometimes dangerous" (p.262, free translation).

[239] 1950/1955, p.774

[240] Wolff, a psychologist who lived and worked among several indigenous populations, and especially having made close contact with the Sng'oi of Malaysia, wrote a beautiful book in which he described a different way of knowing, which he called: "a sense of *knowing.*" He said: "For me it works when I can get out of my mind, when I can experience without having to understand, or name, or position, or judge, or categorize . . . . I am saying this after

the fact, trying to describe something that does not fit into our Western concepts, and therefore there are no words" (2001, p.158).

[241] Jalāl al-Din Rumi, 1995, p.256

[242] Jung, 1988, p.350

[243] 1887/1974, p.34

[244] 1995, p.309

[245] In the previous chapter, named "The constellation," three structures of attention were mentioned and established, in order to deepen the phenomenological understanding of Hellinger's work; those were: the body, the family, and the orders of love.

[246] Hillman has argued that, "[b]esides being an object, [which has been a very common and usual conception,] the body is also an experience" (1965/1997, p.145).

[247] 1988, p.980

[248] In this respect it is worth mentioning Jung's remark that, "[t]he stomach, according to Paracelsus, is the alchemist in the belly" (1966c, p.19); "hence philosophy was in essence an alchemical procedure" (p.27) which had to produce an effect in "the body."

[249] Jung, 1988, p.980

[250] Prior to Jung, Nietzsche said something in the same sense, in the chapter titled "On immaculate perception" (the title is not a coincidence,) from his book *Thus spoke Zarathustra*. He boldly wrote (addressing the humanity of his time and place) how "[y]our spirit has been persuaded to despise what is earthly, but not your entrails: and *they are what is strongest in you!*" (1894/2005, p.106). Such sentence, which of course, having come from Nietzsche, cannot be taken literally as only the entrails, refers to what is bodily. Hence, he continued a few lines later: "So dare for once to believe yourselves—yourselves and your entrails! Whoever does not believe himself, always lies" (p.107).

[251] 1954b, p.82

[252] 1894/2005, p.30

[253] This is the title of Nietzsche's chapter: "On the despisers of the body," from *Thus Spoke Zarathustra*.

[254] 1999, p.125

[255] Thinking is not a function only of the head and the brain; the whole organism participates, as Damasio pointed out (1999). However, an individual body is part of a larger organism, the family system; therefore, it thinks and feels accordingly. Thinking without having sensed and perceived the current state of this larger organism might be narrow, rigid, and dangerously biased. The body, naturally, is the individual field of experience by which one can sense and

perceive the influence of greater systems: familial, cultural, spiritual, etc. To despise such bodily experiences could be the same as deciding to remain not-conscious; oftentimes, one's tragedy of choice.

[256] Jung, 1988, p.350

[257] This is, indeed, Nietzsche suggestion too, who said that, "[a]bove all, one should not wish to divest existence of its *rich ambiguity*" (1887/1974, p.335). This boldness to leave the concept of the body without a clear definition, almost as an anti-concept, is in fact a very old teaching, as Ray pointed out, "[t]he fist step on the Tibetan yoga path is to progressively strip away everything we *think* about what our body is. Eventually, we arrive at a point where we have no mental picture left and we actually *know nothing* of what or how the body may be" (2008/2014, p.52).

[258] 1992, p.111, free translation

[259] Ortega was a great homeopathic medicine physician; he was considered a practitioner of great understanding of Hahnemann's legacy, even his continuator and the man who completed the work. He co-founded "Homeopatía de México," a school that strictly follows Hahnemann's *unicist* model.

[260] 1950/1955, p.23

[261] There are some lines by Rumi, regarding evidently the divine, saying: "They try to say what you are, spiritual or sexual?/ They wonder about Solomon and all his wives" (Jalāl al-Din Rumi, 1995, p.37).

[262] There is a passage in Jung's *Red Book*, where Philemon told him: "Spirituality and sexuality are not your qualities, not things you possess and encompass. Rather, they possess and encompass you . . . No man has a spirituality unto himself, or a sexuality unto himself. Instead, he stands under the law of spirituality and of sexuality" (2009b, p.352). Therefore, he considered that, "[t]o the psyche, spirit is no less spirit for being named sexuality" (1954b, p.52).

[263] Just like Rumi wrote, in his poem titled *One Strong brushstroke down*: "Don't squint and frown/ trying to distinguish soul from body" (Jalāl al-Din Rumi, 1995, p.336). Jung was well aware that, "[i]t is due to our most lamentable mind that we cannot think of body and mind as one and the same thing; probably they are *one* thing, but we are unable to think it" (1950/1955, p.33). (Mind is the English word for the German *Geist,* which also means spirit.) In this sense, the body can be seen as the place where the sensorial knowledge converges and gets integrated, but also where the intellective knowledge takes form; moreover, it can be seen as the mirror that gives sensorial knowledge to autonomous images that are not present in the physical world. Everybody has experienced this vastly, every night in dreams. To expand on this see the essay *Theory of Visionary Knowledge* (Corbin, 1987, pp.230-232), and *The Imago Templi and Secular Norms* (Corbin, 1975, pp.165-166).

[264] Nietzsche, 1887/1974, p.35

[265] The body can also be considered, as Jung well said, as "the particular capacity of acuteness of consciousness . . . which restricts you to a certain place in space and a certain moment in time" (1988, p.349); but even such operational definition is ambiguous due to the accuracy and attunement of consciousness. Jung was well aware that the "unconscious processes are constantly supplying us with contents which, if consciously recognized, would extend

the range of consciousness" (1971, p.194). Therefore, one's physicality, as the embodiment of "the unconscious[,] appears as a field of experience of unlimited extent" (1971, p.194).

[266] There is a great insight by Jung, who wrote that, "[m]atter is an hypothesis. When you say 'matter,' you are really creating a symbol for something unknown, which may just as well be 'spirit' or anything else; it may even be God" (1958, p.477). One can also read in Jung's *Red Book*: "to explain matter is arbitrary and sometimes even murder. Have you counted the murderers among the scholars?" (2009b, p.230). In fact, such an insight resembles very much Nietzsche's posture and perspective (previously mentioned).

[267] Dodds argued, tracking the notions since the ancient Greece, that "[b]etween *psyche* . . . and *soma* (body) there is no fundamental antagonism" (1951, p.138). In this book, for the purposes of a better general understanding, the words "body," "bodies," "bodily," and "embodiment" will still be used to refer the physical experiences and domain, but in a broader, wider, and deeper sense than usual, not at all limited to the so-called material perspectives and material causality.

[268] "It is an almost ridiculous prejudice to assume that existence can only be physical" (Jung, 1966b, p.11).

[269] Interestingly enough, Jung mentioned that "[t]he adversary is the somatic man," which could be understood as that which is related to the autonomous functions of the corporeal existence, because he was well grounded in a perspective that acknowledges that "a living body is indispensable part of the personality" (1952/1968, p.94). However, he was well aware also that the somatic is psychic, realizing then that the ailments in the physical body, were also psychic *matters*, and that the bodily issues could not be left behind as mere carnal issues, because the body is required for the psychological experience—which could be better said as: the experience of being human is ineffably corporeal.

[270] Jung, in an essay delivered in 1934, acknowledged that "the illusion still continued to flourish that psychological treatment was some kind of technical procedure" (p.157); and several decades later people still believe that learning therapy is about learning a mixture of techniques. "It has long been imagined that psychotherapy can be practiced 'technically,' as though it were a formula, a method of opinion, or a colour [*sic*] test[;]" however, "the point is not the technique but the person who uses the technique" (Jung, 1964b, p.159).

[271] In some way, this resonates with Socrates, who said in Plato's third book of the *Republic*: "I, for my part, do not believe that a sound body by its excellence makes the soul good, but on the contrary that a good soul by its virtue renders the body the best that is possible" (1989, p.648).

[272] in Bly, Hillman, & Meade, 1992, p.113

[273] "A technique is always a soulless mechanism, and whoever takes psychotherapy for a technique and vaunts it as such runs the risk, at the very least, of committing an unpardonable blunder" (Jung, 1964b, p.168).

[274] Neumann, 1969, p.118

[275] Neumann, a close collaborator and pupil of Jung, observed that "[the] inclusion of the unconscious always entails inclusion of the body at the same time" (1969/1990, p.118); meaning that it would affect the body's organic

functioning. He argued that "the totality of the body, in its unitariness and centredness [*sic*], works unconsciously as a natural phenomenon in everything organic" (p.118), in an autonomous way, as if it were the integrated or disintegrated work of many psychic contents (or figures).

[276] I am cautious when I say this, acknowledging the magnificent and groundbreaking therapeutic methodology developed by Peter Levine, called *Somatic Experiencing*. It is probably the most insightful and exquisite, as much as respectful and loving technique when it comes to addressing issues about corporeal matters. His methodology did not start as a technique addressing matters pertaining the soul, it was fundamentally a corporeal technique; therefore, the chosen naming for it seemed the appropriate one: *Somatic Experiencing*. However, I do realize that Levine's brilliant genius is still moving extensively into other disciplines, his methodology still in the making, and his technique still developing deeply—possibly already into psychic transgenerational issues, as he revealed in his book *Trauma and Memory* (2015, pp.161-170); and into spiritual experiences, as he revealed in his book *In an unspoken voice* (2010, pp.347-356). Like he pointed out, "spiritual transformation emerges from a 'refining' of the instincts" (2010, p.283), in other words, from engaging with one's physicality. In the light of this, I acknowledge that in a near future we might be able to refer to the physical body using the term "somatic," again, without meaning mere carnal issues, but implying physical matters that have to do with the family system, the dead, soul and the spirit.

[277] Hellinger, 2008/2009, p.47, free translation

[278] There is an alchemical passage, quoted by Jung in order to point towards *dark matters*, saying: "Man is generated from the principle of Nature, whose inward parts are fleshy, and from no other substance" (1952/1968, p.110), where he is clearly referring to the *temenos* (p.107), which is indeed the "body" as a container, a vessel, but conceived as the alchemical *lapis*. One can assume that the "body of flesh" itself is a field (a terrain) in which alchemical transformations can take place, and where the "*sol niger*, the black sun of alchemy" (p.110), that Jung mentioned, shines with its "dark light". This corresponds to what Zavala, called "an invisible light, an invisible sun, an invisible wisdom . . . this light was an intuitive comprehension of the circumstances, an illumination art. One could designate this phenomenon in our modern psychological language [quoting Jung] as an 'unconscious, instinctive wisdom'" (1977, pp.26-27, free translation). In such a sense, one could think that an individual is not born only because of biological casualties, but because of an instinctive supremacy that moves throughout the generations, aiming to enlighten the flesh.

[279] There is a passage in Jung's *Red Book,* where Philemon told him: "sexuality approaches our soul as a serpent. She is half human soul and is called thought-desire . . . She bears up the too-crafty thoughts of the earthly, those thoughts that creep through every hole and cleave to all things with craving. Although the serpent does not want to, she must be of use to us. She flees our grasp, thus showing us the way, which our human wits could not find" (2009b, p.353).

[280] Such view of life is not limiting the scope only to the individual notion of it; on the contrary, it rather acknowledges that the essential quality of any individual is its *aliveness*, and any other characteristic is but an accidental feature that is necessary for the experience of life in such a way. Even the idea of "individuality" itself is of a secondary order, being *life* and the light of Nature, the "quinta essentia," as Zavala claims (1977, pp.29), what we all are.

[281] Kerenyi, 1976

[282] Kerényi argued that, "[b]ecause life includes heredity—otherwise it would not be life—it transcends the limit of the individual, mortal, living creature and proves in every individual case, regardless of whether or not heredity is actually realized, indestructible. Life presupposes heredity and possesses the seed of temporal infinity" (1976, p.xxviii). Kerényi sustained this idea based on the marked differences between the Greek words *bios* and *zoë*, the first meaning finite characterized life, and the second infinite indestructible life. He wrote: "*zoë* is the thread upon which every individual *bios* is strung like a bead, and which in contrast to *bios*, can be conceived only as *endless*" (1976, p.xxxv). According to Kerényi, it is in this sense that Socrates claimed, in Plato's *Phaedo*: "So soul is immortal" (Plato, 1989, p.87). This idea comes close to Hellinger's notion of *being in the service of life,* in the sense of being in the service of something greater that moves through individual lives but transcends them spatially and temporally.

[283] 1956, p.129

[284] Jung, 1988, p.403

[285] It is worth noticing what Jung wrote in a letter to Joan Corrie, in reference to his *Septem Sermones ad Mortuous*: "The primordial creator of the world, the blind creative libido, becomes transformed in man through individuation & out of this process, which is like pregnancy, arises a divine child, a reborn God, no more (longer) dispersed into millions of creatures, but being one & this individual, and at the same time all individuals, the same in you as in me . . . The child is a new God, actually born in many individuals, but they don't know it. He is a spiritual God. A spirit in many people, yet one and the same everywhere" (in Jung, 2009b, p.354 footnote).

[286] Hellinger, 2008/2009, p.47, free translation

[287] Jung, 1988, p.403

[288] In Hellinger's view, this dynamic reality is strongly influenced by invisible loyalties to the family of origin and family members of the past—on a first instance.

[289] Hellinger, 2008/2009, p.147

[290] Jung, 1988, p.433

[291] Ibid, p.433

[292] Jung realized that, "if we can reconcile ourselves to the mysterious truth that the spirit is the life of the body seen from within, and the body the outward manifestation of the life of the spirit—the two being really one—then we can understand why the striving to transcend the present level of consciousness through acceptance of the unconscious must give the body its due" (1964b, p.94).

[293] Hillman has observed how with the mainstream psychological jargon and practices "[w]e forget and literalize the soul inside the skin, the mind inside the skull, the dream, the emotion, the memory inside the 'me' to the neglect of the collective psyche, the *anima mundi* in which we live our lives all day long" (2007, p.232). This reflection opens a powerful critique to most psychotherapies that try to alleviate the individual in isolation and within confined consultancy rooms.

[294] Jung, 1952/1968, p.91

[295] Jung, 1952/1968, p.91

[296] Nietzsche mentioned that "[a] 'scientific' explanation of the world, as you understand it, might therefore be one of the *most stupid* of all possible interpretations of the world, meaning that it would be one of the poorest in meaning" (1887/1974, p.335); and even when this was said more than thirteen decades ago, it still seems to apply in many cases—unfortunately. Similarly, Jung wrote that, "[o]rdinary reasonableness, sound human judgment, science as a compendium of common sense . . . afford no answer to the question of psychic suffering and its profound significance" (1958, p.330)—there is *something else.* Hence, he boldly criticized the scientific approach, which he considered "an excellent way of getting rid of the inconvenient emotional components of conscience, notwithstanding that these are the real dynamics of the moral reaction . . . [and without which] the phenomenon of conscience loses all meaning" (1964b, p.446).

[297] 1952/1968, p.280

[298] Jung, 1960/1969, p.200

[299] It is worth considering Jung's peculiar notion of *instinct,* saying that: "[i]t is even probable that archetypes are the psychic expressions or manifestations of instinct" (1960, p.255). He even wrote that, "the unconscious psyche must consist of inherited instincts, functions, and forms that are peculiar to the ancestral psyche. This collective heritage is by no means made up of inherited ideas, but rather of the possibilities of such ideas—in other words, of *a priori* categories of possible functioning. Such inheritance could be called instinct, using the word in its original sense" (1954b, p.34). The word stems from the preposition *in,* which denotes "marking bounds or limits within" (Onions, 1996, p.466), and the Latin *stinguere,* meaning to prick (p.478); hence, instinct etymologically suggests an "innate impulse." Jung, for a time, considered that "[e]very psychic phenomenon is instinctive that does not arise from voluntary causation but from dynamic impulsion, irrespective of whether this impulsion comes directly from organic, extra-psychic sources, or from energies that are merely released by voluntary intention—in the latter case with the qualification that the end-result exceeds the effect voluntarily intended" (1921/1971b, p.451). However, he realized that, "[i]nstinct is not an isolated thing, nor can it be isolated in practice. It always brings in its train archetypal contents of a spiritual nature, which are at once its foundation and its limitation" (1954b, p.81). It could be said that instinct is the creative principle of life, the movement of the living, the will to live, the will to live more, and the *will to power* (in Nietzsche's sense)—consciously or not.

[300] In the end, like Van der Kolk insightfully addressed it, "the body keeps the score" (2014); that is, the physical body manifests the unresolved issues, the unattended difficulties, the toughness of life, and the traumas, inevitably—until attended, resolved, and redeemed from them. He reveals groundbreaking insights in regards to trauma, and particularly, in *Paths to recovery* (part five of the book, pp.205-348), he acknowledged the importance of "creating structures" that allow individuals to find a better place within their families and systems.

[301] Jung, 1988, p.1239

[302] There is an interesting dialogue in Plato's third book of the *Republic,* where Socrates inquired about physical health, and asked whether the bodily habit of athletes was the best, and after receiving an affirmative answer, he

questioned further: "Don't you observe that they sleep away their lives, and that if they part ever so little from their prescribed regimen these athletes are liable to great and violent diseases?" (Plato, 1989, pp.648-649).

[303] One of Jung's description of the unconscious part of the psyche is that it is "hard and immitigable as granite, immovable, inaccessible, yet ready to come crashing down upon us at the behest of unseen powers" (1954, p.177); and of course one cannot take such statement in plain literality, because it does not make sense. One might rather think that Jung meant that the unconscious (aspect of the) psyche is not a thin-air speculation, but a real, serious "thing," that gains more recognition when sensed and felt—although this unfortunately happens often only through accidents, illnesses, misfortunes, tragedies, symptoms, severe pains, or some kind of *concrete* event; however, it does is accessible and movable through the adequate methods.

[304] Jung, 1988, p.1239

[305] Hausner, 2008/2009, Kutschera & Schäffer, 2002/2006

[306] 2008/2009, p.43

[307] Jung, first and foremost a physician, acknowledged that "[the doctor] is bound to recognize that there are many diseases and states of suffering which, not being susceptible of a direct cure, demand from both patient and doctor some kind of attitude to their irremediable nature" (1950/1955, p.697); because in many instances the disease is bound to an attitude of the sufferer, and unless the individual changes it—alone or with the help of the physician—the disease will remain. Therefore, observing something quite bold and hard to comprehend, he wrote: "it is very important that the doctor should not strive to heal at all costs . . . Sometimes it is really a question whether you are allowed to rescue a man from the fate he must undergo for the sake of his further development" (1976, p.131). Hellinger's attitude, when helping people, is not different from this.

[308] Jung, 1952/1968 p.282

[309] There are many videos available from live seminars in which Hellinger helped people with some kind of disease. One can watch some examples in "Family constellations and their contribution to health" (Hellinger, 2007).

[310] 1952/1958, p.297

[311] 1952/1967, p.167

[312] Jalāl al-Din Rumi, 2003, p.180

[313] Of course, like Durand observed, alchemy *should not* be reduced to "a method—or, worse still, a recipe—for making gold [in a literal sense] . . . What the adept does through his work and meditation is to make manifest the unity of the world, particularly the world of metals, while at the same time unifying himself" (1976, p.88).

[314] It has been a great mistake to consider Jung's theoretical insights and visions a disembodied discipline; he clearly stated that, "[i]n the alchemical tradition 'philosophia,' 'sapientia,' and 'scientia' were essentially the same . . . [and] in some strange way imagined as being quasi-material, or at least as being contained in matter" (1966c,

p.26). He knew from Paracelsus, for instance, that "the physician must know alchemy in order to diagnose human diseases from their analogy with diseases in minerals. And finally, he himself is the subject of the alchemical process of transformation, since he is 'ripened' by it" (p.20). Rumi, long before Jung and Paracelsus, wisely mentioned in his poem titled *Solomon to Sheba*: "The *alchemy* of a changing life is the only truth" (Jalāl al-Din Rumi, 1995, p.188).

[315] *Sensuousness* is not a very common term. In this work, it is used following Jung, "not in the vulgar sense of *voluptas,* but [as] a psychological attitude in which the orienting and determining factor is not so much the emphasized object as the mere fact of sensory excitation . . . [therefore] this attitude might also be described as reflexive, since the whole mentality depends on and culminates in sensory-impressions" (1921/1971b, p.312). It is not a sensualistic attitude, as if it were a matter of pleasure-displeasure, nor mere sensationalism, which could be considered as an "extreme empiricism" (p.311).

[316] Jung, 1988, p.800

[317] Ibid.

[318] Thus, following the insights offered by Ray, "perhaps surprisingly, what we fear or are anxious about is never the external world in itself—rather, it is our own body, what it already feels and what it already knows" (2008/2014, p.110).

[319] Jung wisely mentioned, long time ago, that, "it should not be forgotten that science is not the *summa* of life, that it is only actually one of the psychological attitudes, only one of the forms of human thought" (1921/1971, p.41); a good advice in the age of neuroscience. He wisely wrote once: "One has to look at the history of science: how many have *been* right, and how few have *remained* right!" (1961, p.133)—it might seem advisable to remain wondering about impossibilities, rather than only believing scientific truths.

[320] Grinberg-Zylberbaum, 1994 & Jodorowsky, 2005.

[321] Jung, 1933, p.219.

[322] Jung wrote in his *Red Book*: "matter that is stripped of the divine radiance of force is empty and dark" (2009b, p.288). There are some lines by Rumi, from his poem *A king inside who listens*, saying: "There are many people with their eyes open/ whose hearts are shut. What do they see?/ Matter" (Jalāl al-Din Rumi, 1995, p.321).

[323] Jung's view was that, "[m]atter is a quality of an existence which is absolutely psychical" (1988, p.986); in other words, matter is psyche, the flesh is soul.

[324] Jung, 1988, p.355

[325] 1894/2005, p.131

[326] Ibid.

[327] Jung knew this too, quite well; he wrote: "he who accepts what approaches him because it is also in him, quarrels and wrangles no more, but looks into himself and keeps silent" (2009b, p.301).

[328] Jung, when commenting on the contents of the complex, mentioned that, "such contents are somehow associated with physiological reactions, with the processes of the heart, the tonus of blood vessels, the condition of the intestines, the breathing, and the innervation [*sic*] of the skin" (1950/1955, p.71).

[329] 1992, p.79

[330] 1992, p.90

[331] 1992, p.105

[332] Hillman, 1992, p.80

[333] 1933, p.91

[334] One has to be aware, also, like Guggenbühl-Craig suggested, that moralism does not make illnesses fall into the categories of sins for one's psychological failures or lack of adaptation, like psychosomatic medicine easily tends to do (1995, pp.105-112). Oftentimes, regrettably, physical illnesses and pains have been regarded as the consequence of negative personality traits of the person, as if being shy and apprehensive were the cause of cramped intestines. Such diagnoses blame it all on the person's inabilities, and tend to humiliate more than heal. When this perspective is in charge, as in many psychotherapeutic and bodywork settings, the soul escapes, runs out of the room, and one is left alone with the therapist, reduced to flesh, bones, and viscera with one's personality in disorder. Therefore, it is highly recommended to acknowledge that when addressing bodily issues, the theory or body-metaphor requires the perspective of the soul (the complex and the unconscious) in order to attend the tissues beyond only sensation.

[335] Hillman insisted vastly on this, hence he quoted Sendovingius in saying that: "The greater part of the soul is outside the body." See *Anima Mundi* (1992c, pp.89-130).

[336] The Native American scholar Deloria Jr. has observed how "[w]ith science [in many cases]... we have inherited a strange body of doctrine that has limited our understanding considerably[,]" almost crippling intelligence, and certainly seriously damaging life on Earth. Moreover, "[w]ith Darwin's popularity, and the addition of Marxian and Freudian thought in the last century, we have created a society in which science reigns supreme" (2002, p.15), but in which life has been reduced only to what science can say about it—sadly, foolishly, and shamefully. One can reflect more on this observation when one thinks of some Western's paradigms commented by Deloria Jr, as it is the *monogenesis* of the world and the universe, the notions of *time as real and linear*, the divisive (and very schizophrenic) *binary thinking*, the *stability of the solar system*, or the *homogeneity and interchangeability of individuals* (p.15). Any of these "Western" world paradigms have been addressed through the Judeo-Christian traditions or through Westernized science, but those are not the only possibilities, it is only that many Westernized intellectuals have insisted just on those two ways of "thinking." As Deloria Jr. wisely comments, "Western science is totally dependent on Western religion for its worldview" (p.14), and it has been a great enterprise in the Western "thinking" traditions to give scientific answers to issues for which Western religions had already given the answers, as if only one or the other were correct, "as is the custom in the Western intellectual tradition, ... [posing] questions that can be answered

only in binary form—yes/no, right/wrong" (p.13); or, in the worst of all cases, to think that both are correct, without being aware that at the core it is still the same limiting paradigm. If one pushes Deloria's critique further, one might find that such ideas can shatter the ontological and epistemological premises of the Western worldviews. Those who are ignorant (of other traditions) think that only Westernized science or Westernized religion are the only ontological and cosmological ways of seeing and knowing which can explain life. Like he boldly observes, "[w]e like to believe that the histories created by Western science and religions are the proper way to understand the world" (p.125). If one can experience the depths of psyche one might realize that *science is only a modern myth;* and in fact it can limit understanding if one tries to explain everything through it, as it happened to the Mexican scientist Grinberg-Zylberbaum when trying to explain the miraculous healings by Pachita through the lens of his psycho-physiological education and his Eastern philosophical biases. Pachita repeatedly said that it was the spirit of Cuauhtemoc (the last Aztec *tlatoani*) the agent that did the healings, while Grinberg-Zylberbaum stubbornly wanted to fit Pachita's ability to heal with his *Syntergic Theory*. He wrote that Pachita found his theory interesting, but that she insisted that it was not she who did the healings, but Cuauhtemoc, *El Hermanito* (1994)—indeed, a blowout to both, Western intellect and (dominant) Western religions.

[337] This has become a fashionable statement among modern and post-modern intellectuals; and, like Jung wisely observed, "[a]mong these moderns there are of course some of those who are negative, destructive, and perverse natures—degenerate and unbalanced eccentrics—who are never satisfied anywhere . . . in the hope of finding something *for once* which will compensate at low cost for their own ineptitude" (1958, p.336).

[338] One can easily compare indigenous ways of living with Westernized ones, and rapidly realize Westernized men aim to live within concrete walls, literally and metaphorically, in architecture and thinking traditions, in philosophy and city planning; while other cultures acknowledge and live according to the fluid nature of reality, without implying that they are nomads. Moreover (and for worse), it is the tradition of the Westernized man to live according to what is concretized in writing, either graved on stone or written in a book, even if he borrows it from some Eastern or Middle-Eastern text. It is not surprising that the current hardly debatable *scriptures* are also the scientific journals. Westernized education has been concretized by the scriptures, religious or scientific, as if that which is written is or becomes "the truth;" whereas in other traditional and much older cultures, education is guided by a lived experience, and truth flows and is renewed throughout the generational stream of life. In some non-Western traditions, like Deloria Jr. observes (2002, p.ix), it is not conceived that man, and woman, "evolve" their beliefs, but that they "remember;" what a striking difference! Evolution could indeed be a fallacy, and "has nothing to offer us[;]" like he wisely claims, it is presented through "illogical dogmas, simplistic reasoning, and fantastical fictional scenarios" (p.88). It seems like a very cheap idea that has even infected conscience studies, and now people *believe* that conscience has evolved through the historical time of the Earth—if one inquires deeply on such assumption, one can easily find the presuppositions.

[339] Rumi wrote, in *The Fragile Vial*: "The body is a device to calculate/ the astronomy of the spirit./ Look through the astrolabe/ and become oceanic" (Jalāl al-Din Rumi, 1995, p.14). In a similar vein, Ray argued: "The body's aim . . . is always to fill us out, round us out, bring us to our own completion" (2008/2014, p.238).

[340] Hillman, 1992, p.51

[341] 1992, p.80

[342] This is also the homeopathic medicine's view, where "disease, is therefore a vital process, a series of phenomena that have place in the plane of energies, within the prodigious enigma that we denominate life." Disease, then, is an "energetic imbalance" (Ortega, P.S. 1992, pp.115-116, free translation). This is similar to the radical views of the New Germanic Medicine, which claims that any so-called "disease" by conventional medicine "is an intelligent biological happening, with a determined telos, which we need to interpret and comprehend again under the light of embryology and behavior studies" (Hamer, 1994/2005, p.16, free translation). Jung, in his early writings, when studying dementia praecox, was "incline[d] to the view that on the basis of a *disposition* (italics added) whose nature is . . . unknown . . . an unadapted [*sic*] psychological function arises which may develop into a manifest disturbance and *secondarily* induce symptoms of organic degeneration" (1960, p.156). This view of psychopathology can be applied to pathology in general, where a certain pre-disposition of psychic order posits the individual in a situation (an atmosphere) in which his or her organism is more vulnerable to the affections of life—that often end up manifesting organically. The organic manifestation of disease, from this view, is not prior to the psychological disturbance (as it was Jung's observation regarding dementia praecox and schizophrenia). It rather points to an affective disposition in one's psychic atmosphere, which might be determined by *how does one stand,* or *how does one find oneself* (*Befindlichkeit*) in regard to other psychic autonomous contents. Therefore, it can be assumed as accurate the idea that, "the symptom is really the effort of the diseased system to cure itself" (Jung, 1964b, p.168).

[343] Jung knew this too. In the famous Tavistock Lectures, delivered for an audience of persons involved in the medical profession, he mentioned: "The doctor especially should never lose sight of the fact that diseases are disturbed normal processes and not *entia per se* with a psychology exclusively their own" (1950/1955, p.6).

[344] 1992, p.126

[345] Jung commented: "The theory of knowledge [epistemology] does not of course figure in the medical curriculum, but is indispensable to the study of psychology" (1950/1955, p.524). In order to explore psychic issues and unconscious contents, one requires an epistemology that can see through and into psyche, so to speak; otherwise, that which one claims to know might be limited by a narrow theory of knowledge. A very experienced constellations facilitator suggested that, one requires "a way of seeing solutions using information beyond our normal objective reality . . . [which] involves waiting, listening, and allowing an organic healing movement that comes from a field beyond the cognitive mind" (Ulsamer in Mason Boring, 2012, p.20).

[346] 1933, p.91

[347] Artwork, embodied imagination, dreamwork, theatrical therapies, automatic narrative writings, and other techniques might serve this purpose; there is, however, the risk of getting trapped in the symptomatic or the superficialities, remaining with images or ideas that might resemble great symbolism, but not getting into the essentials. Jung even called *intuition* "a sort of divination, a sort of miraculous faculty" (1950/1955, p.14), a way to perceive things that are not physically present, but which are nevertheless actual; therefore, he defined it as "a sort of perception which does not go exactly by the senses, but it goes via the unconscious" (p.15). Jung, here, planted the seed for a new way of getting to know things, maybe an old one that had been forgotten, a different way of knowledge; he broadened the field of epistemology.

[348] Jung noticed, since his early writings, that the complex had "numerous somatic innervations" and "chronic effects" (1960, pp.41-51); this being so, because "[e]motions and affects are always accompanied by obvious physiological innervations" (Jung, 1950/1955, p.10). The powerful and insightful work of Somatic Experiencing, developed by Levine, which precisely addresses the autonomous nervous system and all things related (namely all organs, systems, and biological processes) could offer greater insights for dealing with that which Jung called the complex. If Levine's work, which addresses and heals the physical, is paired with investigations regarding how the unconscious aspects of the complex manifests somatically and observed in lived experience through the constellations work, then a powerful practice might widen the healing arts; this might be a new medicine path, but only time will tell.

[349] Jung observed that, "on the one hand the ego rests on the *total field of consciousness*, and on the other, on the *sum total of unconscious contents*" (1951/1959, p.4). The first part of Jung's observation might be acceptable, the notion of "I" rest on the beliefs, desires, thoughts, and all sensorial, emotional, and mental processes that one is, and has been aware of; however, the second part of his observation is simply overwhelming. The notion of "I" also rests on a terrain where there are many more contents than one could ever be aware of and many more than one could ever count.

[350] This is just like the Heraclitus fragment numbered as B89 by Diels-Kranz, which has been translated as: "Heraclitus says the universe for those who are awake is single and common, while in sleep each person turns aside into a private universe" (Waterfield, 2000, p.38). It has also been translated as: "The waking have one world in common. Sleepers meanwhile turn aside, each into a darkness of his own" (Heraclitus, 2001, p.63); so that, while all individuals share a public consensus of life, they also live, simultaneously, within a dreamlike world, a psychic configuration: the complex. The fragment has also been translated as: "Heraclitus says that for those awake there is a single common world, but that asleep each enters a private world" (in Barnes, 2001, p.62). This makes one think that it is not only during night-dreams that each lives in a private world, but also while being deeply immersed in the (psychic) complex one lives asleep.

[351] The term "force" is to facilitate understanding, but it is rather meant as in subatomic physics, where "the concept of force is therefore no longer useful" . . . "there are no such forces, but only interactions between particles, mediated through fields, that is through other particles. Hence physicists prefer to speak about interactions" (Capra, 1975, p.203). This is indeed close to Jung's notion of such a term, who said that, "[f]orces are phenomenal manifestations; what underlies their relations with one another is the hypothetical idea of energy, which is, of course, entirely psychological (1961, p.124).

[352] Jung, 1960/1969, p.103

[353] Jung, 1988, p.1214

[354] Jung, for instance, was aware "how often a single unpleasant impression produce in some people an unshakable false judgment, which no logic, no matter how cogent, can dislodge!" (1960, p.43). This is often the case in persons in whom the religious view and practice speaks more about the person's psychic configuration than truthful conviction and devotion. Some people turn to religious practices and spirituality because they cannot deal with their bodies and

the Earth, or because they cannot stand their mothers, or simply because money, relationships, and the professional life mean to face one's own unresolved life.

[355] Rumi, in his poem *Muhammad and the huge eater*, wrote, "Don't bore mouse holes/ in the ground, arguing inside some/ doctrinal labyrinth./ That intellectual warp and woof keep you wrapped/ in blindness" (Jalāl al-Din Rumi, 1995, p.66). Jung too knew that, "[e]ven a man with a highly developed intellect can go badly astray because he has never learnt to use his intuition or his feeling, which might be at a regrettably low level of development" (1950/1955, p.250). And it is not rare to see an even lower level of embodied consciousness in intellectuals; despite their high capacity to argue and write lucidly, there seems to be a lack of capacity to perceive the needs of the body and perceive how do these relate to a greater field of human interaction. Sometimes the exquisite capacity for literacy in regards to economics, social, political, or whatever intellectual issues is only a cover up for the illiteracy in regards to one's own bodily matters.

[356] 2009b, p.251

[357] Jung wrote in his *Red Book*: "Because there are so many among us who can talk about anything, pay heed to what they live" (2009b, p.301), and also on how they die; wisdom and genuine knowledge might not rely on what they wrote, but more on how they lived, loved, laughed, *and* left. In some indigenous traditions it is known that a man's life can be known by the way he leaves this world.

[358] 1964b, p.153

[359] 1956, p.97

[360] 1950/1955, p.263

[361] It is worth to mention some of Hillman's insights regarding the mythic figure Pan, the god of nature, from his book *Pan and the nightmare* (2007b), where he partially relates him to instinct (p.19), stating that, "[h]e lives in the repressed that returns . . . . [as if] we are returned by instinct to instinct" (p.27), whether that occurs by oneself or to oneself. Hence, Hillman related it to phenomena like: "rape, masturbation, nightmare panic, seduction by nymphs, and other Pan-induced events that force us out of civilized habits" (p.9). These insights, which could seem altogether too poetic, strive towards developing awareness of that which is corporeal, because, indeed, panic remembers bodily issues, and vice versa.

[362] Jung, 1933, p.178

[363] Hillman, 1992, p.119

[364] Jung, 1988, p.347

[365] Woodman, a Jungian analyst who focused for decades on body-soul rhythms, argued that, "[u]nless the images arise from the body, at least in part, the imagination cannot do its healing work" (1993, p.29); in simpler words, one can spend a life-time speaking about and analyzing images from anything else, that is, images that constellate

any kind of possible situation, but if they are not related to *one's embodiment*—symptoms, ailments, pains, diseases, relationships, sexuality, eating and sleeping patterns, etc.—there will hardly be any transformation and healing.

[366] Nietzsche, in a passage titled *Why we are no idealists*, wrote: "ideas are worse seductresses than our senses, for all their cold and anemic appearance, and not even in spite of this appearance: they have always lived on the 'blood' of the philosopher, they always consumed his senses and even, if you will believe us, his 'heart'" (1887/1974, p.333).

[367] Corbin considered that "the humanities are becoming aware of the metaphysical (or more simply, the *transnatural*) condition which constitutes their very essence . . . discovering that the I and the World, the *modes of being* of the personal subject and the *regions of being* which it explores, are not two things which get juxtaposed, but presences within each other, an *interpresence*, an indissoluble correlation and structure" (1990/1998, p.23). He called this "the *phenomenological* orientation of the humanities[,]" which, he observed too in the physical sciences.

[368] Hellinger, 2008/2009, p.154, free translation

[369] Deloria Jr. commented that the Sioux conceived that "generations were tied together as if they were all present in the flesh" (2009, p.149).

[370] Jung wrote that "[o]ur psychic prehistory is in truth the spirit of gravity, which needs steps and ladders because, unlike the disembodied airy intellect, it cannot fly at will" (1952/1968, p.62). He might have implied that one, in any case, requires walking on solid ground and theories that ground one to Earth. It is not in vain that Jung commented in his last book, that, "[t]he less we understand of what our fathers and forefathers sought, the less we understand ourselves, and thus we help with all our might to rob the individual of his roots and his guiding instincts, so that he becomes a particle in the mass, ruled only by what Nietzsche called the spirit of gravity" (1961/1965, p.236).

[371] Hellinger, 1996/2002, p.139, free translation

[372] Zavala, following Jung, stated simply that, the "light of nature is the all penetrating world-soul, that force of nature" (1977, p.29, free translation) that moves everything and every "body."

[373] The mention of strife is in relation to Empedocles, who claimed in the fragment B20 of the Diels-Kranz numeration: "...in splendid mass of human members: now by Love we all come into one, limbs which have acquired a body when life is thriving at its peak; now again, divided by evil Conflicts [strife], each wanders apart along the shore of life" (in Barnes, 2001, p.15). Kingsley argued that this is one of those fragments that have been tremendously misunderstood. He explained a mystical idea of critical importance: "to use Love and Strife instead of being used by them" (2010, p.448).

[374] Dalai Lama, 2005b, p.39

[375] This notion (community of fate), coined by Hellinger, will be explained in the chapter titled "Family."

[376] Hillman, 1992.

[377] Oxford dictionaries

[378] Onions, 1966, p.574

[379] Dodds argued that in ancient Greece, when considering the *miasma,* the ideas of pollution, curse, and sin were already fused together (1951, p.37).

[380] 2001, p.25

[381] It corresponds to the fragment B98 of the Diels-Kranz numeration, translated also as: "souls smell things in Hades" (in Barnes, 2001, p.64). In these translations one requires a figurative and allegorical understanding, in order to avoid literalisms. In depth psychology, the idea and image of *Hades, the realm of the dead,* should never be taken and considered from the Christian concept of Hell, nor from Dante's description of Inferno, but as Hillman suggests in *The dream and the underworld* (1979), as "a psychological realm now, not an eschatological realm later" (p.30). In such sense, following Hillman, Hades can be considered as "the unseen one and yet absolutely present [domain of soul]" (p.31), where there is "the final cause, the purpose, the very *telos* of every soul and every soul process" (p.30). It is a psychological way of experiencing and seeing life, where everything "become[s] deeper, moving from the visible connections to the invisible ones" (p.30). The realm of Hades, although one might not see it by the ordinary ways of seeing, "is not an absence, but a hidden presence—even an invisible fullness" (p.28). Hillman has said that Hades, the Greek name for the underworld, "is the mythological style of describing a psychological cosmos" (p.46); and entering the underworld, he said also, "refers to a transition from the material to the psychical point of view" (p.51). It is a *way of seeing* and "speaking of images that are at the same time invisible" (p.51), images that are absent, but whose presence is part of one's psychic complex. When considering Heraclitus fragment from such allegorical perspective, then the idea that "the soul is known by scent" takes a different sense. It elicits the notion of an atmosphere with some smell, which is not the literal public smell in the air, but the *essential* odors of the *psychic terrain* in which every individual lives.

[382] Hahnemann explained *acute diseases* as those "rapid morbid processes of the abnormally deranged vital force, which have a tendency to finish their course more or less quickly, but always in a moderate time[;]" and chronic diseases as those "of such a character that, with small often imperceptible beginnings, dynamically derange the living organism, each in its own peculiar manner, and cause it gradually to deviate from the healthy condition" (1833/2009, p.93). However, he clearly stated that, "[t]he true natural *chronic* diseases are those that arise from a chronic miasm [*sic*]" (p.97).

[383] Ortega, 1992, p.183, free translation

[384] 1992, p.183, free translation

[385] Ibid.

[386] By "disposition" I do not mean a genetic or physical determination, because that could limit and narrow understanding. I rather mean a psychic positioning (*Aufstellung*) that is dynamic and that can be changed—naturally, this positioning implies an affective circumstance (a surrounding energy) that is influenced

according to how does the individual find himself in such an atmosphere (*Befindlichkeit*). For example, an individual was within a physical atmosphere where he, through other people, was in contact with influenza (Spanish flu) and yet he was not physically affected. But, the moment that he felt a deep fear because of a legal issue that he was attending, his physicality became weak, feeling without enough strength to face the situation; this revealed him that his psychic positioning was not the best, it was without enough support, therefore, his disposition allowed his physicality to be affected by the disease.

[387] "[This is] what really constitutes the miasma: the subjacent morbid disposition that only permits us an apparent and incomplete health, ready to transform those diverse morbid dispositions into obvious alterations of clear disease" (Ortega, 1992, p.382 free translation).

[388] Ortega, 1992, p.126

[389] Hahnemann considered that, "it is only the vital force, deranged to such an abnormal state, that can furnish the organism with its disagreeable sensations, and incline it to the irregular processes which we call disease" (1833/2009, p.53). Hence, "[i]t is only the morbidly affected vital force alone that produces disease" (p.53).

[390] This is one of the main differences between homeopathic and allopathic medicine. Hahnemann considered that the latter, mostly "employs, in order to keep in favour [*sic*] with its patient, remedies that immediately suppress and hide the morbid symptoms by opposition (*contraria contrariis*) for a short time (palliative), but leave the disposition to these symptoms (the disease itself) strengthened and aggravated" (1833/2009, pp.xvi-xvii).

[391] 1960, p.211

[392] Hahnemann defined disease as: "*dynamic derangements of our spirit-like vital principle in sensations and functions, that is to say, immaterial derangements of our state of health*" (1833/2009, p.11). In simpler words, the root of the disease is not in the organic sensations, as if it were a matter of the cells, nerves, and organs, but in the immaterial interaction between oneself and the other contents of the complex—whether those are physical and actual (like mother and father), or psychical and virtual (like the dead and the ancestors).

[393] Jung, therefore, recommended: "go to school once more with the medical philosophers of a distant past, when body and soul had not yet been wrenched asunder into different faculties" (1954b, p.83). It is worth noticing that Jung studied the writings of Paracelsus and considered him of great influence (Jung, 1966c, pp. 3-29), and the latter has also been considered the forefather of Homeopathic medicine (Torres & Reig, 2018, pp.115-116). It is also worth recalling some Socratic insights through Plato's *Charmides*, where he said: "the cure of the soul, my dear youth, has to be effected by the use of certain charms, and these charms are fair words, and the temperance is implanted in the soul ... [it] is the great error of our day in the treatment of human beings, that men try to be physicians of health and temperance separately (1989, p.103).

[394] 1999, p.15, free translation

[395] 1999, p.215

[396] 1845/2014, p.23

[397] Similarly, the Dalai Lama mentioned that *all* our actions spring from the "overall state of mind and heart,"—from one's *disposition and motivation*—, which is called *kun long* in Tibetan (1999, p.81). He explained also that the *kun long* reflects what in Tibetan is called *nyong mong*, literally meaning "that which afflicts from within" but often translated as "afflictive emotions . . . such as hatred, anger, lust, pride, greed, envy, and so on" (p.86). Such afflictions, he wrote, "are the very source of unethical conduct. They are also the basis of anxiety, depression, confusion, and stress, which are such a feature of our lives today" (p.87). Hence, he wrote too that, "[m]urder, scandal, and deceit all have their origin on afflictive emotion" (p.87). Hahnemann, similar to the Dalai Lama, insisted that, "[by] noteworthy observations on himself he [the physician] will be brought to understand his own sensations, his mode of thinking *and his disposition* (the foundation of all true wisdom) (italics added)" (1833/2009, p.128 footnote). Following this argument, we could say that, if one is not aware of one's *kun long*, that is, if one is not aware of one's violent, selfish, and destructive chronic afflictions, then the miasma, the origin of disease, remains unchanged and intense—and the body unaltered and insane.

[398] Ortega claimed that the years and decades of suppressing disease with allopathic medicines enhanced alterations, and "these changes in that which is mental have been produced so suddenly and generally that the result is a transformation in the human being, generically speaking, and that constitutes what could be called the 'collective miasma'" (1992, p.370, free translation).

[399] 1992, p.184

[400] A similarity of the allopathic method and medicine with the socio-political and international policies for dealing with conflicts is no coincidence. Trying to get rid of the "bad" elements, whether germs, bacteria, viruses, persons, or peoples, seems, from a Homeopathic standpoint, a terrible mistake that will just keep on going throughout the generations, sickening individuals, societies, nations, lands, and the world in general. The allopathic paradigm is to kill what it considers to be the "pathogenic" elements; it is therefore a paradigm or war and destruction, with no chance for a harmonious way of life until the so-called "sickening elements" are totally eradicated—as if such idea would be ever possible.

[401] Jung considered that, the predisposition to what he, in his young age, called *dementia praecox*, consisted in an abnormal sensitiveness (1960, p.219). Somé (who will be considered later in the book) however, said that from his Dagara (West African tribe) perspective, such sensitivity is not seen as something dysfunctional, but a calling form the spirit world (Somé in Marohn, 2003). Dick Russell wrote a beautiful book, titled *My mysterious son* (2014), where he brilliantly weaved the chronological situation of his son, with personal observations, some of his son's journal writings, a shamanic perspective, and the clinical picture of what has been called schizophrenia but which reveals an abnormal sensitiveness that reaches far into the lineages and the collective miasma.

[402] Oxford dictionaries.

[403] Jung said, when speaking about consciousness, that, "[the subjective components of conscious functions] are usually a sort of disposition to react in a certain way, and usually the disposition is not altogether favourable [*sic*]" (1950/1955, p.23). In simpler words, he meant that, the individual's reactions to the environment, throughout

life, move him or her into a position in relation to other psychic contents (figures, persons, presences), and that constitutes his or her psychic disposition—which at times is uneasy, and favorable to disease.

[404] 1960, p.218

[405] Hahnemann considered that, "[a]lmost all the so-called mental and emotional diseases are nothing more than corporeal diseases in which the symptom of derangement of the mind and disposition peculiar to each of them is increased, whilst the corporeal symptoms decline (more or less rapidly)" (1833/2009, pp.157-158). In simpler words, even the so-called mental or psychological disturbances are the result of a chaotic disposition, the miasma—diseased relational patterns with, and among, the psychic contents and figures (the complex).

[406] *Dementia praecox*, as Jung used it at the time, was an unfortunate name given to an undifferentiated conglomerate of psychopathological conditions. He said that when "speaking of the psychogenesis of mental disease . . . [he meant in] a vague and misleading way 'dementia praecox,' . . . [which] gathered all those hallucinatory, catatonic, hebephrenic, and paranoid conditions, not showing the characteristic organic process of cellular destruction" (1960, p.213). At the time he wrote: "[s]tatistically, this group of illness contains by far the largest number of cases of psychosis." Dementia praecox, he said also, was what his mentor Bleuler, for a time, called "schizophrenia" (1960, p.155).

[407] 1960, p.219

[408] At the Tavistock Lectures Jung mentioned: "*Similia similibus curantur* is a remarkable truth of the old medicine," which is in fact the basic principle of homeopathic medicine, but he warned how "as a great truth it is also liable to become great nonsense. Medical psychology, therefore, should be careful not to become morbid itself" (1950/1955, p.6). Jung, without knowing, foresaw what the pluralistic homeopathy (which is a homeopathic view that does not take into account the miasmas but only the physical maladies) would become, a great nonsense.

[409] 1992, p.404, free translation

[410] Psoriasis stems from the Greek *psōríāsis,* which stems form *psórā* that means "itch," but is related to the Sanskrit *bhas,* which means to "crush, chew, devour" (Onions, 1996, p.720). Sycosis stems from the Greek *súkōsis,* which stems from *súkon* that means fig (p.895). Syphilis stems from the "title of a poem, in full, 'Syphilis sive Morbus Gallicus' (syphilis or the French disease), [from] 1530, by Girolamo Fracastoro," which "is the story of a shepherd *Syphilus,* represented as the first sufferer; . . . *Syphilus* [however] is of unknown origin" (p.897). Ortega described briefly each of these three miasmas in *Introducción a la medicina homeopática* (1992, pp.423-444).

[411] Ortega, 1999, p.63

[412] 1999, p.75

[413] 1999, p.83

[414] 1999, p.91

[415] 1999, p.93

[416] Ortega, 1999, p.115

[417] One can bridge this Homeopathic observation and principle with Hellinger's notion of rupture of the orders of love and their consequences. A disordered view of life leads to a disordered functioning of the organism, and viceversa; the cause of the disorder and therefore its solution lies in the complex, the psychic terrain, the miasma, on which the individual lives, loves, and dreams.

[418] 1999, p.113

[419] Ortega, 1992, p.408

[420] Ortega, 1999, p.213

[421] Ortega, 1992, p.204

[422] 1999, p.135-144

[423] Ortega meticulously wrote a miasmatic classification and definition of symptoms, where he observed, for example, that feeling abandoned, bored, calmed, credulous, mortified, shy, and/or nostalgic would correspond to a psoric constitution; feeling ambitious, greedy, dictatorial, frivolous, industrious, loquacious, extravagant and/or exhuberant would correspond to a sycosic constitution; and feeling rage, destructiveness, envy, cruelty, rancor, and or ferocity would correspond to a syphilitic constitution. For the complete list of observations see *Introducción a la Medicina Homeopática* (1992, pp.463-477, 513-515).

[424] 1999, p.137

[425] Ortega, 1999.

[426] In a very similar way, Jung considered that, "[t]he genius, too, has to bear the brunt of an outsize psychic complex; if he can cope with it, he does so with joy, if he can't, he must painfully perform the 'symptomatic actions' which his gift lays upon him: he writes, paints, or composes what he suffers" (1957, p.100); in other words, even the genius sees, and lives, the world through the chronic miasma.

[427] This is parallel to an idea of Hillman, that "perceptions are filtered through the prism of the psyche" (1992b, p.41). In such sense, any human action is a direct result of the way one perceives, and it is intended to participate in such field of perception; however, if the perceived is heavily tinctured, so will the actions. For example, if one's way of perceiving is highly tinctured by the syphilitic (destructive) coloring, so will be the motivations, reflections, intentions, wordings, and actions of the person. Hillman claimed that "[w]e stand inescapably in the light of one or another color band, giving us a definite perspective and bias" (p.41); however, this coloring through which we perceive (and love, and see the world) is not static, but dynamic, it can be changed, and possibly enlightened. It is not a quantitative view of disease, in which one measures how many copies of a certain virus live in an individual's

organism, or measuring how big is the tumor, but acknowledging the qualitative characteristics of the miasma, which colors all domains of life and enhances specific ways of pathologizing.

[428] This is one of the reasons why Hahnemann insisted that, "the ascertainable physical constitution of the patient (especially when disease is chronic), his moral and intellectual character, his occupation, mode of living and habits, his social and domestic relations, his age, sexual functions, &c., are to be taken into consideration" (1833/2009, p.49).

[429] 1999, p.218

[430] This relates to Hahnemann's insistence on attending the "totality of the symptoms" (1833/2009, p.51), which would inevitably include psychic and affective matters; but it also alludes to an important critique, stating: "the old school physicians, not knowing how else to give relief, have sought to combat and if possible to suppress by medicines, here and there, a single symptom from among a number in diseases—a *one-sided* procedure" (p.51 footnote).

[431] Ortega, 1999.

[432] Ortega, possibly quoting Hahnemann (but without any clear reference), mentioned that, "the knowledge of the miasmatic theory gives the solution and that which fulfills the perfect realization of the homeopathic method" (1992, p.444, free translation). In other words, if the miasmatic theory is unbeknownst to the homeopathic physician, then such a physician is not aligned with homeopathy. Similarly, if the complex theory is unbeknownst to the psychologist, the miasma will remain unattended, unresolved, and the soul unredeemed.

[433] Ortega, 1992.

[434] 1992, p.408

[435] Real Academia Española, free translation

[436] According to Onions, the word stems from the Arabic *tarhah,* and means "what is thrown away," which stems from *taraha,* that means "reject;" see the etymology of the English word *tare* (Onions, 1996, p.903). From the constellations' observations, it is quite interesting that many diseases and chronic illnesses are in relation to members of the family and the community of fate that are or were *rejected* and excluded, as if thrown away from the community—breaking the orders of love, firstly the right of belonging, secondly the order of complete number, and thirdly the order of priority. Maybe the *taras* are physical conditions that manifest a serious relational disorder.

[437] Ortega, 1992, p.452, free translation

[438] 1992, p.407

[439] Onions, 1996, p.58

[440] Jung advised that "[t]he real toxin is to be sought in the complex, and this is a more or less autonomous psychic quantity" (1954b, p.87).

[441] Ortega, 1999.

[442] This is similar to Rumi's lines, from his poem titled *Backpain*, saying: "There are values in pain that are difficult/ to see without the presence of a guest" (Jalāl al-Din Rumi, 1995, p.337). The lines suggest that behind physical pains, there are presences waiting to be seen, waiting to be acknowledged, and included; but if one does not *host* the presences, as guests, then one *sees* nothing and remains only with the pain—the *hospital*, therefore, could also be the place where one acknowledges those in need of one's psychic look, attention, and love. Maybe, in a time to come, hospitals will become also the places where individuals can host the psychic guests from one's lineage that need attention, and in such a way much of our unresolved, unanswered, and unredeemed will become clear.

[443] Hellinger has observed that there is a kind of love behind many diseases, which cause is in the psychic realm (1996/2002, p.150); a kind of love that might be blind, ignorant, or disruptive to the orders that he has discovered.

[444] Hahnemann, in 1818, long before Hüsserl and the phenomenological vogue, wrote in the preface to the second edition of his opus magna, *Organon of Medicine*: "Unaided reason can know nothing of itself (*a priori*), . . . every one of its conclusions about the actual must always be based on sensible perceptions, facts and experiences if it would elicit truth" (1833/2009, p.ix). Hence he wrote, "[t]he unprejudiced observer . . . takes note of nothing in every individual disease, except the changes in the health of the body and of the mind (*morbid phenomena, accidents, symptoms*) which can be perceived externally by means of the senses" (p.50). Ortega, alluding to this passage of the *Organon* (paragraph 6), argued that, "we must get rid of all investigation that is not corroborated by the experimental, the experience" (1992, p.271). Therefore, like Hahnemann advised, "every physician ought to be . . . a good observer" (1833/2009, p.128 footnote). It is curious how, on the one hand, homeopathy is not regarded as a serious medical path, by many; one the other, it is outstanding how detailed it is in its observations, taking into account even the patient's feelings, thoughts, actions, motivations, intentions, desires, and all kinds of sensations. If done right, it requires the rigor of a serious phenomenologist: "a good observer."

[445] This is so, because, "[t]he affection of the morbidly deranged, spirit-like dynamis (vital force) that animates our body . . . and the totality of the outwardly cognizable symptoms produced by it in the organism . . . are one and the same" (Hahnemann, 1833/2009, p.54). In other words, symptoms (which are visible) *are* the manifest individual's affectivity—the individual's psychic position, disposition, and movement (which are invisible without the proper epistemological techniques, like the Constellations work).

[446] Ortega remarked that from the perspective of molecular biology, immunology is important because it implies "whether the living organism knows how to react to an unexpected aggression by adapting and inventing an original response; or by obeying to a situation for which its genetic patrimony has prepared it" (Bussard in Ortega, 1992, p.270, free translation). One can assume that it is the same psychically speaking. It is important because it implies whether the individual knows how to react (or rather *pro-act*) to an unexpected condition or encounter by not getting entangled and not letting such situation affect him or her, or by simply obeying his or her group conscience, and remaining loyal to it in spite of the uneasiness and eventual disease. It is quite interesting to note that immune, from its etymological origin, the Latin *immunis,* means "exempt from a service or charge," in the sense of not doing a

communis service (Onions, 1996, p.463). Psychically and homeopathically speaking, immune would mean, on a first instance, to be exempt of doing a service to the main individual's *communis* (the family), that is, being indisposed (invulnerable) to the uneasiness of the family—either past or present—and hereditary diseases. (See the chapter titled "Family" to deepen into the notion of family as a *communis*, a community.)

[447] It is worth noticing a parallel advice in Homeopathic medicine. Hahnemann, when insisting on the need of physicians for trying the medicines—also named as *medicinal diseases*—on themselves, mentioned: "Let it not be imagined that such slight indispositions caused by taking medicines for the purpose of proving them can be in the main injurious to the health. Experience shows on the contrary, that the organism of the prover [sic] becomes, by these frequent attacks on his health, all the more expert in repelling all external influences inimical to is frame and all artificial and natural noxious agents, and becomes more hardened to resist everything of an injurious character, by means of these moderate experiments on his own person" (1833/2009, p.128 footnote). However, this should not be confused with vaccination, because that is based on a bacteriological view; Hahnemann rather based his whole approach on the dynamic view of the individual—motions and emotions within the web of life relations, and strictly observed in sensations, motivations, intentions, desires, and actions. Besides this, there is a tremendously deep spiritual teaching from Kabbalah, where it is said that a truly spiritual person, an elevated soul, is one who is willing to feel pain in order to help another person. (Berg, M., 2010, min. 20'00"- 40'26")

[448] In a similar sense, Jung mentioned: "It would be vain to imagine . . . that one could disembarrass oneself of one's own weight and thus get rid of the ultimate and most fundamental of all premises—one's own disposition" (1950/1955, p.771). Ortega, in a quite allegorical way, when commenting Hahnemann's *Organon,* mentioned that the disease, which is a dynamic agent, perturbs the instinctive existence by torturing, as if it were a malignant spirit (1992, p.349); maybe it is not all that malignant in itself, but indeed a presence (a psychic figure) with whom one is entangled in an instinctive and sickly way.

[449] Jung considered that an "*applied* concept of energy always deals with the behaviour [*sic*] of forces, with substance in motion; for energy is accessible to experience in no other way than through the observation of moving bodies" (1960/1969, p.28). In such sense, and following Jung, it is quite accurate to imagine "entities" and personify them with "bodies" that are moving in one's psychic terrain and which are in relation to oneself, producing an intensity of affection—affection as the qualitative susceptibility of being affected. When speaking of psychic energy, therefore, one is not speaking of a quantitative concept, but of a quality of intensity that can just be observed and *sensed and felt* through its effects.

[450] This can be related to what Jung, in his early writings, meant by "imago," which should not be confused with image. He said that it was "a technical term . . . [for] a living independence in the psychic hierarchy, i.e., possesses that *autonomy* which wide experience has shown to be the essential feature of feeling-tone complexes." He also said that for later writings he would "use the term 'archetype' instead, in order to bring out the fact that we are dealing with impersonal, collective forces" (1952/1967, p.44footnote). In other words, the relation of a individual with a particular living image that inhabits his or her terrain is an *imago,* an inevitable archetypal situation that is out of one's control and will, and, moreover, that is of a trans-personal nature; it could be thought that all human relations generate imagos, and imagos are inter-related between themselves, just as in life relations with persons are interdependent, as one can see when a relational shift with a certain person can create an unexpected shift with a third person. Just so, archetypal situations always affect one another. For instance, the memories from

one's own father, which could seem like a relationship with a conglomerate of felt-sensed images (an imago), will always be governed by the archetypal forces of fatherhood—such a relationship will never be free of its archetypal duress. Not only that, such a relationship will tincture other relationships and perspectives; it will color one's vision, understanding, behavior, and every sphere of life. Much of Hillman's work is precisely this, explained thoroughly in a poetic style, sustained by mythic imagination, and appropriately named: Archetypal Psychology.

[451] This notion is close to the esoteric claim of *the circle whose center is essentially its circumference,* explained in more detail by Corbin, for instance, (1990/1998, pp.165-171); it gives the idea of a terrain in which one finds oneself, but which is also no-where and no other than oneself.

[452] 1894/2005, p.30

[453] In Jung's view the unconscious has a "multitudinous quality" (1988, p.1404) with which one had to deal, cope, negotiate, and eventually integrate. The so-called unconscious is not one single entity that holds one's dark side and repressed memories, it rather is an uncountable multitude of presences and one's relationship to them.

[454] The image of the actual world and the extremely polluted environmental situation is no coincidence; but, like Jung wisely wrote, "[n]o culture of the mind is enough to make a garden of your soul" (2009b, p.236). Just like Machado, one should ask oneself: "What have you done with the garden that was entrusted to you?" (in Bly, Hillman, & Meade, 1992, p.99)—from the poem titled: *The wind, one brilliant day.*

[455] Hahnemann, commenting on the chronic miasmas, conceived that, even "the most robust constitution, the best regulated mode of living and the most vigorous energy of the vital force are insufficient for their eradication" (1833/2009, p.97). From this standpoint, it is clear why is it that individuals who had a healthy eating regimen, who exercised regularly, who kept a balanced lifestyle, can suddenly present a severe disease that either diminishes brutally their so-seemingly state of health, or even brings them to the deathbed and finishes their existence. In Hahnemann's words, "[chronic miasmas] never disappear of themselves, nor can they be diminished, much less extinguished, by the most vigorous constitution, or the most regular mode of life and strictest diet" (1845/2014, p.23). He pointed his observations quite clearly: "unless they are thoroughly cured by art, they continue to increase in intensity until the moment of death" (p.23).

[456] Jung made this comparison of the Wagnerian leitmotif and the feeling-tone complexes, where "our actions and moods are modulations of the leitmotivs [*sic*]" (1960, p.38, footnote). His observation is quite sharp, implying that our actions and moods, despite the everyday context, are variations in tone of a recurring theme; the relationship's entanglements within the terrain (the psychic complex) *are* the leitmotifs—and that is why an individual's real issue is not in the everyday actions and moods (modulations), but in the structure of the main theme (an archetypal situation) that is played over and over, at different tones, sometimes in a low key, sometimes in very high key, but repeated nevertheless throughout the entire drama of life.

[457] Oxford dictionaries.

[458] Hillman wrote extensively on the archetypal view of any situation, and the archetypal nature of every human act, and also thoughts, feelings, behaviors, and ways of understanding, relating, loving, and even dying. See (1992b,

2005, 2007). He even claimed that any way to look at the world, life, death, the divine, God, and so on, is but an archetypal *seeing through* (1992), because one never gets out of archetypal ways of being.

[459] The idea of care might imply a "nursing fantasy," and it has been the dominant fantasy of many psychotherapeutic schools, and which Hillman has strongly criticized (1992). Of course, the notion of "care" might go beyond the "nursing fantasy," but one has to be aware, especially within the therapeutic framework, of what archetypal pattern is becoming the structuring dynamic for such an action.

[460] The idea of cure, if associated with the allopathic medical model implies a getting rid of, or a fighting against, something, which is not the paradigm of Homeopathic medicine. For the latter, Hahnemann mentioned: "*cure is only possible by a change to the healthy condition of the state of health of the diseased individual*" (1833/2009, p.56). But, as he wisely continued: "This spirit-like power to alter man's state of health (and hence to cure diseases) . . . can never be discover by us by a mere effort of reason; it is only by experience of the phenomena it displays when acting. . . that we can become clearly cognizant of it" (p.56). Similarly, during a constellation, the solution (cure) cannot be discovered unless one experiences the affective display of the representatives, because only then it is that one can fully recognize what is the needed motion that will alter the psychic arrangement—the *diathesis*. This is phenomenology at its best.

[461] This comes close to Aizenstat's work with dreams, which he has coined and copyrighted as *Dreamtending* (2009). The mystic poet, Rumi, wrote in his poem titled *The dream that must be interpreted*: "This place is a dream./ Only a sleeper considers it real" (Jalāl al-Din Rumi, 1995, p.112), referring evidently to this place that is often called "the real world." But he continued saying: "But there's a difference with *this* dream./ Everything cruel and unconscious/ done in the illusion of the present world,/ all that does not fade at the death-waking" (p.112). This idea, indeed similar in many traditions, considers life, the world, and others, in a dream-like way, but one achieves wakefulness by attending them, whether they appear to one in a night-dream, a nightmare, or during the day—which is also a dream.

[462] Hahnemann, clearly mentioned that for the "*examination of a case of disease* . . . the physician [requires] nothing but freedom from prejudice and sound senses, attention in observing and fidelity in tracing the picture of the disease" (1833/2009, p.102)—one can assume that he was an empirical phenomenologist. Jung's perspective was similar; he commented and warned that, "it is much easier to make conjectures over the head of the patient than to see what the empirical material really means" (1964b, p.168).

[463] Ortega, 1992, pp.187-188

[464] Hahnemann observed that, when searching for a homeopathic remedy, "the *more striking, singular, uncommon and peculiar* (characteristics) signs and symptoms of the case of disease are chiefly and most solely to be kept in view" (1833/2009, pp.133-134). Similarly, when inquiring about individual's situation in order to facilitate him or her a constellation, it is the most advisable deed to ask for striking, singular, uncommon and peculiar events in his or her family of origin. This would mean that common events or generalized situations, as if saying only such things as depression, unemployment, uncertainty, and the like, do not give sufficient information for displaying the complex—on most cases.

[465] Ortega, 1992, pp.189-201

[466] This is akin to a fundamental insight by Hahnemann, stating: "*A weaker affection is permanently extinguished in the living organism by a stronger one, if the latter (whilst different in kind) is very similar to the former in its manifestations*" (1833/2009, p.59). For example, a man whose affective disposition is in the service of his mother's grief, and being sickly but blindly entangled with her sorrow, could find a healing solution by representing and experiencing (during a constellation) another man's affection, if such a man's situation is similar or stronger in the entanglement with his own mother—and only if the constellation comes to a healing resolution, of course. Hahnemann, in a way, knew this principle; therefore he commented about his insight: "Thus are cured both physical affections *and moral maladies* (italics added)" (p.59 footnote). For a medical explanation of this homeopathic principle see chapter one: "El método de sanación de la naturaleza", meaning *the healing method of nature* (Torres & Reig, 2018, pp.27-42).

[467] Hahnemann insisted on this as he wrote: "how small, in other words, must be the dose of each individual medicine, homeopathically selected for a case of disease, to effect the best cure? To solve this problem, and to determine for every particular medicine, what dose will it suffice for homeopathic therapeutic purposes and yet be so minute that the gentlest and most rapid cure may be thereby obtained . . . [will not be through] the work of theoretical speculation; nor by fine-spun reasoning, not by specious sophistry can we expect to obtain the solution of this problem. Pure experimentation, careful observation, and accurate experience alone can determine this" (1833/2009, pp.189-190).

[468] Ortega, 1992, pp.197-201

[469] The homeopathic medicine procedure resembles some old alchemical ideas that Jung revised from the *Theatrum Chemicum*. He wrote, quoting Gerhard Dorn: "This truth is the 'medicine, improving and transforming that which *is no longer* into that which it *was before* its corruption, and that which *is not* into that which *ought to be.*' It is a 'metaphysical substance,' hidden not only in things, but in the human body: [according to Dorn] 'In the human body is concealed a certain metaphysical substance known to very few, which needeth no medicament, being itself an incorrupt medicament' . . . this virtue and heavenly vigour [*sic*] can be freed form its fetters; not by its contrary . . . but by its like" (Jung, 1951/1959, pp.161-162). The aim of the homeopathic medicament is not to annihilate pathogenic elements that are corrupting the physical body, but to liberate the vital force within the individual, and "restore to health by means of smallest doses of simple medicines carefully selected according to their proved effects, by the only therapeutic law comfortable [*sic*] to nature: *simila similibus curentur*" (Hahnemann, 1833/2009, p.38). It is important to mention that the best rendering of his therapeutic maxim would be "let likes be treated by likes," rather than the popularized "likes cures likes," that comes from a common error and misspelling of the Latin phrase: *similia similibus curantur* (rather than *curentur*), and which was not Hahnemann's—see *Organon*'s Appendix and endnotes (Dudgeon in Hahnemann, 1833/2009, p.206).

[470] For a great variety of examples in regards to parents, children, siblings, couples, dead ones, and some other topics, see *On Life & Other Paradoxes* (Hellinger, 2002, pp.59-75). Healing words, which Hellinger, in the context of Constellations, called phrases of solution, always have to do with reconciliation and respect (2001/2008, p.272). At the same time, as he said, "if they are correct there is an immediate resonance [with the actual persons involved]" (p.273). These healing words, in some ways, are an incantation, a powerful medicine, a *pharmakon*—if they come from the right place. In this respect, there is a profound kabbalistic teaching about words, where it is said that for the person to say the "right words" first he has to connect to the world of speech, and then the light of the Creator will

speak through the throat of the person. Hence there is a verse in *Malachi 2:7* (Old Testament) saying: "The mouth of the kohen [priests] keeps the mind," meaning that it is not the person speaking, but something greater through him (Berg, M., 2013, min. 9'30"-18'05").

[471] Hahnemann observed that, "there are enormously powerful things (forces) which are perfectly destitute of weight, as for example, caloric, light, &c., . . . [just as] the irritating words that bring on a bilious fever, or the mournful intelligence respecting her only son that kills the mother" (1833/2009, pp.190-191 footnote). But, just as these enormously powerful forces can be used destructively, just so they can be used in unsuspected ways to restitute the state of health of any person. The important issue to consider is that the healing effect of such forces (words or sentences) has to be said by a specific person, not just by a close friend, a physician, a lover, or a stranger; and such a person is most of the times someone from one's family system. Hence the value of the Family Constellations, because when one is in such a setting, one can say the appropriate words to the (representative of the) person that one needed to—or listen them from him or her. For instance, one can say certain things to one's mother that one has never said before; or one can hear a few words from someone who would normally not say such things; or one can even say and listen things from someone who already passed away—a dead person. This would be one approximation to what Laszlo referred to as "healing with information rather than with biochemical substances and invasive methods" (2014, p.82). If these insights were to be taken to their ultimate consequences, a new medicinal path would emerge, one based on community, presumably a *medicine-community*°—as already happening in Mexico.

[472] In the last paragraphs of the *Organon* (1833/2009, pp.194-200), Hahnemann made some remarks on sensitivity and animal magnetism, and he clearly explained that a slight touch can alter the vital force, if performed by a special person. Changaris wrote a beautiful book explaining the importance of touch, its implications, its benefits, and how it needs to be properly introduced into the therapeutic settings, in order to deepen the healing practices—including psychology (2015). During a constellation, which is framed within a limited physical setting, a brief time, and intended to find healing resolutions, the representatives often touch a person who needs it, whether that is a son, a daughter, a grandchild, etc.; when this occurs, liberating and powerful emotions take place, and those with good-enough training to observe the body will attest that also an important shift occurs in the spontaneous movements in the functioning of the autonomous nervous system—a proven demonstration of the healing power of touch when it is used with genuinely loving intentions, within a healthy environment, and by the appropriate persons.

[473] The Homoepathic *pluricist* view—and method—is the one that considers and treats diseases separately, not seeing the disease as part of the holistic way of being; as such, it is not a strict Hahnemannian method, only a derivate, which Ortega categorically and emphatically warned that it should not be considered Homeopathy (Ortega, 1992, p.117).

[474] Ortega, 1992, p.117

[475] Ortega, 1992, pp.157-167

[476] Hahnemann referred to this notion of pure experimentation as "the sole and infallible oracle of the healing art" (1833/2009, p.58).

[477] Hahnemann controversially wrote: "the material medica [*sic*] of the old school [that is, allopathic medicine,] . . . is founded mainly on conjecture and false deductions *ab usu in morbis*, mixed up with falsehood and fraud" (1833/2009, p.34). This became one of his most important critiques to the old school.

[478] From the view of depth psychology, it is worth reading Hillman's mockery and critique of "psychology's former favorite mirrors—machines, monkeys, and infants"—because it promotes a view and notion of man which is "naïve, inarticulate, uncultured" (1992, p.221), and maybe altogether futile and wrong. From the standpoint of Homeopathic medicine, one has to add that departing investigations and insights from the sick man is also gravely wrong. This harsh assertion, which might sound all too provocative, was indeed Hahnemann's way to discover the homeopathic principles and, more importantly, the physical effects of the remedies. In Homeopathy, Hahnemann was the mature healthy individual with whom he tested the effects of substances, at first. He tested with himself, and from such experiments he discovered the psychic effect of hundreds of mineral, vegetable, and animal substances, as biased, ambiguous, presumptuous, and subjective as it may sound. However, he also documented his conclusions with observations by many other physicians who used a variety of substances (1833/2009, pp.207-237). He wrote this account of observations from other physicians, he said, in order "to show that the art of curing homeopathically might have been discovered before my time" (p.207). Ortega, following Hahnemann, explained that the only way to discover the inherent virtues of the remedies, is to test them on healthy individuals, and from the acquired observations proceed to apply them on diseased individuals (1992, pp.285-286). In the case of Constellations, it might have been Hellinger himself and his extensive observations during decades, while helping thousands of individuals—but such is only the best guess. Jung knew this very well too from the old alchemists, and he quoted Dorn saying that, "we cannot be resolved of any doubt except by experiment, and there is no better way to make it than on ourselves" (Dorn in Jung, 1951/1959, p.163). Like Hahnemann said: "Those trials made by the physician on himself have for him . . . inestimable advantages" (1883/2009, p.128). Therefore, a healing aim that is based on the observation of apes or other animals, in the emphasis of linguistic programming or cybernetic allegories, in the behavior and attitudes of infants, or from the loving and living ways of sick people (sick in the homeopathic sense of the word), seems far from reaching the insights needed to provide healing and promote health. Probably this is altogether too provocative, but it is foundational of the healing arts and needs to be said, maybe, at some point there will be a lengthier explanation.

[479] Hellinger's vitality, strength, and joyfulness, in his eighty-sixth year of life, might prove that his insights and the orders of love are not capricious. The word *health,* in fact, stems hypothetically from the Germanic *xailaz,* that means whole (Onions, 1996, p.432); one can think that maintaining or regaining one's health implies striving towards wholeness—psychic wholeness presumably.

[480] Hellinger & Hövel, 1999.

[481] Hellinger said (in an international seminar in Mexico City, not available in video yet), for example, that, in his experience in South Africa, where he lived sixteen years, he perceived inconceivable for a Zulu child to speak wrong about his or her parents. In respected psychology Institutes, however, I have experienced doctorate professors speak badly (and cheaply) about their parents. It would be worth considering Socrates' saying, from Plato's fifth book of the *Republic*: "I believe that involuntary homicide is a lesser fault than to mislead opinion about the honorable, the good, and the just" (1989, p.690)—this issue will be reviewed at length in the chapter titled: "Honor."

[482] This could seem like a contradiction to what Hellinger has insisted upon in the last years, that is, facilitating constellations without any intention, even without the intention of helping or healing. Because of that, one could say that the constellations have no therapeutic aim at all. However, when a constellation is facilitated in such a way, a therapeutic effect arises organically—not because the facilitator aimed for it, but because the consultant desired it. It is, of course, a paradox. So, when speaking of the "therapeutic aim" of the constellations, I am referring to the intentions of the individuals seeking for help and resolutions, and therefore asking to be constellated. Hellinger, in this respect said: "I do not orient myself towards diseases nor to the fact that someone gets healed or not. I work with the system. I look if forces that sicken are acting in the family. I bring them to the light" (2001/2008, p.199, free translation).

[483] Ortega, 1992, p.117

[484] Socrates, according to Plato's *Charmides,* had mentioned something strikingly similar, when saying that: "the cure of many diseases is unknown to the physicians . . . because they disregard the whole, which ought to be studied also, for the part can never be well unless the whole is well" (1989, p.103).

[485] Ortega 1999.

[486] Jung, who was a physician and a psychiatrist, boldly mentioned: "psychotherapy made approximately the same mistake as did the old school of medicine when it attacked the fever in the belief that this was the noxious agent" (1964b, p.173). His remark seems indeed very close to those made by Hahnemann, Ortega, and Homeopathic Medicine. Hahnemann wrote in the *Organon* that the so-called *local maladies,* if considered only "as mere local affections, and at the same time to treat them only, or almost only, as it were surgically, with topical applications—as the old school have done from the remotests ages—is as absurd as it is pernicious in its results" (1833/2009, p.145). He clearly commented that, "no external malady (not occasioned by some important injury from without) can arise . . . without the co-operation of the whole organism, which must consequently be in a diseased state . . . so intimately are all parts of the organism connected together to form an indivisible whole in sensations and functions" (p.146). Once (in previous editions of the *Organon*) he even worded such insight quite clear: "[an external malady] could not make its appearance at all without the whole consent of the rest of the health, and without the participation of all the rest of the sensitive and irritable parts of the living organs of the whole body" (p.276 endnote). He ventured to comment: "How stupid, how criminal, is not therefore, the procedure of ordinary physicians who regard the external malady as not belonging to, and as separated from, the rest of the body" (p.281 endnote).

[487] 2008/2009, p.76, free translation

[488] Peter Levine, who for decades has worked extensively with people suffering from all kinds of trauma, and after having researched vastly, wrote: "Generational transmission [of trauma] is a compelling possibility that we cannot and should not ignore" (2015, p.168). More so, when trying to understand and explain how this happens, he referred to homeopaths, "[who] have long recognized this kind of generational information exchange through their understanding of 'miasma,' a term referring to a cloud of contagious power that has independent life of its own and must be treated by influencing the patient's 'energy/information field'" (p.167).

[489] Hahnemann wrote that, "disease (that does not come within the province of manual surgery) considered, as it is by allopathists, as a living thing separate from the living whole . . . is an absurdity" (1833/2009, p.53). Ortega made it clear too, as he said: "If we use the word disease or diseases, we do it considering them always as symptomatic entities that traduce the way of being of the individual and never as foreign beings to the sick person. A true disease is always a state of existence" (1992, p.431, free translation). One can see the similarity of this view with that of Jung, who considered that, "[t]he psyche reflects, and knows, the whole of existence, and everything works in and through the psyche" (1954b, p.90); any physical condition fulfills a psychic necessity, something that the soul needs. In this sense, Heraclitus saying is quite accurate, "[t]herefore good and ill are one" (2001, p.37), which corresponds to Diels-Kranz fragment B58 in the Diels-Kranz numbering, also translated as "[they are one,] good and bad" (in Barnes, 2001, p.51).

[490] Although the word integral stems from the Latin *integer* which means "whole quantity," the etymological sense of it rather points toward "making up a whole, made up of parts which constitute a unity" (Onions, 1966, p.479), but not considering the part as a whole in itself. Therefore, by integrative practice one can consider the sum of perspectives that attend issues from a multi-disciplinarian basis, but still from a divided notion of reality, in which the disease and the human entity are different phenomena. Such practices aim to integrate a variety of ways of living in order to get rid of the disease, but they would not consider the disease as part of the momentary wholeness that the individual lives in. From a holistic perspective, the disease fulfills something that otherwise would be lost.

[491] Onions, 1996, p.445

[492] Jung considered that, "the symptomatology of illness, is on the one hand destructive, but it is at the same time an attempt at healing" (1988, p.1232). Ortega, when speaking of his medical patients, argued similarly that, "oftentimes a disease helps them to return to well-being" (1992, p.329 free translation). It is worth noticing Hausner's standpoint, where he clarifies that "the constellations coordinator [or facilitator] does not consider disease as a problem, but rather sees in it its function and that it is an attempt of a solution" (2008/2009, p.46, free translation). Hausner has been one of the world leading persons in treating diseases from the constellations standpoint (after Hellinger himself, of course). In a similar sense, Hillman mentioned that, "[s]ymptoms remind us of the autonomy of the complexes; they refuse to submit to the ego's point of view of a unified person" (1992, p.49). That is, complexes remind the individual of contents (presences, persons, images) that his ego forgets or rejects; but that does not make the complexes evil or malignant processes. Because of this, Jung used to say that, "the complex forms something like a shadow-government of the ego" (1954b, p.87); that would explain why "the body" gets ill, even if the individual wills to be healthy—because the will, oftentimes but not always, is a function of the ego.

[493] 2008/2009, p.25

[494] 1954b, p.89

[495] 1954b, p.95

[496] Jung was of the idea that, "one cannot treat the psyche without touching on man and life as a whole, including the ultimate and deepest issues, any more than one can treat the sick body without regard to the totality of its functions—or rather, as a few representatives of modern medicine maintain, the totality of the sick man himself"

(1954b, p.76). This assertion sounds indeed quite similar to the homeopathic medicine view, where it is clear that the disease is related even to one's private ways of living, loving, thinking, and philosophizing. Hence, Jung argued close to the end of his life: "it is impossible to treat the whole man solely within the framework of a medical specialism" (1950/1955, p.357). Hahnemann, long before Jung, explained this medical idea clearly in the first edition of *Organon* (although this paragraph does not appear in the later editions); he wrote: "the human organism in its living state is a complete whole, a unity . . . . This vital unity does not permit a disease to remain only local, completely and absolutely local in our body, . . . The rest of the body always sympathises [*sic*] more or less, and expresses this sympathy by some symptom or other" (1833/2009, p.259). Of course, this holistic principle includes as much the psychic as the organic. In such a sense, one can think, for example, that it is not only the liver what is sick, but that might be a manifestation of constant anger, rage, and frequent thoughts about being right and deserving to be angry; it might not the gall bladder itself what gets sick, but that it shows the individual's killing and death desires as well as his or her entitlement to put people down and ridicule them. However, one should beware of thinking that it is only about feelings, sentiments, and emotions, like many schools of psychotherapy have claimed, because that would leave the psychic terrain unnoticed, unattended, and unredeemed.

[497] It is worth considering Socrates's suggestion, according to Plato's *Charmides,* where he said: "Suppose that there is a kind of vision which is not like ordinary vision, but a vision of itself and other sorts of visions, and of the defect of them, which in seeing sees no color, but only itself and other sorts of vision" (1989, p.113). There are also some lines by Rumi, in his poem *Chinese Art and Greek Art,* saying something similar: "They [the Sufis] make their loving clearer and clearer./ No wantings, no anger. In that purity/ they receive and reflect the images of every moment,/ from here, from the stars, from the void" (Jalāl al-Din Rumi, 1995, p.122). However, Rumi's advise is quite important: "You're an artist/ who paints both with existence and non/ . . . but remember, *You are not your eyes*" (Jalāl al-Din Rumi, 2003, p.14), from the poem *You are not your eyes.*

[498] Ortega, 1992, pp.203-209

[499] Ortega meant that in homeopathic medicine, the *vitalistic* "is simply the recognition of life in its dynamic expression, hence its undeniable and acceptable 'a fortiori'" (1992, pp.244-245, free translation). Moreover, he commented Hahnemann's shift of words by the end of his life, from vital-force to vital principle, which he considered as a great modification in the philosophical views. Ortega argued that rather than being only a set of forces, by stating it as a principle, it denotes "the unmistaken prevalence that Hahnemann gives to the dynamic of Being, the principle or primordial, the primal, the most important and that which gives or imprints the characteristics of living, acting, or of existence to Being" (p.356 free translation). The way Hahnemann, in his old age, conceived the dynamic of the life-principle is similar to the (extremely powerful) idea of "choosing life," encouraged and transmitted by the Kabbalists—but this is not the place to deepen into the parallel.

[500] Hahnemann referred to Psora as "*the oldest* miasmatic chronic disease known. The oldest history of the oldest nations does not reach its origin" (1845/2014, p.24). He considered that "[s]everal varieties of *psora* have already been delineated by Moses 3400 years ago . . . [where] *psora* appears to have specifically infected the external parts of the body . . . It is not my object to relate here the different names by which the various nations have designated the more or less malignant varieties of leprosy . . . Names are of no consequence here, since the essence of this miasmatic itch is every where the same" (p.25). With these comments one could easily and inadvertently digress into a discussion about leprosy. However, kabbalists teach that *tzarat* (the disease which is described and has been

translated as leprosy in the third book of Moses) is not merely leprosy but a code word for disease, and the root of all disease. It does not mean the specific disease known nowadays, and almost extinct, as leprosy, but a human condition of pain, suffering, and cause of death. In simpler words, kabbalists consider that any person experiencing *tzarat*, leprosy, is a person experiencing darkness: pain, suffering, and difficulty. Surprisingly, kabbalists teach, darkness has a purpose in Creation; darkness awaits to be healed too, by man. M. Berg explained that this is the reason why the translation of the Old Testament from the original Hebrew would be "and he sees that the leprosy has been cured from the leper," meaning that darkness got healed too, and fulfilled its purpose in the thought of Creation (Berg, M., 2014, 0'1"- 19'05").

[501] 1960, p.227

[502] It is worth mentioning Dodds account of the ancient Greeks, who, he said, "accepted the idea of inherited guilt and deferred punishment . . . due to a belief in family solidarity which Archaic Greece shared with other early societies and with many primitive cultures" (1951, pp.33-34). He also pointed that, "[i]t appears from Plato that in the fourth century fingers were still pointed at the man shadowed by hereditary guilt, and he would still pay a *cathares* to be given ritual relief from it" (p.34). Moreover, he mentioned, "[there was] a universal fear of pollution (*miasma*), and its correlate, the universal craving for ritual purification (*catharsis*)" (p.35). From his scholarly writings, Dodds argued that "[t]here is no trace in Homer of the belief that pollution was either infectious or hereditary. In the archaic view it was both, and therein lay its terror: for how could any man be sure that he had not contracted the evil thing from a chance contact or else inherited it from the forgotten offence of some remote ancestor?" (p.36). Dodds, also, in order to deepen into these ideas, gave references from the Old Testament, Joshua 7:24, Jeremiah 31:29, and Ezekiel 18:20; and John 9:2 from the New Testament, as well as several references from Plato (*Theaetetus, Republic, Laws*) and Plutarch.

[503] 1960, p.244

[504] Somé, for instance, wrote a passage told by his grandfather, where he told him: "[i]f you do not abide by the ancestral law, you tacitly ask for your own punishment" (1995, p.42).

[505] 1961, p.166

[506] Rilke, 2000, p.39

[507] Probably a lot of people would resonate with Suzuki's saying: "You are not the master even of your own body which seems to be most intimate to you" (1956, p.199). Jung, similarly, commented how common it is the to equate ego with body, logically thinking that "[the ego] is supposed to be in full possession of the body." But, "[i]t is not" (1950/1955, p.72), it is a fallacy, and, more so, one of life's greatest ironies. The more one equates the ego, the "I," with the body, the more unpredictable, uncontrollable, and uncontained the body becomes in its autonomous and spontaneous functions.

[508] 2008/2009, p.77, free translation

[509] Hellinger, 2008/2009, p.89, free translation

[510] Taking into consideration the aborted or miscarried children has been a difficult issue to accept, and even Hellinger did not considered them relevant at first, but then he observed the effects that bringing them back into the constellation produced in the living members, and he so he firmly acknowledged the importance of their place within the family system. Jeff Wilson, in his book *Mourning the unborn dead* (2009), did a magnificent research regarding a Japanese ritual and its current adaptation in North America, that addresses precisely the loss of an unborn child, whether miscarried or aborted, and the profound healing that comes from mourning and acknowledging his or her place in the stream of life. Wilson, without being a depth psychologist or constellations facilitator, and without any interest in defending such positions, came to the same conclusions as Hellinger—his conclusions have serious implications if taken seriously, and profound healing could occur.

[511]The notion of "previous partners" refers to important *sentimental* partners that they might have had before meeting the actual person with whom they formed a couple in such lineage. It is as ambiguous as it sounds, where sentimental is nothing but a totally subjective value and experience. For instance, in cases of individuals having had many sexual partners, only few of them, or just even one, might have been of importance in the heart—oftentimes it is the first sexual partner, and those with whom one procreated children. In other cases, there is no need of sexual intercourse for becoming an important sentimental partner, as it could be the case with couples that got split because of their families' interests and/or pressure, and could never consummate their love through the sexual act. It does not seem to be either a matter of the length of time together, because there are many possible exceptions, so many that they are not even exceptions anymore. One has to consider the heart; if it left something in the heart, then it is of importance. It might be worth noticing that Jung wrote an example of how a woman who kept a love situation, with a man other than her husband, in secret, produced a series of unconscious reactions in her daughters and sons, creating a "very oppressive atmosphere in the home" (1954, p.77). Those "silent facts in the background . . . have an extremely contagious effect on the children" (p.77). "Unfortunately[,]" as Jung said, "it is almost a collective ideal for men and women to be as unconscious as possible in the ticklish affairs of love . . . [and] the full fury of neglected love falls upon the children" (1954, p.125).

[512] Just as in the case of the parents.

[513] Hellinger, 2008/2009, p.59-60

[514] Hellinger in Kutschera & Schäffler, 2002/2006, p.11

[515] Hellinger, 2008/2009, p.40

[516] It is, somehow, as if at one's birth, one were united to the body of the family, and even when separated by physical distance or time, one is united to such a family by fate and to its fatal consequences and fatalities; to separate oneself from this fated situation one needs *to know how*. This resonates again with fragment B20 by Empedocles, form the Diels-Kranz numeration, stating: "we are joined together and united by love as limbs/ Which have obtained a body at the prime of life,/ Only later to be torn asunder by evil discord,/ And they each wander separately by the shore of life" (Waterfield, 2000, p.152). This translation is heavily biased in its wording; it translated "strife" as "evil discord." Hence, it presents separation as evil, when in fact separation (to be turn asunder) by strife, that is, strife with one's family fatal consequences is what brings an individual to the shore of life—this is a powerful

paradox. See Kingley's detailed explanation in his book *Reality* (2003), although he refers to this passage in a greater mystical sense and as a Western's way of enlightenment.

[517] 1996/2002, p.32, free translation

[518] 1996/2002, p.14

[519] Kutschera & Schäffler, 2002/2006, p.49, free translation

[520] "There is, prior to consciousness, an unconscious out of which consciousness can arouse, and that is an intelligence which surely exceeds our intelligence in an indefinite way" (Jung, 1988, p.371).

[521] 1961/1965, p.88

[522] 1996/2002, p.41, free translation

[523] Hellinger, 1996/2002, p.30, free translation

[524] There is a powerful kabbalistic concept known as *Meshiach*, from where the word messiah comes. Meshiach, claims M. Berg, following the teachings of R. Ashlag, is when humanity will be able to access and live in a level of consciousness and spiritual reality where no one is higher or lower than the other, where there will be no better or worse, where everyone will be the same. In the kabbalistic jargon they call that they reality of the circular vessels (Berg, M., 2011, min. 0'01"-09'30"). To some extent, and if the facilitator does not block this from happening, constellations allow one to glimpse at this dimension of reality: no person better than any other, and all involved in a movement of life and love.

[525] The idea of being born as a tabula rasa is incompatible with the ontological premises of Vedic and Buddhistic philosophies, for example, where the notion of reincarnation is a key aspect in one's life situations and struggles, because it is the determining factor of *karma*. Presocratic philosophers also alleged some kind of continuity, before birth and after death; one can read, for example, Empedocles fragment numbered B11 by Diels-Kranz, saying: "Fools—they have no far-ranging ideas: they suppose that what did not exist before comes into being/ or that something may die and perish entirely" (in Barnes, 2001, p.130); moreover, he mentioned how a spirit "wraps in an unrecognizable garment of flesh" (p.156), alluding obviously to reincarnation—in fragment B126. In the Kabbalah, what is known as *tikkun* implies a set of situations that the individual soul has to correct in life; therefore it is not entirely free, it needs to attend such aspects in life; one comes into the world with a specific *tikkun*. Jung also considered that "[o]ur mind . . . was not a *tabula rasa* when we were born" (1988, p.941). However, like Jung pointed out, "[t]he fact that the [individual] psyche is not a *tabula rasa,* but brings with it instinctive conditions, just as somatic life does, naturally does not suit a Marxist philosophy at all" (1958, p.304 footnote) or all those sociological, anthropological, philosophical, and even biological fantasies of the psychic homogeneity of men and women at the moment of birth. Jung's view of this was adamant, saying that, "[n]aturally the concrete contents are lacking, but the potential contents are given *a priori* by the inherited and preformed functional disposition . . . They [these patterns of experience] are ideas *ante rem,* determinant of form, a kind of pre-existing ground plan that gives stuff of experience a specific configuration, so that we may think of them, as Plato did, as images, or as inherited functional possibilities which, nevertheless, exclude other possibilities or at any rate limit them to a very great extent" (1921/

1971b, pp.304-305). This "pre-existing ground plan that gives stuff of experience a specific configuration" is what has been described in this book as the *terrain*, the miasma.

[526] 2003, DVD 1, 1:56'

[527] Hellinger 2000/2001, Weber, 1999

[528] 2008/2009, p.43

[529] 2008/2009, p.51

[530] 1950/1955, p.356

[531] Hilman explained, in his seminar titled *Myths of the Family*, how "by understanding the ways in which they perceive and valued of the world, we enter history we extend our span and we increase longevity" (n.d., Part 1, 56'); and he wisely argued that, "each child ruled out, each parent cut off is a lost limb of imagining power and thus shortens life" (n.d., Part 1, 56').

[532] It is often considered that the love of the child towards the parents is so strong that it can assume issues that correspond the parents, as if trying to help them, but in fact it is a main rupture in the orders of love, where the child is behaving as if better, or as if knowing better than them, and breaking the flow of life—from parents to children. For this reason it has been called an *infantile way* for dealing with such issues. It is worth noticing that Hillman had a similar idea when regarding "childhood wounds less as the result of nutritive and sexual traumata than as wounds of love" (1992b, p.61), as effects derived from one's ways of loving—at times a longing, a yearning, a desire, a need, an idealization (p.89) or something else by which the individual brings Psyche to Eros, a bringing of the individual notion of soul to an important relationship in life, even when it could be damaging. Some ways of loving, however, even when seeming pure and innocent, virginal, kind, good-willed, well intentioned, and noble, could alter and disrupt what Hellinger called the order of life, and its *orders of love*, which must flow always from parents to children.

[533] Jung was well aware that, "[o]ur conception of all problematical things is enormously influenced, sometimes consciously but more often unconsciously, by certain collective ideas that condition our mentality. These collective ideas are intimately bound up with the view of life and the world of the past centuries or epochs" (1921/1971b, p.220). But, generally, such ideas "become accessible to consciousness only when the individual possesses so much self-awareness and power of understanding that he also reflects on what he experiences instead of just living it blindly" (p.221). The complex, like Jung saw, is part of cultural, religious, social, and ethnic patterns; hence, there have been some Jungians and post-Jungians who have written about the "cultural complexes."

[534] Hellinger, for example, observed very clearly that, "the relationship of a couple is embedded in a larger field with roots reaching far back in time through the ancestry of each partner." Therefore, he realized that, "[w]e grow from our roots, and are shaped and challenged by our origins, but we are also subject to their limitations" (2001c, p.175). Therefore, Jung's consideration ought not to be overlooked, saying that, "[w]e carry our past with us . . . and it is only by a considerable effort that we can detach ourselves from this burden" (1958, p.93); so that, pretending not to care for the past of one's family might be actually quite foolish, because that would not acknowledge anything, and it would maintain the burden or hindrances just as they are, and oneself blind to them—it seems quite certain that

it is only by considerable effort that one disentangles from the family romance, never through indifference, disdain, rejection, forgetfulness, or un-acknowledgment. Those are only ways to remain unconscious and stupid.

[535] Deren, for instance, commenting on the importance of the ancestors for the maintenance of the family's well-being, according to the Voudon tradition, wrote that "nothing of hereditary's accumulation should be permitted to leak away, to be lost forever" (1953/1983, p.28), because that, she argued, is what sustains the spiritual force of the living. This insight is common in many other indigenous traditions.

[536] 2009, p.149

[537] 1958, p.517

[538] Decades after Jung, Sheldrake saw something similar when he explained the idea of "inheritance of behavioral fields," where "[h]ereditary behavior, like hereditary form, is influenced by the genes, but it is neither 'genetic' nor 'genetically programmed.' On the hypothesis of formative causation, its characteristic patterns are organized by morphic fields inherited by morphic resonance from past members of the same species" (Sheldrake, 2012, p.174). Jung's insight, however, implied more than just behavior, but also attitudes, beliefs, thought patterns, desires, and even life scenarios. If this observation were given more seriousness some disciplines would expand its knowledge in an unprecedented depth.

[539] The most fundamental statement of Buddhism says that nothing (and one can apply this to individuals) has a quality of inherent intrinsic existence; "things exist, but not intrinsically so, existence can only be understood in terms of dependent origination" (Dalai Lama, 2005b, p.112). In this view, one can see that everything that individuals might think to be their inherent qualities, are physical and psychical (including mental) correlates, that depend upon what was given. "[T]hings and events [and individuals naturally] can only be understood in relation to, or in dependence upon, other factors" (p.110).

[540] Jung, 2002, p.218

[541] n.d., Part 1, tape 1, 16:00

[542] Such a disposition can also be called a "congenital sensitiveness" (Jung, 1961, p.249), which predisposes the individual to be more vulnerable to what is happening in the ancestral psychic terrain, as if making the individual more aware of the unresolved, unattended, and unredeemed issues that are pendant in the family and the lineages. Such individuals, with a so-called hyper-sensitivity, might be the tribal soul's response to a generalized anaesthetizing way of life in the families that has not given due attention to psychic matters—matters of life and death indeed—and for which it requires someone to respond to (or be affected by) the calling.

[543] At the beginning of the twentieth century, when researching the origin of the so-called "mental diseases," particularly neuroses and psychoses, Jung already discarded the traumatic standpoint, which considered that traumata were the origin of later psychological disturbances. He opted for a *psychic determination* that was susceptible to be disturbed by events, and would develop a psychological disorder (Jung, 1960, p.269 & 1961, p.132). Such view is in accordance with the Homeopathic medicine pathogenesis of diseases in general, not just "mental diseases." In fact, such view can be amplified to failures, accidents, misfortunes, and happenings of any kind,

where such events are psychic manifestations, not detached from the dynamics of soul, and they can be seen with psychological importance, significance, meaning, and purpose.

[544] This view does not see everybody within an Oedipal configuration. Jung considered that "[b]esides the endogamy-complex there are many other complications which can equally well be compared with mythological motifs" (1960, p.261). Hillman's Archetypal Psychology, and many others inspired by him, explored this idea vastly.

[545] Jung realized that "we are born within certain archetypes . . . certain disturbances" (1988, p.913); archetypes, as Jung said, "are, by definition, factors and motifs that arrange the psychic elements into certain images, characterized as archetypal, but in such a way they can be recognized only from the effects they produce. They exist preconsciously, and presumably they form the structural dominants of the psyche in general" (1958, p.149 footnote). It is worth noticing that archetypes *arrange* psychic life; they indeed structure the homeopathic medicine notion of *diathesis* (the miasma). "From the functional point of view, one could describe them as a system or a functional unit which contains the picture of the conflict, the danger, the risk—and also the solution of it" (Jung, 1988, p.977).

[546] n.d. Part 1, tape 1, 39:00

[547] Hillman proposed a way of seeing (and thinking) that would re-vision and re-imagine the epistemological standpoints of mainstream psychologies and psychotherapies, arguing that they all depart from a fantasy, which unfortunately was (and still is), for many of them, the fantasy of materialism, utilitarianism, and pragmatism—without attention to the psyche (soul). Hence, he introduced not just a way of seeing but also a way of speaking about psychology, based on metaphors and myth; from such *seeing through*, he claimed that "[t]he rules for ordering the imaginal . . . are very close to the dynamics of what we today call psychopathology" (1992b, p.199). He realized that the psychological descriptions of pathology, are nothing but a way of seeing the psyche governed by archetypal fantasies, which in the case of most mainstream psychologies are dictated by nineteenth and twentieth century (European) ways of seeing the world, but nonetheless only fantasies about an unfathomable reality. Hillman sharply noticed how the nineteenth century mind has polluted not just the outer world, but also the current ways of seeing the world, and the ways in which one sees psyche and its afflictions (p.205). Therefore, by way of mythology he discovered that the human ways of being, with its so-called psychopathological aspects, can also be seen through imagination in order to acquire different fantasies, different worldviews, which are in fact actual in cultures around the globe that have survived psychic colonization. Jung, prior to Hillman (of course), also saw the narrow vision of many psychologists, and he even boldly said that "[t]heories in psychology are the very devil" (Jung, 1954, p.7); he clearly foresaw the great danger of many theories that have been popularized, that have been institutionalized, and that unfortunately dictate over social, clinical, and educational practices—psychoanalysis is just one of those.

[548] When Hillman argued that "mythology is the study of pathology" (n.d., Part 1, tape 1, 40:00) one might think that he suggested that in those old stories and old ways of explaining the world and the human origins, there are detailed descriptions of interrelations among the characters and between the characters and other unseen forces, some which might be sick ways or relating, and some healthy ones, but in general old "natural" ways of being on Earth, maybe *as old as mountains.*

[549] Jung, 1950/1955, p.132

[550] Onions, 1996, p.460

[551] It is worth noticing Hahnemann's medical comments on *idiosyncrasies*, "by which are meant peculiar corporeal constitutions which, although otherwise healthy, possess a disposition to be brought into a more or less morbid state by certain things which *seem* to produce no impression and no change in many other individuals" (1833/2009, p.117). In simpler words, there are issues or events that could seem irrelevant to many individuals, but which severely affect an individual, this being so because of his or her *peculiar* disposition—which makes him or her vulnerable to such an affection. For instance, many individuals might not seem to be affected by mentioning the loss of a sibling, but those who have are; and throughout the work of constellations it has been revealed that even the nephews and nieces of such a dead person are oftentimes affected—without them knowing. This occurs because it is part of their psychic constitution and configuration. Just as in homeopathic medicine "the idiosyncrasy is a susceptibility that we have for determined substances" (Ortega, 1992, p.341), just so, there is also a susceptibility to react—most always unconsciously—under determined circumstances or events (favorably or unfavorably), because of the peculiar disposition of the individual—the complex.

[552] Jung mentioned in his last book: "The 'newness' in the individual psyche is an endlessly varied recombination of old-age components" (1961/1965, p.236); where it is important to emphasize that he clearly meant 'psyche,' not only the physicality. He did not refer to the constitution of the physical appearance, but to the patterning of the psychic life and the soul's movements.

[553] This is also because his method is inherently systemic, and does not only look for the individual, but for the whole family. He regards this attitude as "systemic empathy" (2003/2006, p.40) with an aim that he refers as "systemic help" (p.209), never for one individual only.

[554] 2003/2006, p.69, free translation

[555] Hellinger does not consider important the opinions of the individual regarding his or her family members, he claims that he just needs the facts, the events, and with it he can configure (constellate) the family (2006/2007, p.66).

[556] In *Mis antepasados me duelen* (van Eersel & Mailard, 2004) there are interviews with a brief explanation from seven different perspectives (mostly European and all Western) that have regarded the theme of family's antecessors in a therapeutic way.

[557] Hellinger, 2003/2006, p.69

[558] 2009, p.147

[559] Dumas in van Eersel & Mailard, 2004, p.73

[560] This shamefully applies to almost all, if not all, Jungians, but does not apply to Jung, who had a keen observation of the flow of psychic issues, from one generation to another, as one can attest in his early writings. Many of his insights, indeed, anticipate Hellinger. Jung had an *in-sight-full* vision into the psychic systems several decades before Gregory Bateson came with the term "systemic thinking" and popularized it; and he had an acute awareness of the unconscious flow of trans-generational psychic issues also many decades before Eric Berne came to discover it in his transactional analysis. Both, Bateson's and Berne's theories and observations influenced Hellinger, but Jung had

thought of it and written of it way before all of them. Somehow Jung's pupils, followers, and collaborators did not get interested in such observations, and they seemed to have been more seduced by the studies of mytho-religious symbolism.

[561] Jung, of course, knew well that many issues that one claims and feels as "personal" are at their root trans-generational. He commented: "A human life is nothing in itself . . . It is part of a family tree. We are continuously living the ancestral life, reaching back for centuries, we are satisfying the appetites of unknown ancestors, nourishing instincts which we think are our own, but which are quite incompatible with our character; we are not living our own lives; we are paying the debts of our forefathers" (1984, p.320). According to Jaffé (1984), Jung's personal secretary in his last years, it is known that Jung knew his family lineage. On his paternal side, five generations back, there had been a "learned Catholic Doctor of Medicine and Jurisprudence" by the name Carl Jung. The grandson of this man was Jung's great grandfather, Franz Ignaz Jung, who had been a medical practitioner. The son of Franz Ignaz, was Carl Gustav Jung (Jung's grandfather) who had studies natural sciences and medicine. It has been said too, that his grandfather requested "an institution which would accept patients with all manners of illness, the cure of which must be attempted by psychological means as well" (p.38)—in a time when psychology was not in vogue or popular. Jung's father, Johann Paul Achilles Jung, on the other hand, studied theology and was a pastor. However, Jung knew also the rumor that his grandfather, Carl Gustav Jung, had been the illegitimate son of Goethe, a fact that could give him a blood relationship to the author of *Faust*—a book that fascinated him. According to Jaffé, "Jung spoke often of this legend and not without a certain pleasure" (p.36). On his maternal side, his grandfather, Samuel Preiswerk, was also a pastor and "taught Hebrew and Old Testament theology" (p.39); it was said that this man "reserved a special chair for the ghost of his deceased first wife Magdalene [who was not the grandmother of Jung]" and with whom he had "intimate conversations at a specific time" (p.40). Hence, Jung's mother, Emilie Preiswerk, was the one who introduced him to the séances of spiritism (Hillman, 1976b, pp.126-127). If one is acquainted with Jung's complete work, one can see that he, in some way or another, addressed issues concerning theology and religion, medicine and psychiatry, natural sciences and psychology, literature and the humanities, and even spiritism and the occult.

[562] Deloria Jr., 2009, p.138

[563] It is worth noticing Jung's observation, claiming that, "[t]he psyche is a self-regulating system that maintains its equilibrium just as the body does. Every process that goes too far immediately and inevitably calls forth *compensations* (italics added), and without these there would be neither a normal metabolism nor a normal psyche" (1954b, p.152); one can realize that compensations do not only occur to, and in, the personal notion of the psyche, but also collectively—as one can attest when exploring it form the trans-generational view. He "regard[ed] the activity of the *unconscious* as a balancing of the one-sidedness of the general *attitude* produced by the function of *consciousness*" (1921/1971b, p.419); therefore, compensation is an apt term for the autonomous function of the psyche in its need to include what consciousness itself, in its *selection*, has excluded as *irrelevant*. Therefore, "any one-sidedness of the conscious mind, or a disturbance of the psychic equilibrium, elicits a compensation from the unconscious. The compensation is brought about by the constellation and accentuation of complementary material which assumes archetypal forms when the *fonction du réel*, or correct relation to the surrounding world, is disturbed" (1950/1955, p.520). It could be said that disturbances in one's well being, as sicknesses, accidents, failures, and difficulties of many kinds, are compensations on a systemic level, bringing back an equilibrium for something that had been lost or excluded—previous family or community of fate members, presumably.

[564] Hellinger, 2003/2007, p.102

[565] Weber, 1999, p.170

[566] Hausner, during his work with chronic symptoms and illnesses, has observed how "a lot of diseases are in relation to the fate of members of the family who were excluded" (2008/2009, p.308, free translation); and he says also that it is a common observation in the Constellations work "the profound relation that exists between relevant excluded members of the system and the development of symptoms or diseases" (p.159, free translation). This is the beginning of an answer to what Jung wrote, in 1933, saying: "the future still has to discover a pathology of the psyche to match that of the body" (1950/1955, p.795); it seems that *exclusion* is the clue.

[567] "The family consciousness is unjust towards the later generations by doing justice to previous generations" (Hellinger, 2006/2007, p.41, free translation). There is a similar idea by Jung, who said (when referring to the psychic influence on the children) that one "can hardly hold a man responsible for his unconsciousness, but the fact remains that in this matter nature knows neither patience nor pity, and takes her revenge directly or indirectly through illness and unlucky accidents of all kinds" (1954, p.125); and constantly the children are those who pay.

[568] Weber, 1999, p.149

[569] Hausner, 2008/2009, p.218, free translation

[570] Jung, in a similar way mentioned, that, "we can take the theory of compensation as a basic law of psychic behaviour [*sic*]" (1954b, p.153). Unfortunately, this observation by Jung has not been explored sufficiently by the Jungians. It was Hellinger the man who gave detailed descriptions of compensations within the family context and the dynamics of the soul.

[571] St. Just, after her extensive clinical experience as a traumatologist and constellations facilitator, remarked: "I have a theory that what one does for a living or practices as a serious hobby has something to do with unfinished and possibly hidden business of previous generations" (2012, p.167). And, indeed, this theory had already been formulated by Boszormenyi-Nagy and Spark, in relation to what they considered to be family loyalties (1973/2012).

[572] It has already been explained that in the original German the Constellations are called *Aufstellungen*, in the sense of collocation, but the important representatives to collocate are mostly members from one's family—hence: *Familien Aufstellungen*. However, there are some conceptual guidelines (by Hellinger) that were not mentioned, as it is the "identification," "parentification," "the primary and secondary feelings," the balance between the "give and take," and the observations on "bonding" in one's relationships. All those aspects and some more are described and exemplified in Hellinger's first book about this kind of work (Weber, 1999).

[573] Jung realized that, "[t]he child is helplessly exposed to the psychic influence of the parents and is bound to copy their self-deception, their insincerity, hypocrisy, cowardice, self-righteousness, and selfish regard for their own comfort" (1954, p.79); but Jung here did not mean the conscious psychological attitudes, he rather meant the unconscious psychic tendencies that remain unknown if unexplored, and to which the children react. However, it might be that not in all cases the children unknowingly *copy* their parents, but surely they unknowingly and inevitably react to such influence—often with disturbing or disruptive consequences if it is a moral issue.

[574] "What the father kept silent, that comes in the son to be spoken; and often I found the son to be the father's unveiled secret"(Nietzsche, 1884/2005, p.86). One has to be careful not to take Nietzsche's insight in plain literality, since that was not his style of writing; in any case, it is a profound observation.

[575] 1988, p.1097

[576] Ibid.

[577] "Soured arrogance, repressed envy, perhaps the arrogance and envy of your fathers: they burst forth from you as flames and the madness of revenge . . . Enthusiast they resemble: yet it is not the heart that inspires them—but rather revenge" (Nietzsche, 1884/2005, p.86). Jung, when commenting on this passage, mentioned: "This is a great truth," although he acknowledged that "*ressentiment*" was a better rendering (of the original German) than revenge (1988, p.1099).

[578] 1988, p.1097

[579] Ibid.

[580] One can read traces of the notion of trans-generational affection in Plato's second book of the *Republic,* where Adimantus said: "we shall be brought to judgment in the world below for our unjust deeds here, we or our children's children" (1989, p.612). It is important to note, however, that Adimantus, wording what Socrates would reply, said: "our calculating friend [Socrates] will say, here again the rites for the dead have much efficacy" (p.613)—this issue is reviewed at length in the chapter titled: "The dead."

[581] 1988, p.1098

[582] 1988, p.1097

[583] The importance behind these insights is because Jung considered that "[a]ll personal secrets . . . have the effect of sin or guilt, whether or not they are, from the standpoint of popular morality, wrongful secrets" (1954b, p.57). Hellinger revealed something very powerful in this respect, as he wrote: "we have to give off a very disseminated concept, and also a very disseminated theory of knowledge in which our knowledge is based on observation and, also, in communication. In other words, that a son knows of his family only that which was communicated to him, and that, to the son, it would be possible to hide something in the sense that: if it is not communicated to him, he does not know it. This results in an erroneous supposition" (2001/2008, p.258, free translation). Hellinger boldly criticized epistemology (theory of knowledge) as widely known, advocating for a new way of knowing; maybe, an epistemology that takes into account what Jungians called the unconscious, but firmly based in phenomenology.

[584] "In all families there are secrets and taboo-topics . . . However, when systemic events of importance are denied, unspoken or forgotten, such as the conception of a child, a paternity or a violent death, the exclusion of these persons who belong, damage the order in such system. These types of secrets, however, come into the light even if one has a lot of care for covering them. They will be expressed through a behavior or symptomatology in the children of such family, and if not in such generation it will be in next ones" (Hausner, 2008/2009, p.259, free translation).

[585] Onions, 1996, p.906

[586] There is a saying by Jung: "make an image . . . for how can you develop consciousness if you don't figure things out?" (1988, p.1321). He said that, "you can get the patient's mind at a sufficiently safe distance form the unconscious, for instance by inducing him to draw or to paint a picture of his psychic situation . . . In this way the apparently incomprehensible and unmanageable chaos of his total situation is visualized and objectified" (1960, p.260). This, if seen as a phenomenological technique to deal with the *imaginal,* is just like Helligner's way to deal with systemic "identifications;" where such notion is, for Hellinger, "an iterative compulsion in a systemic level which puts in the scene again and repeats arguments from the past, but without giving them a solution" (Weber, 1999, p.173, free translation). It is not until one literally sees the issue objectified, out there, at a distance form oneself, (although this can be done with a symbolical representative and not necessarily with the actual person or thing, or even with a drawing), that one can *dis-identify* from it and realize that it was something one was adopting for oneself, from someone else of the family system, the lineages, or from somewhere else maybe. This, in fact resembles Jung's notion of the term "identification," since he considered that, "[i]dentification differs from imitation in that it is an *unconscious* imitation, whereas imitation is a conscious copying" (1921/1971b, p.440).

[587] "[I]f we don't identify, we have the chance to discover what this poor ego is and we can learn how to deal with the inherited factors of our mind" (Jung, 1988, p.914); in other words, Jung suggested to be aware the inclinations and tendencies of the thoughts, feelings, and behaviors in every fantasy, but well aware of not identifying with them, because only so can one detach and objectify such psychic contents. If one does not see those contents with some distance, then one can easily fall in the false belief that they constitute one's *identity,* and one lets them direct one's life. Hence, Hillman argued that "[o]ur fantasies are not only in the mind, we are behaving them" (1972/2007b, p.48).

[588] Jung knew that a part of the complexes could consist of "completely unconscious fantasy-systems that have a marked tendency to constitute themselves as separate personalities" (1952/1967, p.29).

[589] 1988, p.914

[590] This is a way to see what Jung called the "psychological non-ego that has an influence on man" (1988, p.915). *Fantasies,* from the view of Jung, are products of the unconscious (as a way of saying that they are not ego-willed, or ego-produced), just as dreams (1954, p.105); and he was very well aware that some fantasies could rather belong to life-issues of the grandparents, for example (1954, pp.123-125). Jung wrote: "fantasy is as much taboo as feeling . . . fantasy is for the most part a product of the unconscious . . . it is essentially involuntary and, by reason of its strangeness, directly opposed to the conscious contents . . . [like] dream, though the latter of course is involuntary and strange in a much higher degree" (1921/1971b, pp.52-53). Hence, Jung wrote: "the important thing is not to interpret and understand fantasies, but primarily to experience them" (1971, p.225), which would not mean to enact them literally, but to let something be revealed through imagination. However, as he well advised, "we must not take fantasies literally when we approach the question of interpreting them" (p.230), if interpretation ever happens. Jung said clearly: "Fantasy as imaginative activity is, in my view, simply the direct expression of psychic life, of *psychic energy which cannot appear in consciousness except in the form of images or contents* (italics added), just as physical energy cannot manifest itself except as a definite physical state stimulating the sense organs in physical ways" (1921/ 1971b, p.433).

[591] Jung knew from Pierre Janet, since he was quite young, that "once baptized, the unconscious personage is more definite and distinct; he shows his psychological characteristics better" (Janet in Jung, 1957, p.54 footnote).

[592] 1950/1955, p.72

[593] Jung mentioned that, "conscious realization of unconscious fantasies . . . [extends] the conscious horizon by the inclusion of numerous unconscious contents[,]" as if it were extending one's terrain and the number of people dwelling on it; "gradually [diminishes] the dominant influence of the unconscious[,]" as if the recognition of such psychic personae would calm down their insistences and needs; and "[brings] about a change of personality[,]" which would also change one's way of relating and even one's metabolism and embodiment (1971, p.231).

[594] 1921/1971b, p.548

[595] Jung, 1988, p.1232

[596] "Of course it is useless to talk of such experiences if you have not been through them[,]" said Jung, when referring to personifying and the (autonomous) persons of the unconscious (1988, p.1356). The same applies to the revelations that come through the constellations.

[597] 2001, p.55

[598] This corresponds to fragment B20 by Diels-Kranz, which has been translated as follows: "Being born, they wish to meet their doom and they leave behind children, born for their doom" (in Barnes, 2001, p.63). This clearly resonates too with fragment B124 by Empedocles in the Diels-Kranz numeration, stating: "Alas, wretched race of mortals, unhappy ones, from what conflicts and what groans did you come into being" (in Barnes, 2001, p.145).

[599] Jung mentioned that, "[t]he guilt of the parents is impersonal, and the child should pay for it no less impersonally" (1954, p.44); and by such statement he revealed that he was well aware of the "natural ethos," as he called it, which imposes a kind of psychic duty, and at the same time configures fate. Jung was well aware that, "[a]n ethos is and remains an inner value, injury to which is no joke and sometimes have very serious psychic consequences" (1964b, p.445). One might do well remembering Heraclitus fragment B119, in the Diels-Kranz numeration, stating ἦθος ἀνθρώπῳ δαίμων (*ethos anthropos daimon*) often translated as "man's character is his fate" (in Barnes, 2001, p.62), which has also been rendered as "one's bearing is one's fate" (Heraclitus, 2001, pp.82-83), but which can also be plainly translated as: *ethos is man's fate*—an ethos which is *naturally* trans-generational, and psychic, of course—not simply one's character out of the social codes of order and conduct. The word δαίμων (*daimon*), however, can also be read as implying more personal, and even trans-human, characteristics, including then the sense of identity, purpose, meaning, and an old and unfathomable dimension of reality; therefore, the fragment has also been translated as: "Man's character is his guardian spirit" (Waterfield, 2000, p.46).

[600] Jung knew clearly that, "it may happen that parents are unaware of their contents and then their children have to live them" (1988, p.1495); he knew also that even in the case of night dreams there is a trans-generational flow—giving a clear example (p.1495). A few years before he died, he also mentioned: "We have known for a long time that children's neuroses depend on the psychic situation of the parents" (1950/1955, p.358).

[601] 1954, p.79

[602] Jung mentioned constantly how "[people] are naïvely convinced that everything they think, feel, want, and so on, is a product of their wills and is therefore 'arbitrary'" (1954, p.90); and they consciously attribute their ways of life to them, without ever realizing that one's life is deeply affected, influenced, and moved by forces out of the personal sphere of consciousness. Jung knew that, "[n]othing exerts a stronger psychic effect upon the human environment, and especially upon children, than the life which the parents have not lived" (1966c, p.4); oftentimes, it is as if one's life obeyed the psychic influences from previous generations.

[603] James, 1997, p.59

[604] Hillman mentioned that *honor to the parents* was something that was needed to be brought back into psychotherapy (n.d., Part 1, Tape 1), and he realized how damaging it was to do the opposite, but he did not insist on it as Hellinger did, nor did he seem to have seen the difficulties and intricacies for achieving it, or the powerful healing effect it can trigger in the whole being of individuals, families, and societies.

[605] 2008/2009, p.125, free translation

[606] It is worth making clear that the alluded notion of religiosity is not only that of Western mainstream and dominant religions. As Deloria Jr. pointed out, in the West, "[r]eligion has come to be seen by many as a mild form of mental illness or immaturity to be transcended by science in its ability to give us answers" (2002, p.114), or as the "god above god" (p.117) attitude in with which once you have mentioned god, "nothing more can be said" (p.113) and nothing more can be argued or disputed, or even as a kind of superstition that is ought to be overcome by trendy philosophical discourses. The notion and idea of religiosity that will be evoked might be closer to that of "other cultures of the world, [where] religion does not exist in the form we encounter it in the West" (p.137); it rather concerns "ways of living within the cosmos in the most harmonious manner" (p.137). Just like Van Der Leeuw claimed, "it is a failing of modern thought that, in connection with the term religion, it must immediately think of 'gods'" (in Deloria Jr., 2002, p.126).

[607] 2008/2009, p.125, free translation

[608] Jung observed how "one likes to accuse father and mother or a wrong education or enemies in order to excuse oneself for one's defeat" (1988, p.562).

[609] 1961, p.96

[610] Jung was well aware that, "these fantasies are not concerned any more with real father and mother but with subjective and very much distorted images of them which lead a shadowy but nonetheless potent existence in the mind [and body and circumstantial happenings] of the patient" (1961, p.134).

[611] Liedloff came to this conclusions after her thorough observations of the Yequana tribe in the Venezuelan Amazon and their contrasts with the Westernized practices, developing and coining the concept of "continuum," which became the hallmark of her work and life. She realized how children who are deprived of the "in-arms experience" could later as adults express this lack of having been held long enough, behaving in ways of the Casanova

syndrome, gigolos or gold-diggers, the slob syndrome, the martyr, the actor personality, the compulsive academic, or the compulsive traveler, to give a few examples (1975, pp.117-120). In spite of the emphasis being on educating about the concept of continuum and the in-arms experience during the first stage of life, her observations were quite sharp about the effects in adult life. In some sense, Liedloff's work is a precursor of Jirina Prekop's life's work, *Festhalte-Therapie,* which is rather a therapeutic solution for individuals who did not have the blessing of in-arms experience as long as they needed it. It is not so strange that Hellinger wrote an insightful book together with Prekop (Hellinger & Prekop, 1998/2004).

[612] One can confirm that this was Jung's view, and one of his working goals was to help individuals reach psychological maturity, since he said plainly: "analysis itself is a process of quickened maturation" (1950/1955, p.172); however, by analysis one should not think of psychoanalysis and the Freudian schools, but specifically in his method, which was very much based on "active imagination"—explained colloquially during the Tavistock Lectures (1950/1955, pp.168-182).

[613] Jung knew quite well that, "[t]he small world of the child, the family milieu, is the model for the big world[,]" and that "[t]he more intensely the family sets its stamp on the child, the more he will be emotionally inclined, as an adult, to see in the great world his former small world" (1961, p.137). It is obvious, then, that those who still struggle with the way that fate carried them along through childhood, will struggle as well with the world (in childish ways). But, as Jung well said, "[o]f course this must not be taken as a conscious intellectual process" (p.137). It happens without one being aware, like one's body autonomous and metabolic functioning—or malfunctioning: constipated digestion, high or low blood-pressure, bad circulation, disturbing sleeping patterns, hormonal excesses, skin problems, etc.

[614] Hillman urged, a long time ago, to "imagine family beyond the perceptions of childhood" (n.d., Part 1, Tape 1, 53:00); if not, then not just family and one's parents, but also one's life and soul are seen from such perceptions. If one is bold enough, one can even imagine life beyond the human, *all-too-human,* perceptions; and soul too, like he mentioned in the fourth part of *Re-visioning Psychology* (1992), should be imagined as something more than only a human phenomenon.

[615] Jung, in his young years, observed that, "the emotional environment constellated during infancy influences not only the character of the neurosis, but also the patient's destiny even down to its very details" (1973, p.476); but he also argued that "[i]t should be one of the most important aims of education to free the growing child [or even the adult] from his unconscious attachment to the influences of his [or her] early environment" (p.478). One can deduce that it is not childhood what weights most for the unfolding of destiny, but one's inevitable emotionality to the memories and lived experiences of it—whether in gratitude, appreciation, and respect, or in rancor, contempt, and disdain.

[616] Hillman since many years ago warned how "[psycho-] therapy has trapped itself in the family and at the same time condemns family" (n.d., Part 2, tape 1, 2:00); he suggested that the usual psychotherapeutic ways to deal with family might have done more damage to the family than what the family might have done to one. Of course this was prior to the popularization of the Family Constellations, which have also distinguished themselves from usual psychotherapies and the common blaming of one's parents. Hillman claimed that, "it is so ingrained in us that we think we are the result of family" (n.d., Part 2, tape 1, 2:30), suggesting that it is such thinking and narrowed vision which has led to blame the parents and the family for one's misfortunes and misery. He even dared to call such

paradigmatic views as "psychology's demolition of the family" (n.d., Part 1, Tape 1, 18:00), where the mysteries and depths of the psyche are only explained by mom's and dad's "mistakes." Hellinger expressed a similar idea, when saying that "[s]imply to say that families cause illness would be a cheap condemnation of the family" (Hellinger & Hövel, 1999, p.80).

[617] 1894/2005, p.283

[618] Hellinger, 1996/2002, p.92, free translation

[619] There is a kabbalistic teaching where it is explained how "all the light [and blessings] that a child ever receives always comes through the conduits of his mother and his father," this being so because "family is not a coincidence," and "there is a spiritual pipeline, a channel that is drawn specifically in this order" (Berg, M., 2012, min 0'1"- 9'13").

[620] 1996/2002, p.94

[621] The sense of *lack* is in fact the crucial and most important characteristic of the main chronic miasma—*psora*. Hahnemann argued that it was "[i]ncalculably greater and more important than the two [other] chronic miasms [*sic*]" (1833/2009, p.98), namely, *syphilis* and *sycosis*. He wrote: "[psora is] the only real *fundamental cause* and producer of all the numerous, I may say innumerable, forms of disease" (p.98). He claimed that, "this extremely ancient infecting agent has gradually passed, in some hundreds of generations, through many millions of human organisms . . . [and] it can now display such innumerable morbid forms in the great family of mankind . . . produc[ing] an innumerable variety of defects, injuries, derangements and sufferings" (p.99). He listed afflictions from "scoliosis and cyphosis, caries, and cancer" to "deafness, cataract, amaurosis, urinary calculus, paralysis," and many more under the many forms of disease that the psora produces and enhances. If, instead of "infecting agent" one understands a "sickly psychic disposition" (as it has been presented throughout this work), then the sense of lack that Hellinger refers to and the chronic affection of lack that Hahnemann discovered are probably the same. Interestingly, Hahnemann warned that the psora is "increased and disfigured to a monstrous extent by allopathic unskilfulness" (p.154); and similarly, the psychological notion of lack is also increased to a monstrous extent by those unskilled—almost criminal—psychotherapists, who help their patients blame and accuse their parents.

[622] 2003/2006, p.99

[623] Hellinger, 2003/2006, p.99

[624] One can argue, like Socrates, that: "misstatements are not merely jarring in their immediate context; they also have a bad effect upon the soul" (Plato, 1989, p. 95)—from Plato's *Phaedo*.

[625] Hellinger considered that, "bowing is a movement as much of the body as of the soul[,]" and "it is not complete until the person straights up again and keeps his path" (Weber, 1999, p.71, free translation).

[626] 2003/2006, p.100

[627] Regarding an honest and profound bow, one could read in *Ayaz and the king's pearl,* by Rumi, a story in which the courtiers of a kingdom were bowing profoundly and honestly, with the head against the floor, and, like

he observed: "Whoever bows down like they are bowing down/ will not rise up in his old self again" (Jalāl al-Din Rumi, 1995, p.128). Of course it is only a poem, but he who has done right, knows.

[628] Onions, 1996, p.763

[629] Ibid, p.742

[630] Ibid, p.763

[631] Onions, 1996, p.452

[632] It is worth mentioning the similarity with Jung's idea of "union with the instincts," which could be thought as union with the force of life as it was given and as it has taken one at its service. He interestingly mentioned that "the acceptance of the instincts . . . [requires] a specific humility. For you cannot accept your instincts without humility . . . you can only accept them humbly" (1988, p.1307), just as in the case of one's parents, one can only accept them humbly—literally bowing. Then, as Jung said, "you have the simple human fate, the happiness and the misery of ordinary human life, and something on top, because you have accepted it[;]" in other words, if one nods to one's parents one nods to one's life instinct, one's *will to live*, and unexpectedly one feels something else. But, as Jung warned, "[i]f you do it for the tip you hope for, it is no good: you have cheated yourself" (p.1307).Those who do it just because Hellinger has said that it is healing, without genuinely feeling it, cheat themselves deeply.

[633] Jung mentioned that, almost always, "[an individual's] idea of his father is a complex quantity for which the real father is only in part responsible, and indefinitely large share falling to the son" (1951/1959, p.18); therefore, like Jung observed, the individual rarely *sees* his father, he only sees the image that he has made of him. This occurs because perception is not clear, it is tinctured by wishes, desires, expectations, hopes, sensations, and ideas of how the father should be or could be. And when the father does not match with the image, it makes the individual think that "he has every right to feel hurt, misunderstood, and even betrayed" (p.19). Jung commented that such was an example of "the fallacy *enkekalymmenos* ('the veiled one') . . . [a famous old paradox] which stems form Eubulides the Megarian, [and] runs: 'Can you recognize your father?' Yes. 'Can you recognize this veiled one?' No. 'This veiled one is your father. Hence you can recognize your father and not recognize him'" (p.18 footnote). It is worth noting that it happens also with daughters in regards to their father, and with both, sons and daughters, in regards to their mother.

[634] It is a transgression to the life-principle because parents gave life, and if one complains about them, then one is not fully receiving (the force of) life from them. This insight matches with the dynamic derangement that Hahnemann argued that is the cause of all disease.

[635] 1894/2005, p.195

[636] Rumi, in a poem titled *Father Reason,* which addresses the divine father, wrote: "Make peace with this father, the elegant patterning,/ and every experience will fill with immediacy" (Jalāl al-Din Rumi, 1995, p.145); but it could be applied to the earthly father as well, and it would make sense too. Van der Post commented: "the fact that in an age when men and their societies increasingly used the failures of parents, society, and history as excuses and justifications for not being fully responsible for themselves and their reactions, he [Jung] always spoke of his

parents with gratitude and love and referred repeatedly to his 'dear and generous father'"" (1975, pp.79-80). There is a profound kabbalistic explanation of why we see the world in a chaotic way and we do not understand what happens and we get confused. Kabbalists teach that it is because our heart is covered with impurity, but impurity, the Hebrew word *tumá*, comes from *tim tum*, stupidity. Selfishness is what creates the layers of impurity around the heart. When one only sees oneself, only one's suffering, only one's life story, one risks seeing the world in a confused way, not understanding why things happen, always seeing the world in a stupid way—even when supported by great theories and philosophies (Berg, M., 2014b, min. 24'20"- 28'40").

[637] 1964b, p.35

[638] Ibid, p.35

[639] Ibid, p.35

[640] Jung, in his young age, observed that, "misfortune is always too strong an attachment to the parents, so that the child remains imprisoned in its infantile relationships" (1973, p.478), even towards life, the world, fate, and the divine; and maybe not "always," but certainly in many cases.

[641] 1894/2005, p.132

[642] It is quite interesting to notice that the word *blame* stems from the Greek *blasphemeîn,* which stems from *blásphemos,* and means "evil-speaking" (Onions, 1996, p.98); therefore, it is cognate with blaspheme and blasphemous. There is a deep kabbalisitc explanation of the dangers of bad-mouthing and evil speaking, referred to as *lashón hará,* literally, evil-tongue. The root of it being too much emphasis on the external side of life and not being in contact with the internal aspect: the soul, and the realm from where healing comes from (Berg, M., 2016, min 0'1"-28'03").

[643] 1894/2005, p.232

[644] Ibid, p.232

[645] 2008/2009, p.156, free translation

[646] Jung observed in his practice, for instance, that "[e]ven *very intelligent* (italics added) patients are incapable of seeing that from the very beginning they owe the complications of their lives as well as their neurosis to dragging their infantile emotional attitude along with them" (1961, p.137). It becomes clear that even great intellectual persons might still be attached to the emotional family atmosphere—and one can see that in many psychologists and philosophers, psychotherapists and professors of any discipline, not to mention the many priests who seem to get into such practice because of their disturbed psychic atmosphere, and end up sexually abusing children—mostly boys. It could not be more clear that intellectual skill, many long years of studies, and even a rigorous discipline, do not necessarily free an individual from his (or her) psychic disturbances and chronic miasma.

[647] Jung observed and said, for instance, that, "it is sufficiently obvious, and has been confirmed over and over again by experience, that what the doctor fails to see in himself he either will not see at all, or will see grossly

exaggerated, in his patient; further, he encourages those things to which he himself unconsciously inclines, and condemns everything he abhors in himself" (1954b, p.115).

[648] There are some lines by Rumi, from his poem *Eastern Mystery*, saying: "I ask that lovers no longer be shy or concerned/ with right and wrong, with reputation/ or recognition" (Jalāl al-Din Rumi, 2003, p.162). This is one of the greatest paradoxes of this beautiful Earth: the more one elevates love beyond the boundaries of this Earth, beyond its rights and wrongs that bring some people close and some others away, the more one honors this Earth, and the more grounded and embodied one's love for others becomes.

[649] There are some beautiful lines by Rumi, from his poem *Green ears*, where he wisely wrote: "When you think your father is guilty of an injustice,/ his face looks cruel" (Jalāl al-Din Rumi, 1995, p.239), as it often happens when a lot of children (and child-like adults) look at their father only form their own mother's perspective; but, "[w]hen you make peace with your father,/ he will look peaceful and friendly" (p.239). Even if the parents never saw each other again after the sexual encounter which generated the conception of the individual, or even if the individual is born out of a rape, the gift of life demands honor to both, because the father is such a figure only because of *that* specific woman who became the mother, and vice versa, and such an act allows one to enjoy the world's coloring. One realizes then, like Rumi said, that, "[t]he whole world/ is a form for truth" (p.239).

[650] Hillman, n.d., Part 1, Tape 1, 8:00

[651] This rather seems as another clumsy concept, like that of "normality," which is not based on psychic facts, but it is "based on statistical expectations" (Hillman, 1997, p.134), and from which we have now the monstrous category called abnormal psychology—which is incapable of *seeing through* (like Hillman) and seeing into the depths of its matter of study (psyche). Maybe it is only the human concept of "functionality" (in the family) that which is dysfunctional; it does not do justice to psychic matters and the aims of soul.

[652] 1998, p.143

[653] Hellinger has said that "[i]t's not a child's place to understand nor to forgive [in relation to what his or her parents did,]" because it's "presumptuous" (Hellinger & Hövel, 1999, p.15).

[654] Hillman made a bold critic to those models and methods of psychotherapy which give great importance to childhood and emphasize the developmental stages, having built up psychologies from a developmental view; he sees them actually as a burden, because those therapies keep individuals (and even their own theories) within the perspectives and paradigms of the child, and "the child always needs therapy, because is always growing and always feels abandoned" (n.d., Part 1, Tape 2, 2:00). Hillman foresaw, some decades ago, the need to end psychotherapy—and especially leave behind the perspectives based on childhood and development.

Hellinger has also considered "ridiculous" the many schools of therapy that urge their clients "to kill their parents (in fantasy, of course), or beat them or scream out their anger" (Hellinger & Hövel, 1999, p.79), because they actually do more psychic damage with all that.

[655] It is one of the most important aspects in Constellations work to realize that anyone who is part of the family, has the right of belonging to the family (Hellinger, 1996/2002, p.101); and one can also see that if one does not

know to which system does one belong, and who does this system include, then one has lost a very important place in the world—one is then psychically *displaced,* and in such psychic *dis-position* one is *disposed to disease*. And when individuals are displaced, it is not surprising to see them behave individualistically, for their own and nobody else, without honor, respect, concern, or care for community, further generations, the land, the waters, or the rest of the living beings. Many social problems, and many of the so-called ecological problems too, can be seen as the result of a massive psychic displacement—and this in fact suggests a very insightful way to address such problems and devastations.

[656] After these insights, Heraclitus fragment numbered B43 might be considered applicable. It has been translated as: "It is more important to quench insolence than conflagration" (2000, p.46); and also rendered as: "Insolence needs drowning worse than wildfire" (2001, p.67). Insolence, precisely, stems from the Latin *insolent*, which means arrogant, therefore used in the sense of "contemptuous of dignity or authority" (Onions, 1996, p.477).

[657] One can also draw a genealogical tree and see that one's life involved many people passing on life—the more one reaches into the past, the more one realizes how insignificant a single life is if considered only for itself. This, however, might not have the impact that has being in front of one's blood antecessors, embodied through representatives, or in some sort of ritual setting, but it is a way to start acknowledging them.

[658] Socrates, in Plato's tenth book of the *Laws,* mentioned: "thou hast forgotten in the business that the purpose of all that happens is . . . to win bliss for the life of the whole; it is not made for thee, but thou for it" (Plato, 1989, p.1459).

[659] Jung mentioned that, "although parental *imagos* [*sic*] (italics added) can be released from the state of projection and withdrawn form the external world, they continue, like everything else acquired in early childhood, to retain their original freshness" (1954b, p.96), and one might feel the original love. Hellinger realized the importance of this too, and with a different wording said almost the same: "Many disorders and illnesses arise from a conflict that results from refusing to acknowledge systemic ties . . . I then try to reactivate the positive side of the original love" (1999, p.81); this, of course, would mean that the bond remains, but as a healthy one, in its original freshness.

[660] 1887/1974, p.104

[661] Onions, 1996, p.760

[662] Hillman considered that "[h]istory provides parentage to psychic events, giving them background in race, culture, and tradition" (1998, p.143). We are unable to understand much of our psychological lives and individual destiny unless we look way back into the lineages and realize how the greatest part of our fate was crafted from the crucial events that the previous generations of our family endured. And for doing so one requires first a general knowledge of historical events and circumstances, because only then an undiscovered history of our family will emerge, one in which we see greatness, passion, courage, and many other virtues, but most importantly the flow of love and the force of life.

[663] Jung mentioned: "The true history of the mind is not preserved in learned volumes but in the living organism of everyone" (1938/1966b, p.41). One's "body" is nothing but the result of hundreds of generations of human beings, and one's being is the latest embodied actualization of such mixture (an *idiosyncrasis*), as if carrying the entire history

of all those who lived before in the blood lineages; hence, one's life can be seen as a repetition of old (almost mythic) patterns of living and loving, as archetypal ways of dwelling on Earth. By archetype, following Jung, "[i]n no sense it is a question of [only] inherited ideas, but inherited, instinctive impulses and forms that can be observed in all living creatures" (1960, pp.261-262); the physical "body" acts and reacts in ways that are not foreign to the history of the human being, it obeys *dominants of consciousness* even in its hormonal secretions.

[664] Meade in Eliade, 1958/2005, p.xviii

[665] 1988, p.944

[666] "Behind our consciousness is the whole collective unconscious which lives down in the body, and that is eternally caught in the past: we cannot change it" (Jung, 1988, p.944).

[667] Hillman, 1998, p.143

[668] Jung, 1958, p.500

[669] Hillman has observed that "historical 'facts' may be but fantasies attached to and sprouting from central archetypal cores . . . [which conform] psychological realities of passionate importance," that "[give] the soul a feeling of destiny, an eschatological sense of *what happens matters.*" He has quite sharply and poetically seen through history, and realized that "[it] is but the stage on which we enact the mythemes of the soul" (2005, p.33). In other words, Hillman did not discard historical facts as a mere way of remembering events, as if a murder or a rape were not so if one remembers them differently; he rather points out that the so-called historical events were also governed inescapably by archetypal situations, and such events *in fact* gave body and place to a psychic movement, which most often, when tough, are so incomprehensible that one ends up calling them destined and fated. If such psychic movements are perceived not only personally, but trans-generationally, then one can understand better the importance of previous family deeds and misdeeds, and how one is an outcome of them and *in fact* their continuity.

[670] "The first form of the complex cannot be other than the parental complex, because the parents are the first reality that the child comes into conflict" (Jung, 1933, p.80). It becomes clear that any dealing and coping with the complexes have to begin with one's parents, because of their priority in (Earthly) time and (psychic) importance for any individual. Jung knew quite well the imperious necessity of "freeing man from his family fixations, from his weakness and uncontrolled infantile feelings" (1952/1967, p.414), which would otherwise would block libido to family ties (and that applies to women too); because, as he knew also, [t]he blocking of libido [or psychic energy] leads to an accumulation of instinctuality and, in consequence, to excesses and aberrations of all kinds" (1952/1967, p.169). This observation, of Jung, in fact confirms that many problems in society for which there have been all kind of conjectures and explanations—from sociological and economical, to neurophysiological, pedagogical, political, etc.—might be at their core an unresolved and collective infantilism; in other words, a lack of psychological mature men and women. "The immaturity of man [and woman] is a fact that must enter into all our calculations" (Jung, 1954b, p.109). Hellinger, in fact, throughout the Constellations work observed that addictions (and alcoholism included) are mostly in relation to a rupture in the orders of love, where there is no honorable place for the father in the son's or daughter's heart (even when adult). He has even said that the more disdain there is for the fathers (in general, throughout the world), often because of women and the "mothers," the more that drug-addiction rises (Hellinger, 2000/2001, pp.122-126). In his view, the addiction is a revenge and at the same time an expiation for not

being able to "take the father," so to speak, to take the father in the heart, in an honorable way; and this is mostly a dynamic that is caused by the mother, because from where or who else would the child get those terrible ideas about his or her father? This, which by the way also applies to bulimia, said Hellinger, should be taken into consideration when treating addictions (Weber, 1999, pp.321-322). It has been a general observation, for example, that, "[a]scetics lack their mother; addicts lack their father" (2002b, p.26).

[671] Hausner, 2008/2009, p.67, free translation

[672] Jung wrote in one of his *Black Books*, which would latter became the *Red Book*: "May one man carry another's burden, has become an immorality. May each carry his own load; that is the least that one can demand anyone to do" (2009b, p.339 footnote).

[673] This would be an example of what Jung called "neurotic suffering" which "is an unconscious fraud and has no moral merit, as real suffering" (1954, p.78); as it is the case when individuals deeply suffer for situations that in fact pertain their parents, grandparents, or even to someone prior to them. Moreover, such neurotic suffering, "infects" the children, if there are any, and is "often passed on from generation to generation" (p.78)—as a curse.

[674] Weber, 1999, p.297, free translation

[675] Some persons might be tempted to argument against this, but it is worth remembering Hellinger, who has observed how "for the majority of persons, the suffering according to the systemic dynamic is way more important and also way easier than the solution[,]" because in such a way "if the person suffers and goes through bad times, feels innocent and united to his [or her] parents" (Weber, 1999, p.142, free translation). This revelation has profound and serious implications for healing, happiness, and well-being—if one dares to explore it in oneself.

[676] 1887/1974, p.262

[677] "Love in a family is responsible for illness as well as health" (Hellinger & Hövel, 1999, p.80). Again, this insight is much too profound, and deep revelations about the human condition might change if taken into consideration seriously.

[678] Hellinger wrote sometime that to renounce of God might mean to renounce of one's family and its values (2000/2001b, p.92).

[679] 1952/1967, p.414

[680] Jung, 1952/1967, p.414

[681] In this regard, Jung gave two clear examples; one is that of a "the stepmother who identifies herself with the daughter and, through her, marries the son-in-law; or the father who thinks he is considering his son's welfare when he naïvely forces him to fulfill his—the father's—wishes, for instance in marriage or in the choice of profession" (1964b, p.37). Both cases imply a lack of freedom because of a psychic influence from the parents, most of the times unconsciously, even when the individuals—sons or daughters—might think that they chose it free-willingly. This is

so because the individuals try to help their parents live their unfulfilled life, and they unconsciously sacrifice their own happiness, freedom, health, purpose, and fulfillment for such aims—*even if it costs their life*.

[682] Jung, 1952/1967, pp.414-415

[683] Jung, 1961, p.285

[684] This concept of libido is quite different from Freud's and the psychoanalytic school, for Jung "[l]ibido is intended as an energic [*sic*] expression for psychological values. A psychological value is something that has an effect, hence it can be considered from the energic standpoint without any pretence of exact measurement" (1960, p.190). "Libido is intended simply as a name for energy which manifests itself in life-processes and is perceived subjectively as connotation and desire . . . It brings us into line with a powerful current of ideas that seeks to comprehend the world of appearance energically. . . suffice it to say that everything we perceive can only be understood as an effect of force" (1961, p.125). Hence, he firmly argued regarding Freud's view, that, "there is nothing for it but to abandon the sexual definition of libido, or we shall lose what is valuable in the libido theory, namely the energic point of view" (1961, p.118)—those Jungians (in particular) who stick to the notion of libido as the sexual energy have greatly misunderstood, misinterpreted, and misread Jung. He claimed that "the libido concept . . . signifies nothing more than the energy of the life process. Its laws are the laws of vital energy" (1921/1971b, p.212). "The natural flow of libido . . . means complete obedience to the fundamental laws of human nature, and there can positively be no higher principle than harmony with natural laws that guide the libido in the direction of life's optimum" (pp.212-213). In this sense, a blockage of libido, or a hampering of it, could be the cause of physical disease and chronic illness, homeopathically speaking. However, it is worth noticing Jung's saying that, "[t]he release of libido is obtained through ritual work. The release puts the libido at the disposal of consciousness, where it becomes domesticated. From an instinctive, undomesticated state it is converted into a state of disposability" (1921/1971b, p.210 footnote). It is clear then, that a constellation (ritual) can purify and cleanse (generate a catharsis) the psychic terrain (chronic miasma), and thus release psychic energy (libido) that was directed without awareness towards certain contents or persons (an unconscious process), and make this life-force available for other activities, other places, other persons, and even other intentions—indeed, as if a powerful beast would have been tamed and were dwelling in one's house (*dómos*). There is a beautiful passage by Rumi, from his poem *Zikr*, where he said: "Don't try to control a wild horse by grabbing its leg./ Take hold the neck. Use a bridle. Be sensible./ Then ride! There is a need for self-denial" (Jalāl al-Din Rumi, 1995, p.115).

[685] Jung also realized, in his early years, how "[t]he first moves towards friendship and love are constellated in the strongest possible manner by the nature of the relationships with our parents, and here as a rule one can see how powerful is the influence of the family constellation" (1973, p.475); and not only at early stages of life, but even later in one's couple relationships, when one decides to marry. He fully realized, for instance, that "[m]any an unhappy choice of profession and disastrous marriage can be traced to such a constellation" (p.476). Jung was well aware that "[i]t is the strength of the bond to the parents that unconsciously influences the choice of husband or wife, either positively or negatively" (1954, p.191), and also at second or third marriages. Surprisingly this also affects in one's work, profession, productivity, and prosperity—one can read this from Hellinger, who wrote a short book titled *Success in life success in business* (2009b). Therefore, it seems corrrect to follow Jung in saying that: "The place of the father is taken by the society of men, and the place of the mother by the family" (1964b, p.36). In order to deepen into these insights, it is worth noticing the etymological roots of the words matrimony and patrimony; the first stems

form *mater*, the second from *pater,* hence *patri*, and both with the suffix *mōnium,* used as *–mony* (Onions, 1996, p.562, 658), which is "related by gradation to *–men*" (p.588) in the sense of "expressing the result or product of an action" (p.569).

[686] It is not meant in the sense that literal matrimony and patrimony have to be given by the parents. It rather means that one can be married but without the blessing of a loving and caring relationship, one can have a house but without the blessing of a home, one can have money but not the blessing of prosperity, one can have a successful company but not the blessing of working on one's vocation, one can have professional success but not the blessings of friendship, and so on.

[687] It is worth to mention Somé's observation, inquiring "if the epidemic of breast cancer is not symptomatic of the denial of the mother in the Western culture" (1999, p.265). From such reflections, that are in fact close to Hellinger's, one can realize that just as dishonor could enhance severe physical diseases, a genuine attitude of honor might avoid them—or even cure them.

[688] There are some beautiful lines by Rumi, from his poem *All rivers at once*, saying: "Your father and your mother were playing love games./ They came together, and you appeared!/ Don't ask what love can make or do!/ Look at the colors of the world" (Jalāl al-Din Rumi, 1995, p.92).

[689] 1894/2005, p.277

[690] There is a beautiful passage in the poem *The long string* by Rumi, where he wrote that a rich man asked a Sufi whether he wanted a coin of silver that day or three the day after, and the Sufi answered: " I love the half coin I have already in my hand/ from yesterday more than the promise of a whole one/ today, or the promise of a hundred tomorrow" (Jalāl al-Din Rumi, 1995, pp.81-82). Like the mystic clarified: "A sufi is the child of *this* moment" (p.82).

[691] The word "numinous" was coined by Otto when struggling to find a better word for holy or sacred (the German *heilig*), but without the supremacy of its ethical associations, and without the rationalizations and moralizations of the term. He rather referred to it as a *sui generis* concept "irreducible to any other", and as something that "cannot be strictly defined." He considered that the numinous "cannot, strictly speaking, be taught, it can only be evoked, awakened in the mind; as everything that comes 'of the spirit' must be awakened" (1923/1958, p.5-7). Jung, influenced by Otto, mentioned that, "[t]he numinosum is either a quality of a visible object or the influence of an invisible presence causing a peculiar alteration of consciousness" (1938/1966b, p.4).

[692] Onions, 1996, p.617

[693] Otto, 1923/1958, p.6

[694] Otto, 1923/1958, p.10

[695] Ibid, pp.12-24

[696] Otto, 1923/1958, p.26

[697] There are some lines from a poem titled *Offering,* by Mcgrath, which actually address in gratitude the effort and sacrifice that a father has to do for his child, acknowledging the lose that he undergoes (and of course that it could apply to any mother too). It says: "you gave us/ All the lost honey of a young man's years—/ Steering through the vicious seas of those bitter times . . . / Ah . . . dearest father, dear/ Helmsman!" (in Bly, Hillman, & Meade, 1992, p. 144).

[698] Otto, 1923/1958, p.11

[699] This notion of the numinous is simple, accessible, sensuous, and potentially universal, and, yet, it was far from being mentioned in the book *The idea of the numinous* (Casement & Tacey, 2006). I have to make clear that, contrary to the writings of the above mentioned book, it is not an "idea" but an experience; one only knows the warmth of the fire if one has been close enough, never if one has read about it in books, heard elusive speeches and explanations of it, or if one has seen it from a safe distance.

[700] 2003/2006, p.184, free translation

[701] Just as one can read in the (translated) words of the Persian mystic who long time ago, in his poem *Nod to what is,* said: "Hafiz says God is fully known only through love, which accepts *everything.* Love reveals the universe as a cosmic playground where everything and being participates in a single, magnificent Game" (Hafiz, 2006, p.21).

[702] This might be very close to Jung's consideration and notion of religiosity, saying that, "[i]ndeed, this is the original meaning of the word *religio*—a careful observation and taking account of (from *relegere*) the numinous" (1958, p.596). Jung's statement clearly suggests that to be religious is not because one follows a religion, but that one is aware, that one observes and respects, the numinous and luminous quality of this existence of flesh. It sounds as no coincidence that Somé also mentioned that, "what we call respect should be a religion into itself" (2005, Disc 1, Track 2). Corbin, for instance, considered that, "[t]he religious mode of apprehension is a growth of transparence of the divine. And it is always concrete, unique things (events, lived situations, images) which serve as support for the relation lived and experienced 'in the present'" (1990/1998, p.26). Therefore, he continued, "it cannot be communicated as if it were some sort of technique" (p.26); in other words, it must be experienced! Hellinger, when explaining about constellations, commented: "This work, and what it brings into the light, has a religious dimension or spiritual dimension . . . It obligates us to recognize the earth and to recognize that in multiple ways we are intermingled with something earthly . . . It seems to me that many religions orient themselves in the direction for dissuading us from looking into this reality" (2001/2008, p.364, free translation).

[703] Somé, 2005, Disc 2, Track 3

[704] Hillman, when writing about the issues faced in the consulting room, claimed that "problems are not merely classifiable behavioural [*sic*] acts, nor medical categories of disease" (1997, p.43), and such an insight would be applicable also to psychoses and insanity. He argued that such problems "*are above all experiences and sufferings, problems with an 'inside'*" (pp.43-44), not mere mistakes of the communicative action or the environmental situation (like Bateson and Watzlawick thought sometime ago); if by "inside" one does not consider the individual interiority, but rather the *terrain,* the chronic miasma, then it is very clear that it is in relation to the autonomous psychic activity.

[705] Hillman, for instance, considered that, the "[r]ecognition of the 'reality' of the 'unconscious' is a recognition of the depths, fullness, richness of the psyche, that it has contents, that it is not a *tabula rasa*" (1992, p.125), and, moreover, that we are not all constituted and configured in the same way. Jung observed that more often than not, "[e]veryone thinks that psychology is what he himself knows best . . . Instinctively [every individual] supposes that his own psychic constitution is the general one, and that everyone is essentially like everyone, that is to say like himself" (1964b, p.134). As a consequence, "[p]eople are profoundly astonished, or even horrified, when this rule quite obviously does not fit" (pp.134-135). People who believe that we are all born the same have severe limitations for acknowledging the psyche, its motion, its depths, and its healing and its knowing potentials. Naturally, like Jung observed too, differences are often thought as "a mistake that must be remedied as speedily as possible, or a misdemenour [*sic*] that calls for condign punishment" (p.135). He realized that, "[it is the] prejudice of simple-minded persons that everybody is exactly the same as them" (p.135), and a lot of psychologists, despite their expensive education, seem to suffer this simple-mindedness.

[706] For a more detailed explanation on this description see *The psychogenesis of mental disease* (Jung, 1960), particularly the chapters "Mental disease and the psyche," "On the psychogenesis of schizophrenia," "Recent thoughts on schizophrenia," and "Schizophrenia," which he re-visioned and wrote throughout several decades. Jung even gave the clear advice when treating such persons, patients with, or with proclivity to, psychotic illnesses; he warned to be careful with persons whose "mythological layer of the psyche is uncovered, for these contents have a fearful fascination for the patient" (1954b, p.15), and an amateurish psychotherapy might only trigger the psychosis.

[707] Jung, in 1935, at the Tavistock Lectures, when answering a question regarding the difference between the dissociation in hysteria and the dissociation in schizophrenia—which would be equivalent to ask the difference between neurotic and psychotic dissociation—said: "with schizophrenia it is a deep dissociation of personality; the fragments cannot come together any more" (1950/1955, p.100). Rather than taking this statement in a dogmatic way, one can realize that the crucial issue to consider is the notion and dynamic depths of the "personality."

[708] It is worth mentioning that Jung was well acquainted with schizophrenia and psychotic individuals, unlike Freud and many of his followers, who never lived or worked in an asylum, like Jung did. For such reasons Jung has been considered, besides a true pioneer, a man of great vision (*because he actually ventured to see*) into *the depths of soul* when exploring and treating severe psychological disturbances—the so-called psychosis. "Depth psychology" (*Tiefenpsychologie*) was in fact coined by his mentor Bleuler, but Jung did not stick to that term (Jung, 1961, p.229); unfortunately, the term came to be mixed and confused with psychoanalysis and other psychotherapies that do not reach as far into the psyche, and do not conceive the unconscious as Jung, and do not speak of it as Jung did—the Freudian view of the unconscious is only one example, which is the one that has been widely popularized and that has permeated a variety of psychologies, psychotherapies, universities' studies, and even the common-citizen jargon. It is very important to note that almost all descriptions, diagnosis, treatments, and understandings of psychosis, even outside the psychoanalytic traditions, have departed from Freud's views, when in fact he did not treated psychotics—it would not be a surprise that it is all wrong, and a great error.

[709] This refers to what has been called the *structural standpoint of the psyche* in Freudian literature, which in fact resembles a kind of nineteenth century industrial machine, with repression of forces, and sublimation, and an investment of force for determined and functional labors which were, in fact, constant and supervised by an over-looker (an *über-Ich*), with some negotiated discharge and release of tension, a kind of pressure release in order

to avoid overheating (or impulsive acting), and a cauldron of instinctual behaviors heating up and moving the gears of the whole machinery, with the futuristic illusion of progress, production, and profit, at the cost of a great discontent—it rather reveals the thoughts and mis-understandings of their time and place, more than the structures of the psyche. Such perspectives speak more about the psyche of Freud and the Freudians, including all the different struggling hordes that follow and do as the primal "father" figure until today, than about a universal structure of the psyche—how can they be so blatantly blind (so Oedipal) to that fact? Jung clearly wrote, when old, in 1953: "I could not make up my mind to accept the sexual theory of neurosis and still less of psychosis . . . Freud's one-sided emphasis on sex must be a subjective prejudice" (1950/1955, p.438).

[710] Jung "believe[d] that incest and the other perverted sexual aspects . . . [which were] essential contents of the regressive tendency . . .[observed through the lens of the Freudian psychological theory]" were really something else that the patients were seeking in the mother or the father, say: "the universal feeling of childhood innocence, the sense of security, of protection, of reciprocated love, of trust, of faith—a thing that has many names" (1954b, pp.32-33). Hellinger's healing resolutions, indeed, are very close to Jung's view, where it is often observed through the Constellations work that many individuals, asking for help, are in fact seeking such things that Jung mentioned, form their father or mother. It is not that such individuals got fixated in childhood, or that they regressed, but that something was missing from their childhood—even when they were very advanced already into adulthood.

[711] One has to make clear the distinction and point of departure—which is no small issue to be overlooked. Jung mentioned: "Freud . . . derives the unconscious from the conscious, which is along the same rational line ['There is nothing in the mind that was not in the senses']. I put it the reverse way . . . consciousness really arises from an unconscious condition." (1950/1955, pp. 9-10). Therefore, Jung "adopted a standpoint affirming the psychogenesis of schizophrenia, and emphasized that the symptoms (delusions and hallucinations) are not just meaningless chance happenings but, as regards their contents, are in respect significant psychic products" (1960, p.227); in other words, the suffering of schizophrenics is accomplishing something, as if it were a way in which (the great) psyche is telling or doing something. Jung did not discard those contents as only mental rubbish; and one can attest this since he was professionally young, by 1909, when he mentioned that, "we are intellectually still so dense and lethargic that our ears cannot hear and our minds cannot grasp the mysteries of which the insane speak" (1950/1955, p.337). Hillman said that, "[l]eading away from experience leads also away form understanding the data as they are presented" (1997, p.49), therefore, he conceived understanding "based on sympathy, on intimate knowledge, on participation" (p.49), never based on diagnostic manuals. However, by sympathy he warned not to consider "merely an identification with the other's viewpoint and sharing his personal suffering[,]" because that would only be *personal commiseration* (p.150); he rather encouraged *"knowledge of the objective psyche"* as "an *understanding of the personal level of the psyche in the light of knowledge of the impersonal level*" (pp.150-152).

[712] It is worth noticing Jung's thought and insight regarding "the famous 'birth trauma' [which] has remained such an obvious truism that it can no longer explain anything, any more than can the hypothesis that life is a disease with a bad prognosis because its outcome is always fatal" (1958, p.516). Several decades before the psychoanalyst Janov popularized the "Primal Scream," and which would be the hallmark of his "birth trauma therapy," Jung anticipated him and discarded it. Hellinger, in fact, would experience the primal scream himself and learn from it, but he would also dismiss it, not considering the great panacea and healing process that many believe it to be.

[713] 1961, p.261

[714] Hahnemann conceived that, "[t]hey [the usually termed mental diseases] do not, however, constitute a class of disease sharply separated from all others, since in all other so-called corporeal diseases the condition of the disposition and mind is *always* altered; and in all cases of disease we [physicians] are called on to cure the state of the patient's disposition" (1833/2009, p.156). In other words, it is what Jung called the "complex" that which must be attended.

[715] It is worth noticing the comments of Jung, even when young, when he wrote about schizophrenia: "[p]sychogenesis has long been discussed, but it is still a modern, even an ultra-modern problem" (1960, p.233); it seems that he was very well aware that such disturbance needed more psychological exploration and research, not mere studies that co-relate brain chemicals with behavioral, intellectual, and social functions.

[716] Jung, wrote that, "[p]resumably the psyche does not trouble itself about our categories of reality; for it, everything that *works* is real" (1954b, p.52). (There is an etymological relation between the German *werken* (to work), *wirken* (to have an effect) and *Wirklichkeit* (reality).) Psychotic fantasies and hallucinations, therefore, belong to the real. He mentioned that, "[p]ersons with natural introspection ability are capable of perceiving fragments of this autonomous or self-activating sequence without too much difficulty, generally in the form of visual fantasies, although they often fall into the error of thinking that they have created these fantasies, whereas in reality the fantasies have merely occurred to them" (1954b, p.11). Psychotics or potentially psychotics, suffer from powerful fantasies that they experience, that they see, that happen to them. Therefore, Jung said: "we may conclude that what the artist and the insane have in common is common also to every human being—a restless creative fantasy which is constantly engaged in smoothing away the hard edges of reality" (1960, p.177).

[717] Van der Post wrote how Jung considered that, "[t]he fault of not understanding the deranged . . . lay with the psychiatrists and their failure to realize that even in the most gravely disturbed spirits, there was embedded something fundamental also of themselves" (van der Post, 1975, p.113).

[718] In 1949, Jung stated that, "[t]he fundamental reason for this [the misunderstanding of psychoses] is that the doctor . . . seldom or never has the necessary epistemological premises at his command. Instead of which, if he reflects at all and does not merely observe and register, he has usually succumbed to a philosophical or religious conviction and fills out the gaps in his knowledge with professions of faith" (1950/1955, p.651). This is akin to a fragment by Heraclitus, numbered 86 by Diels-Kranz, which has been translated as: "What is not yet known those blinded by bad faith can never learn" (Heraclitus, 2001). It is not surprising that Hellinger had not only the Catholic theological background (since he was a priest), but was also well acquainted with Parmenides and Heraclitus, and some other pre-Socratic philosophers, Lao-Tse, Western mystics, Western philosophers, and even Shamanism.

[719] 1950/1955, p.349

[720] Jung said that, "[u]nfortunately only too often no further knowledge reaches us of the things that are being played out on the dark side of the soul, because all the bridges have broken down which connect that side with this" (1960, p.178).

[721] Jung was well aware that other, more primal, cultures "[do] not seek the cause of insanity in a primary weakness of consciousness but rather in an inordinate strength of the unconscious" (1960, pp.243-244), which, he knew, was a

conception of insanity with "a special characteristic which we should not overlook: it ascribes personality, initiative, and willful intention to the unconscious—again a true interpretation of the obvious facts" (p.243). This way of explaining insanity is not foreign to the idea of possession (in Jung's term), and it is indeed "a correct interpretation . . . [being as if] invaded by autonomous figures and thought-forms" (p.243).

[722] Onians, 1996, p.720

[723] In this regard it is worth mentioning Jung's view of such things, which unfortunately anticipated most of the actual understanding of what today are psychotic situations: "modern psychiatry behaves like someone who thinks he can decipher the meaning and purpose of a building by a mineralogical analysis of stones" (1960, p.160). Every psychiatric case is understood chemically, but hardly ever explored, not to say understood, psychically. Jung offered a comparison, saying that when exploring psychosis only through chemistry "would be tantamount to treating the Cologne cathedral in a text-book of mineralogy, on the ground that it is consisted very largely of stones" (1960, p.123); it completely leaves out sense, meaning, purpose, symbolism, communal, social and ritual functions, spiritual connotations, etc.

[724] From Jung's perspective it is clear and emphatic that "Freud's theory of sexuality . . . [is], at bottom, hostile to spiritual values ... psychology without psyche" (1958, p.333); it is a rather damaging view of life and soul. Jung had a clear standpoint when referring to psychosis; he wrote: "I could not base the theory of dementia praecox [as schizophrenia was known at the time] on the theory of displacements of libido sexually defined" (1960, p.121). Those who still think that Jung has something to do with Freud, or that both views are similar, are only reading Jung's writings through Freud's views and concepts. Jung did not give value to the idea of the libido getting sexually fixated, which would be the cause of psychological disturbances and the etiology of psychoses according to Freud and Freudians; he conceived the whole issue differently, and rather said: "[w]hen Freud speaks of the early infantile fixation, it is merely the fixation to the psychical background" (Jung, 1988, p.939). Moreover, it is the fixation to the *psychic ground*, the incapacity and inability to find a better way to move (a dynamic) in one's psychic terrain, and find oneself in better relation to the others.

[725] Etta, the mother of a schizophrenic young man wrote to the father of their child: "All the kind and gentle probing questions from therapy sessions really don't work with him. Or most people" (Russell, 2014, p.207). She realized that something else is needed than the usual therapeutic methodology. Maybe a trip to Africa, a soul retrieval journey, or something in which ancestors are involved, as Russell, the father of the young man, discovered.

[726] During his time, Jung realized that "with the aid of psychoanalysis the rationalizing mind of the West . . . [had been] brought to an inevitable standstill by the uncritical assumption that everything psychological is subjective and personal" (1958, p.517); and such bias is unfortunately still the predominant paradigm of anything psychological. He admitted that "[t]he question of archaic behaviour and thought-forms [as it is the case with psychosis] obviously cannot be dealt with solely from the standpoint of personalistic psychology" (1960, p.255); Jung was indeed a precursor, in a way, of systemic thinking and collective solutions—something still new today or unthinkable for many disciplines. But, "because we are living so much in our personal psychology, in personal relations, in personal projections—we are so linked and cemented with human society—that we cannot perceive or conceive anything impersonal" (Jung, 1988, p.969); he was definitely a pioneer of transpersonal psychology. Hillman realized that too, as he, many years later, pessimistically warned: "[t]he horizon of the psyche these days is shrunk to the personal" (1992, p.181).

[727] 1971, p.290

[728] Malidoma Somé mentioned to Russell, the father of a schizophrenic young man: "Your job is basically the humanization of the spiritual emergency, such that people can gradually step away, distancing themselves from the easy labeling of clinical psychotics, schizophrenics, which is a reflection of a profound misunderstanding. Because the structure of the world afforded by people like these has not been studied sufficiently" (Somé in Russell, 2014, p.265).

[729] Jung mentioned that, "[the] breakdown of ideas is distinctive of schizophrenia ... [and it] has this peculiarity in common with a quite normal phenomenon, the *dream*" (1960, p.257). "The dream [however] ... is an autonomous and meaningful product of psychic activity" (1961, p.25), and "no psychic (or physical) fact is accidental" (p.25). Jung considered that, "[t]here is something individual in the dream: it is in agreement with the psychological disposition of the subject];]" and he rhetorically asked: "In what does this disposition consist? It is itself the result of our psychic past" (p.26), which, of course, seen and understood trans-generationally, it is not only personal. "Dreams are unquestionably products of unconscious psychic activity" (Jung, 1954, p.154).

[730] It is worth noticing Jung's saying regarding visions: "I must, as a psychiatrist, emphatically state that visions and their accompanying phenomena cannot be uncritically evaluated as morbid ... Visions, like dreams, are unusual but quite natural occurrences which can be designated as "pathological" only when their morbid nature has been proved" (1958, p.420); but, even when morbid, such visions are not accidental or random, they show something of psychic importance. Jung explained that, "the voices heard by the insane seem to belong to definite personalities who can often be identified, and personal intentions are attributed to them. And in fact, if the observer is able ... he will discover in them something very like motives and intentions of a personal character" (1950/1955, p.312). Therefore, when commenting on *hallucinations,* he said that, "it is as though the psychic content had a life of its own and force its way into consciousness by its own strength" (1950/1955, p.461), claiming that it "also occurs in the sphere of the normal."

[731] 1950/1955, p.353

[732] The word symptom originally stems from the Greek *súmptōma* used in the sense of "chance, accident, mischance," stemming from *sumpíptein,* composed of *sún,* which means "together," and *píptein,* which means to "fall" (Onions, 1996, p.896).

[733] Jung mentioned: "in its basic structure, the human psyche is as little personalistic as the body. It is far rather something inherited and universal" (1960, p.243); therefore, insanity cannot be studied, and treated, as something that pertains only to the individual suffering it—Jung saw the intricacies of it, and foresaw the need of a systemic approach. Hellinger's constellations, particularly multidimensional constellations, so it seems, became an approach that pointed in the right direction.

[734] Jung was well aware that "we cannot make an insane person responsible for his insanity" (1988, p.913).

[735] "The way to a psychiatry of the future . . . can only be by way of psychology" (Jung, 1960, p.162); but unfortunately it has been the opposite direction that which has prevailed: drugs to anaesthetize sufferers, every child, everyone who might be extremely sensitive to the depths of psyche—to psychic matters. Jung acknowledge this

problem when he wrote, in 1952: "When I was working in 1906 on my book *The Psychology of Dementia Praecox* (as schizophrenia was then called), I never dreamt that in the succeeding half-century psychological investigation of the psychoses and their contents would make virtually no progress whatever" (1950/1955, p.349). Nowadays, more than half a century after such words, schizophrenia and psychosis have even become pejorative, and those diagnoses are used for labeling something that most probably has not been correctly understood. There are many judgments and accusations towards Jung, for instance, claiming that he was a madman and that his theories are proper of a psychotic man. If one sticks to the psychoanalytic view or to the (common) psychiatric understanding, Jung himself and his visions fall into a category that is pejorative, and naturally misunderstood; but a completely other story it is if one realizes that being psychotic is a gift of hyper-sensitivity towards the depths of psyche, which if not delivered to the world, becomes an un-easiness, indeed a dis-ease and a dis-order. One can attest this by re-viewing Jung's *Red Book* (2009b), which it is nothing more that his own way of dealing with his gift, and which he used for becoming a visionary of the depths of the soul. For those unprepared ones who see it and naïvely read it without the proper knowledge, the *Red Book* is nothing but the outcome of a crazy man. The ignorant ones might consider it as unintelligible as Nietzsche *Thus spoke Zarathustra*, or as incomprehensible as Goethe's *Faust*. Shamdasani, who translated the Red Book, and edited it, argued: "This is the most laboriously worked item in Jung's corpus" (Hillman & Shamdasani, 2013, p.116). Hence, Hillman pointed out, "this book is so crucial because it opens the door or the mouths of the dead. Jung calls attention to the one deep, missing part of our culture, which is the realm of the dead . . . we're living in a world which is alive with the dead, they're around us, they're with us, they *are* us" (idem, p.83).

[736] It is worth mentioning that Jung did not gave a detailed classification of psychoses; unlike Freudians, psychoanalysts, psychiatrists, and people influenced by them, Jung did not gave much importance to the labeling of disturbances, and he did not worry in discussing the etiology and characteristics of the schizoid, paranoid, the borderline, and all those diagnostic inventions—Hellinger is very similar to him, indeed. Hillman expressed that "classification is such a trap in psychiatry, sociology, or any of those fields whose main concern should be with understanding human behaviour" (1997, p.42); he argued how "Jung alone among the great psychologists refused to classify people into groups according to their suffering" (p.43), He considered precisely that to be Jung's virtue, "to have alone recognised [*sic*] the gross inadequacy of only outside descriptions" (p.43). Jung, when speaking to medicine doctors regarding the psychological treatment, said it quite clear, "the diagnosis is a highly irrelevant affair" (1954b, p.86), therefore, he claimed, "in psychotherapy the recognition of disease rests much less on the clinical picture than on *the content of complexes* (italics added). Psychological diagnosis aims at the diagnosis of complexes and hence at the formulation of facts which are far more likely to be concealed than revealed by the clinical picture" (p.87).

[737] Franklin in Russell, 2014, p.242

[738] Franklin is Russell's son, who has suffered schizophrenia since he was an adolescent. However, throughout his father's marvelous book, *My mysterious son*, one can realize that Franklin is indeed pointing towards something else, towards a much bigger need that requires to be acknowledged in order to be attended. The insights of the book reveal a new way to approach this psychological condition called schizophrenia, not just for Russell's son, but for humanity altogether. Franklin's comment "We've gotta get into the unconscious" can mean many different things, depending on the epistemological point of departure. From a psychoanalytic (Freudian, Lacanian, etc.) point of view, it would remain within the personal unconscious. From Jung's point of view, it would go as deep as the world unconscious, way beyond the personal and family unconscious, even reaching the other-than-human psyche. In Russell's book one

can notice that Franklin's condition reveals that Jung's view of schizophrenia points into the right direction: it is something beyond the personal, it is something else calling us, and asking us to attend it, through the voices of the so-called mad, crazy, or insane.

[739] Van der Post wrote about Jung's learning and discovery that, "even from the nature of some specific hallucination, delusion, psychosis, or neurosis how a personal story was clamouring [*sic*] to be carried on and lived" (1975, p.120). However, it might not be a story that corresponds to the person's life events, but to his or her trans-generational family, or even to his community of fate.

[740] Jung mentioned that "[i]n insanity we do not discover anything new and unknown; we are looking at the foundations of our own being, the matrix of those vital problems on which we are all engaged" (1960, p.178). Those who are simply called "crazy" or "mentally ill" might be only an embodiment of what is happening to humanity in general, as a collective species. He observed that, "[t]he psychopathology of schizophrenia . . . demonstrate the production of archaic material beyond a doubt . . . [in which] one thing is certain: it contains an indefinite number of motifs or patterns of an archaic character, in principle identical with the root ideas of mythology and similar thought-forms" (1958, p.490); therefore, one can assume, many insane are embodying the deep human suffering—most possibly for some purpose. As an anecdote, I can tell that when Hellinger was asked, in an international seminar in Mexico City in 2009, his opinion about autism (which is akin to schizophrenia), he "did" a multidimensional, silent constellation to see such issue, with more than ten representatives, from both genders and a wide age range, and after a while of movements and something which seemed to be the embodying severe suffering, he stopped it and said nothing more of it. He simply stated that they (the autistic) were fulfilling a function. Maybe the seminar will be someday available in a video for the public; certainly one can only speculate about such constellation, but indeed the situation displayed something purposeful that seemed of mythical proportions. "So long as we know only the causality or the historical development of a normal or psychic phenomenon, but not its functional development, i.e., its purposive significance, it is not really understood" (Jung, 1950/1955, p.652).

[741] Somé, for instance, said that, from the Dagara perspective, "[a] person who is suffering from serious psychological problems is said to have left his spirit somewhere[,]" and, he continued "[l]iving away from your double is like living with chaos, terror, and insecurity" (1995, p.186), quite similar to what Westerners would claim to be schizophrenia or madness. Jung, in fact, commented that, this phenomena, also known as "Loss of soul[,] amounts to a tearing loose of part of one's nature; it is the disappearance and emancipation of a complex, which thereupon becomes a tyrannical usurper of consciousness, oppressing the whole man. It throws him off course and drives him to actions whose blind one-sidedness inevitably leads to self-destruction" (1921/1971b, p.226). It is as if the individual were lost in his own psychic terrain, which is extended in depth and highly populated, and while being lost some psychic figure would lead the physicality and consciousness towards its doom. In fact, Jung considered that certain psychotic states of mind were just like demonism, which he defined as: "a peculiar state of mind characterized by the fact that certain psychic contents, the so-called complexes, take over the control of the total personality in the place of the ego, at least temporarily, to such a degree that the free will of the ego is suspended" (1950/1955, p.648).

[742] Jung considered that, "[u]ndoubtedly a psychological cause hardly ever produces insanity unless it is supported by some specific predisposition" (1960, p.218); in simpler words, insanity is hardly ever produced by situations that happened in life, i.e., lack of a good enough breast (a well-known explanation in Freudian psychoanalysis), a faulty communication within the family, trauma, abuse, bullying, parents' divorce, early deaths, or similar events. "It can be

stated, however, almost with certainty that the psychological predisposition leads to a conflict, and thus by way of a vicious circle to psychosis" (p.218).

[743] Jung claimed that, "the psyche does not merely react," in the sense that it is not something that can be well-programmed or not. In other words, it cannot be thought and conceived as Watson's, Skinner's, and Bandura's black box of behaviorism, a mere response resulting from the integration to the external stimuli throughout one's existence; "it gives its own specific answer to the influences at work upon it, and at least half the resulting formation is entirely due to the psyche and the determinants inherent within it" (1961, p.287). Every individual psyche has its own telos, its *Ananké* (as Plato stated), its *tikkun* (as Kabbalists claim), its *karma* (as Hindus and Buddhists know). Only extremely naïve and simplistic people, although they elaborate their theories quite complicatedly, could think that the psyche is *only* the result of what has happened to the individual throughout his (or her) life—those people have difficulties with the word and notion of *depth,* they even reject it or avoid it, and they assume that because they do not see and know life, psyche, and the world in-depth, then it must be just as they see. Hence, Hillman has warned: "behaviorism sounds too willful, too Protestant, too American, altogether too humanistic" (1996, p.259), and, he suggests, the soul ought to be imagined beyond the all-too-human ideas and ideals.

[744] While some spiritual traditions and teachings would insist on a kind of path to be lived or desired, from a depth psychological view, that is, seeing it from psyche, *all* lives are valuable and fulfill a function. For some Christians, for instance, homosexuality is seen as spiritually wrong, as well as for most Jewish and Moslems. Most Jewish also insist on procreation, as if a single individual with no descendants were unfortunate or not so fortunate as those with five children. Some other traditions would suggest that having no children is a way to be more detached from the world of illusion, and would consider it better. There are many ways through which some spiritual traditions pose (and suppose) a kind of superiority of being, or ways to be a better spiritual being; but being better is always in relation to someone who is worse, always. Many of those (pseudo-) spiritual paths consider a madman as spiritually inferior in regards to a sane individual. From a view that sees from and for (the great) psyche, all individuals are part of it, without insistence on the better ones and the worse ones, the inferior ones and the superior ones; with such view, no one fails, all can be well-loved. This might be what Heraclitus stated in fragment B75 by Diels-Kranz, translated as: "Even a soul submerged in sleep is at hard work, and helps something of the world" (Heraclitus, 2001); in other words, even when an individual only lives by unknowingly acting and reacting to his or her psychic terrain (the complex), which is indeed like a dream, is also fulfilling something for his family system, his fellow kin, and the world. It is as if those who suffer a so-seemingly incurable insanity might be healing something at the depths. Hence, the fragment has also been translated as: "We all work together to one end, some knowingly and consciously, others unknowingly—so Heraclitus, I think, says that even those asleep are workers and fellow-workers in the events in the world" (in Barnes, 2001, p.62).

[745] 1996, p.256

[746] Rilke, 2000, p.78

[747] It is very interesting to consider that Jung's *confrontation with the unconscious* (1961/1965, pp.170-199), which he also named as his *Nekyia*, was indeed an attentive perception to issues regarding the dead. The Nekyia which alludes to Homer's Odyssey passage where Ulysses journeys to the *land of the dead* seems to have been greatly misunderstood by most Jungian analysts and depth and archetypal psychologists. They have considered it a confrontation with the unconscious and even a *creative illness,* as Ellenberger suggested (1970, p.672), and so they

have thought that a Nekyia is basically a deepening down into one's unconscious and one's darkness, very much in the sense of a personal (almost Freudian) notion of the unconscious, but they have never realized the actual objectivity of the dead and their needs, nor did they ever considered it a real visit to the land of the dead—as Homer considered it, and as Jung clearly said: "*Nekyia* is therefore an apt designation for the 'journey to Hades,' the descent into the land of the dead" (1952/1968, p.53footnote). Moreover, psychotherapists and psycho-theorists have confused it with subjective imagery, analytical processes, difficulties, diseases, tough years, and even unlucky times, but hardly ever with the actuality of *the dead* (νεκρός), from which the word *Nekyia* (νέκυια) comes from. This seems to be an enormous mistake, having produced a terrible misdirection and profound disorientation—it is not surprising that most Jung-inspired psychologists, psychoanalysts, and practitioners do not speak of the dead or of the land of the dead, and some are even scared of it. Shamdasani saw it quite clear, as he remarked: "A shift occurs immediately when you stop thinking of Jung's work in terms of the imperative to come to terms with the collective unconscious. If you shift from that language to *the confrontation with the dead* (italics added), accepting the lament of the dead, one's understanding changes dramatically in that one enters a world and the problems one takes up and is confronted with are not one's own" (Hillman & Shamdasani, 2013, p.163).

[748] It is worth noticing Jung's dialogue with the anchorite, in his *Red Book*, who told him (although with words that are pejorative and racist in today's English): "I learned to understand that those uneducated Negroes unknowingly already possessed most of what the religions of the cultured peoples had developed into complete doctrines" (2009b, p. 272). "Negroes" (for the sake of this passage) can be simply taken as the designation of "black people," alluding to the color *negro*; and "uneducated" possibly refers to people who have not been inculcated and indoctrinated into the Westernized mindset. In any case, this makes one conjecture that Jung suspected or even knew that some peoples from Africa, who had not been contaminated by the Mediterranean, Middle Eastern, and Western education and religions, who "had heard neither of Osiris or the other Gods" (p.272), including the Jewish and the Christian Gods, knew of the numinous quality of existence and the Earth, and that they could explain it "in a more simple language" (p.272).

[749] One can read his autobiographical rendering in his book titled: *Of water and the spirit* (1995).

[750] Somé, 2005, Disc 2, Track 1

[751] Somé, 2005, Disc 1, Track 1

[752] Jung, for instance, said once that, as a Protestant or Catholic, "you can step into Buddhism, say, or theosophy, or something of the sort; and if it leaves you dissatisfied, what remains? Nothing but your shadow, all the things you don't like" (1988, p.258); probably all those issues in relation to a trans-generational background that some people would rather not ever face, i.e., slavery, human exploitation, child abuse, assassination, war murdering, land grabbing, rape, sexual abuse, torture, financial fraud, etc. Jung questioned the Western's fascination for yoga, which could still apply today: "[w]hat is the use of imitating yoga if your dark side remains as good a medieval Christian as ever?" (1958, p.500). It is not that he was pessimistic, or that he undervalued yoga, but he was well aware that, during his time, for many Westerners it was only a "spiritual fake" (p.500), as it would be the case these days too. "People will do anything, no matter how absurd, in order to avoid facing their own souls. They will practice Indian yoga and all its exercises, observe a strict regimen of diet, learn theosophy by heart, or mechanically repeat mystic texts from literature of the whole world" (1952/1968, pp.99-101). Nietzsche had seen this too, and therefore he wrote a bold and powerful critique about his contemporary men, in the chapter "On the land of culture," from *Thus*

spoke Zarathustra. He wrote: "how should you be *capable* of belief, you colorfully sprinkled creatures!—you who are paintings of all that has ever been believed! . . . All ages gossip against each other in your spirits; and even the dreams and gossip of all ages were much more real than your waking life is!" (1894/2005, p.104).

[753] Jung stressed much the fact that, "[t]he individual gets cut off from his roots if he tries to use the roots of other people" (1988, p.1477); he rather encouraged everyone to find his or her own source of wisdom.

[754] Since his first written works Hillman wrote about this, he was well aware that "[i]n non-western cultures . . . the souls of the dead are taken regularly into account and their lot fully considered, with prayer, with ancestor worship, with ritual observation, and through soul-mates, names-sakes, offspring, and friends. Communication with the dead continues" (1997, p.84). He argued that this is a "psychological realism" based on the "empiricism of the soul's imagery and beliefs, evidenced in the practices and attitudes of most cultures" (p.84). Through the eyes of Westernized science, this is blatant superstition; through the eyes of indigenous wisdom, it would be stupid not to acknowledge this. In his posthumous book "Lament of the dead", Hillman argued: "I think it's more a matter of realizing that there is a porous permeability between the living and the dead . . . And it seems to me that this offers a completely different way of realizing that the day world is permeated with the other world—in all kind of small ways, that they're always inner voiced, that the dead are cautionary figures" (Hillman & Shamdasani, 2013, p.25).

[755] 2009b, p.342

[756] Somé, 2005, Disc 1, Track 2

[757] Disc 1, Track 1

[758] Disc 1, Track 3

[759] One can suppose that Jung suspected this too; there is a passage in his *Red Book*, where Philemon rhetorically asked and answered: "Why don't they [the dead] stay quiet? Because they have not crossed over to the other side" (2009b, p.342).

[760] Disc 1, Track 3

[761] Jung knew that, "the dead need salvation" (2009b, p.297). Shamdasani also saw this clearly throughout Jung's work, and he argued: "There's the idea in Jung that his psychology is not just for the living, it's for the dead" (Hillman & Shamdasani, 2013, p.184).

[762] Disc 1, Track 3

[763] "[T]hat the dead do not know that they are dead" is not such a strange idea for some, as Jung said when commenting on the *Bardo Thödol*, the Tibetan Book of the Dead; it is an assertion to be found "just as often in the dreary, half-baked literature of European and American Spiritualism" (1958, p.518), and it is even a common and popular, almost folkloric, knowledge that still remains from ordigenous traditions of countries like Mexico, although often not taken with uttermost seriousness; it has become a sort of tourist attraction with a tremendous lack of awareness of its profound implications. However, Jung also wrote, "generally speaking, we have nothing in the West

that is in any way comparable to the *Bardo Thödol,* except for a certain secret writings which are inaccessible to the wider public and to the ordinary scientist" (1958, p.523). Hence, Shamdasani, after studying Jung's writings in order to edit the *Red Book,* clearly pointed out that for Jung "[t]he questions of the living, the problems of the living, the suffering of the living can be answered, or addressed, only through attending the dead" (Hillman & Shamdasani, 2013, p.175). Shamdasani's use of words is as precise and bold as it is shattering for those claiming to be Jungians: *only* through attending the dead.

[764] 2008/2009, p.138, free translation

[765] Jung commented that, "[i]t is a primordial, universal idea that the dead simply continue their earthly existence and do not know that they are disembodied spirits" (1958, p.518), unless they liberated themselves at death, as it is claimed of some monks, gurus, shamans, or mystics (but which is not the case of the great majority), or at least until something is done for them, as Somé insists. Corbin argued that in Ismaili gnosis, for instance, "to leave this world it does not suffice to die. One can die and remain in it for ever [*sic*]. One must be living to leave it" (1983, p.58). There is even a passage by the great Sufi Mystic Ibn Arabi where he claimed: "I ask of God, both for myself and for my brothers, that when our lives reach their end the person who performs the prayer for the dead over us should be a servant whose 'hearing, sight and speech' are God. May it be so for me, for my brothers, for our children, for our fathers, our wives, our friends, and for all Muslims among men and among the jinns" (in Addas, 1989/1993, pp.288-289).

[766] 2008/2009, p.168

[767] This idea that I call a "psychic look," would be often referred, in the Constellations' work, as an "unconscious identification." It has been observed that the psychic (instinctual) pull to look to someone from the community of fate is a strongly influencing behavior that has marked effects in the actuality of the individual who's look has been pulled. There are some lines by Nietzsche that precisely addressed these nuances, he wrote: "For the longest time, conscious thought was considered thought itself. Only now does the truth dawn on us that by far the greatest part of our spirit's activity remains unconscious and unfelt" (1887/1974, p.262). In simpler words, many thoughts, feelings, and actions, and even intentions, decisions, and inclinations are directed by an unknown activity—hence unconscious, inadverted, and unperceived—that is utterly important for the soul, regardless of the individual's will.

[768] Hellinger has observed and remarked this in many seminars; he has made a distinction between *complete and incomplete dying,* and one can read the transcript of several cases and testimonies from participants in his book *Farewell* (1998/2003), but, he advised, "[o]f course, you can't simply take this as given and apply it. Every soul needs to find its own individual way" (p.23). Naturally, these affirmations could be too difficult to understand for those individuals who require experiences to fit their intellectual theories, but, like Hahnemann wrote: "How insignificant and ridiculous is mere theoretical scepticism [*sic*] in opposition to this unerring, infallible experimental proof" (1833/2009, p.191).

[769] 1966c, p.9

[770] Hellinger, 2003/2007, 2006/2007.

[771] Dodds argued that, "[t]he Greeks had always felt the experience of passion as something mysterious and frightening, the experience of a force that was in him, possessing him, rather than possessed by him. The very word *pãthos* testifies to that . . . it means something that 'happens to' a man, something of which he is a passive victim . . . [where] his reason . . . is in suspense" (1951, p.185). In the light of this, it is not difficult to relate such circumstantial affections with Jung's notion of being possessed, and which is the cause of psycho-pathology.

[772] 1988, p.1189

[773] It is worth noticing Jung's clear statement: "the unconscious is the ghostland, *the land of the dead* (italics added)" (1988, p.1189); but unfortunately, like he observed, "[p]eople are far more inclined to accept the possibility that they suffer from a neurosis, or even a slight psychosis;" as he said, "they prefer to think that they have obsessions or compulsions rather than explaining their symptomatology by the presence of ghosts" (p.1189)—the similarities with Somé's view are stunning. Not in vain Jung mentioned that, "that ghost land . . . forms the weak spot in us" (1988, p.1197). It should be noted that Jung also said, in regards to ghosts: "it doesn't matter whether you weigh them, or photograph them. That is absolutely irrelevant" (1988, p.1274). Jung clearly suggested that, "the dead are not in a different place from the living. There is only a difference in their 'frequencies'" (1950/1955, p.315). In a poetic yet insightful way he said: "we need to revere what has become and to accept the dead, who have fluttered through the air and lived like bats under our roofs since time immemorial" (2009b, p.297).

[774] 1988, p.1252

[775] 2008/2009, p.189

[776] There is a very important passage by Jung, in his *Red Book*, where he realized that *respect and a reverence* is required for what has become, and that, he said, is the *law of love* (2009b, p.297), which means "accepting the lament of the dead" (p.297 footnote). Hellinger, similarly pointed out: "The dead do not want expiation but respect. And that is what counts . . . And the asking of a blessing is that expression of respect" (2001/2008, p.232, free translation). But, as Jung revealed, "if you have no reverence for what has become, you will destroy the law of love[,]" in other words, you will feel the need to take revenge for the dead—supported by all kind of justifications and arguments. Jung saw it extremely clear: "You will be forced to restore what was before, namely violent deeds, murder, wrongdoing, and contempt for your brother. And you will be alien to the other, and confusion will rule" (2009b, p.297). Those who do not acknowledge the great pain and great suffering of the dead in their lineages, live it unconsciously as if it were personal, and that inevitably leads to more conflict, and particularly to revenge and much bloodshed—they get possessed by feelings of the dead, and enact their desires. Percy B. Shelley's last lines of his poem *Hellas* is to the point:

"O cease! must hate and death return?

Cease! must men kill and die?

Cease! drain not to its dregs the urn

Of bitter prophecy!

The world is weary of the past—

O might it die or rest at last!" (in Quiller-Couch, 1955, p.719).

[777] Hellinger, 2003, p.68

[778] Hillman pointed it out very clearly, as he said: "the use of the phrase 'the dead' is hounded with frightening things—it belongs to the other side" (Hillman & Shamdasani, 2013, p.175).

[779] 2008/2009, p.138

[780] Jung, in a reflection, suggested: "Live the life of the day and do not speak of the mysteries, but dedicate the night to bringing about the salvation of the dead" (2009b, p.296). Hillman got this clear when commenting on Jung's *Red Book*; he mentioned to Shamdasani: "our task is nothing to do with getting better, and the path of individuation and so on and so forth. The task is living with the dead" (Hillman & Shamdasani, 2013, p.85). And Shamdasani's reply was even more radical as much as to the point: "What we take to be our individuation, in a personalistic sense, or our quest, or however one frames it, is not such. It is taking up the unredeemed dead, or taking up the tasks left by the dead, or the individuation of the dead" (p.85).

[781] Rilke, 2001, pp.173-175

[782] 2008/2009, p.138

[783] "For that *humanity might be redeemed form revenge*: that is for me the bridge to the highest hope and a rainbow after lasting storms" (Nietzsche, 1894/2005, p.86).

[784] Dodds realized that some ancient Greeks knew that "clean hands are not enough—the heart must be clean also." Therefore, *catharsis* was "the mechanical fulfillment of a ritual obligation . . . [and] cleansing could pass by imperceptible gradations into the deeper idea of atonement for [trans-generational] sin" (1951, p.37); in such a sense, he said that, "the techniques of catharsis are not rational but magical" (p.154). Hellinger, not far from this, considered that, "[i]f we can do something of value in the memory of the dead, then the strength from the dead enters into the good that we do" (2003, p.68).

[785] 2008/2009, p.138, free translation

[786] 2005, Disc 1, Track 3

[787] 1993, p.97

[788] Somé, 1993, p.98

[789] In one of his books, Somé wrote briefly about the importance and the design, setting, and choreography (the ritual motion) of the "grief ritual," but reading about it is one thing and experiencing it is another thing. The grief ritual, as presented by Somé, is a five day event in which the community stops everything else, and gathers for acknowledging the pain and sorrow that we all share and that we all carry throughout life, and just then we all help each other to heal. The ritual is as powerful as it is beautiful and deep.

[790] Somé explained that, "the Dagara people don't comprehend the idea of private grief . . . the person who is sick belongs to the entire community" (1999, p.220). Hence, the grief ritual is always a community concern, and the healing that occurs embraces all participants.

[791] Rumi beautifully wrote, in his poem titled *A dying dog*: "Tears are worth more than money./ Tears are blood distilled into water" (Jalāl al-Din Rumi, 1995, p.333). Tears in this sense are not just emotionally soothing, but they even purify and cleanse the soul—one's terrain. There are some lines addressing this idea, in the poem *Sunflower* by Jacobsen, stating: "Let the young rain of tears come./ Let the calm hands of grief come./ It is not as evil as you think" (in Bly, Hillman, & Meade, 1992, p.111).

[792] 1993, p.57

[793] Shamdasani recognized that, "[t]he first task that Jung finds himself confronted with is the reanimating of the dead, acknowledging their presences exist and haunt us. Acknowledging that the dead *are*, and they have presences, they have effects" (Hillman & Shamdasani, 2013, p.176).

[794] Jung wrote, in the *Red Book*, while scrutinizing and dialoguing with his "I" (ego), in regard to the dead: "'What is this?' Their souls have accomplished as much as they could. Then they encountered fate. It will also happen to us. Your compassion is sick" (2009b, p.335). This reveals a powerful insight; feeling bad for their life is a cheap expression of love towards them, and, moreover, it steals away their dignity, it gives them no honor, it minimizes their destiny—and in the end, to do all this is sickening for oneself.

[795] 1993, p.57

[796] There are some lines by Rilke, titled *Sonnets to Orpheus VIII*, where he poetically described this. He wrote: "Where praise already is is the only place Grief/ ought to go, the water spirit of the pool of tears; she watches over our defeats to make sure/ the water rises clear from the same rock/ that holds up the huge doors and the altars" (in Bly, Hillman, & Meade, 1992, p.110). In other words, grief clears the soul—one's psychic terrain—and it makes the water of life (one's vital force) rise and flow. Hillman, towards the end of his life regarded the famous Jungian term of "individuation" as "the opening to the dead and the deeply personal. And the deeply personal is connecting back through history, it's connecting to all that's been left out and forgotten . . . .The process [of individuation] is one of connection or restoration or remembrance. Why we don't call it that? The process of remembering. Anamnesis. (Hillman & Shamdasani, 2013, p.96). In Voudoun, Deren mentioned, it is known that the death rituals help to keep unbroken "the chain by which the divine heritage of the race is extended forward" (1953/1983, p.45).

[797] 1996/2002, p.105

[798] Deren wrote on the importance of the ancestors for the earthly maintenance of well-being, according to Voudoun, and she emphatically pointed that, "[t]his service for the ancestral dead is not a nostalgia or sentimentality . . . It is not a moment of return to the past; it is the procedure by which the race incorporates the fruit of previous life-processes into the contemporary moment, and so retains the past as a ground gained, upon and from which it moved forward to the future. The living do nor serve the dead; it is the dead who are made to serve the living" (1953/ 1983, p.28). Hence, even though one experiences great pain and grief during the death rituals, if done properly one also feels that such grief has reached someone else, just like Rilke wrote in *Sonnets to Orpheus VIII*: " She [Grief] is

awkward, but all at once/ she makes our voice rise, sideways, like a constellation/ into the sky, not troubled by her breath" (in Bly, Hillman, Meade, 1992, p.110).

[799] Hellinger, 2003/2007, p.9, free translation

[800] 2003/2007, p.9

[801] Jung, considering the events form the Second World War, and writing the brief essay *After the Catastrophe*, mentioned that, "although collective guilt, viewed on the archaic and primitive level, is a state of magical uncleanness, yet precisely because of the general unreasonableness it is a very real fact" (1964b, p.197); moreover, it is something that might be there, polluting one's terrain like a miasma, without one even knowing, like a not-conscious un-easiness, an unconscious disease—an invisible dynamism of psychic figures that lurk in the dark of one's terrain, waiting to be seen. "If collective guilt could only be understood and accepted, a great step forward would have been taken" (Jung, 1964b, p.217). Unfortunately, like Hillman pointed out with impressive clarity when commenting on the importance of the dead, just in the last one hundred and fifty years one encounters "slavery, civil war, brutalities of all sorts, Chinese oppression, it's just so huge, all the deaths of the Indians, and animals . . .We enter the realm of the dead overloaded to begin with" (Hillman & Shamdasani, 2013, p.182).

[802] There is a passage of profound insight in Jung's *Red Book*, where his soul asks him: "Will you accept what I bring?" And after he humbly accepts, his soul tells him that there are many different war and killing artifacts from their fathers, and "everything the battles of yore have littered the earth with[,]" but also "all the superstitious hatched by dark prehistory[,]" as well as "fratricide, cowardly mortal blows, torture, child sacrifice, the annihilation of whole peoples, arson, betrayal, war, rebellion" and even "epidemics, natural catastrophes, sunken ships razed cities, frightful feral savagery, famines, human meanness, and fear, whole mountains of fear" (2009b, p.305); and he accepts it all. Such a passage reveals that which is needed in order to attain a trans-generational wholeness: a deep reverence to all that had to occur in order for one to be born and be alive. The *Red Book*, in Shamdasani's view, was, for Jung, "an attempt to come to an affirmation of the fullness of life . . . . Including what is most horrific in it. It's a realization that if you rejected part of existence then you've rejected, in a way, all of it" (Hillman & Shamdasani, 2013, p.21). One can perceive Nietzsche's influence in the affirmation of life: when you say yes to a single joy, you've said yes to all woe as well (1894/2005, p.283).

[803] Jung, for instance, wrote: "The number of unredeemed dead has become greater than the number of living Christians; therefore it is time that we accept the dead" (2009b, p.297). This profound insight, if taken seriously, would bring attention to those who were massacred in order to have the actual globalized Western world: Native Americans, indigenous from Central and South America, Australian aboriginals, almost all Africans, Indians, Mongolians, Tibetans, Japanese, and the list goes on and on.

[804] Rumi wrote, in his poem *The stupid things I've done*: "Look on the terrible things I've done,/ and cause herbs and eglantine to grow out of them" (Jalāl al-Din Rumi, 2003, p.133). But, as the mystic poet pointed out, one has to *look on* first.

[805] 1996/2002, p.100

[806] 1996/2002, p.100

[807] Shamdasani argued that Jung realized this quite boldly, saying: "What he [Jung] grapples with is the weight of human history and ancestry. He realizes that he can't move forward without going back, without understanding the implications that the past weighs on him" (Hillman & Shamdasani, 2013, p.38).

[808] In the ninth elegy, Rilke wrote a profound reflection regarding the dead:

"Yet . . . the living are wrong when they distinguish so clearly:

Angels, it's said, are often unsure

Whether they pass among the living or dead.

Ever-racing, the current whirls each generation

Through both these kingdoms. In both it outsounds them" (1998, p.25).

[809] 2007b, p.124, free translation

[810] Hillman also mentioned that "[t]he dead other goes on existing as a psychological reality with whom one communicates[,]" and "[the] claim that these psychic realities are only internal images or only objectifications of one's subjectivity" is foolishly "a comfortable rationalism" (1997, p.85).

[811] Jung wrote that, "whoever well-meaningly tears you away form the dead has rendered you the worst service, since he has torn your life branch from the tree of divinity" (2009b, p.296). One can well consider the following: Have not most psychotherapies done this? Are not these practices a great error? It is no surprise that the Westernized man behaves quite shallowly, childishly, selfishly, and with less and less concern for the divine.

[812] Jung, for instance, knew that: "a medicine man . . . must be able to talk to the dead, he must be able to reconcile them. For the dead are the makers of illness, causing all the trouble to the tribe" or, in contemporary terms, to the family system (1988, p.1402). Hellinger, indeed and with no doubt, is a medicine man in Jung's sense, since he clearly reconciles the dead and gives them peace. Mike Haney, form the Lakota and Seminole tribes, mentioned: "[t]here is a general feeling among my people that a lot of our failures today are a direct result of not taking care of our ancestors" (in Budnik & Johnson, 1994, p.229). Kingsley's argument, based on Old Greek philosophy, is very similar: "The greatest prophets in ancient Greece were as famous for looking into the past and into the present as they were for looking into the future. They were able to see things in the present that are so obvious we miss them, and see things in the past that hold us down and hold us back" (1999, p.109). In this sense, Hellinger (through his method) has helped to look deep into the past and into the present in order to release people from the issues that hold them down, that hold them back, and hold them from a fulfilled life.

[813] in Deloria Jr., 2003, pp.172-173

[814] Jung said that, "the unconscious is not only a storehouse of life, but is a storehouse of death in which there are many corpses" (1988, p.1256); the differences with the Freudian idea of the unconscious, that has influenced Gestalt approaches, rational-emotive, cognitive-behavioral, bodywork, existential, humanistic, and even hypnotic, or linguistic psychotherapies, are striking, as well as all those popular *avant garde* life-coaching techniques, which focus mostly on motivational and inspirational stimuli.

[815] Wilhelm, the great sinologist who translated the *I-Ching*, mentioned that, in ancient China it was thought that certain psychic remnants of individuals who died remained as "capacities, tendencies, or forces[;]" therefore, he wrote, life was conceived as a continuation "upon broken-down remnants of the dead" (1962, p.24).

[816] 1999, p.130

[817] 1995, p.9

[818] Shamdasani, after studying extensively Jung's writings, saw this idea in Jung's *Red Book*, and he stated how "[h]e comes to the realization that unless we come to terms with the dead we simply cannot live, and out of that our life is dependent on finding answers to their unanswered questions" (Hillman & Shamdasani, 2013, p.1).

[819] Like Jung mentioned, "the past and the future are one: whatever is left over from the past still lives, and the germ of the future is living in the unconscious too" (1988, p.1257).

[820] 2001c, p.270

[821] 2001c, p.270

[822] This is similar to what Jung suggested and encouraged to do, "make a compromise with them, to lay them or to integrate them properly" (1988, p.1402); it is worth asking: why is it that Jungians have not stressed upon this? Only Shamdasani, after editing the Red Book, which he considered "[a] modern 'Book of the Dead'[,]" commented that "there are passages where he [Jung] says that what is required is to be alone with one's dead and to recognize them, that is the work one has to take on" (Hillman & Shamdasani, 2013, p.84-85).

[823] When Somé speaks about "the land of the dead," he refers properly to their final destination, where they are at ease, in contradistinction with that in-between space where they are not-at-ease and generate disease for those still living. Somé argued that "over there [in the land of the dead] . . . they have a sense of community that is far way more exacting than the way we do have here" (2005, disc 1, Track 2), and if one omits someone inadvertently, he says, some things might not work out in the best ways for those still living.

[824] Jung wrote: "Every step upward will restore a step downward so that the dead will be delivered into freedom" (2009b, p.296). Hence, Shamdasani's words about Jung's work are: "One could say he's offering therapy for the dead" (Hillman & Shamdasani, 2013, p.164).

[825] 1993, p.57

[826] Lindsay said it beautifully in the poem *Rain:* "Only boys keep their cheeks dry./ Only boys are afraid to cry" (in Bly, Hillman, Meade, 1992, p.102).

[827] Hillman, 1972, p.239

[828] Hillman, inspired by William James, argued that "emotions are gifts of the spirit" (1972, p.232), which is an experience of "being moved" by the *pneuma* (p.234). He even ventured to propose a "pneumatic view of emotion" which would do justice to "the prophetic, poetic and erotic frenzy[,]" where the "craving for ecstasy and inspiration" could be explored in depth (p.236). In any case, he also reverted "the affirmation that emotion is 'material', reason 'spiritual'" (p.238), inverting the old adage that emotion is "only flesh and only body" and spirit only "intellect and reason" (p.237), because, he sharply argued, "today's conscious mind is all too only too often the rational instrument of materialism in all sorts of forms while the emotions demonstrate spirit" (p.238); this is, indeed, a powerful insight worth to be considered and explored—and very close to Somé's account of the Dagara rituals. It is worth noticing that emotion stems from the Latin *émovêre*, which means to move, in the sense of going out, or forth (Onions, 1996, pp.310, 333); quite a different etymological origin and connotation to that of feeling, which is rather to examine or perceive by touch (p.349), or affection, which is a disposition or inclination (p.17). Emotion denotes a quality of *being moved*, and feeling would consist in the rationalized value of the experience. Hellinger's constellations, but particularly the multidimensional constellations, which he claimed are movements of the spirit-mind, indeed are very *emotive* happenings; moments where one can move out of one's inclination or disposition by means of dynamic force that one feels as a quality in the air—the pneuma. It is not surprising that after a constellation, one's affection and psychic disposition (*Stimmung und seelische Zustand*) can be drastically shifted. Jung, for instance, "use[d] *emotion* as synonymous with affect" (1921/1971b, p.411); and the corollary would be that one's affectivity (and physical innervations), which is determined by one's position and disposition in the psychic terrain, is an intense, but impersonal, quality of psychic movement—as if one were moved by something else. "Emotion is the thing that carries you away" (Jung, 1950/1955, p.25); moreover, "[a]n emotion catches you, sits upon you; you cannot get rid of it . . . You may say you have an emotion, but usually the emotion has you—that is the trouble" (Jung, 1988, p.1184). Hillman, therefore, inspired by Blake and Swedenborg, considered emotions as *divine influxes,* as "a gift that comes by surprise . . . rather than a human property" (1992, p.177). There are also some lines by Rumi, from his poem *The purpose of emotion,* saying: "Call it *spirit, elixir,* or *the original agreement*/ between yourself and God. Opening into that/ gives peace, a song of being empty, pure silence" (Jalāl al-Din Rumi, 2003, p.52).

[829] Somé has commented that, "it is the duty of the living to heal their ancestors. If these ancestors are not healed, their sick energy will haunt the souls and psyches of those who are responsible for helping them" (1995, p.10). Jung also mentioned something strikingly similar: "the spirit of those who died before their time will live, for the sake of our present incompleteness, in dark hordes in the rafters of our houses and besiege our ears with urgent laments, until we grant them redemption" (2009b, p.297). This perspective of the dead requires an ontological shift, an attunement to a wider and more embracing notion of reality, a comprehension of the plasticity of this time-space dimension in which not only we are influenced by our ancestors, but in which we can heal them too, like Somé insists, and in which we can redeem them too, like Jung foresaw.

[830] 2005, Disc 1, Track 3

[831] Disc 1, Track 3

[832] Disc 1, Track 3

[833] Jung observed that: "What we call temptation is the demand of the dead who passed away prematurely and incomplete through the guilt of the good and of the law" (2009b, p.297); and therefore, he advised: "as long as you know about the dead, you will understand your temptation" (p.297 footnote).

[834] 2005, Disc 1, Track 3

[835] 2005, Disc 1, Track 3

[836] This process is similar to "the rites of reclamation" performed in Voudoun rituals, as described by Deren where she stated that, "[a] year and a day following the death of a person, the family undertakes to reclaim his soul from the waters of the abyss below the earth . . . Thus the aid of his knowledge, the disciplines of his moral authority, and the inspirations of his intelligence are re-incorporated as a functioning force in the reality of his family's daily life" (1953/1983, p.46).

[837] Hellinger has insisted throughout the years that, "this work [the constellation work] is not a psychotherapy" (2003/2006, p.166, free translation).

[838] Jung, too, was aware of "the psychological need of the living to do something for the departed" (1958, p.523); where he did not meant it only as a form of cathartic relief for those who remain in life, but as something that helps the dead, indeed.

[839] Somé also acknowledges that while some people put the dead in caskets and drive them as fast as possible to the cemetery, as if putting them out of sight, for the Dagara "[the dead] are still as important to the living as they were before" (1995, p.47), and that one needs to see the dead bodies, in order to mourn them and help them walk "home." These rituals, however, are not of a sentimental character, as if they would only be meant to relieve the pain of those who stay alive; they have an ontological quality and purpose. As (only) an example, one can read the thorough critic of the Western's contemporary ways of dying by Ariès, a renowned French historian, who has observed that in the past (in France and many parts of Europe), before the eighteenth century, and for many centuries, it was believed that there was a *coexistence of the living and dead* (1975/2007, p.28), as if there had been an acknowledged and well-accepted *promiscuity between the living and the dead* (p.35). He even claims that there was a *familiarity with the* [exposed bones or corpses of the] *dead* (p.35), something that might be quite difficult to imagine nowadays in most Western cultures. In Ariès view, death has become shameful and it has been censored (p.72); and one can realize that it is not only the notion of death, but also the realm of the dead what has been denied and strongly censored, keeping Western societies within the narrowness of what contemporary scientific materialism can get to know. He also glimpses that the repression of grief and its impossibility to express it publicly might aggravate the "traumatism" of having lost a loved one (p.77); but, unlike Somé, Ariès only speculates about it, as if it were only for the benefit of those who remain living, as it is already well-known in some thanatological practices in the Westernized world, but without getting to know that grieving is also in benefit of the dead, and further generations that come into life. Grieving, which for some Westernized "thinkers" is only a display of emotion, with some kind of psychological importance for the individual who lost someone, is in fact, following Somé's insistence, addressed as a

psychic necessity of ontological importance to maintain the community's well-being. One could think that it is sick, selfish, and stupid not to grieve.

[840] 1995, p.47

[841] Jung, giving voice to a dead one, wrote something similar in his *Red Book:* "the dead hear your prayers since they are still of human nature and not free of goodwill and ill will" (2009b, p.342). Wilhelm, when writing about death in ancient China, wrote too that, "[t]he dead . . . still hear what is said in their presence—wherefore in China it is the custom to speak no evil in the death chamber but to say everything as if one were in the dead man's company, so that he will not be upset and will have time to complete his release from the corporeal" (1962, pp.25-26).

[842] One might even venture to think that Hellinger, during his 16 years as a missionary in South Africa, got autochthonous influences about the process—but even when he said that he observed some Zulu rituals, he has not made specific references to them in such respect. He has said, however, that he learned about the orders of love form them. Deren mentioned that in Voudoun "[i]t is felt that if [the major death ritual, the ceremony of *dessounin*] is neglected, the family would suffer greatly and be plagued" (1953/1983, p.45).

[843] That might be the reason why Jung consider the unconscious (the land of the dead) to be a *graveyard* or a *blossoming field* (1988, p.1257), indeed just like the image and notion of the psychic terrain, that could be stinking with corpses or blooming with roses. The terrain can be a disgusting pestilent place (miasmatic) or a beautiful fragrant garden, certainly. Moreover, one day, like Machado wrote, the wind could come and tell you: "In return for the odor of my jasmine/ I'd like all the odor of your roses[,]" and if you have no roses, the wind could just take away everything else—from the poem titled: *The wind, one brilliant day* (in Bly, Hillman, & Meade, 1992, p.99). In Voudoun, Deren mentioned, there is a preoccupation "to re-activate the souls of the dead, to consult them for advice, and to demand their constant intervention" (1953/1983, p.45). Following this image, there is also a verse in the Zohar, in the portion of *Chayei Sarah*, stating: "For there is a field, and there is a field. There is a field in which all blessings and holiness dwell, as it is written: 'Like the smell of a field which Hashem [God] has blessed'... And there is a field, in which destruction, defilement, extinction, killings and war reside..." (In Berg, M., 2001, vol. 4, verse 17).

[844] 1999, p.196

[845] Similarly, Black Elk told Neihardt, while telling him an anecdote of tough times in which he had to speak to his people: " . . . we have had visions. In those visions we have seen, and also we have heard, that our relatives who have gone before us are in the Other World that has been revealed to us, and that we too shall go there . . . We must depend upon the departed ones who are in the new world that is coming" (Neihardt, 1932/2008, p.203). Eliade, when commenting on tribal societies and the religious history of mankind, said that, "[e]ven in developed societies the dead will be regarded as the possessors of arcane knowledge, and prophecy or poetic inspiration will be sought where the dead lie buried" (1958/2005, p.37). Mason Boring explained that, "[w]ithin the framework of Native [American] tradition, the ancestors can be understood as existing parallel to us. They are dead, but they are not gone" (2012, p.28). More so, Hellinger clearly considered that, "the dead did not vanished, we see that they intervene in multiple ways, and they are even closely united to us and they still keep needs and expectations from us" (2001/2008, p.370, free translation).

[846] Hillman & Pozzo, 1983, p.183

[847] Jung, giving voice to a dead one, wrote in his *Red Book*: "Community with the dead is what both you and the dead need. Do not commingle with any of the dead, but stand apart from them and give to each his due. The dead demand your expiatory prayers" (2009b, p.342). Jung, so it seems, was well aware of such psychic necessity; most of his followers have not, so it seems, but the dead have made their call louder—and mainstream ways of institutionalized psychotherapy seems more insufficient and inefficient than ever. Hillman, by the end of his life, in conversations with Shamdasani about Jung's *Red Book*, saw it with tremendous clarity: "the biggest of all collective problems, as we've discussed, is the suppression of the dead. Not hearing the voices of history. Not hearing what we've lost. And the fear of the dead" (Hillman & Shamdasani, 2013, p.151). It is not surprising that Mason Boring, a Shoshone medicine-woman, mentioned that, "[t]alking with ancestors has in fact been the one identifying mark of the heathen" (2012, p.14).

[848] Jung wrote, in his old age, that "[d]ream symbols are the essentials message carriers from the instinctive to the rational parts of the human mind. . . [in order to] understand the forgotten language of the instincts" (1964, p.37). And without being adamant about such statement, one can realize that through dreams some things are revealed. Somé shared a very similar idea, saying that "[f]or indigenous Africans, dreams and visions are evidence of the Spirit portraying the way to us. What is shown to you in that manner is actually an invitation from a higher realm to consecrate yourself to the production of something that is going to benefit the greater community" (1999, p.72)—an inherent systemic view of dream. Pete Catches, a Sioux elder mentioned: "In our culture, we look upon the spirits as one of us, one of the Lakota people who have gone before us" (in Budnik & Johnson, 1994, p.17). Dodds argued that from the tradition of the ancient Greeks, "dreams though not divine, may be called daemonic" (1951, p.120); which should not be misunderstood as demonical or malignant. (This will be explained further in the chapter titled: "Destiny.") Dodds mentioned that in such a tradition, "[a] dream-figure can be a god, or a ghost, or a pre-existing dream-messenger, or an 'image' (eidolon) created specially for the occasion; but whichever it is exists objectively in space, and is independent of the dreamer" (p.104); this, in fact, resembles what Corbin called the *mundus imaginalis*. Kingsley pointed this in clear words: "what we don't understand is that sometimes beings communicate to us through dreams, in the same way that they try to communicate through outer events" (1999, p.164). Dreams are no small things, especially when a dead relative appears in one of them.

[849] Jung said, for example, that: "when someone is threatened with dissolution[,]" as it could be a psychosis, "it is as if these particles could not be united, as if the ancestral souls would not come together" (1988, p.1402); what a huge difference when speaking of insanity as that from mainstream psychologies, psychiatric, and psychoanalytic views. "I am telling you all this in order to explain that other aspect of the dead: it is not only the dead body, but the spirits of the dead" (p.1402). Shamdasani is probably one of the very few who stated it boldly and without fear: "It is the ancestors. It is the dead. This is no metaphor. This is no cipher for the unconscious or something like that. When he [Jung] talks about the dead he means the dead" (Hillman & Shamdasani, 2013, p.2).

[850] Hillman & Pozzo, 1983, p.116

[851] Van Kampenhout, for instance, wrote that, "within the shamanic context, when a person is sick, it is considered that the totality of the family and communitarian system needs healing" (2007b, p.31, free translation).

[852] Somé refers to this as the expensive "professionalism that masks ignorance better than you do" (2005, Disc 1, Track 2), and in which one is deceived by psychologists, psychotherapists, physicians, priests, and professors, and where one can be told any kind of absurdity or stupidity only because it is backed up by the credentials of their profession. If one re-visions the Western intellectual traditions (in many fields of studies), it is something that has happened often, all-too-often, and there would be no reason for believing that it is not happening today.

[853] Van Kampenhout, for instance, wrote that "in the shamanic thought, the failure in life is diagnosed more than often as the lack of strength [from the ancestors] than the lack of resources (material or [so-called] psychological)" (2007b, p.59, free translation).

[854] Jung knew well that "[c]oncepts are coined and negotiable values; images are life" (1963, p.180). One can easily go from fear, to anxiety, back to fear, and suddenly into confusion and depression, before getting into apathy and indifference; but a whole other thing is to see images, having to deal and cope with personifications—persons of the psyche. They populate one's terrain, and they might help one to grow it into a beautiful garden.

[855] There is an African saying: "when a human being descends from Heaven he/she descends into a human society" (Bührman, 1984, p.245). How different from the modern Western views of life where the human descends only into a physical "body" (in its most narrow and utterly personal notion of it).

[856] Jung, 1950/1955, p.658

[857] Jung, 1964b, p.201

[858] Hillman, when commenting about the *Red Book* with Shamdasani, asked him: "Part of [Jung's] cosmology is the continuing, living power of the dead. Would you say that?" To which Shamdasani answered: "That's pivotal. In his view, we have to find a place for the dead in order to enable our own living" (Hillman & Shamdasani, 2013, p.173). Unfortunately, Jungian psychotherapy, in general, has not been able to digest the depth of this insight, and has been unable to take these implications seriously. Hellinger, however, showed the path, a well-trodden path for shamans like Somé.

[859] 1988, p.303

[860] Somé, 2005, Disc 2, Track 1

[861] Maybe that is what Empedocles claimed, in fragment B111 by Diels Kranz, saying: "And you will lead from Hades the power of dead men" (in Barnes, 2001, p.117); also rendered as: "And you will bring out of Hades the energy of a man who has died" (Waterfield, 2000, p.142). It is worth considering that, according to Kingsley, Empedocles was not merely a philosopher but also a *magician* (1996). Kingsley scholarly explored the historical account about Empedocles having worn bronze sandals, and he discovered that, "in the ancient world a bronze sandal was a symbol connected specifically with underworld ritual and magic" (p.238). And he pointed out too that, "[b]ronze for the Greek had a special affinity with the dead" (p.239). Hence, Kingsley argued, "it is certainly

no accident that the closest parallel from ancient literature to Empedocles' image of a person capable of descending to and returning form the underworld at will is the account by Lucian of the practices of a Zoroastrian magus at Babylon" (p.226)—from where the Greeks got the word *magus*.

[862] 2005, Disc 1, Track 5

[863] Jung commented in his *Red Book*: "To give birth to the ancient in a new time is creation . . . The task is to give birth to the old in a new time . . . these are all things which are the inborn properties of the human nature" (2009b, p.311).

[864] "Shouldn't the philosopher be able to rise above a faith in grammar?" (Nietzsche, 1886/1998, p.35). There are some beautiful lines by Rumi, from his poem *No Flag,* stating: "I used to want buyers for my words./ Now I wish someone could buy me away form words" (Jalāl al-Din Rumi, 2003, p.163).

[865] Jung observed that, mostly, the scholar "throws himself away in all the books and thoughts of others . . . [and does not realize that] his soul is in great need" (2009b, p.264); therefore, "you see those old scholars running after recognition in a ridiculous and undignified manner" (p.264). Hence Hillman argued that, "the questions that occupy you have been handed to you. That's one of Jung's main thoughts, that one" (Hillman & Shamdasani, 2013, p.26). And Shamdasani's response was: "You're being used by the dead. And the sooner you realize that the better" (p.26).

[866] For example, Habermas's *Theory of the communicative action* and the idea of the *public sphere* would be a completely different notion if one were to realize the (psychic) atmosphere influenced by the dead-not-yet-at-peace on those living and the impact it has on their public and private ways of life. Bateson's *ecology of the mind* is indeed faulty and incomplete, if it cannot see what many indigenous and autochthonous cultures see and claim as objectively real (not mere subjective visions), and that around which they organize many life events: the dead and the ancestors. Bandler's and Grinder's *study of the structure of the subjective experience (and what can be calculated from it)* would have an entirely different way of perceiving, processing, and practicing if the objectivity of the dead, and the logical psychic structuring which includes them, were acknowledged—it becomes understandable why, for people like Somé, most of the Western intellectual tradition can be risible.

[867] Hillman and Shamdasani called this our *epistemological insecurity*, where "we don't really know what we're doing . . . we have to articulate another [epistemology]. . . I still think we have to find other forms . . . . forms of elaborating what the dead want to say" (Hillman & Shamdasani, 2013 p.14). Hellinger's work is a way of getting to know what the dead need; another is by divining, like Somé. In any case, Hillman and Shamdasani saw the necessity for a different epistemology, a different way of knowing—one which includes the world where the dead reside.

[868] 2009b, p.297

[869] Van Kampenhout's work with trans-generational issues, deeply influenced by Hellinger, but also enriched by Shamanism and Jewish mysticism, has opened a path to address the pending issues from the dead and what he called as the *tribal soul* (2007).

[870] Nietzsche, for instance, knew that "[t]hose who know that they are profound strive for clarity. Those who would like to seem profound to the crowd strive for obscurity" (1887/1974, p.201). Indeed, in many disciplines that study the human being and well-being, the wording and their theories have become so sophisticated that hardly anyone outside such fields of knowledge understands.

[871] This view of life, even when not exactly the same, is compatible with the views of life that ontologically depart from reincarnation and previous lives, like some Ancient Greek, the Kabbalistic, the Vedic, the Buddhistic, the Tibetan, and the Dagara, among many others. Empedocles, for instance, mentioned, in fragment B38 of the Diels-Kranz numeration: "Listen now to a further point: no mortal thing/ Has a beginning, nor does it end in death and obliteration;/ There is only a mixing and then a separating of what was mixed,/ But by mortal men these processes are named 'beginnings'" (Waterfield, 2000, p.145). In fragment B8 of the Diels-Kranz numeration he also claimed: "Another thing I will tell you: there is no birth for any mortal thing, nor any cursed end in death; only mixing and interchange of what is mixed, those things are—but men name them birth" (in Barnes, 2001, p.129). Jung, for instance, when writing about the dead, reflected that "[they are] not just your dead, that is, all the images of shapes you took in the past, which your ongoing life has left behind, but also the thronging dead of human history, the ghostly procession of the past" (2009b, p.296). Moreover, he openly wrote: "It is the mind of our unknown ancestors, their ways of thinking and feeling, their way of experiencing life and the world, gods and men . . . [an] archaic strata [which] is presumably the source of man's belief in reincarnation and memories of 'previous existences'" (1959b, pp.286-287).

[872] "Man 'possesses' many things which he has never acquired but has inherited . . . He is not born as a *tabula rasa*, he is merely born unconscious" (Jung, 1961, p.315). One can even venture to say that those "things" can possess the man (or woman) that has inherited them, as one can see that those persons who have very fixed ideas might be possessed by ideologies, those with very solid views might be possessed by someone's way of seeing the world, or those with stubborn compulsions, inclinations, and behaviors that make them very one-sided might be possessed by the leftovers, unfinished desires, strange cravings, or unfulfilled wishes of previous persons in their lineages. Suicide, for example, can be understood quite differently from this perspective. Hillman, for instance claimed that "the suicidal crises, because it is one of the ways of experiencing death, must also be considered necessary to the life of the soul" (1997, p.76), as if an individual were pulled to commit it, or as if he or she were achieving something through it. When this is seen trans-generationally, one can perceive that in many cases it is an imperative impulse of a dead one, not-yet-at-peace, who needs to experience death, but who has not achieved properly—and therefore requires someone still living to help him (or her), but if the living one believes his feelings and thoughts to be subjective (of a mere personal nature) and does not acknowledge the objectivity of an other member of the soul that is present in his or her affective atmosphere (the terrain), then he or she ends up acting out the suicide. This is indeed close to Hellinger's view on suicide, and it reveals a very different way to approach it, prevent it, attend it, and resolve it, than those which are based solely on motivation, socialization, optimism, and conscious processes. Hillman, in one of his first books, warned that "[w]henever treatment directly neglects the experience as such and hastens to reduce it or overcome it, something is done against the soul" (1997, p.23); in simpler words, the experience of a proper, complete, death has to be allowed for the dead-not-yet-at-peace, it is a psychic necessity! If suicidal prevention cannot see this and strongly neglects this need by enhancing optimism, by denying thoughts about death and avoiding commentaries about death and the dead, and with excessive attention to physical and social life of the suicidal individual, as it has been promoted vastly, it leaves the problem still unattended and unresolved, and indeed the whole perspective is *against the necessities of the soul.* Seen in this way, suicidal impulses are not the individual's

need for a symbolic death, that is a cheap rhetorical abstraction, but instinctual pulls that in fact acknowledge the distress of an actual psychic dead one who needs to accomplish and fulfill the process of death—this could be done by rituals, constellations, prayers, or symbolic enactments.

[873] Some quite clearly stated that, "the present state of restlessness that traps the modern individual has its roots in a dysfunctional relationship with the ancestors" (1995, p.9). By the end of his life, Hillman stated: "That is the collective symptom. The loss of the contact with the dead" (Hillman & Shamdasani, 2013, p.24).

[874] Waterfield, 2000, p.39

[875] This corresponds to fragment B88 in the Diels-Kranz numeration, also translated as: "the same thing, there are present living and dead, the awake and the sleeping, young and old; for the latter change and are the former, and again the former change and are the latter" (in Barnes, 2001, p.63),

[876] "In many Native traditions . . . [d]istress or lack of ease may result from someone who had died not being at peace" (Mason Boring, 2012, p.23).

[877] There is a very strange fragment, by Heraclitus, not for nothing called "the obscure," saying: "Corpses should be disposed of more readily than dung" (Waterfield, 2000, p.46), corresponding to fragment B96, and also translated as: "corpses should be thrown out more readily than dung" (in Barnes, 2001, p.64), and also rendered as: "Corpses, like night soil, get carted off" (2001, p.53). It not taken literally and simply, as in the sense of only disappearing the dead bodies, it could be thought of in the sense of doing something for the dead ones, in order for their earthly life (the corpses) to be properly dissolved and their psychic energies rapidly carted off—because they indeed stink like dung, and propitiate a terrible bad smell in one's terrain, a morbid psychic atmosphere, and invisible and trans-generational miasma. There is a speech by Aspasia, in Plato's *Menexenus,* that Socrates divulges to a friend, saying: "And as for the dead, she [the city] never ceases honoring them, celebrating, in common for all, rites which become the property of each, and in addition to this, holding gymnastic and equestrian contests, and musical festivals of every sort . . . you ought to bear your calamity the more gently, for thus you will be most endeared to the dead and to the living, and your sorrows will heal and be healed. And now do you and all, *having lamented the dead in common according to the law* (italics added), go your ways" (Plato, 1989, p.198). This idea of honoring the dead is place-based, aiming for the well-being of the city in general; therefore, Socrates, when dialoguing about the founding of a city, in the fourth book of the *Republic,* mentioned the importance of "the burial of the dead and the services we must render to the dwellers in the world beyond to keep them gracious" (Plato, 1989, p.669). However, it could also be considered without a specific place, but regarding a specific people, like the Jews did with all the Second World War victims—they built memorial museums around the world, specially in cities where there are big Jewish populations, in order to keep them present, honor them, and maintain their well-being as an ethnic group.

[878] Disc 2, track 2

[879] St. Just, after thorough clinical practice regarding individual and social trauma, acknowledge this idea clearly: "In unresolved trauma, the past is always with us. The path toward historical resolution entails a cultural necessity to acknowledge and integrate the good, the bad and the mythic if we are to be fully present with our current crises" (2012, p.189). In other words, there is a very important necessity that requires resolution in order to move towards

a brighter future: to acknowledge the dead, individually and collectively, within families as much as within cultures and nations.

[880] Jung, when commenting on the symbolism of Christ, wrote: "The scope of integration is suggested by the *descensus ad infernos*, the descent of Christ's soul to hell, its work of *redemption embracing even the dead* (italics added). The psychological equivalent of this is the integration of the collective unconscious" (1951/1959, p.39). Jung mentioned that such biblical passage suggested a symbolic integration of the unconscious; however, it is the literal embracing of the dead, through symbolic rituals, what integrates psychic contents that were not at ease, and generating disease. Hence, Hillman when commenting on the importance of the *Red Book*, said: "what needs to be returned is not just what he [Jung] experienced with these particular dialogues and the work of the *Red Book* but the weight of human history, which is the crucial thing, the dead. The dead have to come back" (Hillman & Shamdasani, 2013, p.66). Quite rightly Mason Boring pointed out that "Constellation work is one of the first methodologies used by modern Western culture in which the dead are considered so intimately. It seems responsible to acknowledge that a technology that has been globally employed by human beings for thousands of years may have a place and can be respected" (2012, p.140). In this regard, van Kampenhout's work with the ancestors is not only a methodology but also a new technology for Westerners, the result of his learnings and experiences from shamanism and constellations, something that he coined (and copyrighted) as *Systemic Ritual* (for which there are no books available yet, but his workshops).

[881] These insights can be read in relation to a quite cryptic fragment by Heraclitus, who supposedly said: "During the night a man kindles a light for himself. Just as when dead-but-alive, with sight extinguished, he contacts death, so when sleep-but-awake, with sight extinguished, he contacts sleep"(Waterfield, 2000, p.44). This corresponds to fragment B26 in the Diels-Kranz numeration, also translated as: "A man in the dusk looks for a light, his sight being quenched: living, he looks on the dead while sleeping; awake, he looks on the sleeping" (in Barnes, 2001, p.63). It could be thought that those under a heavy influences of their psychic terrain live under the influence and affection of many dead ones not-yet-at-peace, without even seeing them, without any sight or insight that their lives are in relation to dead people; therefore, one could agree with Heraclitus in saying that it is like living asleep. Indeed, as if those dead not-yet-at-peace were seeking to contact death through the help of the living; but if those living, inevitably affected by psychic (dreamlike) issues, realize their affection, then they contact and become conscious of the reality of dream, the psychic actuality that configures and conforms their life—and they do something about it.

[882] One can read the similarities of Jung's insights and indigenous perspectives, as well as his awareness of them, since he said: "The unconscious is the land of dreams, and according to the primitive view the land of dreams is also the land of the dead and the ancestors" (1950/1955, p.315).

[883] 2009b, p.342

[884] It is quite interesting to notice that right before the first *Sermon to the dead* begins (in Jung's *Red Book*), the dead say: "We have come back from Jerusalem, where he did not found what we sought. We implore you to let us in. You have what we desire. Not your blood, but your light" (Jung, 2009, p.346). Of course, there are many possible interpretations for the seven sermons, but rather than taking them *just* as metaphorical rhetoric, one could think of them as imaginal reality—that is, considering them as psychical facts.

[885] Jung, 2009b, p.342

[886] 1960, p.193

[887] Kingsley has claimed that the whole Western tradition, including all its intellectual achievements, is the result of Mongolian shamanism, not old Greek wisdom. From Pythagoras and Parmenides, all the way to Plato and Aristotle, who would later influence virtually any western (so-called) "thinker," be it Husserl, Heidegger, Merleau-Ponty, or Deleuze, their philosophies are the result of Mongolian techniques of ecstasy and powerful and *arrow-like* concentration. Kingsley's scholarly documented research is indeed a blowout to the arrogance and pomposity of Western intellectual traditions; he not only reveals their egotistical, narrow, and opaque views of life, the world, and Being, but also their grave mistakes (Kingsley, 2010). He claimed that the beginning of the Western culture is of a Hyperborean origin. Interestingly enough, Jung exclaimed: "I'm the Hyperborean stranger" (2009b, p.275). Corbin, for instance, wrote that, "the *Hyperboreans* symbolize men whose soul has reached such completeness and harmony that is devoid of negativity and shadow" (1972/1994, p.40). Kingsley's argument, however, had been partly pointed out by Dodds in his chapter "The Greek shamans and puritanism," (1951, pp.135-178).

[888] Jung, 1960, p.193

[889] Kingsley's remark is very clear about someone who had the knowledge of a shaman: "[someone] able to travel to the world of the dead and back again not for any personal gain but for the sake of the living as well as the sake of the dead" (2003, p.57).

[890] 2009b, p.239

[891] Hellinger plainly said: "The realm of the living is based on that of the dead. All our ancestors are present in our body and still act in a physical level. Also in a soul level the dead still act" (2001/2008, p.377, free translation). Jung reflected that, "[t]here are many graves and corpses in us, an evil stench of decomposition" (2009b, p.300); in other words, a miasma that emanates from those invisible dead ones and which directs the lives of individuals and their metabolic unfolding in the most uncanny manner. Sometimes the stench can be perceived in persons whose smell is not only strong, but, in fact, quite disgusting—although the perception of smell is quite difficult to be measured according to a parameter. Maybe this insight can be considered under a saying by Heraclitus, who claimed that, "[i]f everything were turned to smoke, the nose would be the seat of judgment" (2001, p.38). This corresponds to fragment B7 in the Diels-Kranz numeration, translated also as: "If everything were smoke, the nostrils would tell things apart" (Waterfield, 2000, p.41). Regarding the importance of smell and its relation with intuition, Jung mentioned: "It is also conceivable that intuition in man has taken the place of the world of smells that were lost to him with the degeneration of the olfactory organ . . . I myself have had a number of experiences in which 'psychic smells,' or olfactory hallucinations, turned out to be subliminal intuitions which I was able to verify afterwards" (1950/1955, p.326). If one could understand this in depth, one could only shout, like Williams in his poem titled *Smell!*: "Oh strong-ridged and deeply hollowed/ nose of mine! What will you not be smelling?" (in Bly, Hillman, & Meade, 1992, p.7).

[892] Jung, 1988, p.1221

[893] From Plato's fifth book of the *Republic*.

[894] 1958, p.309

[895] Jung realized that, "[t]he only thing which is beyond doubt is that there are metaphysical statements which are asserted or denied with considerable affect precisely because of *their numinosity* (italics added)" (1958, p.452), and quite comprehensibly they provoke fear or fascination, doubts or disdain, respect or repudiation, or a combination of all those; but, as he wisely claimed, "[m]etaphysical assertions, however, are *statements of the psyche,* and are therefore psychological" (p.511). "A very justifiable fear of metaphysics prevented Freud from penetrating into the sphere of the 'occult'" (p.516); hence, Freud ended speaking about death and the denial of death, mere concepts, dry abstractions, and a lot of *non-sense,* just as his followers would do today, rather than speaking about the dead and the dead-not-yet-at-peace, real psychic figures, autonomous images, and *sensed presences.* Jung, regarding *psychic facts,* clearly advised his readers "not to pooh-pooh them because they do not fit into our scheme of things" (1950/1955, p.328).

[896] Long time ago Heraclitus, the obscure, mocked about this kind of people, saying that, "[d]ogs, by this same logic bark at what they cannot understand" (2001, p.81); this is the fragment B97 by Diels-Kranz, also translated as: "dogs bark at those they do not know" (in Barnes, 2001, p.65). This coincides with Jung, who said: "The average person distrusts and readily suspects anything that his intelligence cannot grasp" (1954, p.137).

[897] Jung, 1958, p.309

[898] Rumi wisely advised: "Don't talk too long to skeptics or those who claim to be atheists" (Jalāl al-Din Rumi, 1995, p.59), it's a waste of time—form a poem titled *Sexual urgency, what a woman's laughter can do, and true virility.*

[899] Jung suggested, when commenting on the *Bardo Thödol,* that "every serious-minded reader must ask himself whether these wise old lamas might not, after all, have caught a glimpse of the fourth dimension and twitched the veil from the greatest life's secrets" (1958, p.524); and this applies of course to the insistences of Somé, a shaman who has shared profound knowledge for the benefit of all, not merely for the cause of marketing a strange therapeutic technique, as many psychotherapists and life-coaches do in the Western world, or for the sake of branding a new kind of foreign spirituality, like some people would do in their desire for following a fashionable path. Jung, in 1950, wrote: "It is high time humanity took cognizance of the nature of the psyche . . . Psychology needs a tremendous widening of its horizon" (1950/1955, p.320).

[900] This is in reference to Plato's seventh book of his *Republic.*

[901] in Barnes, 2001, p.112

[902] Rilke, 2000, p.24

[903] Rumi wrote in a poem titled *Joy at a sudden disappointment:* "Don't grieve for what doesn't come./ Some things that don't happen/ keep disasters form happening" (Jalāl al-Din Rumi, 1995, p.171).

[904] In a poem titled *Emptiness,* Rumi wrote: "We look back and analyze the events/ of our lives, but there is another way/ of seeing, a backward-and-forward-at-once/ vision, that is not rationally understandable" (Jalāl al-Din Rumi, 1995, p.27). Nietzsche wrote, most possibly referring to himself: "on the whole I do not know whether I do not have

more reason to be grateful to my failures than to any success" (1887/1974, p.243). Rilke similarly acknowledged: "What we choose to fight is so tiny!/ What fights with us is so great!" Hence, in many occasions, like he said, this is how one grows: "by being defeated, decisively,/ by constantly greater beings" (in Bly, Hillman, & Meade, 1992, p.299).

[905] Onions, 1996, pp.246, 260

[906] Weber, 1999, p.39

[907] Nietzsche, wrote in his passage *Personal providence:* "For it is only now that the idea of a personal providence confronts us with the most penetrating force, and the best advocate, the evidence of our eyes, speaks of it—now that we can see how palpably always everything that happens to us turns out for the best" (1887/1974, p.224).

[908] Jung gave a very wise warning, saying that, "it is a fundamental error to try to subject our own fate at all costs to our will. Our will is a function regulated by reflection; hence it is dependent on the quality of that reflection" (1971, p.59).

[909] The notion of remembering one's purpose is the exact opposite to those existentialist claims that say that one seeks for meaning, finds it, or possibly builds it up out of the social and philosophical constructs available—in which Viktor Frankl was possibly the maxim psychological exponent, with his book *Man's Search for Meaning.*

[910] 1952/1968, p.212

[911] Hillman has called this "the monotheism of ego-consciousness" (2007b, p.3), which could be thought of as the insisting imperative that one path, one language, and "my God," of whom I happen to know the names, and which are the correct ones. This critique would not be in opposition to a monistic view of the world, life, and the Spirit. In any case, be it in the religions or in other spheres of knowledge, it seems that "[the] essential battle against Western history's monotheistic unconsciousness necessitates a battle against the monotheism's professional minions" even if those are dressed as "secularism and scientism" (2007, p.283).

[912] Jung "conclude[d] that Western man does not possess the monopoly of human wisdom and that the white race is not a species of *Homo sapiens* specially favoured [*sic*] by God" (1954b, p.82).

[913] Jung, for instance, warned that, "[t]he insights of the East [or Middle-East]. . . have no meaning for us if we close our minds to our own problems, jog along with out conventional prejudices, and veil ourselves our real human nature with all its dangerous undercurrents and darknesses" (1966c, pp.58-59).

[914] Jung, 1966c, p.60

[915] Rumi wrote a poem, titled *A song about a donkey,* where he warned "the dangers of imitating others in your spiritual life." He narrated the story of a man with a donkey who met some poor Sufis, who later sold his donkey and made a feast with the money, and the man joined them in celebration the whole night, where they repeatedly sang that the donkey was gone, and it is not until the day after that he realized that the donkey was not there. Rumi

acknowledged that: "The imitation here/ came form the man's desire to be honored./ It deafened him to what was being / so constantly said" (Jalāl al-Din Rumi, 1995, p.251).

[916] Growth, in this sense, is an obvious metaphorical process, but, as Hillman suggested, "[not] as quantitative growth . . . [but as a movement] downward and inward, and backward toward ancestral spirits and germinating seeds from which we have sprung" (1977, p.165). This could fit what Heraclitus said, "[t]he way up is the way back" (2001, p.45), corresponding to fragment B60 by Diels-Kranz, as if one's way "home" required one to look back, so that every step back is also the way up. The fragment has also been translated simply as: "The path up and down is one and the same" (in Barnes, 2001, p.51); and also as "Road: up and down, it's still the same road" (Heraclitus, 2000, p.39). But, as Waterfield suggested, it has a cosmological connotation in relation to fragment A1 from the Diels Kranz numeration, saying: "As it is condensed, fire becomes moist, and then as it is further compressed it becomes water, and as water solidifies it turns into earth; this is the downward road" (Heraclitus, 2000, p.43). This ontological account will be explored further in the chapter titled "Soul." This, however, also resonates with some lines by Rumi, from his poem *Town and country*, saying: "The way is usually downward, through humility and grief into union" (Jalāl al-Din Rumi, 1995, p.340). It is worth mentioning that Jung wrote a very similar reflection in his *Red Book,* saying: "he who strives for the highest finds the deepest" (2009b, p.300).

[917] Suzuki sharply asserted, "a borrowed plumage never grows" (1956, p.97).

[918] Onions, 1996, p.347

[919] Jung, 1971, p.62

[920] 1961, p.301

[921] 2007, p.17, free translation

[922] Nietzsche wisely claimed that, "[a]ll great problems demand *great love,* and of that only strong, round, secure spirits who have a firm grip on themselves are capable. It makes the most telling difference whether a thinker [or an individual] has a personal relationship to his problems and finds in them his destiny, his distress, and his greatest happiness" (1887/1974, p.283).

[923] Jung considered that, "[i]t is the man without amor fati who is neurotic; he, truly, has missed his vocation, and never will be able to say with Nietzsche (Cromwell in the English translation), 'None climbeth so high as he who knoweth no whither his destiny leadeth him'" (1954, p.183).

[924] This had been detailed in Plato's tenth book of his *Republic.* Jung, aware of this, quoted the famous dictum: "*Ducunt volentem fata, nolentem trahunt* (the fates lead the willing, but drag the unwilling)" (1950/1955, p.222), which is indeed suitable for the explanation. However, prior to Plato, Empedocles also said something about necessity, in the fragment B115, according to Diels-Kranz: "There is an oracle of necessity, an ancient decree of the gods,/ eternal, sealed with broad oaths" (in Barnes, 2001, p.115).

[925] Somé mentioned that, "[w]hat the villager see in the physical disease is simply the aftermath of something that has happened on the level of energy or relationship" (1999, p.73).

[926] Wilhelm wrote that there was a time in China, in which in Buddhism, in Taoism, and even in Confucianism "the life blood, the life in the blood, apparently played a great part[,]" because it was known to help prolong existence. "[I]n the secret religious teachings of Orient," he said, "by making the blood healthy, that is, by ridding it of its dross and overcoming the limitations and obstacles in its way . . . [one could] flow continuously and by this continuous flowing never fall behind the time." He mentioned that when the blood "fulfills its inner circulation without hindrance, then it constitutes the strength within strength and is for mankind . . . the substratum of corporeal life" (1962, p.34).

[927] Wilhelm mentioned that, for prolonging life, "methods made use of introspection to carefully observe the life processes as well as what furthers life and what hinders it" (1962, p.34).

[928] The mention of "virtues and vices" in this sense relates to Jung's notion of the *personality*, which he conceived in a trans-generational way. Hence, he acknowledged that, "as little as we are our inherited virtues we are our inherited vices" (1988, p.914).

[929] Jung gave a very clear example of this, where he acknowledged that the role of women and their ways of being and loving were changing; but, as he observed, a woman "[could be] unaware that love, her most personal, most prized possession, could bring her into conflict with history" (1964b, pp.129-130), in simpler words, that the changes were breaking with that with which women had been accustomed. However, Jung rhetorically asked: "But who, if it comes to that, has fully realized that history is not contained in thick books but *lives in our very blood* (italics added)?" (p.130); and he noticed that in such cases, an individual is "caught between two universal forces—historical inertia and the divine urge to create" (p.130).

[930] Weber, 1999, pp.172-173

[931] Hellinger explained that, during the identification one is like the person one represents; and such person does not appear before one's eyes, and because of that one can not love such a person; but once one sees the person represented (by someone), then one can love such person and the identification is dissolved (2000/2001, p.417); this is almost the same as "objectifying" a psychic content, seeing it out there rather than claiming it personal. It is a way to acknowledge what Jung called the objective psyche. Hillman had already wrote about this, saying that, "[t]he very recognition of the 'others' as not mine, disowning them, limits their scope of action. They can be heard but not literally obeyed . . . Disowning thus prevents . . . identification" (1992, p.180).

[932] "Possessed" in Jung's term.

[933] Rumi wrote, in his poem *Where are we*: "What is the body? That shadow of a shadow/ of your love, that somehow contains/ the entire universe" (Jalāl al-Din Rumi, 1995, p.15). Jung commented: "This interior microcosm was the unwitting object of alchemical research. Today we would call it the collective unconscious, and we would describe it as 'objective' because it is identical in all individuals and is therefore *one*. Out of this universal One there is produced in every individual a *subjective* consciousness, i.e., the ego" (1951/1959, p.164). In many cases, as it has been explained before, the ego is equated with the most intimate and most personal notion: the body, although also the most neglected and most unexplored. However, just like Gendlin, developer of *Focusing*, a method based on a special body awareness, said, "[y]our physical felt body is in fact part of a gigantic system of here and other places,

now and other times, you and other people—in fact, the whole universe" (1978, p.88). The body usually senses and feels the microcosm, but since it is part of the macrocosm it can also sense it and feel it, and, more so, within the adequate framework (as in a constellation) it can act upon it and change it on a grand scale—as if the micro could contain and embody, for a brief time, the consciousness of the macro. Anngwyn St. Just facilitates constellations where this can be observed and experienced—to a certain degree.

[934] Jung realized that, "illness is not a gratuitous and therefore meaningless burden;" he knew that one ought to show any man that "it is *his own self*, the 'other' whom, from childish laziness or fear, or for some other reason, he was always seeking to exclude from his life" (1964b, pp.169-170). It is quite interesting that Jung noticed that it is *a childish attitude* that which excludes others from life, from one's psychic terrain—in other words, immaturity, infantilism, stupidity.

[935] This imaginal place is similar to the allegorical image of oneself being a *guesthouse*, presented by Hellinger, in a story by the same name (*La Posada*) (Weber, 1999, pp.110-111). Of course, this is also similar to the image presented long time before by the thirteenth century Sufi mystic, Rumi, in his poem titled *The Guest House*, which says: "This being human is a guest house . . . Be grateful for whomever comes, because each has been sent as a guide from beyond" (Jalāl al-Din Rumi, 1995, p.109). Hence, Jung said: "we must first accustom ourselves to the thought that, even in our most intimate psychic life, we live in a kind of house which has doors and windows to the world, but that, although the objects of this world act upon us, they do not belong to us. For many people this hypothesis is by no means easy to conceive" (1971, p.217).

[936] This notion of the "field" was influenced by Sheldrake's concept of *morphic* and *morphogenetic fields*; the later, he said, "are spatial structures detectable only through their morphogenetic effects on material systems" (2009, p.63). However, "[they] differ radically from electromagnetic fields in that the latter depend on the *actual* state of the system—on the distribution of charged particles—whereas morphogenetic fields correspond to the *potential* state of a developing system and are already present before it takes up its final form" (p.68). Hence, when explaining the cause of form, he stated bluntly, "[t]hese structures have physical effects, but they are not in themselves a type of energy; they act as 'geometrical' or spatial causes" (p.49). Family situations and relational patterns can be observed through a constellation, as it indeed shows a structuring field that moulds and directs energy and the manifestation of patterns (in attitude, behavior, symptoms, etc), but the field when observed through a microscope is non-existent, it is not an energy. If one were to look for this field in the laboratory, one might miss it entirely; one can only perceive it through its effects in the manifestation of form—when taking about family constellations, in the manifestation of familial and relational patterns, as if they were relational forms. Sheldrake's view of how change in "form" can happen is to the point, "although energy can be regarded as the cause of change, the *ordering* of change depends on the physical structure of the fields" (p.49). When speaking of change in relational patterns (which could be claimed as: relational forms), energy is not enough, but an ordering and re-ordering of the structuring field. Hence, Hellinger's insight about bringing back the system into the *orders of love* is not just crucial but essential.

[937] Hillman argued that, "if we speak from the heart, we must speak imaginatively" (1992c, p.4). He relates such a faculty to the Sufi notion of *himma*, or the Greek *enthymesis*; the latter stems from the prefix *en*, which means in, and *thumós*, meaning passion or courage (Onions, 1996, p.311), but which Corbin (Hillman's source), following Ibn 'Arabi, refers to as vital force, soul, heart, intention, desire. This is what "creates as 'real' the figures of the imagination" (p.5), arguing that, "the task of consciousness . . . lies in recognizing . . . that what it experiences as life, love, and the

world is … its own *enthymesis* presented outside as the macrocosm" (p.13). From Hillman's view, then, it is clear that, "[t]he world is a place of living images, and our hearts are the organs that tell us so" (p.16); in this sense, following Corbin, "the heart's characteristic action is not feeling, but sight" (p.28), not sentimentalism, but seeing and looking! Sticking to the etymological origin of such words, *to see,* implies "following with the eyes" (Onioins, 1996, p.806), and *to look,* etymologically speaking, rather indicates "to direct one's sight" (p.536); both refer to something other than "me," whereas sentiment stems from the Latin *sentire, to feel* (p.810), and that is excessively personal, always about "me." The heart, as Hillman suggested, "can be disentangled form confessional personalism" (1992c, p.32); otherwise, as he sharply saw "[t]he image is imprisoned in its feeling, rather that the feeling released into images" (p.36). "[H]*imma* in the heart recognizes them, not ourselves …. [and such] is a religious care with the impersonal, the persons of the imaginal" (pp.36-37). Rumi wrote, in his poem *Be melting snow*: "God is in the look of your eyes, in the thought of looking, nearer to you than yourself" (Jalāl al-Din Rumi, 1995, p.13).

[938] Jung might have been right when saying: "Reason becomes unreason when separated from the heart, and a psychic life void of universal ideas sickens from undernourishment" (1950/1955, p.311). Most certainly, like Wallace wrote: "That's what misery is,/ Nothing to have at heart" (in Bly, Hillman, & Meade, 1992, p.166)—from his poem titled: *Poetry is a Destructive Force.*

[939] The concept of loyalties in this context is taken from Boszomrenyi-Nagi and Spark, who wrote extensively on the unconscious arrangement of familial reciprocity and relationship, see: *Lealtades invisibles* (1973/2012). Loyalty, together with devotion and commitment, are "the main determinants of family relationships. They derive from the multigenerational structure of justice of the human universe, created from the historical patrimony of actions and attitudes between its members" (p.28, free translation). Hellinger, who took this concept from their work, observed how loyalties work in family constellations and developed many therapeutic insights from there. However, it is wise to remember that Hellinger's procedure was phenomenological and rigorously empirical, that is, not taken merely from books, but observed in lived experience.

[940] There is a fragment by Empedocles, numbered B105 by Diels-Kranz, stating: "The heart, nourished in the ebb and flow of seas of blood,/ Is the main seat of what men call understanding,/ For understanding is the blood around the heart" (Waterfield, 2000, p.158). According to Waterfield, "what makes blood responsible for understanding is presumably the fact that it can give an undistorted view of things" (p.326). One could say that, not being able *to see* one's relational patterns and psychic contents would sicken one's heart and pollute one's blood, which in consequence would diminish understanding in general. The fragment has also been rendered as: "Nourished in seas of churning blood/ where what men call thought is especially found/ for the blood about the heart is thought for men" (in Barnes, 2001, pp.155-156).

[941] Jung mentioned that, "the objectivity of the psyche … [is] the reality of the unconscious … [which in fact is] a most significant and important reality" (1988, p.1176); how else can one know things about the autonomous movements of the unconscious and the psyche if such notions are always attached to one's subjectivity? Van der Post mentioned that it is a common assumption to equate "without" with "objective" and "subjective with "within;" but that might be a great mistake, actually. He rather "believed that they were by no means synonymous and that there was something as objective *within* the human being as the objective *without,* and that men were subject to two great objective worlds, the physical world without and a world within, invisible except to the sensibilities of the imagination" (1975, p.21). Corbin also mentioned something quite similar, and indeed groundbreaking. He wrote:

"In short, the *ontology* of the *imaginal world* presupposes a metaphysics of the active Imagination, and in the absence of such a metaphysics there can be no visionary knowledge" (1987, p.230).

[942] Wilhelm commented that in ancient Chinese alchemy, where one "must not expect to find any scientific chemistry[,]" there was a "psychic technique" in which "the magic power of imagery was brought into practice" (1962, p.35); and it is worth mentioning that through the "[a]ttention directed to these images . . . [one] exerts an effect upon the bodily life as a result of which fluids are produced which circulate in the blood" (p.36). In other words, and applied to this written work, through the intimation with images, or representatives who embody one's essential images (as in a constellation), one can generate an effect upon physical life, "and the blood, which may have been about to stagnate, is provided new life energy; thus a new circulation of blood is brought about" (p.36). Although there are slight differences between what Wilhelm described as "meditation" (p.35) and the work of constellations or active imagination, either way "it is evident that what is involved is in principle the gradual, subtle perception . . . which meditates not upon itself but upon what may be forthcoming from the soul, from the blood" (p.36). This technique, in fact, resembles much of Hillman's writings about *the thought of the heart*, where he argues that, alchemically, the heart is not the blood pump, but "the circulation itself" that is "making us all heart, heart all through us" (1992c, p.72). Durand also mentioned that in the writings of Paracelsus, a forefather of Homeopathic medicine, "one can already foresee the 'imaginative' faculties becoming preeminent" (1976, p.90).

[943] Just like Rumi claimed in his poem *Ayaz and the thirty courtiers*: "There is destiny,/ but don't deny your individual freedom" (Jalāl al-Din Rumi, 1995, p.345).

[944] Jung realized "a general human precondition, the inherited and inborn biological structure which is the instinctual basis of every human being . . . Every normal human situation is provided for and, as it were, imprinted on this inherited structure, since it has happened innumerable times before in our long ancestry" (1961, p.302). If this is understood systemically, like Hellinger did, it becomes quite clear why Jung said that, "[a]t the same time this structure brings with it an inborn tendency to seek out, or to produce, such situations instinctively" (p.302). Jung, precisely when commenting on "magic," wrote: "The only comparable effect capable of psychological verification is that exerted by unconscious contents, which by their compelling power demonstrate their affinity with or dependence on man's totality, that is the self and its 'karmic' functions" (1951/1959, p.140). Therefore, he suggested: "We could conceive this as hereditary influences, vestiges of ancestral life, although this idea does not suggest as much as karma does to the Indian" (p.140 footnote). These observations of Jung precisely foresaw, in a very close way, what many decades later Sheldrake called *morphic resonance* (2009), which is "*a causal influence from previous similar forms*. This influence would require an action across space *and* time unlike any known type of physical action" (p.82). However, Sheldrake explained it as "[a] resonant effect of form upon form across time and space [that] would resemble energetic resonance in its selectivity, but it could not be accounted for in terms of any known types of resonance, nor it would involve a transmission of energy" (p.85). Hence, he conceived it as the influence of the past manifesting its presence in the repetition of form. "Unlike [other] kinds of resonance, [acoustic, electromagnetic, electro-spin, or nuclear magnetic resonance,] morphic resonance does not involve a transfer of energy form one system to another but rather a nonenergetic transfer of information" (Sheldrake, 2012, p.121).

[945] Jung realized, for instance, that, the "[p]arents have the strongest effect upon the child not only through its inherited constitution, but also through the tremendous psychic influence they themselves exert. . . . the uneducatedness and unconsciousness of adults works far more powerfully than any amount of good advice,

commands, punishments, and good intentions" (1954, p.131). Hence, he, rhetorically but wisely, asked: "How are we to protect our children from ourselves, if conscious will and conscious effort are of no avail?" (1954, p.42).

[946] Hellinger, 1999, p.102

[947] Nietzsche realized this too, and giving the example of scholars as an allegory, wrote: "There are philosophers who are fundamentally merely schematizers; for them the formal aspect of their fathers' occupation has become content . . . one pays the price for being the child of one's parents" (1887/1974, p.290). In simpler words, although one receives the gift of life from them, if one loves them childishly one might risk suffering the way they suffered, and one might be heavily content with such a life—and such a lie!

[948] It is worth mentioning that Jung had also commented also the same insight regarding conscience, saying that, "[w]e can refuse to obey this command by an appeal to the moral code and the moral views on which it is founded, though with an uncomfortable feeling of having been disloyal" (1964b, p.445).

[949] Jung, for instance, mentioned: "Jesus is the perfect example of a man who preached something different from the religion of his forefathers" (1958, p.477), meaning that he was bold and courageously enough to be disloyal. "Christ was disobedient to his mother; Christ was disobedient to his tradition" (Jung, 1950/1955, p.280). This is probably one of the main insights of Jung's *Red Book,* where he mentioned: "if I am truly to understand Christ, I must realize how Christ actually lived his own life, and imitated no one. He did not emulate any model" (2009b, p.293). Therefore, he boldly wrote: "If I thus imitate Christ, I do not imitate anyone, I emulate no one, but go my own way, and I will also no longer call myself a Christian" (p.293). In a latter passage Philemon, regarding Christ, exclaimed: "everyone would have to take their own life into their own hands, faithful to their own essence and their own love" (p.356); in other words, being loyal to no one else, but oneself.

[950] Jung also mentioned this issue about loyalty. When lecturing about Paracelsus, he said: "A loyal son . . . will make amends for his father's guilt. All the father's resignation will turn into consuming ambition in the son. The father's resentment and inevitable feelings of inferiority will make the son an avenger of his father's wrongs. He will wield his sword against all authority, and will do battle with everything that lays claim to the *potestas patris*, as if it were his own father's adversary" (1966c, pp.4-5). The previous co-relations should not be taken as a fixed rule, but as an example; in any case, what stands out are the inevitable "heavy punishments," like Jung called them, due to being loyal to one's family—because this of course, applies too with the mother, the grandparents, great-grandparents, any blood-antecessor, and even not-blood related persons from one's community of fate.

[951] In the poem titled *Craftmanship and Emptiness*, Rumi wrote: "The mother and the father are your attachment/ to beliefs and bloodties/ and desires and comforting habits/ Don't listen to them!/ They seem to protect,/ but they imprison" (Jalāl al-Din Rumi, 1995, p.25). However, beware because this does not imply disrespect and dishonor. This might be similar to Heraclitus's fragments numbered B73 and B74 by Diels-Kranz, saying: "we should not act and speak like sleepers . . . nor like children of our parents" (in Barnes, 2001, p.65), in other words, acting and speaking while being heavily entangled in the psychic complex.

[952] In fact, Narby postulated an interesting hypothesis, suggesting that the DNA, as it has been widely described by scientists, corresponds to animated essences common to all forms of life, of which the shamans speak about and with which they communicate (1995/1997, p.125). That which Narby referred as "animated essences" is similar

to imaginal presences, that is, autonomous psychic figures. The word "animated" is often used to qualify "living" entities, but its etymological origins, the Latin *anima* (air, breath, life, soul), the Greek *ánemos* (wind), and the Sanskrit *ániti* (breathe) (Onions, 1996, p.38), have a psychic as much as a biotic connotation. In this sense, animated refers to figures of soul (psychic presences) as much as to living entities.

[953] Jung mentioned that, "[t]he concept of the archetype is a specifically psychological instance of the 'pattern of behaviour' [*sic*] in biology. Hence it has nothing whatever to do with inherited ideas, but with modes of behaviour" (1954b, p.124 footnote). At the time he said regarding biological investigations: "the most important of these are the E.P.S. [electrophysiological studies] phenomena, which medical psychology should no account ignore. If these phenomena rove anything at all, it is the fact of a certain psychic relativity of space and time, which throws a significant light on the unity of the collective unconscious" (pp.124-125). It seems that Jung foresaw some of Rupert Sheldrake's interests and discoveries. Hellinger claimed that, in his opinion, Sheldrake's notion of the "extended mind" and the "morphic fields" are the best explanation—form a biological standpoint—of the Family Constellations (Hellinger 2005/2008b, p.45). Sheldrake himself wrote that his research on morphic fields and morphic resonance would not only expand the theories regarding inheritance, among many other theories, but would actually shift the focus in regards to memories. Rather than retrieving them from stores inside the brain, he suggested that there is a transfer of memory by resonance, which would be close to Jung's notion of a collective unconscious (2012b, p. 209). He even ventured to write that, "[m]emories themselves do not decay at death, but can continue to act by resonance, as long as there is a vibratory system that they can resonate with" (2012b, p.210). If these, among other of Sheldrake's experiments and investigations, are taken seriously into account, a new biology will arise, indeed.

[954] Jung was well aware that one "ought to really describe the phenomenology of those psychic processes which manifest themselves in the course of treatment and do not have their counterpart in medicine" (1954b, p.93).

[955] "With hygiene and prosperity alone man is still far from health" (Jung, 1951/1959, p.181). Ortega argued that, "[i]f a patient who lives in an insane an unhygienic habitat moves to a hygienic place, he or she will not fully recover the state of health if the affliction has a miasmatic depth" (1992, p.382, free translation).

[956] The *holo-field* is similar to a dreamscape, one is there, as part of it, and yet the dream feels as if it were inside oneself, or as if it would have been one's mind production, one's imagining fiction, but at the same time, it is non-tangible, not-provable, real as much as actual, invisible as much as unfathomable, and, most importantly and never to be dismissed as minor characteristics, non-local and non-separatable. The dream and the holo-field have two virtues that break the illusion of this physical world: non-locality and non-separatedness; they crack the manifested world and allow us to glimpse a deeper dimension of reality. There are some lines by Rumi, saying: "When the soul lies down in the grass,/ the world is too full to talk about./ Ideas, language, and even the phrase *each other*/ doesn't make any sense" (Jalāl al-Din Rumi, 1995, p.36). The *holo-field*, as described, might fit with what Lazlo referred to as the "nonlocal interaction-generating field" (2014, p.12), because, he argued, "there is an urgent need for a paradigm in which nonlocality is a basic feature" (p.8).

[957] This is close to what Jung conceived, saying that, "Natural man is not a self—he is the mass and a particle in the mass, collective to such a degree that he is not even sure of his own ego . . . [he is] a *variété*" (1952/1968, p.81).

[958] Ortega, when writing about the homeopathic remedies, claimed that it is sufficient that one cell of the living organism gets stimulated with the medicinal virtues in order for the effects to begin and move on throughout the whole organism, with indubitable results (1992, p.200). Of course that if the *holo-field* is non-local, then a single cell cannot be the field itself, and yet, paradoxically, it is an opening for such an interacting-generating field to produce its observable effects. For a further deepening into this understanding, Lazlo's concept of the akasha field is very useful. He argued that, "the first task of the medical practitioner is to adapt the M-dimensional [manifested] interactions of the organism for optimum conformance with the A-dimensional [Akashic] information" (2014, p.58); that is, to adapt the interactions of the manifested domain of reality of an individual (attitudes, behaviors, intentions, motivations, etc.) with the hidden, non-visible, psychic reality (what Hindus have called for centuries: Akashic Records). For Lazlo, "[t]he organism is a psychosomatic system, in constant interaction with its surroundings. It is sensitive to information form the M[anifested]-dimension as well as form the A[kasha]-dimension" (p.58). In other words, disturbances like pains, illnesses, and so forth, are also in relation to a greater domain of information other than merely the physical reality; they might have its root-cause within a deeper field of reality that is non-local, timeless, and yet present—and so the healing solutions.

[959] Some beautiful lines by Hafiz resonate with these insights, as if he had spoken of a *holo-field*: "For a divine seed, the crown of destiny,/ Is hidden and sown on an ancient, fertile plain/ You hold the title to" (2003, p.13).

[960] Onions, 1996, p.255

[961] 1996, p.8

[962] Ibid, p.8

[963] 1996, p.9

[964] Corbin, who deeply influenced Hillman's perspective in this respect, wrote a scholarly syncretistic work titled the *Man of Light* (1971/1994), and when speaking of the angel he refers to it also as *the Hermetic idea of Perfect Nature* which "is described as 'the philosopher's angel'" (p.16), as a "the 'Witness in Heaven,' the suprasensory master" (p.17), "the 'Heavenly Twin'" (p.34), "the Heavenly Guide" (p.89), "the Witness of light" (p.91), "the *shāhid* . . . the being whose beauty bears witness to the divine beauty, by being the divine revelation itself" (p.92). Corbin studied mostly Persian theology, but he argued that, "the Greek equivalents of these Iranian notions tend to fix the play of transparitions upon the vision of a determinate figure, namely that of the *Agathos Daimon*—that is to say, upon a figure which in every case becomes the tutelary angel or celestial *paredros*"(1983, p.23). *Agathos Daimon*, which could be translated as "good spirit," was the ancient Greek spiritual companion that granted health and wisdom, later called the genius by the Romans; *paredros* is a Greek transliteration that meant he who sits close by, used in the sense of an advisor. He argued that, "in the same context the figure Τύχη (fate, destiny) was identified with the figure which dominates the Hermetic horizon, *Agathos Daimon,* who appears simultaneously as a Hermetic divinity and as the personal 'good daemon,' the δαίμων πάρεδρος, the celestial *paredros* or partner—that is to say, the helping, tutelary angel—a gratuitous gift obtained by prayer" (1983, p.26). It is important to note, however, that the Greek Τύχη is usually meant in the sense of "luck;" therefore, its Roman equivalent was "Fortuna." Hence, Corbin claimed, "Τύχη is *Agathos Daimon,* who is a divine figure as such and also a *daimon paredros,* the personal angel of each soul" (1983, p.27).

[965] Somé recalled a saying by one of his tribe elders: "When the spirits have a plan for someone, he survives even the unsurvivable" (1995, p.185).

[966] Rumi rhetorically asked, in a poem titled *The long string*: "Who am I/ standing in the midst of this/ thought-traffic?" (Jalāl al-Din Rumi, 1995, p.84), and one can ask as well, who am I, standing in the midst of this city-traffic, in the midst of this family context, in the midst of this nation, in the midst of this culture, and this time of humanity? Kingsley's point about this cannot be clearer: "there can be no serious enquiry that doesn't end in the discovery of one's own divinity" (2003, p.319). More so, in his words: "we are all *daimôns* who keep passing from life to death and then from life to death and life again" (p.358).

[967] 1961, p.314

[968] Jung wrote in his *Red Book* that sometimes "the daimonic comes as something so insipid and worn out, so mild and stale, that it makes you sick" (2009b, p.264).

[969] Onions, 1996, p.985

[970] Corbin, for instance, referred to "the idea of *vocation* with all its mysterious, imperative, irrational and inexorable connotations. The idea of vocation serves perhaps better than any other for recapitulating all that is suggested by the idea of the Angel, conveyed to us in the theme of . . . glory . . . and destiny" (1971/1994, pp.96-97). He claimed that, "the essential, undeniable idea of individuality is seen in fact inseparable from angelology because it provides a basis for the idea of the Angel just as the idea of the angel is its own foundation" (p.97).

[971] Somé spoke briefly about this idea, and the need for "people taking responsibility for the total growth that everyman is entitled to; not this kind of mental lobotomy that modernity imposes on people, so that they can become classified by profession" (n.d., 14'00"). He has observed that, when being "under the cloak of what you may call the minimalism of history, which is quite fashionable in modernity . . . you're supposed to live a life purposeless, giftless; yet in order to survive, you have to show that you have a gift . . . and you end up writing a thing that is called a curriculum vitae" (2005, Track 6), and more than often one ends up being shamefully proud of it; but that is not vocation in its *deep* sense. Some's view of vocation indeed redeems all those who did not go to school, and it acknowledges that even those excessively educated are not a pinch better than the rest.

[972] 2005, p.313

[973] There are some lines by Rumi, from his poem *The well of sacred text,* saying: "there is an essence inside variability/ always quivering with joy of returning/ to the origin" (Jalāl al-Din Rumi, 1995, p.346).

[974] 1996, p.45

[975] 1996, pp.63-91

[976] Hellinger commented a similar idea, claiming that: "[t]here is a sense of personal determination, or calling, or purpose that touches you to the core and is beyond conscience" (1999, p.43); he referred to is as that special-ness that

each person experiences and that cannot be deduced from the parents, something that "is lived like a task . . . [and with which] we find ourselves in the service of something greater, either way" (2008/2009, p.38, free translation).

[977] The translated words of the Sufi mystic, Ibn 'Arabî, explained that, "[t]he form of the Angel, 'the tree of his soul from which he plucks the fruit of knowledge,' is . . . his transconscience, his divine or celestial counterpart, of which his conscious ego is only a part emerging in the visible world" (in Corbin, 1969/1998, p.305). Bamford, following Corbin's writings, claimed: "The task of each soul, then is to achieve *angelicity*, that is, 'the state of being that is its own species' (in Corbin, 1990/1998, p.XLIX); moreover, "one's angel in this sense, is none other than a soul's knowledge of itself as knowledge of its angel." In other words, "human beings, as individuals, are angels, celestial beings; and as such, by definition, are exiled or fallen . . . [and such a notion would naturally involve] an 'ascent' or 'return'" (p.XLIX). This account of one's angelic nature derives from Iranian philosophy, and particularly to its esoteric teachings; it might not apply to the popular and vulgar ideas, images, conceptions, and preconceptions of angels in exoteric traditions.

[978] 1996, p.90

[979] Hillman has insisted that, "the spirit of psychology is lamed by materialism, literalism, and the genetic viewpoint towards its subject matter, the psyche" (2005, pp.134-135), and, as a consequence, many people can hardly think beyond these categories, narrowing the spirit of life to what science discloses to the masses, and to what they can understand from it. In a similar way Bamford, following Corbin's work, stated: "the intellect assumed a shadow-form in the abstractions of reason and the tyranny of literalism. Meanwhile the soul—the most truly human essence—fell by the wayside; and the angelic world—the true Imagination—was lost" (in Corbin, 1990/ 1998, p.XXI). Like Corbin claimed: "Instead of a *phenomenon*, an *epiphany* of being, we are left only with a kind of ghost of being" (p.18). Hillman, therefore argued that, "[l]iteralism is an ego viewpoint; it means blocked into an ego . . . Only I am literally real" (1992, p.48), and only that which I understand from science is right. Rumi, similarly, wrote in a poem titled *Limb-Shadows*: "But why does reason keep me from drowning/ in your love. What use is this/ being rational inside majesty?" (Jalāl al-Din Rumi, 1995, p.309).

[980] Somé argued this by realizing how differently one lives when one knows: "I'm coming into this world, because I have the gift of healing to give;" he considered this the most important aspect in life, "because at the core of our identity is the gift of healing that we brought with us to these world." He sees that "identity is connected with gift and healing, that identity is connected with purpose; all of these concepts are sustained and held together by the notion of ancestry" (2005, Disc 2, Track 2). It comes clear, then, that ancestry, in this sense, is not the self-replicating genetic pool that biologists speak about and that Somé dismisses as unimportant and uninteresting; ancestors are rather daimonia—those who have been called and con-fused with the jinn, geniuses, angels, spirit-guides, otherworldly figures, wise presences, and so on. Hence Somé mentioned about Hillman, whom he knew well, "[w]ere it not because he came across very strong things in terms of his perception of the psychological profession, it is the kind of thing that could have toppled him over the edge. That's why he basically lived on the edge all his life" (in Russell, 2014, p.267).

[981] Somé claimed that, "confusion of one's true identity really comes form the tyranny of the material world" (n.d., 55'00"), and that would include the tyrannical idea that enslaves an individual to believe that he (or she) is only a biological offspring of a certain family, a mere family *chutzpah*. Kingsley argued precisely that the *daimon* is

"wrapped up and inserted into a whole sequence of bodies made from flesh and blood . . . that will fit to perfection, but—and this is the paradox—always remain alien to what it really is" (2003, p.363).

[982] 1996, p.89

[983] Hillman has warned that accounting "for life occluded revelations by analogies with nature commits a 'naturalistic fallacy,' that is, assuming that psychic life obeys only natural laws as described, for instance, by evolution and genetics" (2005, p.315).

[984] Jung wrote in his *Red Book*: "giving form to God has sapped us completely. We are not only poor but have become sluggish matter throughout, who would never be entitled to share in divinity" (2009b, p.288).

[985] Hillman's view, inspired by Plato, considered that "a person is born with an innate paradigm that is not identical with the genetic endowment and that gradually gives way in middle childhood as genetic factors kick in" (1996, p.135); so that, in spite of one's life being heavily influenced and affected by the genes, inheritance (physical and psychical) and the family, there is still *something else* which is felt as not from this world, because it was not learned, acquired, received, given, or conditioned in this world.

[986] Corbin, when writing about the notion of the Perfect Nature (or Angel), realized that there was a controversial issue: "why should there be only one Active Intelligence? To answer this question calls for a decision as to whether all human souls are identical in species and essence, whether each soul differs from another in kind, or again whether they are not perhaps grouped essentially in spiritual families composing many different species" (1972/1994, p.20). Corbin cited the philosopher, Abû'l-Barakāt Baghdādî, to answer his inquiry: "for each individual soul, or perhaps for several together having the same nature and affinity, there is a being in the spiritual world which throughout their existence watches over this soul and group of souls with especial solitude and tenderness, leads them to knowledge, protects, guides, defends, comforts them, leads them to victory; and this being is . . . called *Perfect Nature*. This friend, defender and protector is what in religious terminology is called the *Angel*" (p.20). Rumi, regarding the "Friend", wrote in a poem titled *The servant who loved his prayers*: "Forget your figuring. Forget your self. Listen to your Friend./ When you become totally obedient to that one,/ you'll be free" (Jalāl al-Din Rumi, 1995, p.90). Grinberg-Zylberbaum, who did (what could possibly be called) an autoethnographic research on Mexican shamanism—which he also called Mexico's autochthonous psychology—, transcribed a conversation with a native healer, by the name of Don Lucio, who, in fact, mentioned something very similar, alluding that each individual belongs to a kind of spiritual herd which is guided by a spiritual pastor, and that remaining with one's spiritual nature was indeed healing (n.d., pp.90-111). Goodbird, the Indian, narrated a passage of a Native American medicine man, known as Bush, who cried desperately when lost and in despair: "O gods, I am poor and I suffer! I want to find my god. Other men have suffered and found their gods" (in Deloria Jr., 2006, p.12); however, Deloria Jr. explicitly clarified that the word "gods" *is* "a mistranslation or deliberate changing of words to convey meaning of experience." He mentioned that, "[i]n the Indian context, of course, we are talking about spirits" (p.12); but possibly, one could as well call them daimons—and one could genuinely cry: "I want to find my daimon!"

[987] Hillman suggests that aside to, or, even, rather than, psychodynamics, there should be *psychodaimonics*; a kind of awareness to what is "a daimonic inheritance, a gift and curse from the invisible ancestors" (1996, pp.144-145). This is a bold move from that which studies only genes, biological structures and fields, and psychological dynamics, relationships, and patterns, to a vision that recognizes the call and calling of the spirit world. Somé, actually

encouraged a very similar view in this respect, and he proposed to ask oneself in regard to those belonging to one's lineage who have passed away: "What is it that this loved one wanted to accomplish during his or her lifetime, and somehow failed short of reaching completion" (2005, Disc 1, Track 3); Somé seemed not to have meant those activities related to the mundane, but to the depths of life, soul, and the spirit.

[988] Hillman, for instance, when exploring Jung's legacy, considered that, "[a]n individual fate requires more than the individual to carry it; it calls up legendary figures, 'ancestors'" (1976b, p.134)—although he did not speak of them as daimons.

[989] 2005, Disc 2, Track 2

[990] Hillman claimed that, the "daimon's nature and the soul's code cannot be encompassed by physical means—only curious thought, devotional feeling, suggestive intuition, and daring imagination" (2005, p.315). Corbin claimed that, "[t]o lose this archetypal dimension is literally to cease to have an angel, it is to die as a soul can die: to cease to answer for one's celestial partner, which can then no longer answer for its earthly soul (1983, p.18).

[991] Some insisted on the fact that "there is not just an intellectual or physical dimension of us, but there's also an equally powerful spiritual dimension of ourselves, which if we were to reconcile it with our own mind and body, would produce an extremely potent person in us" (n.d., 23'40").

[992] Somé claimed that this is "probably the more crucial part ... we are spirit that have occur here ... with a special mission" (n.d., 30'15"). He said that from the Dagara perspective "our true nature is spiritual" (1995, p.20). Hillman argued that "[f]or millennia and most everywhere, it was palpably evident that divine and daimonic figures appeared as persons. But the scientific *Weltanschauung* with its cut between observer and observed severed us from that witness, and its testimony became magical thinking, primitive belief, superstition, insanity" (1972/2007b, p.23).

[993] Philemon told Jung, in the first of the Sermons of the dead: "you must not strive for what you conceive as distinctiveness, but for *your own essence*. At bottom, therefore, there is only one striving, namely the striving for one's essence" (2009b, p.348). Later, after the sermons, Philemon also mentioned: "everyone would have to take their own life into their own hands, faithful to their own essence and their own love" (p.356); in other words, imitation of another's path, or another culture's path only hinders one's way to one's deep wisdom.

[994] The Dalai Lama addressed that, "[n]ihilism, materialism, and reductionism are above all problems from a philosophical and especially a human perspective, since they can potentially impoverish the way we see ourselves" (2005, p.12).

[995] Jung wrote in his *Red Book*: "Some would rather abandon themselves to despair than adhere to a worldview completely removed from the well-trodden paths of their habitual behavior [or habitual thinking]. They would rather venture into pathless, dark land at the risk of perishing there, even if it should outrage all their cowardice" (2009b, p.368). Hence, he also observed that, "[i]f one has no religious beliefs, then one does not like to admit the feeling of deficit, but prates loudly about one's liberal-mindedness and pats oneself on the back for the noble frankness of one's agnosticism" (1958, p.452); more than often one prefers to fool oneself with the writings of post-modern philosophers and clowns than acknowledging one's ontological ineptitude and cosmological poverty.

[996] Somé, 1999, p.73

[997] In this respect, it is worth considering the similarity to Corbin's view of the *angel*, inspired by Iranian Sufism, and also called *shāhid*, where he claimed that just "[a]s you look upon the *shāhid*, so does he look upon you, and such yourself are. Your contemplation is worth whatever your being is worth; your God is the god you deserve; He bears witness to your being of light or to your darkness" (1971/1994, p.92).

[998] 1996, p.9

[999] Deloria Jr. commented also about this, although not explicitly; he wrote: "We need to see where we have been before we see where we should go, we need to know how to get there, and we need to have help on our journey" (2006, p.xix). He referred to the "spirit world." Jiménez words, from his poem *I am not I*, are indeed profoundly philosophical as much as they are powerful and mystical: "I am this one/ Walking beside me whom I do not see/ . . . / The one who will remain standing when I die" (in Bly, Hillman, & Meade, 1992, p.367).

[1000] In some lines by Rumi, he wrote: "Your features did not begin in semen./ Don't try to hide inside anger/ radiance cannot be hidden" (Jalāl al-Din Rumi, 1995, p.74). There is also a Zen koan by the sixth (Chinese) Patriarch, who said: "If thou comest for the faith, stop all thy hankerings. Think not of good, think not of evil, but see what at this moment thy own original face doth look like, which thou hadst even prior to thy own birth" (Suzuki, 1956, p.71).

[1001] In a similar way, Rumi wrote in his poem *Body Intelligence*: "Keep wanting your connection/ with all your pulsing energy. The throbbing vein/ will take you further/ than any thinking" (Jalāl al-Din Rumi, 1995, p.152). There is also brief but concise article, titled *As far as longing can reach*, by Peter and Maria Kingsley (2006). Hillman also rendered a piece of writing to this issue, in his essay *Pothos* (2007), which is "the longing towards the unattainable, the ungraspable, the incomprehensible, the idealization which is attendant upon all love and which is always beyond capture[;]" in simpler words, "love's spiritual portion" (p.183). This attitude "rather makes us aware of always being in a syzygy with another figure . . . [who] is attainable only through imagination" (p.190). Therefore, Hillman argued, this attitude "refers to our angelic nature, and our longings and sea-borne wanderings are the effects in our personal lives of transpersonal images that urge us, carry us, and force us to imitate mythical destinies" (p.191). Rumi even claimed: "This longing/ you express *is* the return message" (Jalāl al-Din Rumi, 1995, p.155), from *Love Dogs*. Jung, also aware of the importance of longing, wrote: "If you do not acknowledge your yearning, then you do not follow yourself, but go on foreign ways that others have indicated to you" (2009b, p.249); in other words, without longing one is lost and vulnerable. Rilke wrote: "O you, my deepest soul,/ place trust in me so I will not displease you;/ within my blood runs rampant dreadful din;/ I know this longing I hold in" (2001, p.51).

[1002] Somé claimed that, "without grief we cannot reach the depth of connection with that spirit that can stir us out there in the pursuit of the very purpose that is assigned to each one of us" (n.d., Tape 1, side 1, 37'40"). Rumi, in the poem *Love Dogs*, similarly wrote: "The grief you cry out from/ draws you towards union" (Jalāl al-Din Rumi, 1995, p.155). This might be close to the notion of "deep lament," which some Native American tribes express during the solo walks that have been translated as *vision-quests* (Black Elk & Lyon, 1990). Rumi, also wrote: "Lament! And let the milk/ of loving flow into you" (Jalāl al-Din Rumi, 1995, p.157), from *Cry out in your weakness*.

[1003] 2000, p.74

[1004] "Everything about grief is like gold . . . . It is the most direct language of surrender, the language of acknowledgement and recognition of our own feebleness, the feeling of disconnection that we experience, which in turn becomes the medicine for the restoration for that connection . . . it is something very profound" (Somé, n.d., 35'55").

[1005] 1954, p.112

[1006] Jung, having realized that "organic therapy fails completely in the treatment of neuroses, while psychic methods cure them" (1958, p.329), expressed openly the idea of the psychotherapeutic process being a "healing fiction" (p.331), from where (most probably) Hillman developed insightful arguments and wrote a book by the same name, *Healing Fiction* (1983). In this book the later argued that "[psychological] case histories are a way of writing fiction" (p.5), because they "deliteralize our life from its projective obsession with outwardness . . . [moving] us from the fiction of reality to the reality of fiction" (p.48), and he argues that in case histories there is "the gift of finding oneself in myth" (p.49). However, what could be misinterpreted as a kind of picturesque method of hermeneutics, and in fact something well-known in Freudian and French psychoanalytic and philosophical circles, was indeed, presented by Hillman, as a way to know oneself through a *pandaemonium of images.* He claimed that "[k]now thyself in Jung's manner means to become familiar with, to open oneself to and listen to, that is, to know and discern, *daimons* (italics added)" (p.55). He fully realized that "[t]he land of the dead is the country of ancestors, and the images who walk in on us are our ancestors" (p.60), although he did not mean only literal blood progenitors, but "ancestral culture" too; in any case, he considered that "[k]now thyself is revelatory, non-linear, discontinuous . . . [a] biography thoroughly gone into the imaginative act . . . [a process of] self-understanding healed by active imagination" (p.80), where one would attend "Psyche first, then world" (p.81), and always asking *what does the soul want.* But, as he claimed, this might be achieved only as a "realization of itself in its images, itself a fiction among fictions" (p.106), as if oneself were a fiction (the personal notion of life) embedded in another fiction (the world), yet, aiming for *Gemeinschaftsgefühl* (community) (pp.106-109) and the *communal sense* (pp.117-129). However, what could seem simply as an imaginary, almost childish, elaboration of a personal historicity process, is in fact, as Hillman suggested, a *healing art* (pp.78-81) and "a healing of the imaginal body" (p.73). Moreover, what he presented as the process of knowing oneself, which for Freud and his followers would "mean knowing one's past personal life, a whole life recalled[,]" is indeed a much deeper issue, it clearly "means archetypal knowing, a daimonic knowing" (p.62). This whole way of seeing, which could seem way too fantastical, is in fact quite close to what Somé told about the Dagara, whose "view of reality is large[;]" he claimed that "[i]f one can imagine something, then it has at least the potential to exist" (1995, p.8). He even explained that "[they] have no word for fiction" (p.9), but not because they conceive reality as only material, on the contrary, because their worldview is much more embracing. He claimed, "[i]n the world of my people there is nothing but reality, alone without its opposite" (1995, p.254); one can fully understand, then, that fiction cannot be conceived as non-real.

[1007] 2009b.

[1008] Hillman suggested that, "*récit,* or recitation," is a way to come "to a new realization of 'experience'. . . . [which means] an account of events experienced, rather than my experiencing[;]" and this breaks up the identification with experience which confession reinforces . . . as possession, *my* sins" (1992c, pp.32-33). Experience, he said, "does not have to be owned to be held" (p.34).

[1009] Hillman argued that "we are saved form the personalism of feeling[,]" that which makes us think that we possess such feelings, "by bringing those feelings to persons who are not we, who are beyond our notion of experience" (1992c, p.36); "so that the *himma* in the heart recognizes them . . . as true Persons[;]" and then we can talk to them, and establish a "dialogical situation," like Jung did; such, is "the supreme act of Creative Imagination" (Corbin, in Hillman, 1992c, p.36), where "we move the heart from its confessional mode of experiencing to a prayerful response to its images" (p.37). Rumi, in a poem titled *A mouse and a frog,* wrote: "*Lovers pray constantly*" (Jalāl al-Din Rumi, 1995, p.80), where the notion of "lover" might be he who talks and listens to his divine nature. Hence, in some other poem he wrote: "Listen to the presences inside poems,/ Let them take you where they will" (p.99).

[1010] Visions are not to be taken as imaginary allegories of one's psychological context. In this same sense, Corbin warned against "[reducing] these visionary narratives to allegories, as if a discovery of their hidden meaning consisted in a regression to the level of conceptual evidence, where esoteric doctrine as such is supposed to be situated" (1990/1998, p.162). Kerényi's observation seems important: "In accounts of ancient religions too little attention has been paid to the visionary faculty." And this has been so, he said, because most often "historians of religions have no visions" (1976, p.14).

[1011] Hillman said that, "you find your genius by looking in the mirror of your life" (1996, p.259); one can assume, however, that he did not mean literally to gaze oneself in the mirror, or to look only at the physical, social, professional, public, and material life, but also to see into the psychical—most of which can only be *seen through* creative imagination. Jung, of course, knew this very well, and he wrote: "I have no small opinion of fantasy . . . All the works of man have their origin in creative imagination" (1954b, p.45). This insight is also close to some ancient Greek views, like that of Hesiod, who considered that "creative thinking is not the work of the *ego*" (Dodds, 1951, p.81). Hence, Jung wrote: "[i]nstead of using the term 'creative fantasy,' it would be just as true to say that in the practical psychology of this kind the leading role is given to *life* itself; for while it is undoubtedly fantasy, procreative and productive, which uses science as a tool, it is the manifold demands of external reality which in turn stimulate the activity of creative fantasy" (1921/1971b, p.58); in other words, life's creative principle moves through the human species, and individuals, by being at the service of something greater, create. In this respect, before comparing this notion of fantasy to what other theorists might say, it is worth reading Jung's sharp critique, which remains valid: "The Freudian interpretation reduces fantasy to causal, elementary, instinctive processes. Adler's conception reduces it to the elementary, final aims of the ego. Freud's is a psychology of instinct, Adler's an ego psychology" (p.60). This critique is valid for contemporary views on fantasy and imagination, regardless of those being related to Freud or Adler or not, in the end, they are only names, only representatives of such views, but views that are nevertheless actual in many disciplines, professions, and intellectual and educational circles. Jung warned, "[b]oth reduce fantasies to something else and treat them merely as a semiotic expression" (p.63), and he emphasized the distinction between 'semiotic' and 'symbolic,' the latter, he considered, severely misused by Freud (p.63 footnote), and most probably by *all* Freudians too. "It is therefore short-sighted to treat fantasy, on account of its risky or unacceptable nature, as a thing of little worth" (p.63).

[1012] 2001, p.63

[1013] This corresponds to the fragment B78 by Diels-Kranz, which has also been translated as: "Unlike divine nature, human nature lacks sound judgments" (Heraclitus, 2000, pp.37-38); also rendered as: "For man ways have no insights, divine ways have" (in Barnes, 2001, p.68). Empedocles also mentioned, in fragment B132 by Diels-Kranz: "Prosperous is the man who has gained the wealth of divine thinking" (Waterfield, 2000, p.154), also translated as: "Happy is he who has gained the wealth of divine thoughts" (in Barnes, 2001, p.117). By God or divine one could well assume, in this case, the spiritual nature, and so one could safely say with Socrates: "real wisdom is the property of God" (Plato, 1989, p.9). Kingsley, following ancient Greek philosophers, also wrote: "only one type of knowledge has any genuine substance or value—the kind originating directly from a divine source" (2003, p.338).

[1014] The *Red Book* opens with the following lines: "The years, of which I have spoken to you, when I pursued the inner images, were the most important time of my life. Everything else is to be derived from this" (2009b, p.vii); this introductory passage was written in 1957, ca., four years before his death. He knew very well, that these kind of "images sprung from the life, the joys and sorrows, *of our ancestors* (italics added); and to life they seek to return, not in experience only, but in deed" (1971, p.89). It is worth noticing Hillman's remark, saying that, "Jung shifted the main analogy for the individuation process form the hero myth in *Symbols of Transformation* (in German 1911) to *Psychology and Alchemy* (in German, Eranos lectures 1936 and 1937)" (2005, p.117); during those in-between years he developed a dedicated and delicate attention to what would become the *Red Book*. This was "a shift from the rational and voluntary faculties of the soul to its third faculty, the imagination" (p.117). In spite of this, many followers and Jung-inspired people, with more than a thousand faces, have stubbornly defended the heroic psychological viewpoint, rather than allowing a transformation of their way of life into the alchemical. Hillman has called this "[the] profound *psychological* error: The internalization of the ideal hero into a personality cult of individual self, which leaves the city without foundation and our therapeutic psychology deluded" (2006, p.115); in plainer words, cities have become places of isolation, alienation, degradation, consumerism, and, paradoxically, severely apolitical, while psychology in general has become ineffective, inefficient, and insufficient to the actual psychic needs of the political animal: the *anthropos*. Nietzsche wrote clear statement addressing this issue: "For this is the secret of the soul: only when the hero has abandoned her is she approached, in a dream, by the—over-hero" (1884/2005, p.103). Nietzsche was alluding to the Greek myths, so that he meant Ariadne when he wrote "she," Theseus when he wrote "hero," and Dionysos when he wrote "over-hero." This idea was reviewed later thoroughly by the mythologist Kerényi, in the subchapter titled "Ariadne" from his book *Dionysos* (1976, pp.89-125), and he claimed that, "the union of the two archetypal images, the divine pair Dionysos and Ariadne represent the eternal passage of zoë [indestructible life] into and through the genesis of living creatures" (pp.124-125).

[1015] There is a passage in Jung's *Red Book,* where a professor diagnosed him with "religious madness" and considered his hearing of voices as hallucinations; surprisingly, Jung replied "[w]ith all due respect . . . may I say that it is absolutely not abnormal, but rather the intuitive method" (2009b, p.295), where, in fact, he alluded to have understood "precisely the genuine and right intuitive method [of Henri Bergson]" (2009b, p.294 footnote). Jung considered that "the psychic content appears before the intuitive, as a quasi-hallucination" (1921/1971b, p.312); this could be thought of, indeed, as plain madness to the uneducated, ignorant, or materialist.

[1016] Hillman rhetorically asked: "But what if [the soul's] nature is not natural and not human?" And he boldly ventured further, saying: "Suppose what we seek is not only something else, but somewhere else, in fact, having no 'where' at all despite the call that beckons us to search" (2005, p.315). There is a beautiful rendering of such insights in a poem by Rumi, titled *Wean yourself;* he wrote that if one would tell an embryo how vast and intricate the outside world is, with wheatfields and mountains, and orchards, galaxies, sunlight and friends, the embryo would tell: "*There is no 'other world'./ I only know what I've experienced./ You must be hallucinating*" (Jalāl al-Din Rumi, 1995, p.71). This is what Hillman commented about Jung's notion of something *deeply personal* (Hillman & Shamdasani, 2013, p.41), or also that which is the *profoundly personal* (p.99).

[1017] 1954, p.175

[1018] Jung explained: "the irrational fullness of life has taught me never to discard anything, even when it goes against all out theories (so short-lived at best) or otherwise admits of no immediate explanation" (1958, p.602). Hence, he wrote: "The final appeal to reason would be very fine if man were by nature a rational animal, but he is not, on the contrary, he is quite as much irrational" (1954b, p.78). He wrote that, "[t]he irrational is an existential factor which, though it may be pushed further and further out of sight by an increasingly elaborate rational explanation, finally makes the explanation so complicated that is passes our powers of comprehension, the limits of rational thought being reached long before the whole of the world could be encompassed by the laws of reason" (1921/1971b, p.454). For a scholarly account on the importance of the irrational for life, wisdom, health, healing, community, and the divine, see *The Greeks and the Irrational* (Dodds, 1951).

[1019] Jung, in his *Red Book*, wrote some interesting reflections on the irrational: "Divine madness—a higher form of the irrationality of the life streaming through us—at any rate a madness that cannot be integrated into present-day society—but how? What if the society were integrated into madness?" (2009b, p.295). Jung's comments can be understood better under Corbin's insight, who realized that the Delphic proverb "Know Thyself" was probably indicative that a "human consciousness discovers *in* itself, *in front of* itself, and *behind* itself, a presence which is at once *oneself* and *other* that oneself" (1990/1998, p.23). Dodds argued that, for Empedocles and other ancient Greeks, "[t]he occult self which persisted through successive incarnations . . . [was] not '*psyche,*' but 'daemon' . . . [and] the function of the daemon is to be the carrier of man's potential divinity and actual guilt" (p.153). Empedocles, in fragment B115 by Diels-Kranz, mentioned, possibly about his own origin: "Among them am I too now, an exile form the gods and a wanderer" (in Barnes, 2001, p.114); also rendered as: "Now I too am one of these, an exile form the gods, a wanderer. Putting my trust in the insanities of strife" (Waterfield, 2000, p.154).

[1020] 2000, p.80

[1021] One can read that Jung knew this quite well, from the ancients who named it *Heimarmene*, "the dependence of character and destiny on certain moments of time" (1952/1968, p.34); and knew too that it was also called "the compulsion of the stars" (1921/1971b, p.212), suggesting an astrological sense.

[1022] "Hillman considered myth as "the primordial metaphor of family" (n.d., Part 1, Tape 1, 8:00); therefore, he encouraged us to study myths as a way to study family structures, because, as he clearly understood, "[m]yths have a place for what is wrong and yet necessary" (1997, p.80).

[1023] Some forces are so great that the only way to explain them is as archetypal. Michael Berg has explained how, from a kabbalistic understanding, there are forces that run through us that are not *us*, that are older than us, as if they were part of the fabric of this world. In this sense, he gave the example of Korach's uncontrollable jealousy for Moses, which was a repetition of Cain's jealousy for Abel (because they were the reincarnation of one another, respectively), which he felt as a great force for no reason—because it was the effect of the the "snake's venom" on Adam and Eve when they ate the apple. (Berg, M., 2017, min. 09'20"- 13'15").

[1024] 1966c, p.97

[1025] Somé has observed how this attraction towards the *fashionable* "is a translation . . . [of] the lost pieces of the puzzle of one's identity, one's purpose; and so, this is why you go from one delusion to another delusion and it's an endless thing" (n.d., 53'00")—one can especially see this in fashionable philosophies, where people are going from Marx, to Foucault, to Deleuze, to Giegerich, to Zizêk, and so on, endlessly. Rumi, the Sufi mystic, acknowledge this in his poem *The sheik who played with children*, mocking those very well-educated individuals who think they possess knowledge: "Those people who have it worry/ if audiences like it or not./ It's a bait for popularity./ Disputational knowing wants customers./ It has no soul." Jalāl al-Din Rumi, 1995, p.46). Corbin's remark is worth mentioning: "philosophy is vain and sterile if it is not a preparation and guide which leads to mystical experience. Likewise, mystical experience without previous philosophical training is in serious risk of going astray" (1990/1998, p.102). In Kingsley's writings one can also find this idea; he said: "Really there can only be one kind of knowledge. And rationality is simply mysticism misunderstood" (2003, p.148).

[1026] 1954, p.145

[1027] Jung observed and wrote to himself: "Your values want to draw you away from what you presently are, to get you ahead and beyond yourself[,]" as it is the case with very industrious persons, even scholars; "[y]our being, however, pulls you *to the bottom* (italics added) like lead" (2009b, p.264)—the spirit of gravity (described as the inevitable heaviness of being) has been associated in alchemy with lead.

[1028] Hence, Nietzsche advised: "Live in *ignorance* about what seems most important to your age. Between yourself and today lay the skin of at least three centuries. And the clamor of today, the noise of wars and revolutions should be a mere murmur for you" (1887/1974, p.271).

[1029] Hellinger also mentioned: "As far as I have been able to see, the soul doesn't follow the rules of the *Zeitgeist*" (1999, p.153).

[1030] This vision of reality seems as old as mankind. Octavio Paz, the Mexican essayist and poet, in the prologue to Castaneda's book, *Las enseñanzas de Don Juan* (*The teachings of Don Juan*) (1968/2000), but alluding also to *Una realidad aparte* (*A separate reality*) (1971/1974) and *Viaje a Ixtlán* (*Jorney to Ixtlán*) (1972/1975)—which compose Castaneda's first three books—, wrote that, "Castaneda might have doubted of the reality of everyday reality, denied by the prodigious, as of the reality of the prodigious, denied by humor[;]" that, he continued, "is not less powerful than the paradoxes of Nagarjuna, Diogenes, or Chuang-Tseu" (Paz in Castaneda, 2000, p.21, free translation). Therefore, he argued (summarizing Don Juan's teachings), "the brujo aims with all those manipulations to break the vision of everyday reality, upsetting our perceptions and sensations, annihilating our feeble reasoning, devastating our certitudes—in order for the *other* reality to appear" (Paz in Castaneda, 2000, p.21, free translation).

[1031] Jung claimed that, "Man belongs not only to an ordered world, he also belongs in the wonder-world of his soul . . . Man lives in two worlds. A fool lives here or there, but never here and there" (2009b, p.264). This is very similar to Hillman's insistence on the *rediscovery of the soul*, which "shows itself in the reawakening of emotion, fantasy, and dream, in a sense of mythological destiny penetrated by the transpersonal, and by spontaneous acausal time[,]" if this is allowed, Hillman argued, "[one *cures*] from a chronic identification of the soul with outer events, places, and people" (1997, p.79), as if one were *only* an outcome of the family's blood and fate. Hence, Rumi wrote in his poem *Tending two shops* that, "You own two shops, / and you run back and forth." But he emphasized: "Live in the nowhere that you come from, even though you have an address here" (Jalāl al-Din Rumi, 1995, p.75).

[1032] There is a passage by Rumi, from his poem *Two friends,* saying that there is an underground water that moves "without sound, and without repetition[,]" and he affirmed: "Where we are now is narrow fantasy/ that comes from there, and the actual, outside world/ is even narrower. Narrowness is pain,/ and the cause of narrowness is manyness" (Jalāl al-Din Rumi, 1995, p.88).

[1033] Hellinger briefly, but clearly, mentioned a very similar notion when he said: "There is a depth that flows through everything and is beyond the boundaries of time . . . sometimes there are situations in which one comes into contact with this depth, and the hidden orders of things become visible. This is contacting the greatness of the soul" (1999, p.63).

[1034] 2009b, p.229

[1035] Ibid, p.229

[1036] Kingsley's remark is quite similar, as he pointed: "When rationality is really combined with irrationality, then we begin to go beyond them both . . . we start seeing illogicality of everything that normally is considered so reasonable" (1999, p.171).

[1037] 2009b, pp.234-235

[1038] Nietzsche knew something very similar regarding the power of imagination, as he said: "Oh, these men of former times knew how to *dream* and did not find it necessary to go to sleep first. It is quite enough to love, to hate, to desire, simply to feel—and right away the spirit and power of dream [the spirit of the depths] overcome us, and with your eyes open, coldly contemptuous of all danger" (1887/1974, p.123).

[1039] There is a passage in a poem by Rumi, titled *Why am I so blessed?,* where he wrote: "You shout, *Rise and dance,/* and they do, the ancient dead, the newly dead,/ so happy to be out in the air again,/ the graveyard looks like a marketplace/ on a holiday./ I am not saying these things/ to appear visionary and spiritual/ I have seen this happen in ways I cannot express" (Jalāl al-Din Rumi, 1995, p.312). Eliade, after researching tribal societies and their rites and symbols of initiation, also mentioned that, "death is never final, for the dead return [as ancestors]" (1958/2005, p.34).

[1040] Plato, 1989, p.7

[1041] This is indeed close to the words by the Iranian mystic Sohravardî, who said that "[s]ome souls learn nothing except from human masters; others have learned everything from invisible guides known only to themselves" (in Corbin, 1971/1994, p.20). Deloria Jr. compiled a book with stories of Native American medicine men, and in most cases it was powerful *presences* those who shared them wisdom and taught them, either in visions or dreams, whether appearing in a human, animal, mineral, or some other form from the natural world (2006). Jung also wrote that, "on the assumption that the contents of the psyche are realities, all these figures . . . might well be endowed with a higher form of consciousness transcending that of the ordinary human being. Experience shows that such figures always express superior insight" (1952/1968, p.302). However, he also gave the warning that "[a] wrong attribution may bring about dangerous inflations . . . [or] disasters that may result" (p.304).

[1042] Jung wrote in one of his *Red Book* drafts: "My visions are truth for I have beheld what is to come. But you are not supposed to believe me, because otherwise you will stray form your path, the right one, that leads you safely to your suffering that I have seen ahead" (2009b, p.300 footnote); therefore, he reflected for himself: "May no faith mislead you, accept your utmost belief, it guides you on your way." Bamford, when commenting on Corbin, also wrote that, "[t]he human being individuates, becomes fully human, only in his one-to-one encounter with his angel" (in Corbin, 1990/1998, p.XLIX), in other words, with his original nature.

[1043] Jalāl al-Din Rumi, 1995, p.128

[1044] Keats in Quiller-Couch, 1955, p.748

[1045] 1995b, p.xvii

[1046] Hillman conceived that, "[t]he soul is less an object of knowledge than it is a way of knowing the object, a way of knowing knowledge itself" (1992, p.13). Hellinger, making a critique, also noted that: "Theology attempts to uncover the mystery and thereby turns it into an object; science sometimes does the same with nature, and psychology with the soul" (2002b, p.20).

[1047] Jung wrote: "quite correctly, it seems to me, for in one of its aspects the psyche is not individual, but is derived from the nation, from the collectivity, from humanity even. In some way or the other we are part of a single, all-embracing psyche, a single 'greatest man,' the *homo maximus*, to quote Swedenborg" (1964b, p.86).

[1048] 2008/2009, p.123

[1049] 2008/2009, p.132

[1050] Rumi, in a couple of lines gave an image for these insights: "Fish don't hold the sacred liquid in cups!/ They swim the huge fluid freedom" (Jalāl al-Din Rumi, 1995, p.123).

[1051] Jalāl al-Din Rumi, 1995, p.269

[1052] 2008/2009, p.140, free translation

[1053] Jalāl al-Din Rumi, 1995, p.82

[1054] It is worth noticing Jung's remark that, "[a]rchetypes are like riverbeds which dry up when the water deserts them, but which it can find again at any time. An archetype is like an old watercourse along which the water of life has flowed for centuries, digging a deep channel for itself" (1964b, p.189).

[1055] Jung mentioned insistently on the need to "broaden our conventional conception of the psyche" (1954b, p.90).

[1056] Jung considered that, "time and space are relative for the unconscious, so that unconscious perception, not being impeded by the space-time barrier, can obtain experiences to which the conscious mind has no access" (1950/1955, p.313).

[1057] 2008/2009, p.156

[1058] 1996/2002, p.53

[1059] Rilke wrote some beautiful verses in his *Prayers to a lowly God*, where he voiced Abel, saying: "Everybody will have to walk my path/ all will fall victim to his wrath, all will be lost on him./ . . . The night has remembered me, but not him" (2001, p.13).

[1060] Hellinger, 2003/2006, 2005/2006

[1061] Jung wrote in his last book: "Inner peace and contentment depend in large measure upon whether or not the historical family which is inherent in the individual can be harmonized with the ephemeral conditions of the present" (1961/1965, p.237). If one relates this insight to the Homeopathic medicine view of the individual, it becomes clear that the treating and healing of one's chronic miasma, depends largely on the reconciliation and harmonization of one's historical family within oneself, which is like a field with all their presences, a psychic terrain.

[1062] 2003/2006, p.12, free translation

[1063] Jung wrote the following reflection in his *Red Book*: "Why do fools go out and preach the gospel to the negroes[?] . . . what do they teach others when they themselves stand up to their necks in the black mud of deception and self-deceit? . . . they preach love to be able to run away from themselves, and to do others what they should do to themselves" (2009b, p.341). And he continued his reflection saying: "These hypocrites and liars . . . prefer to love others" (p.341) because they cannot stand themselves, or because they are not strong enough to see into the atrocities of their people, their lineages, and their family. I truly wonder if most of those people are not weaklings who need to go abroad in order to see great suffering in others—a great pain that they cannot bear themselves. But, like Jung wisely wrote: "everything begins with yourself" (p.341), otherwise you are a coward, a liar, and a farce!

[1064] Jalāl al-Din Rumi, 1995, p.142

[1065] 2003/2006, p.10, free translation

[1066] There is a passage in Jung's *Red Book*, where Philemon told him: "You have neglected yourself, your garden is full of weed, and you want to teach your neighbor about order and provide evidence for his shortcomings" (2009b, p.343); in other words, if the miasma (the terrain) is neglected, then, even philanthropic activism and charity could stink—and could do more damage than having done nothing. Somewhere (which I cannot trace now), Somé mentioned the answer given by one of the elders of his tribe, after him having asked the elder about those industrious enthusiasts, self-named altruists, that go to Africa aiming to help the people, and the elder's answer was as picturesque as wise: "Beware if a naked man offers you a shirt." If one were to say it with Homeopathic medicine jargon, one would say: "Beware if sick people come here to share with you their industriousness, their ways to govern, to do politics, to teach, and that which could be calamitous: their ways to heal! Are they healed?"

[1067] Jung, 1959b, p.287

[1068] Ibid, p.287

[1069] Jung wrote that, "[w]e are very far from having finished completely with the Middle Ages, classical antiquity, and primitivity, as our modern psyches pretend" (1961/1965, p.236); but more importantly, there are entirely different ways of being and knowing from old cultures, that have been parodied as ridiculous or inferior, when in fact those cultures had powerful ways of healing, moving, traveling, seeing, knowing, living, and loving. Some seem altogether lost, but some others are still living in the unconscious embodiment of many individuals from all regions on Earth.

[1070] "I always say that our psychology has a long saurian's tail behind it, namely the history of our family, of our nation, of Europe, and of the world in general" (Jung, 1950/1955, p.81).

[1071] 1961/1965, p.237

[1072] Jung mentioned that, "[i]f our impressions are too distinct, we are held to the hour and minute of the present and have no way of knowing how our ancestral psyches listen to and understand the present—in other words, how our unconscious is responding to it" (1961/1965, p.237).

[1073] Jung, 1959b, p.287

[1074] Jung knew well, that "[w]e have merely succeeded in forgetting that an indissoluble link binds us to the men of antiquity" (1952/1967, p.4), and maybe to men prior to our recorded history of that which we call antiquity, men of former times, not only former epochs, but former ages, former aeons maybe. This perspective would take a much deeper relevance, a groundbreaking importance indeed, if inquired about the cultures of antiquity and ancient men in the way that Kingsley wrote about "Parmenides and other people like him": "They were people who deliberately, consciously, laid ground for our lives as we live them and for existence as we know it; who shaped our world, structured the ways we think and operate at a far deeper level than we are even aware of" (2010, p.253).

[1075] Deloria Jr. commented that, the Sioux, for instance, as well as some other Native American cultures, "had a saying that each generation must think of 'seven generations' when considered important actions or were faced with an impending crisis" (2009, p.148), in which one would think of three generations "back" in time, and three "forward," completing seven with one's generation; this clearly reveals that they had an ontological understanding of psychic issues, knowing that the actions and intentions of today will remain and be active later, long after one's death. Vernon Harper, an elder from the Cree tribe, mentioned: "Our people have also always considered the unborn generation in their decision making. We ask ourselves: 'How is something going to affect our children?' . . . So each generation has to be conscious of what they are doing" (in Budnik & Johnson, 1994, p.133). Van Kampenhout (without him being a Native American, but having studied with them) claimed that in traditional shamanic cultures, it was asked to think in the next seven generations, because in such a way one teaches the youth that indeed seven generations have already prayed for them, and then a powerful bridge with the ancestors is built (2007, p.63). This idea resonates with a saying by Empedocles, in which he referred to Pythagoras, in fragment B129 of the Diels-Kranz numeration, stating: "Among them was a man of immense knowledge,/ who had obtained the greatest wealth of mind,/ a master especially of every kind of wise deed./ For when he reached out with all his mind/ he easily saw every thing/ in ten or twenty human generations" (in Barnes, 2001, p.161).

[1076] 1952/1967, p.177

[1077] Jung considered that, "consciousness itself demonstrably comes from an older unconscious psyche" (1964b, p.443). Mason Boring commented on the fact that through our ancestry "there is a remembrance of old songs and ceremonies and a different way of knowing" (2012, p.24).

[1078] 1951/1967, p.177

[1079] "Marrow," which is the "soft substance in the cavity of the bones," stems, hypothetically from the Indo-European *mozgho,* but it has been known, since long ago, that it is a "central or vital part" (Onions, 1996, p.557).

[1080] It is not in vain that Jung enigmatically wrote: "the psyche is therefore all-important; it is the all-pervading Breath, the Buddha-essence, it is the Buddha-Mind, the One, the Dharmakaya. All existence emanates from it, and all separate forms dissolve back into it" (1958, p.482).

[1081] Berg, 1986.

[1082] There is an interesting passage, in the poem titled *Moses and the shepherd,* by Rumi, where Moses scolds a shepherd for the way he talked to God, considering it insulting, and later, after a revelation, he goes after the shepherd and says to him: "I was wrong. God has revealed to me/ that there are no rules for worship./ Say whatever/ and however your loving tells you to. Your sweet blasphemy/ is the truest devotion. Through you a whole world/ is freed" (Jalāl al-Din Rumi, 1995, p.167). The shepherd knew, however, by the time that Moses went back to him, that, "[t]his is certainly not like/ we thought it was" (p.168).

[1083] I cannot explain here in what does it consist, but one can read more of this in *La conexión astral,* originally titled as *Astrology: The star connection* (Berg, 1986/1989), *Days of power: Part one* (Berg, 2005), and *Days of power: Part two* (Berg, 2006); although, in these books, according to this perspective, it is not alleged as one's culture myth of origin, but everybody's story of origin; they are not the spiritual tales of some people, but the spiritual unfolding of *all* humans' and divine's conscience. This implication deserves thorough and profound study, as well as practical living experiences—which seem to require a life-time dedication, not just some scholar investigation.

[1084] This understanding of such (Biblical) "stories" requires a different perspective from that of history and historicity, which imply a line of consecutive events throughout a straight time-line. Rather than considering such "stories" as only myths—in a pejorative sense—, or improbable facts, one requires to *live* them as mythical facts, that is, understand them as happenings that are taking place in the soul, and in which one is taking place too. This necessarily implies an imperative re-vision of the concepts and notions of time and myth. More so, this would also imply that many taken-for-granted scientific assumptions were reviewed as well, since "[w]e pride ourselves on being able to separate fact from fiction, science from myth, but we don't see that our science itself is what is always has been: a fragile mythology of the moment" (Kingsley, 2003, p.254).

[1085] Onions, 1996, p.218

[1086] Jung considered that, "cosmogonic myths are, at bottom, symbols for the coming of consciousness" (1951/1959, p.148).

[1087] 2009, p.149

[1088] In the Yuwipi ceremony, for example, which is particular of the Native Americans of the Plains, "all generations are represented. The generational aspects of the yuwipi are made more consistent by the fact that all yuwipi spirits, human and animal, are actually spirits of those who once lived on earth" (Powers in Deloria Jr., 2006, p.85). This allows the participants "[to] feel the sense of continuity between the living and the nonliving" (p.85).

[1089] Jung, when bridging the religious contributions of the East with those of the West, wrote that, "it would be far more to the point to find out whether there exists in the unconscious an introverted tendency similar to that which has become the guiding spiritual principle of the East" (1958, p.483). Van Kampenhout, who studied different versions of Shamanism, and some Kabbalah too (after discovering that he was partly Jew), mentioned, for instance that the Jews indeed have a special soul that others do not have, but that such special soul is not individual, but tribal; and, moreover, all other peoples have that something extraordinary too, but according to their ancestral connections (2007, p.62). From these kinds of insights, it would seem far more important to realize one's ancestry, than to pray to a foreign (image of) "God."

[1090] Jung, 2002, p.196

[1091] 1958, p.188

[1092] Somé, 1995.

[1093] Jung, 1954b, p.34

[1094] 1964b, p.32

[1095] Eliade too, from his research of tribal societies, considered that, "[i]t was the mythical Ancestors who lived the primordial drama that established the world in its present form—and consequently it is they who know and can transmit this lore" (1958/2005, p.40).

[1096] Onions, 1996, pp.394, 677

[1097] Jung clearly stated, in 1936: "I am interested in the undeniable differences in national and racial psychology" (1950/1955, p.565). He might have kept quiet during and right after the holocaust of the Second World War and the terrible idea of a superior race. However, it is worth noticing, and not to be overlooked, that in 1948, when founding the C.G. Jung Institute in Zürich, Jung said: "racial psychology, folklore, and mythology in the widest sense became the subject matter of complex psychology" (1950/1955, p.472). In 1949, in the prologue for a book of Esther Harding, he wrote: "one part of the psyche is explicable in the terms of recent causes, but another part reaches back into the deepest layers of our racial history" (1950/1955, p.519). Close to the end of his life, in 1953, he wrote: "Just as the human anatomy has a long evolution behind it, the psychology of modern man depends upon its historical roots and can only be judged by its ethnological variants" (1950/1955, p.489). He suggested that the individual could only be understood in relation to his ethnic origin, that also holds the pattern of the individual's divinity—the daimon. The word ethnic stems from the Greek *ethnos*, and was used originally in the sense of "nation" (Onions, 1996, p.329); however, such connotation does not refer to the actual political nations, but to the races, the peoples. Therefore, as Onions pointed out, the Ecclesiastical Greek *tà éthne* rendered the Hebrew *gōyim*, which was the word used to refer to non-Israelitish nations. And even among the Israelites, there is a marked difference between those who are Cohen (or Kohen) and the rest.

[1098] Deloria Jr., when commenting the inherited relationship between ethnicity, religiosity, and land, wrote: "The traditional objection to this concept is that it would create religious wars[;]" therefore, champions of Unitarianism advocate for a universal religion. But, "[t]he past history of the West is eloquent testimony to the fact that a universal religion crossing ethnic lines does not lessen wars; it tends to increase them" (2003, p.293).

[1099] Russell lines, having himself experienced it personally, are descriptive of this idea: "For the first time, I felt the power which the Anglo-Saxon so fears and admires in the black man. A raw, vital, earthly force. Screaming of blood and birth and harmony and uniqueness. Nature. The African, curing his ills with jungle herbs and tilling his field with oxen, lived near the heart of things . . . the need to explore an inner world before we presume real knowledge of the outer" (Russell, 2014, p.129).

[1100] There are also interesting epistemological peculiarities and devises of some other, so-seemingly, remote peoples like the Australian Aboriginals, the Maori, the Mongolian, the Eskimo, the Polynesian, the Tibetan, the Hindus, and the Chinese, among others.

[1101] 1958, p.296

[1102] 1921/1971b, p.45

[1103] 1958, p.296

[1104] Jung observed, for instance, how "[c]ausality is one of our most sacred dogmas. There is no legitimate place in our world for invisible, arbitrary, and so-called supernatural powers—unless, indeed, we descend with the modern physicist into the obscure, microcosmic world inside the atom, where, it appears, some very curious things happen" (1964b, p.54). He reflected that, "[a]s the time-factor is indispensable to the concept of causality, one cannot speak of causality in a case where the time-factor is eliminated (as in precognition)" (1950/1955, p.500).

[1105] It is worth noticing that the English word *man,* which is part of the word *woman,* stems from the Germanic *mann,* which stems from pre-Germanic *manw,* or *mane,* which stems from the Sanskrit *mánu,* that means "man" or "mankind," but which stemmed originally from *Mánu,* the "progenitor of mankind" (Onions, 1996, pp.549-550) according to the peoples of those lands; in other words, their ancestor. In the words of Kingsley: "Human existence is nothing but the divine life unlived" (2003, p.340), and, more so, "[i]mmortal life is everywhere, sacred, inextricably entangled—and aching in the depths of its being to return home, to be back again where it comes from" (pp.359-360).

[1106] 1958/2005, p.40

[1107] Eliade, venturing to understand the so-called "primitive" cultures, claimed: "the primitives are not so much interested in what we call 'history,' that is, in the series of irreversible events taking place in linear, historical time. They are concerned rather with their own 'sacred history,' that is, with the mythical and creative acts which founded their culture and institutions, and bestowed meaning upon human existence" (1973, pp.xv-xvi).

[1108] Jung, 1961/1965, p.235

[1109] 1958, p.112

[1110] Rumi wrote in a poem titled *Story water*: "Water, stories, the body,/ all the things we do, are mediums/ that hide and show what's hidden" (Jalāl al-Din Rumi, 1995, p.172), a powerful presence that is oneself, and yet something else, as if personal and unique and impersonal and infinite.

[1111] in Deloria Jr., 2003, p.59

[1112] Jung considered that, "[t]his end-result is a true *antimimon pneuma,* a false spirit of arrogance, hysteria, woolly-mindedness, criminal amorality, and doctrinaire fanaticism, a purveyor of shoddy spiritual goods, spurious art, philosophical stutterings, and Utopian humbug, a fit only to be fed wholesale to the mass man of today. That is what the post-Christian spirit looks like" (1951/1959, p.35). In other words, he considered that there was a growing danger among Westernized peoples: the fake sense of spirituality (antimimon pneuma).

[1113] 1958, pp.463-464

[1114] 1958, p.495

[1115] It is worth reflecting on Jung's claim that, "the unconscious is the matrix mind . . . the Universal Mind . . . the Australian *aljira* . . . and its characteristic qualities are its dream manifestations, its ancestral world of thought-forms, and its timelessness" (1958, p.490).

[1116] Jung's friend, Laurens van der Post, acknowledged: "we Europeans have destroyed primitive societies and even more sophisticated cultures the world over by taking away or rejecting the story which was seed and essence of their history, their present and future . . . we have been thieves and killers of some aboriginal story and so deprived them of their own particular reason for being what they were—indeed, had at one stroke deprived both their yesterdays and today of meaning and purpose" (1975, p.125). Similarly, Standing Bear, a Sioux Chief, mentioned not too long ago: "The white man is still troubled by primitive fears . . . And he hates the man who questions his oath across the continent" (in Deloria Jr., 2003, p.59).

[1117] 1988, p.1401

[1118] Jung once said: "ancestral souls are included within you. At all events, you are a collection of ancestral spirits, and the psychological problem is how to find yourself in that crowd" (1988, p.1401). On the one hand, this statement refers to all those psychic persons who dwell one's terrain, from the trans-generational lineages; but on the other, it refers also to the ancestralized persons, the spirits, who might dwell in a different realm. Therefore, the deepest aspect of this insight relies on what Romanyshyn referred to as *Alchemical Hermeneutics,* which "is always an expression of longing" (2007, p.225). He considered that an "[i]nterpretation at the level of soul is not just about deciphering a hidden meaning, it is also about hunger for the original presence that still lingers as an absent presence" (p.225).

[1119] This corresponds to fragment B119 in the Diels-Kranz numeration. It has been given many possible translations, but maybe a plain transliteration is sufficient and better, as long as one makes an effort to understand the words *ethos* and *daimon* in an old Greek sense (as it has been attempted in this work). *Ethos* has been used in the sense of "characteristic spirit, settled character," or similar connotations. It is an old Greek word that means "usage, character, personal disposition," stemming hypothetically from the Indo-European *swedh,* from *swe* in the sense of "oneself" and *dhe* in the sense of place (Onions, 1996, p.329); therefore, the word *êthos* also brings attention to the importance of "place" and finding oneself the right place in the soul.

[1120] Onions, 1996, p.330

[1121] Eudaemonism stems from the Greek *eu,* that means "good or brave," and *daimon,* a word often translated in the sense of "guardian genius" (Onions, 1996, p.330), but which has deeper connotations, significance, and importance—as it has been explored in the chapter titled "Destiny." This idea is not far from that of Deloria Jr., who wrote: "I conclude that our ancestors lived in a strange condition in which they were in touch with spirits constantly, and I see that as a goal for our present activities" (2003, p.xvii). Moreover, like he intuited, "[i]t is this unbroken connection that we have with the spirit world that will allow us to survive as people" (p.xvii).

[1122] Jung realized that, "[w]e are so deeply impressed with the truth of our imprisonment in, and limitation by, the psyche that we are ready to admit the existence in it of things we do not know: we call them 'the unconscious'" (1958, p.479), when in fact it could also be thought of as a the codified archives of one's original nature, and spiritual potency.

[1123] Deloria Jr., 2006

[1124] Somé has commented that ancestral spiritual technologies consist in a kind of "hidden magical knowledge," (2005, Disc 1, Track 1). Philip J. Deloria, the son of the Native American scholar Vine Deloria Jr., similarly wrote: "If we can see the possibilities that our ancestors experienced . . . we can recapture the reality of spiritual power" (in Deloria, 2006, p.xv).

[1125] From a poem titled: *The Negro Spears of Rivers.* (My most sincere apologies for the use of the word "Negro,"—if it could seem derogatory—such is the title of the poem.)

[1126] in Bly, Hillman, & Meade, 1992, p.101

[1127] Jung wrote: "'Magical' is simply another word for 'psychic'" (1971, p.195). If one imagines this insight under the writings of Freud, Lacan, or many other "thinkers" who have written about the psychical aspects of life, it makes no sense, it is completely absurd, and it is even considered pejoratively as "primitive thinking" due to a lack of maturity; the difference between these kind of "thinkers" and Jung compromises irreconcilable ontological premises. If Jung's premises are bodily comprehended, one can claim, like Romanyshyn quite sharply wrote, that, one "bear[s] witness to the unconscious as the epiphany of an *other* world beside matter and mind, an epiphany whose ontological surprise is an epistemological shock" (2007, p.255), and a shattering of one's preconceived ideas and assumptions, in spite of their philosophical refinement. That might be why Wallace Black Elk mentioned that, "it's really hard to train a Harvard University graduate" (1990, p.113); for very educated people, in the Westernized sense, he said, "[g]reen is green, tree is tree, rock is rock" (p.113), one could hardly make them understand that "trees talk" (p.34).

[1128] Jung realized that "every civilized human being, however high his conscious development, is still an archaic man at the deeper levels of his psyche" (1964b, p.51); but it is important to mention that he clarified that "the word 'archaic' means primal, original" (p.50).

[1129] And maybe, one might be able to claim along with Rumi, that: "We come into the presence of the one/ who was never apart from us" (Jalāl al-Din Rumi, 1995, p.125), form his poem *Gnats inside the wind*.

[1130] There are some beautiful lines by Rilke, who wrote: "You haven't turned cold yet, it's not too late/ to dive into your expanding depths,/ where life reveals its intent" (2001, p.19), as if it were a spiritual dream with an ontological intention.

[1131] Following Heraclitus, one could say that: "time is a game played beautifully by children" (2001, p.51), from the fragment B52 by Diels-Kranz. However, it has also been translated as: "Eternity is a child at play, playing draughts: the kingdom is a child's" (in Barnes, 2001, p.50).

[1132] Jung suspected all this, in a way, although he did not expand further upon it. He acknowledged, for instance, that "the most primitive aborigines in central Australia have the very elaborate idea that when they perform their totem rites, it is not themselves but as their ancestors in the alcheringa times. They identify themselves with the divine heroes" (1996, p.93). Therefore, he explained in a public seminar, it would be like saying: "I am no longer Dr. Jung, I am Zarathustra, and then I can say the most outrageous things because I speak with the voice of the centuries—I am talking under the cloak of a great ancestor, and afterward I take off my paint and am an ordinary citizen again" (p.93).

[1133] 1996, p.93

[1134] Jung alleged that, in order to comprehend this, "we must go back to the age of myths, which did not explain everything in terms of man and his limited capacities but sought the deeper cause in the psyche and its autonomous powers. Man's earliest intuitions personified these powers as gods, and described them in the myths with great care and circumstantiality according to their characters. This could be done the more readily on account of the firmly established primordial types or images which are *innate in the unconscious of many races* (italics added) exercise a direct influence upon them" (1964b, p.187). He took myths very seriously, and explored them vastly. Hence, he wrote that, "myths are miracle tales and treat of all those things which, very often, are also objects of belief . . . .

Moreover the strange world of myth has suffered no loss of vitality during centuries of reason and enlightenment" (1951/1959, p.35). Therefore, in 1936, when writing about the Germanic situation, for example, he mentioned that, "[b]ecause the behaviour [*sic*] of a race takes on its specific character from its underlying images we can speak of an archetype 'Wotan'" (1964b, p.187). These insights by Jung were decades later supported by Jeremy Narby—although without any mention of Jung—, who claimed that it has been a great error in anthropology, and a hindrance for understanding shamanism, to discard tribal myths as only old irrational stories (1997, pp.19-26). And probably this hindrance is also a burden in sociology and the humanities in general.

[1135] 1964b, p.185

[1136] In this sense, Jung's lines are worth the allegory: "When I say 'Here is the source,' I only mean the spot where the water becomes visible. The water-simile expresses rather aptly the nature and importance of the unconscious. Where there is no water nothing lives" (1950/1955, pp.704-705). Therefore, he said: "If one depreciates the unconscious one blocks the channels through which the *aqua gratie* flows" (p.705). Consider Heraclitus's fragment numbered B36 by Diels-Kranz, saying that: "Death for souls is the birth of water, death for water is the birth of earth, and earth is the source of water, and water is the source of soul" (Waterfield, 2000, p.44); also rendered as: "As souls change into water on their way through death, so water changes into earth. And as water springs from earth, so water does from soul" (Heraclitus, 2001, p.43). This has also been rendered as: "For souls it is death to become water, for water death to become earth; but from earth water comes into being, from water soul" (in Barnes, 2001, p.63).

[1137] 1981, p.6

[1138] Corbin referred to "[a] little manual of Mazdean doctrine, written in Pahlavi and dating from the fourth century of our era, contains a number of questions the answers to which everyone over the age of fifteen is supposed to know. The first questions are: "Who am I and to whom do I belong? Whence have I come and whither am I returning? What is my lineage and what is my race? What is my proper calling in earthly existence?" (1983, p.1)

[1139] 1988, p.818

[1140] It is worth relating these insights with Heraclitus's fragment numbered B49a by Diels-Kranz, saying that: "We step and do not step into the same rivers, we are and we are not" (Waterfield, 2000, p.41 & in Barnes, 2001, p.70); also rendered as: "Just as the river where I step is not the same, and is, so I am as I am not" (Heraclitus, 2001, p.51), as if one were psychically *riverrunning*, and not. This idea would resonate with Empedocles fragment B15 in the Diels-Kranz numeration, saying: "No wise man in these things would suppose in his mind that while men live—what they call life—for so long do they exist and experience ill and good, but that before they were compacted as humans and after they are dissolved they are nothing" (in Barnes, 2001, p.130).

[1141] Hillman, 1992.

[1142] Hillman borrowed this term and image (which became his "psychological motto") from the English poet John Keats, who wrote: "Call the world, if you please, the vale of soul-making. Then you will find out the use of the world" (Keats in Hillman, 1976, p.120). Hillman, towards the end of his life asserted: "This is who you are, you are floating, you are part of the living stream of imagination" (Hillman & Shamdasani, 2013, p.114).

[1143] Hillman, 1992, p.174

[1144] Ibid, p.189

[1145] Ibid, p.201

[1146] Ibid, p.180

[1147] Ibid, p.190

[1148] Hillman, in 1970, wrote a brief explanation about the reason why of "Archetypal Psychology," which would become the hallmark and name or his psychological movement. He commented: "The problems of the psyche were never solved in classical times nor by archaic peoples through personal relationships and 'humanizing', but through the reverse: connecting them to impersonal dominants" (1970, p.218).

[1149] Rumi wrote, in his poem *The Gazing House*: "No need to wait until we die!/ There's more to want here than money and being/ famous and bites of roasted meat" (Jalāl al-Din Rumi, 2003, p.179).

[1150] Rilke probably had a glimpse of this too, as one can attest from his poem *Walk* where he wrote: "So we are grasped by what we cannot grasp;/ it has its inner light, even from a distance—/ and changes us, even if we do not reach it,/ into something else, which, hardly sensing it, we already are" (in Bly, Hillman, & Meade, 1992, p.423).

[1151] Hence, Rumi wrote in a poem titled *Why am I so blessed?*: "Be relentless in your looking,/ because you are the one you seek" (Jalāl al-Din Rumi, 1995, p.312). Hence, Jung considered that, "[a]nyone who believes that he can simply take over Eastern forms of thought is uprooting himself, for they do not express our Western past, but remain *bloodless* (italics added) intellectual concepts that strike no chord in our inmost being" (1951/1959, p.176). Standing Bear, a Sioux Chief, mentioned: "He [the white man] is too far removed from his formative process. The roots of his life have not yet grasped the rock and soil" (in Deloria Jr., 2003, p.59).

[1152] Jung too, considered that, "[o]ur cerebral consciousness is like an actor who has forgotten that he is playing a role" (1964b, p.155). Hence, he advised that "[man] must know once again that he was merely a figure on the stage" (p.156). Van der Post also glimpsed this, and beautifully wrote: "If I went by what men in command of the social, intellectual, scientific, and artistic scene said, that wide prophetic soul of the world of which Shakespeare had spoken in one of his greatest sonnets seemed utterly deprived of its dreaming on things to come and civilisation [*sic*] no longer in possession of any great dream to serve" (1975, p.36).

[1153] 1992, p.209

[1154] Rilke wrote some beautiful lines, praying: "If you are the dreamer, then I am the dream./ Yet if you wanted to stay awake,/ I would be your will" (2001, pp.23-25); indeed revealing the profound and insightful awareness of one's life being the imagining (dream-like) motion of some intelligent, purposeful agent.

[1155] Hillman, 1992, p.209

[1156] Hillman, inspired by mythological thinking, argued that, "[f]rom the Hades perspective *we are our images* . . . [and] the imaginal perspective assumes priority over the natural organic perspective" (1992, p.207).

[1157] 1887/1974, p.328

[1158] Nietzsche, 1967/2000, p.30

[1159] Kerényi claimed (1976, p.134) that one of Nietzsche's most accurate description of the Dionysian is the following: "If one were to allow one's imagination free rein in transforming Beethoven's 'Hymn to Joy' into a painting, particularly the moment when the multitudes kneel down awestruck in the dust: then one might come close to the idea of the Dionysian. Now slave is a free man, now all the inflexible and hostile divisions which necessity, caprice, or 'imprudent fashion' have established between men collapse. Now, with the gospel of world-harmony, each man feels himself not only reunified, reconciled, re-incorporated, and merged with his neighbor, but genuinely one, as if the veil of Maya had been rent and only its shreds still fluttered in front of the mysterious original Unity" (Nietzsche, 1967/2000, pp.22-23). This is just like Kingsley's argument: "For when we live the illusion to the full, to its furthest limits, we are nothing but reality fulfilling its own longing. In spite of the appearances, regardless of all our seeming limitations, we are simply reality completing itself" (2003, p.258). According to Kingsley, this was one of Empedocles' main teachings, "to be able to see this whole world as an illusion and still function in it as if it's real" (p.449).

[1160] 1887/1974, p.343

[1161] Kerényi in Hillman, 1992b, p.275

[1162] One of the most obscure fragments by Heraclitus could be the one numbered B15 by Diels-Kranz, translated as: "Hades is the same as Dionysus for whom they rave and ritualize" (in Barnes, 2001, p.67), also rendered as: "in fact, Dionysus for whom they rave and celebrate the Lenaea, is the same as Hades" (Waterfield, 2000, p.46); and translated too as: "Dionysus is their name for death" (Heraclitus, 2001, p.89). Hence, Jung wrote: "The divine powers imprisoned in bodies are nothing other than Dionysus dispersed in matter" (1951/1959, p.158 footnote). Kerényi actually considered Dionysus as the *archetypal image of indestructible life* (1976). Hence he wrote: "Just as Dionysos is the archetypal reality of *zoë* [indestructible life], so Ariadne is the archetypal reality of the bestowal of soul, of what makes a living creature an individual. The soul is an essential element of *zoë*, which needs it to transcend the seminal stage. *Zoë* requires soul and every conception of life is a psychogony" (p.124); in other words, a process of soul-making, in which "*zoë* takes the masculine form, while the genesis of souls takes the feminine form" (p.125).

[1163] 2001, p.119

[1164] Ibid, p.121

[1165] 1997, p.231

[1166] 1997, p.231 free translation

[1167] There is a beautiful passage by Rilke, who wrote: "Be heather and heath, spreading far./ Have old and ancient burial mounds,/ hardly known, abound—/ . . . / Create yourself, Silence./ . . . / Be moor, be heath, be plain, so the Ancient One may arrive" (2001, p.93). One could think of a similarity in the image of being heath and conceiving one's embodiment as an extensive *terrain.* Maybe, one's psychic terrain might match the "heart sanctuary" that Rumi alluded to, made "of intention and wisdom and mystical conversation and compassionate action" (Jalāl al-Din Rumi, 1995, p.191), from his poem *The far mosque.*

[1168] Corbin, throughout his works, wrote extensively on the notion of *orientation,* which he claimed is very important in Iranian Sufism because it means the "Quest for the Orient." He wrote a brief chapter on this, in *Man of Light* (1972/1994, pp.1-12). He said, "[t]he *Orient* sought by the mystic, the Orient that cannot be located on our maps, is in the direction of the *north*, beyond the north. Only as assensional progress can lead toward this cosmic north chosen as a point of orientation" (1972/1994, p.2). Orient and origin, in fact, stem from the same etymological root, the Latin *oriri* meaning "rise" (Onions, 1996, pp.632-633). Jung also wrote on this respect, and it is one of the major topics of his *Red Book,* where he said to Izdubar: "I've set out to the East, to the land of the rising sun, to seek the light that we lack" (2009b, p.279); see also *Aion* (1951/1959, pp.123-125). Kingsley's last book, *A story waiting to pierce you* (2010), also mentioned this idea. Rilke wrote a exquisite poem that offers some images about this; it is titled *Sometimes a man stands up during supper*:

"Sometimes a man stands up during supper

and walks outdoors, and keeps walking,

because of a church that stands somewhere in the East.

And his children say blessings on him as if he were dead.

And another man, who remains inside his own house

dies there, inside the dishes and in the glasses,

so that his children have to go far out into the world

towards the same church, which he forgot" (in Bly, Hillman, & Meade, 1992, p.60).

[1169] Jung, 1965, pp.233-234

[1170] Rumi said in a poem titled *A two-headed thing:* "There is something in us/ that has nothing to do with night and day,/ grapes that never saw a vineyard" (Jalāl al-Din Rumi, 1995, p.315).

[1171] Jung, 1953/1971, p.198

[1172] Somé's words explaining what happened after his father died are: "Strangely, I stopped seeing the spirit of my grandfather, he went away . . . instead, my direct parent, who were there [*sic*] for briefing me on the various kind of responsibilities" (2005, Disc 1, Track 5). This resonates with some lines by Stevens, from his poem *The Irish Cliff of Moher,* saying: "Go back to the parent before thought, before speech,/ At the head of the past" (in Bly, Hillman, & Meade, 1992, p.151).

[1173] In some beautiful lines form the poem titled *An awkward comparison,* Rumi wrote: "No image can describe/ what of our fathers and mothers,/ our grandfathers and grandmothers, remains./ Language does not touch the one/ who lives in each of us" (Jalāl al-Din Rumi, 1995, p.177).

[1174] This is similar to Deloria Jr. comments of the spiritual ways of the Native Americans—who were indigenous populations—, he mentioned: "Religion for them is an experience and they have no reason to reduce it to systematic thought and the elaboration of concepts" (2003, p.154). In such a sense, it might even be better to call it "religiosity" rather than "religion," because it is not a set of written concepts, but an empirical practice—*sheer experience.* However, he acknowledged that in the modern and post-modern world, "[t]ribal religions, with their emotional and ceremonial emphasis, are placed at the bottom of the cultural evolutionary scale because they practice rather than preach" (p.154).

[1175] Somé insisted on the need "to transcend our relation to the otherworld, from this kind of religiosity inspired by minimalism, whereby you make an approach to the ancestors or any spirit, from a disempowered place, from a place that make you feel that you're not even entitled to ask for what is already yours" (2005, Disc 1, Track 5). Deloria Jr., similarly, argued that, "[u]nlike other religious traditions, which have an early revelation followed by millennia of critical examination of the premises and substance of the spiritual experience, Indians have access to powers here and now" (2006, p.214)—even though he was referring specifically to Native Americans, the argument is common to many other aboriginal and indigenous peoples.

[1176] This insight would of course elicit reflection and deep considerations on the vital importance of one's father and mother, as well as in the very common religious notion of God the Father, Father Sky, the Creator Father, or the Grandfather, and Mother Earth, the Grandmother, the Begetter Mother, or the feminine aspect of God. In any case, it explains in some way the worldwide notion of deep respect towards one's progenitors, whether in Hinduism, Confucianism, Judaism, Islam, Christianity, and many other religious doctrines or indigenous traditions. The insistence on honoring one's father and mother it is not meant in the sense of one's parents being the universe creators, but representatives who embody the archetypal forces that together generated one's life—one's world genesis, in a way. Jung once wrote: "behind the father stands the archetype of the father, and in this pre-existing archetype lies the secret of the father's power, just as the power which forces the bird to migrate is not produced by the bird itself but derives from its ancestors" (1961, p.321). He claimed that, "[r]eligious statements are, however, never rational in the ordinary sense of the word, for they always take into consideration that other world, the world of the archetype, of which reason in the ordinary sense is unconscious, being occupied only with externals" (1958, p.148). Therefore, he considered that, "the archetype underlies the feeling-tone complexes and shares their autonomy. It is also the psychic precondition of religious assertions and is responsible for the anthropomorphism of all God-images" (1964b, p.449). One could conceive, then, "genuine conscience as the collision of consciousness with a numinous archetype" (1964b, p.453); as if one could say that, one's genuine conscience was one's way of knowing according to one's numinous origin. But, like Jung advised, "[one would] have to add at once that the archetype *per se,* its psychoid essence, cannot be comprehended, that it possesses a transcendence which it shares with the unknown substance of the psyche in general" (p.453). Hence, he said: "the archetypes are complementary equivalents of the 'outside world' and therefore possess a 'cosmic' character. This explains their numinosity and 'godlikeness'" (1951/1959, p.196). In this sense, Hillman argued that, "we do not have to take the archetypes as primary *psychic* structures; the psyche is only the place where they manifest" (1970, p.216). And just like Rilke said when speaking of "mein Gott", I would say when speaking of *my* ancestor: "if this be presumptuous so let it be/ for the sake of my prayer, which so earnestly and forlorn/ lingers across your cloud-clad brow" (2001, p.15).

[1177] Actually, the word *patriarchy* stems from the Greek *patér*, which means father, and *arkhes,* in the sense of ruler; therefore, the patriarch, which is usually considered the "head of the family" (Onions, 1996, p.658), can be considered also within spiritual connotations. Eliade argued that, "in the oldest Australian cultural strata… the gods are called Fathers" (1958/2005, p.25)—but, he did not specify whether it is because gods are like fathers, or because fathers (once they become ancestors) are like gods. However, one has to be extremely careful with the use of the word "god" in this context, because it is a European word that hypothetically stems from the Indo-European *ghu-,* in the sense of "invoke," and which might be a representation of the Sanskrit *hu* (Onions, 1996, p.404), but such a connotation does not necessarily involve the common and popular idea and use and misuse of the word god or God. Deren, who explored vastly the Voudoun tradition, commented that, after the death rituals, "[i]n time, the ancestor becomes archetype… Transposed to this dimension, the summoned voice in the govi [the recipient of such psychic energy] is no longer intimate, advisory; it is an objective oracular authority that booms as if from the bowels of the earth. What was one believed, is now believed in. He who was once respected is now revered … The ancestor has been transfigured into a god" (1953/1983, p.29).

[1178] Onions, 1996, p.14

[1179] Onions, 1996, p.937

[1180] Jung, in his old age, when answering specific questions about his spiritual concerns and alluding to the Pueblo Indians' idea that the sun is the Father, said: "today I do everything that is necessary so that my Father can rise over the horizon. That is my standpoint" (1950/1955, p.281). The Persian mystic Sohravardî, eight centuries before Jung, *recited,* according to Corbin, stories of initiation, devoting particular attention to the encounter with one's angel. In one of those, titled *Story of the Western Exile* (Sohravardî, 1976/2002, pp.121-134 free translation), he alluded to the encounter with one's angel *as if* it were the encounter with one's father; Corbin, in fact, claims that it is equivalent to the *Noûs patrikos* of the neoplatonic tradition (p.120 & 132 footnote). By the end of the story, this imaginal presence (father-angel) tells the man—exiled in the West and exiling himself from the West in order to go East—that there is also a grandfather, with whom he has a relationship as a son, but that this grandfather has a relationship with his own father and grandfather as well, and so on and on. The last lines of Wolfe's poem, titled *For, brother, what are we?,* expresses this notion quite close, saying: "We are the sons of our father,/ And we shall follow the footprint of his foot forever" (in Bly, Hillman, & Meade, 1992, p.123).

[1181] Onions, 1996, p.703

[1182] Onions, 1996, p.939

[1183] The verb "treat" stems from the Latin *trahere,* which means "draw" (Onions, 1996, p.939).

[1184] Moreover, it is an act of *enthymesis,* "the act of meditating, conceiving, imagining, projecting, ardently desiring" (Corbin in Hillman, 1992c, p.5); an act that can only be performed by the heart. Hence, it is not surprising to read Socrates—who alluded to *thymos* rather than spirit (in the original Greek text)—saying: "Have you never observed what an irresistible and invincible thing is spirit [*thymos*], the presence of which makes every soul in the face of everything fearless and unconquerable?" (Plato, 1989, p.621)—from Plato's second book of the *Republic*.

[1185] Somé mentioned that, "it is important that the shadow of Christianity be taken away in the context of our dealing with spirit and with ancestors, to the point where, what is behind the meaning of worship can take the form of demand, demand articulated boldly on the basis of natural entitlement" (2005, Disc 1, Track 4).

[1186] Hillman explained that, "[t]he thought of the heart is physiognomic. To perceive, it must imagine. It must see shapes, forms, *faces* (italics added)" (1992c, p.46). This is quite similar to Kinglsey's remark about "these mysterious beings who know more about us than we understand about ourselves . . . . [those] superiors who quietly watch and wait . . . . And when we feel most alone is when they are closest to us, because they are not separate from our own selves" (2010, p.545).

[1187] These lines, in particular, deserve attention in the original German, saying: "Raum wird auf einem neuen Angesichte./ Es war kein Licht vor diesem Lichte,/ und, wie noch nie, beginnt dein Buch" (2001, p.30). It feels like saying also: "There is room for a new face./ There was no sight of this luminescence,/ and, like never before, your Book begins."

[1188] Rilke, 2001, p.31

[1189] 1961/1965, p.225

[1190] Jung, commented in his last book, *Memories Dreams and Reflections* (1961/1965), how he, since early childhood, experienced two personalities; one was adapted and functional to his contemporary society, the other, was very old. (For a better account of this read the entire book.)

[1191] Jung explained this notion, the "Great Man," during a talk, later published and titled: *Fragments form a talk with Students* (1970, pp.177-181). He even mentioned that after all, "[a]nalysis is a long discussion with the Great Man[,]" making clear that, "[y]ou learn about yourself against the Great Man—against his postulates" (p.178). And ultimately, he dared to say quite boldly and clearly: "Ethics is not a convention; ethics is between myself and the Great Man" (p.179). Therefore, he said: "you must teach the patient about this double possibility; that there is the personal and there is something more in the personality, namely the Great Man" (p.181). Willhard Rhoades, an elder from the Pit River tribe, mentioned something similar: "Every nation, every tribe, every band of people all over the world has certain things to do to honor the Old Man, but they all forgot, and so they are the lost people" (in Budnik & Johnson, 1994, p.111).

[1192] Rilke, 2001, p.121

[1193] It is worth comparing Rilke's verse, with that of young Nietzsche, titled *To the Unknown God*, saying:

I shall and will know thee, Unknown One,

Who searchest out the depths. Of my soul,

And blowest through my life like a storm,

Ungraspable, and yet kinsman!

I shall and will know thee, and serve thee.

(Nietzsche in Jung, 1964b, p.182)

[1194] 2009b, p.272

[1195] 1970, p.177

[1196] Joyce, 2003, p.175

[1197] Jung, 1960.

[1198] 1960, p.151

[1199] Woodger in Hillman, 1972, p.241

[1200] 1989, p.197

[1201] From Plato's *Menexenus.*

[1202] "Alienist" is an old designation for psychiatrist, alluding to that which is foreign. Jung said, when answering a series of questions regarding his perspectives and religious beliefs: "You must consider that I am an alienist and practical psychologist, who has to take things as they *are* understood, not as they *could* or *should* be understood" (Jung, 1950/1955, p.722).

[1203] However, when asked whether his system was "Gnostic," Jung emphatically answered: "The designation of my 'system' as 'Gnostic' is an invention of my theological critics. Moreover I have no 'system.' I am not a philosopher, *merely an empiricist* (italics added)" (1950/1955, p.727). This clear perspective of his work, stated in 1956, close to the end of his life, is in fact radical and controversial. Jung has been considered many things, from a madman and a charlatan to a great theorist and mystic, but hardly ever an empiricist—quite close to Hellinger's practical work, not getting interested in theories, but in *empirical solutions* and what I call the *xailaz praxis* (the practice of healing and wholeness).

[1204] Some of Hellinger's latest works reveal and delve into a mystic worldview and living practice. Those are: *Viajes Interiores,* originally titled *Innenreisen*—meaning Inner Journeys—(2007d), *Mística Cotidiana,* originally titled *Natürliche mystik*—meaning Naturally Mystic—(2008/2008c), and *La Verdad en Movimiento,* originally titled *Wahrheit in Bewegung*—meaning Truth in Movement—(2005/2008b).

[1205] Onions, 1996, p.198

[1206] Jalāl al-Din Rumi,1995, p.247

[1207] 1964b, p.173

[1208] In the same text, Jung wrote: "for instance the function of dreams—stand in radical revision" (1964b, p.173)—where it should be noted he did not write light or slight revision, but "radical."

[1209] 1964b, p.173

[1210] Van der Post, having grown up in South African, having known the Bushmen, befriended with Jung, and aligned with him in many perspectives, commented: "a great deal of the troubles of modern man came from the fact that he himself had a deep, warm, caring, trusting, instinctive, primitive self from which he had not only allowed himself to be divorced but had gone on to despise and repress with a deadly ruthlessness" (1975, p.48). If one changes "primitive self" for "ancestral vestige" one can realize that it is almost the same vision as the one presented in this written work. But, like he wisely warned, "[t]he task of modern man was not to go primitive the African way, but to discover and confront and live out his own first and primitive self in a truly twentieth-century way" (p.51), and that exactly is the aim of this written work. If anyone thinks that the aim is to imitate tribal Africans, he or she has understood nothing.

[1211] Onions, 1996, p.35

[1212] 2007, p.46

[1213] Hillman, although with other words, and with another vision, was aware of the need of "a psychology based not on the 'human' but within the 'divine'" (1992b, p.298). Rumi wrote in his beautiful poem titled *The granary floor:* The human-divine combination is a oneness" (Jalāl al-Din Rumi, 1995, p.249).

[1214] 2007, p.46

[1215] Shamdasani openly said to Hillman: "I moved away from psychology because the whole field looked like a Babel of competing tongues" (Hillman & Shamdasani, 2013, p.201), and he knew that something new is deeply needed, as he said: "I am just wary of the idea that what is required is a new psychology" (p.223).

[1216] "Anyone who manages to experience the history of humanity as a whole as *his own history* will feel in an enormously generalized way all the grief of an invalid who thinks of health, of an old man who thinks of the dreams of his youth, of a lover deprived of his beloved, of the martyr whose ideal is perishing, of the hero on the evening after a battle that has decided nothing but brought him wounds and the loss of his friend. But if endured, if one *could* endure this immense sum of grief of all kinds while yet being the hero who, as the second day of battle breaks, welcomes the dawn and his fortune, being a person whose horizon encompasses thousands of years past and future, being the heir of all the nobility of all past spirit—an heir with a sense of obligation, the most aristocratic of old nobles and at the same time the first of a new nobility—the like of which no age has seen yet or dreamed of; if one could burden one's soul with all of this—the oldest, the newest, losses, hopes, conquests, and the victories of humanity; if one could finally contain all this in one soul and crowd it into a single feeling—this would surely have to result in a happiness that humanity has not known so far: the happiness of a god full of power and love" (Nietzsche, 1887/1974, p.268).

[1217] There is a very important comment by Jung, at the Tavistock Lectures, where he honestly said: "I consider my contribution to psychology to be my subjective confession" (1950/1955, p.125). And he defended his argument by saying: "We cannot help being prejudiced by our ancestors, who want to look at things in a certain way, and so we instinctively have certain points of view. It would be neurotic if I saw things in another way than my instinct tells me to do; my snake, as the primitives say, would be all against me" (p.125). By "snake" and "instinct," in this context, one can understand the whole nervous system and the psychic predisposition that is innervated throughout the embodiment, as well as one's autonomous metabolism and physiological unfolding. Therefore, to be against the snake, which is tantamount to be against one's ancestors, might be sickening, defiling, and deadening. Hence, Jung said: "I take the route that my snake prescribes, because that is good for me" (p.125). Moreover, "people who don't follow the serpent [or snake] suffer from a loss of life; they are drained from within, for the faculty of realization is lacking" (Jung, 1988, p.1299).

[1218] Hillman coined and explained *psychologizing* in his groundbreaking book Re-visioning Psychology, but prior to him, Jung explained that *psychologizing* meant "trying to renew the connection with the realities of the psyche, lest consciousness should flutter about rootlessly [*sic*] and helplessly in the void, a prey to every imaginable intellectualism" (1950/1955, p.659). Hence, this work avoided those dry, bitter, and sour intellectual arguments, as well as the elegant and persuasive sophistry that is based on the work of famous intellectuals or acclaimed academicians; and because of this it might not fit for what it passes as hermeneutics. Therefore, the best way to comprehend the methodology of this written work is by understanding the importance of psychologizing. In simpler words, one has to know that one can only know, and one can only write about, as much as one is able to *see through oneself.* This methodology is not based on conceptual or grammatical logic, but on a psychical observation of an order beyond logic, where, like Corbin claimed, "[t]he truth of the individual's vision [of himself] is proportional to his fidelity to himself" (1969/1998, p.76).

[1219] Jalāl al-Din Rumi, 2003, p.3

[1220] Plato, 1989, p.281

[1221] Socrates, in Plato's *Gorgias,* in fact, was referring to Empedocles, who said: "For it is noble to say twice what should be said" (in Barnes, 2001, p.120).

[1222] in Bly, Hillman, & Meade, 1992, p.163

[1223] The original motto, *Por mi raza hablará el espíritu,* means: "for my race the spirit will speak," said by José Vasconcelos in allusion to a sort of cosmic race.

[1224] Possibly, like Socrates claimed, in Plato's *Menexenus,* "life is not life to one who is a dishonor to his race, and that to such a one neither men nor gods are friendly, either while he is on Earth or after death in the world below" (Plato, 1989, p.196). Van der Post, recalling and commenting on Jung, wrote: "[Jung] scorned the growing numbers in Europe who exchanged their own culture for another as an evasion of the difficult task of truly being themselves and once described such a dubious 'traffic' to me as obscene" (1975, p.210).

[1225] Onions, 1996, pp.234-235

[1226] Rilke wrote:

"Through just one branch which hardly looks like him

is God, the tree, proclaimed at last like spring,

and rustles with maturity amidst a land

where people listen rather carefully—

each one alone like me" (2001, p.43).

[1227] Eliade, 1958/2005, p.xv

[1228] There are some beautiful lines by Rilke, when speaking to "God," saying:

"you homesickness we cannot quite curtail,

you forest within which we lose our trail,

you song we have sung with every silence kept" (2001, p.31).

About the Author

Eugenio Ordóñez holds an M.A. and Ph.D. in Depth Psychology by the Pacifica Graduate Institute. He has facilitated Family Constellations workshops and individual sessions for over 10 years. Besides his academic and clinical education he has delved into the study and practice of Kabbalah. He has also been instructed as an Elder following the spiritual technologies of indigenous Africa.

Read more at https://www.quechelah.org/.